Enriching Our Community.
Expanding Our World.

Given to the
Portland Public Library
by the
James A. Healy Fund

WITHDRAWN

Papist Patriots

Papist Patriots

The Making of an American Catholic Identity

BY MAURA JANE FARRELLY

OXFORD
UNIVERSITY PRESS

OXFORD
UNIVERSITY PRESS

Oxford University Press, Inc., publishes works that further
Oxford University's objective of excellence
in research, scholarship, and education.

Oxford   New York
Auckland   Cape Town   Dar es Salaam   Hong Kong   Karachi
Kuala Lumpur   Madrid   Melbourne   Mexico City   Nairobi
New Delhi   Shanghai   Taipei   Toronto

With offices in
Argentina   Austria   Brazil   Chile   Czech Republic   France   Greece
Guatemala   Hungary   Italy   Japan   Poland   Portugal   Singapore
South Korea   Switzerland   Thailand   Turkey   Ukraine   Vietnam

Copyright © 2012 by Oxford University Press, Inc.

Published by Oxford University Press, Inc.
198 Madison Avenue, New York, New York 10016

www.oup.com

Oxford is a registered trademark of Oxford University Press

All rights reserved. No part of this publication may be reproduced,
stored in a retrieval system, or transmitted, in any form or by any means,
electronic, mechanical, photocopying, recording, or otherwise,
without the prior permission of Oxford University Press.

Library of Congress Cataloging-in-Publication Data
Farrelly, Maura Jane.
Papist patriots : the making of an American Catholic identity / by Maura Jane Farrelly.
p. cm.
Includes bibliographical references and index.
ISBN 978-0-19-975771-8 (hardcover : alk. paper) 1. Maryland—Church history—18th century.
2. Catholic Church—Maryland—History—18th century.
3. United States—Church history—18th century.
4. Catholic Church—United States—History—18th century.
5. United States—History—Revolution, 1775–1783—Religious aspects—Catholic Church. I. Title.
BX1415.M3F37   2012
282'.75209033—dc23   2011016654

1 3 5 7 9 8 6 4 2

Printed in the United States of America
on acid-free paper

Because of Brecon

CONTENTS

Acknowledgments   ix
A Note on Spelling and Dates   xiii

Introduction   3
1. The English Origins of American Catholicism   20
2. Prescience, Pluralism, and Profit   48
3. Inconsistencies and Consequences   95
4. Catholic Commitment in an Inhospitable Climate   136
5. The Inconsistency of Intolerance   188
6. Papists Become Patriots   219

Notes   259
Index   295

ACKNOWLEDGMENTS

This book exists because in 1993, I was lucky enough to get a spot in Mark Massa's extremely popular "Catholics in American Culture" course at Fordham University. I have had very few experiences that I can point to as "life-changing." That course was one of them. In Mark's class, I discovered a love of American religious history that I did not know I had. I also encountered the "Americanist Crisis" in Catholicism for the first time—and anyone who makes it to the fifth paragraph in my introduction will discover that I am still fascinated with that subject, eighteen years later.

Because of Mark Massa's class, I applied for and received a "Divining America" summer fellowship for high school teachers at the National Humanities Center in 1995. There, I met Christine Heyrman—and my life changed again. Christine has proven to be an accomplished guide, a savvy advisor, a sharp critic, and a trusted friend for the last sixteen years. And I have never formally been her student. Every one of her pearls of wisdom has been given to me not because I have been enrolled in one of her courses, but simply because that is who Christine is. We should all aspire to be that kind of person some day.

Very few early-career scholars have the opportunity to receive feedback from a Bancroft Prize winner. I had that, plus feedback from my two Pulitzer Prize-winning journalism colleagues at Brandeis, Eileen McNamara and Mark Feeney. If readers find any portion of this book to be remotely accessible, it will be because I have taken their advice.

My American Studies colleagues also read portions of the manuscript and offered valuable advice on everything from John Courtney Murray's genius, to the importance of cover art, to the rules of Kashrut. They are: Joyce Antler, Jerry Cohen, Shilpa Davé, Tom Doherty, Brian Donahue, Richard Gaskins, and Steve Whitfield. Angie Simeone and Cheryl Sweeney made it possible for me to complete my research, in spite of the administrative responsibilities that come with my position as the director of Brandeis' Journalism Program. I am also grateful to Theodore and Jane Norman and the Tomberg family, who provided Brandeis with the funding that made it possible for me to travel to Maryland a number of times to complete my research.

Maryland, incidentally, is a wonderful state to be doing historical research in. The Hall of Records in Annapolis may well be the Rolls Royce of archives, in terms of its style, efficiency, and precision. The staff there—most especially Robert Barnes—are precious resources. David McDonald and Jenny Ferretti at the Maryland Historical Society in Baltimore also helped me with my research. And Lynn Conway and Nicholas Scheetz at Georgetown University proved to be top-notch professionals who are also incredibly interesting people. Fans of historic restoration have a true friend in Mr. Scheetz.

Boston is a great town to be living in, since there are so many wicked smart people here. I am grateful to the members of my American Religious History Roundtable for reading portions of my manuscript and sharing their experience with me. They are: Peggy Bendroth, Chris Beneke, Stephen Berry, David Hempton, Jim O'Toole, Clifford Putney, Jon Roberts, Randall Stephens, and Don Yerxa.

I have had the good fortune to participate in two fellowship programs for early career scholars—one that focuses on American religion and another that focuses on the American Founding. Without the Young Scholars in American Religion program, I would not have been able to dust off the intellectual cobwebs that accumulated during the several years I spent outside academia, working as a reporter. Thanks to Clark Gilpin, Fay Botham, Heather Curtis, Jon Ebel, Jennifer Graber, Matthew Grow, Everett Hamner, Kip Kosak, Lynn Neal, Jonathan Walton, and most especially Tracy Fessenden.

The Jack Miller Center for Teaching America's Founding Principles and History put me into the orbit of some most unusual creatures—political theorists. Without the JMC, I never would have discovered the work of Michael Zuckert, and chapter 3 would have been impoverished because of that. I am grateful to Mike Andrews, Pamela Edwards, and Rafe Major for their wisdom and support. Readers should also be grateful to the JMC. It was a generous subvention from that organization that helped to make this book affordable.

Thanks to Theo Calderara, my editor at Oxford University Press, along with Lisbeth Redfield and Lynn Childress (whose eagle eye is most impressive). Other friends, family, and colleagues who offered advice and sometimes pulled double-duty as copy editors and indexers are: Michael Bellesiles, Moira Davenport, Deanna Devaney, Eugene, Kathleen, Cassie, Megan, and Gene Farrelly, Laurence Nee, Matthew Richmond, Charley Simmons, and Joan Simmons. Charley, more than anyone else, had to deal with my moods and pontifications.

Finally, I am grateful to my Peters Hill Dogpack for helping me get through a difficult time that happened to coincide with the completion of my draft manuscript. In May 2010, my beloved (and gorgeous) six-year-old collie, Brecon, was diagnosed with cancer. He lived twice as long as the oncologists said he would, but half as long as he was supposed to on the day he was born. He lives on in the people he brought into my life.

Maura Jane Farrelly
Boston, July 2011

A NOTE ON SPELLING AND DATES

In 1490, when he set out to produce an English translation of Virgil's *Aeneid*, the printer William Caxton had to make a decision. "Certainly our langage now vsed varyeth ferre from that whiche was vsed and spoken what I was borne," Caxton wrote at the start of an era that ran from roughly 1450 to 1700, and which linguists refer to now as "The Great Vowel Shift." At the same time that printers like Caxton were starting to leave a standardizing mark on English spelling, dialects across England were competing with one another for what one historian has called "mutual comprehension."

Englishmen, according to William Caxton, were "borne vunder the domyncacion of the mone, which is neuer stedfast but euer wauerynge wexynge one season and waneth & decreaseth another season. And that comyn englysshe that is spoken in one shyre varyeth from a nother." Which version of English, then, should the printer from Kent use? It would be "harde to playse euerye man by cause of dyuersite & chaunge of langage," Caxton wrote in his preface. And so in the end, he decided to use a version of English that would be comprehensible "to clerkys and very gentylmen that vnderstand gentylnes and science."[1] This, after all, was the audience he wanted to attract.

Colonial American historians love to reproduce the spelling they are forced to grapple with in their research. Not only does the spelling highlight how difficult their jobs can be sometimes, but as William Caxton's verbatim observations show, the spelling can help to emphasize the reality that—in the words of the novelist L. P. Hartley—"the past is a foreign country."[2]

Colonial American historians, however, are not the only audience I am interested in attracting. Like all first-time academic authors, I suffer from the delusion that my book might actually be picked up by a history buff who sells cars or crunches numbers for a living, and that some young, eager professor at a Midwestern college might actually use my book in her undergraduate classroom.

I have therefore cleaned up the spelling used by my characters considerably. I have kept enough of the original spelling—I hope—to create that foreign "feel" that is so essential to any truthful rendering of a past that is, by this point, 300–400 years old. But in making my spelling decisions, my standard has been readability, rather than literality. Where I felt the spelling was distracting, I changed it. Anyone who has a need to see the original spelling can use my notes to locate the documents.

Following the lead of the Bancroft Award-winning historian Jill Lepore, I have also modernized my dates in the interest of readability.[3] Before 1752, the official start of the year in England and its colonies was March 25, not January 1. As a consequence, colonial American historians will often refer to "old style" dates as "1691/92" or "1718/19," to reflect the reality that they are imposing a modern calendar onto their research subjects. This, too, can be distracting to a nonprofessional audience. Therefore, whenever I have been able to ascertain that an event occurred or a sentiment was expressed between January 1 and March 25, I have placed that event or sentiment in the following year. Whenever I have not been able to confirm an actual day or month, however, I have simply used the year that I found in the record.

Papist Patriots

Introduction

"Catholics were warned against religious liberty and urged to remain loyal to the faith of their fathers."[1]

So ran the opening sentence in a tiny article that appeared in the *New York Times* on July 31, 1903. The piece was a news brief about a Mass that had been said the day before at St. Mary's Cathedral in Newark, New Jersey. Unlike most news briefs, however, which typically came in over the wire and were used by subscribing newspapers to fill the spaces that had not been purchased by advertisers, this piece was a "special" to the *New York Times*. The paper had actually commissioned it, and neither the *New York World* nor the *New York Journal*—the *Times*' chief competitors—would have it.

Ordinarily a Catholic Mass—especially one across the river in Newark—would not have attracted the attention of the news desk at a paper like the *Times*, which had been working hard since 1896 to increase the scope and reputation of its domestic and international coverage. The religious activities of a bunch of Irish and eastern European immigrants who had settled in an industrial cesspool on the other side of the Hudson River were too provincial and unimportant to interest the educated, urbane, and Protestant readers that the *Times*' Jewish owner, Adolph Ochs, was hoping to attract.

This Mass was special, however, and its message was one that the editors of the *Times* anticipated their Protestant readers would want to hear. As it turned out, the editors' instincts paid off, and the sermon the Reverend John Fox, Vicar General of the Diocese of Trenton, delivered on that warm, Thursday morning at the end of July confirmed Protestants' worst suspicions about the tyrannical nature of Catholicism and its inherent incompatibility with American identity. "The spirit of freedom is running riot" in the United States, Monsignor Fox told the men and women assembled in his church, and Catholics should be careful that they "not be carried away with it."[2] It was a clear repudiation of the very foundation upon which American identity and all that Protestant Americans held dear had been built.

As obnoxious as Monsignor Fox's words must have sounded to the Presbyterians and Congregationalists who read them in the *Times*, the priest's sentiments were actually fitting ones for a Mass that was meant to honor the memory of Pope Leo XIII, who had died a few days before. Four years before his death, the Pontiff had issued an encyclical entitled *Testem Benevolentiae Nostrae*—literally, "Witness to Our Good Will," but the encyclical is more commonly known as the "Letter on Americanism." Its primary purpose was to condemn the unbridled individualism that characterized life in the United States and which some Catholics in the country, much to the Pope's dismay, had come to embrace.

Among the developments in America that had "wrapped the mind in darkness," the Pope lamented, were "the passion for discussing and pouring contempt upon any possible subject" and "the assumed right to hold whatever opinion one pleases upon whatever subject and to set them forth in print to the world." It was a remarkably accurate description of the American cultural landscape, made by a man who had never actually visited the United States. Newspaper publishers like Adolph Ochs, Joseph Pulitzer, William Randolph Hearst, and George William Abell were, in fact, encouraging and rewarding the very passion that Pope Leo decried. Indeed, one can only imagine what Leo might have thought of H. L. Mencken, had he lived long enough to witness the career of this celebrated American journalist. Mencken did not join the *Baltimore Sun* until three years after the Pope had died, but in 1923 he admitted in an editorial that he actually admired the Catholic Church, "in spite of its occasional astounding imbecilities."[3]

Leo's encyclical was a classic expression of the ambivalent, sometimes even antagonistic relationship that Catholicism has had with Enlightenment liberalism and its faith in the rationality and autonomy of the individual.[4] The nature and development of this relationship is a well-worn topic among scholars of Catholic history, particularly among those grappling with that curious animal that so troubled Pope Leo back in the 1890s, the American Catholic. No culture in the world, after all, is more individualistically oriented than that of the United States. "To deal with the topic of Catholicism and liberalism," Philip Gleason has observed, "We must... grasp the nettle of 'Americanism.'"[5]

To that end, several prominent historians and theologians have worked to tell the story of how Catholics—who subscribed to a hierarchical faith that saw itself as a corporate body and the One, True Church—found their place at America's table, where the manners included not just a respect for individual rights but also an emphasis on republican government, a mandate of church–state separation, and an acceptance of religious pluralism.[6] For the most part, these scholars have focused on the nineteenth and twentieth centuries and the transformation of American Catholicism during and after the faith's incarnation as an immigrant church. There is an earlier story, however—one that the theologian John Courtney Murray recognized in 1960, but did not adequately explore. That story is what this book is all about.

For Murray, the making of an American Catholic identity was a seamless process, at least as far as Catholics themselves were concerned. While history certainly testifies to the unwillingness of many Protestants to trust a Catholic presence at their American table, Murray famously insisted in 1960, the year that America elected its first and so-far only Catholic president, that Catholics' participation in what he called the "American consensus" was "unreserved and unembarrassed" from the very beginning. The principles that had guided the architects of the American republic in the 1770s and 1780s were perfectly compatible with the "universe of discourse" that characterized Catholic thought. Calling Thomas Aquinas the "first Whig," Murray argued that Catholics understood the language of liberty, as articulated by the Founders, because the "ethical and political principles" upon which that liberty was based were "drawn from the tradition of natural law," an understanding of God's moral expectations for humanity that Aquinas had addressed extensively in his *Summa theologica*.

"It is not an American belief that free government is inevitable, only that it is possible," Murray noted, reminding Americans that the Founders had insisted that free government could be realized "only when the people as a whole are inwardly governed by the recognized imperatives of the universal moral law." That moral law—which Catholics had understood long before Congregationalists like John and Sam Adams discovered it—kept the individualistic impulses that were an inherent part of any free society in check. According to Murray, the moral law had "rescued" the American Republic from "the fate, still not overcome, that fell upon the European nations in which Continental Liberalism, a deformation of the liberal tradition, lodged itself." The virtue of the American people had kept their independence movement from deteriorating into the mockery of liberalism that France's revolution soon became. It was a great "paradox," therefore, that "a nation which has (rightly or wrongly) thought of its own genius in Protestant terms should have owed its origins and the stability of its political structure to a tradition whose genius is alien to current intellectualized versions of the Protestant religion."[7]

As a Jesuit, John Courtney Murray looked to theology when searching for the origins of what was, in 1960, a relatively easy relationship between American Catholics and the cornerstones of their country's political and cultural identity (the expressed concerns of the Houston Baptists aside). This tactic, however, ensured that Murray's argument remained entirely within the realm of ideas, assuming, but never verifying, that American Catholics had always been "unreserved and unembarrassed" about embracing the "American consensus." In fact, the relationship that Catholics have had with the American consensus is far more complicated than John Courtney Murray allowed.

Historians like Jay Dolan and John McGreevy have looked to experience when trying to understand what the foundational principles of American identity have meant to Catholics in the United States. Unlike Murray, these scholars have acknowledged that for many years—most of

America's existence as an independent nation, actually—the Catholic relationship with American culture was one of "tension." This tension was there not simply because Protestants refused to accept Catholics as equal partners in the American experiment but also because Catholic leaders in Europe and America preached that the republican individualism characterizing American life was incompatible with Catholic identity.

Long before Archbishop Vincenzo Pecci became Pope Leo XIII in 1878, priests in antebellum New York and Philadelphia were warning their parishioners that the "liberty" American Protestants extolled "existed only on paper, and not in fact." True freedom was not the purview of the individual; it could be found only within the community of the Church. Catholics, therefore, needed to protect themselves from their country's cultural obsession with liberty. To do this, they had to withdraw from mainstream culture and eschew Protestants and their tantalizing individualism wherever and whenever possible. From the 1840s until the end of the Second World War, if not the post Vatican II era of the 1960s and 1970s, American Catholicism was characterized by a parochialism that encouraged Catholics to settle in the same urban enclaves and send their children exclusively to Catholic schools. The result was the "ghetto mentality" that historian Garry Wills has said defined his own childhood in the Midwest in the 1940s.[8]

The Catholics who accepted their priests' warnings not to interact with Protestants tended to have an "ultramontane" approach to their faith—that is to say, an approach that stressed the fallen nature of humanity and the idea that people and their governments could overcome the reality of sin only through the wisdom and guidance of the Church. Such Catholics did not exhibit the typical American obsession with individual rights or embrace the American principle of church–state separation as a stand-alone ideal. The separation was important because it allowed Catholics to practice their faith in a country where they were the minority; it was not, however, a noble goal unto itself, and Catholics who deigned to suggest otherwise—laymen like Orestes Brownson or clerical leaders like Isaac Hecker and John Ireland—were loudly criticized by their ultramontane religious brethren.[9]

Ultramontanism was popular among Catholics in nineteenth-century Ireland, where the authority of the local civil government had been rendered understandably suspect by centuries of religious persecution, and the Catholic Emancipation movement of Daniel O'Connell had cultivated a strong sense of sectarian nationalism that defined Protestants as the natural enemy of Catholics.[10] True authority for an Irish Catholic did not lie in Ireland, where English officials ruled with an iron fist, but "over the mountains"—that is, the Alps—in Rome.

Irish immigrants dominated Catholicism in America for many decades—certainly in the pews, but then also from the pulpits, even after the Catholic laity in America had become more ethnically diverse. Ultramontanism, therefore, was a formidable force in American Catholicism for most of the nineteenth and twentieth centuries. Catholicism in the United States had an ultramontane character, in spite of the strong current of "Americanism" that concerned Pope Leo in 1899 and has served as an object of fascination for historians ever since.[11]

Because they have looked to the historical record, rather than to a theological and political ideal, scholars like McGreevy and Dolan have seen the natural conflict between "Catholic" and "American" identity and accepted it for what it was. Because their focus has primarily been on the immigrant church, however, and on Catholicism's transformation in the nineteenth and twentieth centuries, these historians have missed (or at the very least not fully appreciated) that John Courtney Murray was actually onto something in 1960 when he insisted that Catholics had embraced the American consensus—even if his observations were unsubstantiated and his theological explanations smacked of casuistry.

Murray's insistence that early American Catholics had understood the individualistic, rights-oriented language of America's Founders and embraced the notion of republican government was not just pie-in-the-sky, revisionist history, written to attract the attention of the editors at *Time* magazine and assuage Protestant fears about a Catholic presidential candidate. What Murray wrote was true. Before Irish immigration started to take off in the 1830s and 1840s, when Catholics were still just an "exotic minority concentrated ... mostly in Maryland and Kentucky," American Catholicism had a decidedly republican tone. The controversial English journalist Harriet Martineau recognized as much during her travels throughout the United States in the early 1830s. Although she believed it was "the Pope's wish to keep the Catholics of America a colonial church," Martineau observed that the Catholic population in America was "democratic in its politics and made up of the more independent-minded occupations." She noted with delight that "the Catholic religion is modified by the spirit of the time in America; and its professors are not a set of men who can be priest-ridden to any fatal extent."[12]

This republican attitude among Catholics in early America manifested itself in the phenomenon of lay trusteeism, whereby boards of elected laymen governed the "temporal affairs" of their parishes, matters that included everything from when and how a new roof might be placed on a chapel, to the hiring of priests and the payment of their salaries. While there is little evidence to suggest that Catholic lay trustees saw themselves as having any authority over spiritual matters, it is clear that they did believe their priests were there to serve them, much like elected officials. It was common in early America for Catholics to call for the dismissal of priests whose accents were too heavy to be understood by English-speakers, or whose drinking habits rendered them incapable of offering any kind of guidance, spiritual or otherwise. Indeed, in Richmond, Virginia, the lay trustees of one tiny Catholic parish were so dissatisfied with their indecipherable French priest that they wrote to Thomas Jefferson in 1818, pleading with him to use his political influence to pass a federal law that would require the congregational election of all pastors in the United States, regardless of denomination.[13]

Jay Dolan has traced this Catholic republicanism—or what he calls "Enlightenment Catholicism"—as far back as the 1780s, specifically to the episcopacy of John Carroll, the first Catholic Bishop in the United States. The Vatican appointed Carroll precisely because he was a native-born American, a citizen of Maryland who would know how to relate to Catholics who had been raised in the liberal environment of America, where "pluralism," John Courtney Murray has noted, "was the native condition."[14]

To be sure, John Carroll was not an unreserved advocate of every component of "enlightened" ideology. As a member of the clergy, he was sometimes quite vexed by the republican pretensions of the American Catholics he oversaw. Commenting on a disagreement that lay Catholics in Kentucky were having in the 1790s with their priest, Stephen Badin, Carroll used the pejorative word "libertinism" to describe the efforts of the laity to draw up and implement a constitution for their parish.[15]

Still, Carroll had been an enthusiastic supporter of the American Revolution—i.e., the ultimate act of liberal rebellion, albeit in a civil sphere. He traveled to Canada in 1776 in a failed effort to convince the Catholics living there to join the Americans in their bid for independence. Afterwards, Carroll rejoiced when the liberal ideals of the independence movement were extended to the religious sphere, joining his fellow American clergy in calling the Establishment Clause of the First Amendment "a revolution, if possible, more extraordinary than our political one."

For Carroll, the First Amendment was the embodiment of a principle he had often endorsed from the pulpit—namely, that "in matters of faith, everything must be free & voluntary." Such an attitude, expressed by a Catholic leader in the last years of the eighteenth century, contrasts sharply with the dismay expressed a full century later by Pope Leo XIII, when the Pontiff lamented that so-called "lovers of novelty" in America were insisting that "allowance be granted the faithful, each one to follow out more freely the leading of his own mind."[16]

But where did people like John Carroll and the Kentucky lay Catholics who were drawing up a constitution for their parish come from? That is to say, if it is true that America's first Catholics were ardent republicans who understood and embraced the rights-oriented tenets upon which the independence movement was based, what made them that way? How did they reconcile their republicanism with the hierarchical orientation of their Catholic faith? Why did a movement that emphasized individual rights resonate with a people who subscribed to a communally oriented denomination like Catholicism? And how did Catholics reconcile their religious identity with the vehemently anti-Catholic rhetoric of the independence movement? George III's decision to allow the free practice of Catholicism in Quebec, after all, was one of the key developments that convinced the colonists the King could no longer be relied upon to protect their liberties. As many historians have noted, the common cry of the Patriots was, "No King, No Popery."[17]

John Courtney Murray devoted thirteen essays to showing how the natural law tradition prepared Catholics in British North America to accept the political ideology of the Founders, and even then, Murray was still left to wonder why, if the liberal tradition that he called the "American consensus" were so compatible with the Catholic mindset, "the tradition should have so largely languished in the so-called Catholic nations of Europe at the same time that its enduring vigor was launching a new Republic across the broad ocean."[18] France's failure to shake off the mantle of absolutism until well into the twentieth century, the cozy relationship the Catholic Church enjoyed with the civil government in Ireland during the first eighty years of that country's independence, and even the unwillingness of the Catholic majority in eighteenth-century Quebec to sign on to the independence movement of the predominantly Protestant lower thirteen colonies all suggest that something more than just an understanding of natural law was involved in the making of an "American" Catholic identity.

To truly understand where people like John Carroll and the lay trustees who challenged their church in the early years of the Republic came from, we have to look beyond theology to experience—and beyond the experiences of nineteenth-century Catholics in the United States to the experiences of seventeenth- and eighteenth-century Catholics in colonial Maryland. Until Catholicism in the United States started to take on a predominantly immigrant tone, many, if not most of the English-speaking Catholics in the new republic could trace their roots to that Catholic community that had been surviving along the Chesapeake since 1634. In 1808, the year the Diocese of Boston was founded, there were fewer than 1,000 Catholics living in the state of Massachusetts. That same year, however, there were approximately 6,000 Catholics living in Kentucky, nearly all of them migrants or the sons and daughters of migrants from Maryland who had poured into the region after the Revolutionary War in search of land that had not been abused by decades of tobacco farming. For that reason, Bardstown, Kentucky, became a diocese the same year Boston and New York did.[19]

Catholicism survived in Maryland, in spite of the fact that it was technically outlawed in the 1690s. Religious liberty was not restored to Maryland's Catholics until 1776, when political leaders adopted a new state constitution that extended freedom of conscience to all Christians. To understand how an "American" Catholic identity was made, scholars need to turn their attention to the experiences that Catholics had in Maryland both before and during the so-called "Penal Period" that ran from 1689 to 1776.

By an "American" Catholic identity, I mean an identity that was not just distinct from the religious identity that existed in predominantly Catholic countries like Spain and France, where Enlightenment liberalism "languished," according to John Courtney Murray. I mean an identity that was distinct from the national identity that existed—even among Catholics—in eighteenth-century England, as well. To become Americans, Catholics in British North America had to do more than simply find a way of reconciling their faith with the Enlightenment principles upon which American identity would rest—as significant as that was. They also had to see themselves as something other than "English" before they could choose to break away.

Colonial Catholics, after all, did not have a lock on "Enlightenment Catholicism" in the late eighteenth century. In England, too, Catholics displayed a liberal mindset that stressed the importance of individual autonomy within the community of the Church, the limited scope of the Pope's jurisdiction in England, and the need for membership within a particular religious organization to be completely voluntary. Following the death in 1766 of James Edward Francis Stuart—the oldest son of the deposed Catholic King James II—England's lay Catholics adopted an approach to their faith that stressed the compatibility between that faith and their civil rights as Englishmen. In so doing, they embraced the individualistic, predominantly Protestant, English cultural context in which they practiced their Catholic faith. Members of what became known as the "Cisalpine Club" called for the vernacular to be used in Catholic Masses, for ordinary bishops to be elected by the Catholic gentry, and for the Pope's spiritual authority in England to be mediated by a national Catholic Church.[20]

The Cisalpine movement was nationalistic, as much as it was religious— an acceptance, finally, on the part of English Catholics of the Hanoverian succession and, implicitly, the Glorious Revolution. In accepting the ouster of James II and all his Catholic descendents, the Cisalpinists were not turning their backs on the Catholic Church; rather, they were insisting that it was possible to be both English and Catholic, and their campaign was an effort to convince officials in London and Rome that this was the case. The Roman Catholic Relief Act of 1791, which allowed Catholics to practice law in England for the first time in nearly 100 years and to send their children to local Catholic schools, was a sign that in London, at least, some people were listening.[21]

Although the Cisalpine movement was sparked by the death of James Stuart in 1766, the forces that enabled English Catholics to assert themselves in this way were much older than that. They had been building for more than two centuries, in fact, as Catholics learned in the wake of the Acts of Uniformity and Supremacy of 1559 that in spite of the communal and hierarchical orientation of their faith, to be Catholic in England was necessarily to assert oneself individually and to challenge authority on some level. In the late sixteenth and early seventeenth centuries, England's Catholics learned that the survival of their faith required them to own their religious identity in a way that was completely unnecessary in majority Catholic countries like Spain and France.

Maryland's Catholic community was derived from this English community that had been defining itself for nearly 100 years by the time the *Ark* and *Dove* landed at Point Comfort and sailed up the Chesapeake to the mouth of the Potomac River. Many of the same forces that compelled Catholics in England to take responsibility for their faith also compelled Catholics in British colonial America to construct a new and personal understanding of what it meant to be Catholic. Whereas those forces empowered the English to challenge their church to become more compatible with English identity, however, in America, the forces prepared Catholics to accept an entirely new national identity—one that came wrapped in the rhetoric of anti-Catholicism, but which represented Catholics' best hope for a return to the more tolerant times their ancestors had enjoyed during the early years of their colony's existence.

Maryland was founded in the 1630s by a Catholic proprietor who wanted to create a "haven" for his religious brethren in the English-speaking world. For the first five decades of the colony's existence, Catholics there enjoyed a remarkable degree of religious liberty, thanks in part to a law that their proprietor had pushed through Maryland's assembly in 1649. In 1689, however, angry Protestants used the psychological ammunition provided by the Glorious Revolution in England to finally end the era of Catholic rule in Maryland. The result was an eighty-seven-year period that included the run-up to the Revolutionary War, during which time Catholics' rights were trampled upon by paranoid Protestant lawmakers.

On top of their legal marginalization, the nearly 25,000 men and women who subscribed to the Catholic faith in Maryland and nearby Pennsylvania had no formal, institutional structure on which to hang their religious identity. The colonies had no Catholic bishop, and although the Vicar Apostolic of London, Richard Challoner, technically oversaw the English Jesuits who served in the Maryland Mission (which included Pennsylvania), Challoner never actually visited North America. His influence was only ever indirect, touching the colonists' lives primarily through the prayer books he published.[22]

The ratio of priests to laity was abysmal, given how important the services of a priest are to the practice of the Catholic faith. This clerical dearth, combined with the transportation difficulties that characterized colonial life, meant that most Catholics were lucky to see a priest once a month—and some had to reconcile themselves to making their confessions and receiving Communion just one time a year.[23]

In this environment, the decision to remain Catholic was a deliberate one. While the dedication of the priests who served in Maryland was vital to the faith's survival, the fact remains that Catholicism endured in eighteenth-century Maryland because the laity refused to abandon their faith. Circumstances forced these laypeople to redefine their faith in order to maintain it, however. They freely challenged their priests whenever the obligations of Catholicism conflicted with the realities of life in the New World, and they created new obligations for themselves that were designed to make up for the fact that the services of a priest were unavailable for much of the year.[24]

A few Catholics did convert to Anglicanism, and their politically powerful and financially lucrative careers attest to the fact that Catholics in colonial America had every earthly reason to apostatize. Yet, for the most part, they did not. That decision—made every single day by individual Catholics throughout the eighteenth century, on their own, without the constant presence and support of a clerical advisor—facilitated the development of a new Catholic identity that was comfortable with the individualistically oriented language of the independence movement.

The new religious identity that the Maryland experience created was compatible with the new national identity that people like Richard Henry Lee and John Adams formally called for in 1776, thanks to a mechanism that Maryland's Catholics had devised for sustaining their religious identity throughout the Penal Period. That mechanism was a collective "memory" that the eighteenth-century community constructed of a time in Maryland's history when their seventeenth-century ancestors had enjoyed the benefits of full citizenship. The memory was a bit selective. It tended to avoid the reality of religious nepotism in the Catholic Lord Baltimore's government, and it also spoke of toleration in the seventeenth century as if it were a fact, simply because it was a law. The reality was that many of Maryland's early Protestant settlers denied that toleration for Catholics had any place an English colony, and those denials occasionally became quite violent.

The memory that Maryland's eighteenth-century Catholics constructed was not meant to be completely factual, however. In the short term, it was meant to prevent the extension of England's anti-Catholic statutes to Maryland, and in the long term, it was used to sustain the Catholic community during a time when being Catholic had become decidedly inconvenient. The memory preserved Catholic identity, in spite of the inconveniences that came with it, by linking that identity to liberty and tradition and, in so doing, ennobling it.

Unlike Catholics in England, where "professed Papists" had been persecuted for more than two hundred years—or even Catholics in Pennsylvania, where the "Romish" faith was legal, if not exactly tolerated throughout the entirety of the colony's existence—Maryland's Catholics knew what it was like to have toleration, and then lose it. More to the point, they understood that the reason they had lost the toleration that their ancestors had built in the seventeenth century was that their colony was tied to England. The Protestant take-over that had led to the demise of religious toleration in Maryland was an extension of the Glorious Revolution in England—a coup whereby English Protestants who were unhappy living under a Catholic ruler challenged the authority of that ruler, in spite of the decades of tradition that lay behind his authority, and won. As went James II in England, so went Charles Calvert, the third and final Catholic Lord Baltimore, in Maryland.

The Protestant revolution of 1689–1692 was neither the first nor the last time that England's conflicts in Europe spilled over into North America, involving the colonists in deadly contests that, increasingly throughout the eighteenth century, they came to see as somebody else's fight. "France and Spain never were, nor perhaps ever will be our enemies as *Americans*, but as our being the *subjects of Great-Britain*," Tom Paine wrote in the years that followed the French and Indian War. England "did not protect us from *our enemies* on *our account*, but from *her enemies* on *her own account*, from those who had no quarrel with us on any *other account*."[25]

Long before Paine articulated it so eloquently in *Common Sense*, Maryland's Catholics understood that their colony's connection to England was weighing them down. In the 1720s, 1730s, and 1740s, their Protestant neighbors clung desperately to their English identity, filling their houses with British furnishings and sipping their tea from

British china, "so that they might," one historian tells us, "with more credibility think of themselves and their societies—and be thought of by the people in Britain itself—as demonstrably English."[26]

Catholics, however, had no such anxieties about their English identity. The Glorious Revolution had done much more than just bring the age of religious toleration in Maryland to an end. It had firmly established that to be English was to be Protestant. Indeed, throughout Maryland's history, the most restrictive laws against Catholics tended to be passed during times when the colonists were feeling most insecure about their "Englishness." Anti-Catholicism, like tea and china, was a way for the colonists to think of themselves—and be thought of by the British people—as English.

While there was still much about English identity that they wished to claim for themselves—the right to be represented in the legislative deliberations that governed their lives, for starters—Maryland's Catholics understood after 1689 that English identity alone was not going to provide them with the liberty they sought. To claim the rights of Englishmen, they were going to have to assume the mantle of not English identity, but "Marylandian" identity. In 1776, that is precisely what they did.

Maryland's Catholics endorsed, contributed to, fought for, and died for an ideology that rested upon republican principles and mandated a cultural and political break from England. They supported the war and embraced the independence movement in numbers that were greater than those of their Protestant contemporaries, and they did so in spite of the anti-Catholicism in which the movement was couched. They were able to overlook the inflammatory words about their faith that sprang from the pens of people like Sam Adams and James Otis, because they saw those words for what they were—rhetorical devices that served the same effective, albeit inconsistent purpose that the concept of slavery served in speeches like the now-famous one delivered by Patrick Henry in 1775.

Right before declaring "give me liberty or give me death," Henry asked his slave-holding colleagues in the Virginia House of Burgesses whether their lives were "so dear, or peace so sweet as to be purchased at the price of chains and slavery."²⁷ For the colonists, "slavery" was a buzzword—three syllables that perfectly encapsulated every threat imaginable to the inalienable rights of Englishmen. "Popery" was an equally concise way of emphasizing the extent to which liberty could be violated, and just as Patrick Henry was not referring to the labor system that dominated his native Virginia when he compared British rule to "slavery," the *Maryland Gazette* was not referring to people like Charles Carroll of Carrollton, the most prominent Catholic in America and one of only four men from Maryland brave enough to sign the Declaration of Independence, when its editors railed against popery and accused the Protestant king of England of having "armed seventeen or twenty-three papists ... with powers sufficient to force every Englishmen out of [Quebec.]"²⁸

This is not to say that anti-Catholicism in the late eighteenth century was not a manifestation of a genuine fear, that it did not have a nasty side, or that its legislated form in Maryland did not offend Catholic ideas of justice and the proper role of government. It is simply to say that when anti-Catholicism, which for so many years had been a way for the colonists to express their "Englishness," was applied to a conflict with the King and Parliament, Catholics were able to recognize the rhetoric for what it was. They saw that the anti-Catholicism was really not about them, and that the ideology animating the core of the movement was their best chance to re-create the conditions of religious freedom that had characterized Maryland's founding.

In 1960, John Courtney Murray wrote that it was "impertinent" to ask "whether Catholicism is compatible with American democracy." The question, he insisted, should be "turned round to read whether American democracy is compatible with Catholicism."²⁹ It was a polemical and, in many respects, pointless assertion, given that in 1960 what mattered most was not whether American democracy had maintained its "natural law" virtue, but whether American voters believed Catholicism could be reconciled with the values of a democratic society. John

Courtney Murray worked hard to show that it could—in spite of his conviction that the endeavor was a response to impertinence. But even he had to admit that certain varieties of Catholicism could not be reconciled with the Enlightenment ideal. As the great French and Catholic observer of American culture, Alexis de Tocqueville, wrote in 1835, "In France, I had seen the spirits of religion and freedom almost always marching in opposite directions. In America, I found them intimately linked together in joint reign over the same land."[30]

Perhaps, then, the question should be neither whether Catholicism is compatible with American democracy, nor whether American democracy is compatible with Catholicism. Instead, maybe we should be asking how it is that Catholicism became "American." A number of very dedicated historians have already told the story of how Catholicism became American again, in the years that followed its incarnation as an immigrant church. This book, I hope, will help us understand how Catholicism became American for the first time.

1.

The English Origins of American Catholicism

The making of an American Catholic identity was a long and slow process. It accelerated rapidly as the Revolution approached in the 1750s and 1760s, but it began subtly and almost imperceptibly in the sixteenth century, as Catholicism's status in England moved "from monopoly to minority," and Anglo-Catholics were forced by circumstance to adopt an approach to their faith that empowered the laity, allowed for compromise with the Protestant majority, and drew a distinction between religious and national identities that did not exist among the people living in predominantly Catholic countries like France and Spain.[1]

Today, most American Catholics would probably insist that their Church began its life in their country as an Irish one. If they were savvy, they might say that the Church's initial identity was French, becoming increasingly German, then Irish, Italian, Polish, and Hungarian over the course of the nineteenth and early twentieth centuries, before taking on the decidedly Hispanic tone that it currently has in large pockets of United States.[2] Most would also probably insist that America's first Catholics had been poor. And on this point, too, they would be wrong. The fact is that America's first Catholics tended to be quite wealthy—and they traced their roots not to the untamed hills of Ireland or the arable plains of France, but to the wuthering moors of Yorkshire and the fens of East Anglia. It was in England that lay Catholics first learned to take responsibility for their religious identity, and it was English

Catholics who laid the foundation of the first distinctly "American" Catholic identity. It is in England, then, that this story must begin.

The historiography on early modern English Catholicism is extensive, rigorous, illuminating, and rife with controversy and disagreement—almost as much disagreement, actually, as there was within the English Catholic community itself during the early years of the seventeenth century. At that time, Jesuits clashed with secular clergy—that is, priests who did not belong to any particular order—over how much freedom from episcopal control the Jesuits in England ought to be allowed to have. Laypeople also clashed with their priests—particularly the Jesuits—over whether it was possible to swear the Oath of Allegiance that James I implemented in 1606 and still be a part of the Catholic family. That oath rejected the Pope's authority to depose temporal rulers like the Protestant king of England, and laypeople who chose to take the oath were in direct violation of a breve that Pope Paul V had issued against it.[3]

Among historians, the main points of disagreement are the questions of just how loyal English Catholics were to the Protestant sovereign of their country; just how seigneurial, or "gentrified" English Catholicism became—or needed to become—in the decades that followed the passage of the Acts of Uniformity and Supremacy in 1559; whether the faith that Henry VIII challenged when he broke with Rome was "vital" or "moribund" among the inhabitants of England at the time of the Reformation; and whether the Jesuits serving in England concentrated their resources on the Catholic gentry in the southeast, rather than the Catholic commoners in the north and west, because they preferred to "spend their time with their social and educational equals," or because they saw this approach as "the best way to win over influential people and escape the attention that strangers might arouse in humbler homes."[4]

All of these questions have important implications for our understanding of the kind of Catholic identity that took root in England's

North American colonies when, in 1634, Maryland was founded as a haven for Roman Catholics in the British world. Although the colony would never have anything even close to a Catholic majority, its proprietor and governor were both Catholic converts, and the social and legal structure that Cecilius Calvert implemented in his colony was meant to ensure that subscribers to his Catholic faith would be able to worship freely in a way that was denied to them in their home country, while at the same time maintaining—and displaying—their loyalty to the Protestant sovereign of England.

The clerical order that Calvert selected to serve his religious brethren in Maryland (at the priests' own expense, since the proprietor had no intention of formally establishing any church in his colony) was the Society of Jesus, the very order that clashed with seculars and the laity over the parameters of English loyalty—and which some historians have criticized for paying an inordinate amount of attention to the English gentry. The priests who came to Maryland, however, do not seem to have had a desire to advance their "conception of clerical dignity," as historians have alleged about the Jesuits in England. Maryland's clergy did not confine themselves to "educated households" where they could "re-create their student experience" with intellectual conversations that resembled the ones they had had at seminaries and colleges in continental Europe.[5] Indeed, the Jesuits who came to Maryland seemed more interested in converting the Natives who lived in the wilderness than in serving the English settlers who built brick and stone homes with warm hearths and copious libraries.

This tendency that Maryland's priests had to devote themselves to the Natives was actually a point of contention between the proprietor and the Jesuits. The manner in which Cecilius Calvert handled the disagreement has important implications for our understanding of how and why American Catholics became comfortable with the spiritual–temporal bifurcation that would ultimately characterize the cultural landscape in the new United States.

The story of Catholicism's decline in England is a familiar one, but it bears some repeating here. When Henry VIII separated from Rome in

1534, he had no intention of changing his country's theological outlook. Reformers found little in Henry's Ecclesiastical Appeals Act to convince them that the king had embraced the "justification by faith" that was animating the Reformation in Continental Europe. The Act simply declared that the king would have sovereign jurisdiction over all matters involving the Church in England, and while this renunciation of papal authority was enough to prompt Church officials in Rome to excommunicate their former "Defender of the Faith," the Act did not change the theological tenor of the official church in England.[6]

Change did eventually come—even if clothed in a mantle of self-interest. In 1536, Henry nullified all but three of the Catholic Church's sacraments—Baptism, Penance, and the Eucharist. The move was an effort to win the good graces of several Lutheran princes in central Europe whose friendship might come in handy should Charles V, the leader of the Holy Roman Empire, decide to defend the honor of his aunt, Catherine of Aragon. Henry had divorced Catherine shortly after breaking with the Catholic Church, and her nephew Charles quickly made it known that he was not pleased.[7]

None of Henry's "reforms" reflected a genuine interest in the Reformation. His actions, however, did initiate a slow, but monumental movement that thoroughly marginalized Catholics in English society and culminated in 1689 with the Glorious Revolution, which firmly established that to be "English" was to be "Protestant." Among the theological highlights in this transformative process were the introduction in 1549 of the Book of Common Prayer, which radically changed the Catholic liturgy through its use of the English language, and the passage in 1563 of the Thirty-Nine Articles of Religion, which limited the Sacraments to just Baptism and the Eucharist, embraced the Protestant maxim that individuals were "justified by Faith only," and declared that the Catholic belief in a transubstantiated Eucharist was "repugnant to the plain words of Scripture."[8]

What these radical changes actually meant to the bulk of the people living in England during the second half of the sixteenth century is not completely clear. Until recently, the prevailing historiography on early modern English Catholicism painted a picture of religious commitment that was far from vibrant. In spite of recent challenges to this historiography, the picture of early modern English religiosity as lackluster and riddled with folk superstition continues to be powerful, dominating our understanding not just of Catholicism's decline in England but also of the shallow and fitful start that Protestantism got during the first twenty-five years of the English Reformation. Between 1534 and 1558, the Crown changed from being Anglican to Catholic to Anglican again, and the English commoners, with the exception of those who had embraced Calvinism, responded to these changes with little or no interest.[9]

The vast majority of England's Catholics at the time of the Henrician Reformation—80 percent, by one historian's estimate—were "simple illiterates" who "flourished" on mindless recitations of the rosary, augmented their devotions with a wide variety of occult practices, had little or no understanding of the Latin liturgy, and "appear to have shown no coherent reaction at all" to Henry VIII's "breach with the authority of the Pope, destruction of the major religious shrines, and dissolution of all the monasteries and convents" in England. Theirs was a decidedly "popular" religion, rooted in superstition as much as in faith, and requiring little understanding of the theological debates—or their political consequences—that animated the halls of power in England throughout the sixteenth century. "People of this kind come into the Church without difficulty," one priest wrote during the early years of the Reformation. "But they fall away the moment persecution blows up."[10]

There were a few protests against the break with Rome, most notably in Lincolnshire, Lancashire, and Yorkshire, all of which are north of London. The wealthiest 5 percent of the literate population in these counties did not participate in the demonstrations, however—perhaps because theirs was what some priests called a "feigned Catholicism," that is, a devotion to religious practice that was designed to curry favor with Catholic leaders in government rather than with the Church or, more to the point, with God. These fair-weather Catholics stood to gain much from the king's confiscation of Church properties if they just kept quiet and accepted the religious changes. Woburn Abbey, for example, an estate in Bedfordshire that has belonged to the Dukes of

Bedford for more than 450 years now, was a Benedictine monastery before Henry VIII handed it over to John Russell, the First Earl of Bedford, in 1547.[11]

But if the religious landscape in England were dull, it was not merely the fault of the laity. The confiscation of the monasteries would not have happened as seamlessly as it did if the priests and nuns living in those monasteries "had stood fast and joined in with a general lay movement of protest." Many members of the Catholic clergy acquiesced, sometimes eagerly, to the changes Henry implemented, choosing to accept the pensioned retirement that the king promised rather than engage the threats or risk the discipline that would have come with protest. By the first quarter of the sixteenth century, the Catholicism practiced by the majority of the clergy in England had grown stale, dispassionate, and "antiquated." The priests and nuns responsible for maintaining English Catholicism, therefore, were uninterested in inconveniencing themselves for the sake of the Catholic faith, theologically or politically.[12]

By the time Elizabeth I died in 1603 and her Scottish cousin, James, assumed the throne, Catholicism had become, in the words of one historian, "a branch of the English nonconforming tradition." Catholics were as marginalized from the centers of power as the Calvinists with whom they shared nothing except an opposition to the Church of England. No one harbored the expectation that England would one day return to being a Catholic nation, and even the Jesuits, who had clashed angrily and publicly with the secular clergy in the 1580s over whether the laity should be allowed to attend Anglican services so as to avoid having to pay recusancy fines (the Jesuits did not think that they should), had resigned themselves to the fact that Catholicism in England was only ever going to be a minority faith.[13]

Exactly how small this minority Catholic community was at the turn of the seventeenth century is difficult to determine. To confine one's analysis just to the recusant rolls—that is, the surviving lists of people who chose to pay the fines first levied during Elizabeth's reign rather than attend Anglican worship services, as the civil law commanded—would be to miss a significant level of Catholic commitment and behavior among many of the so-called "church papists" who very carefully lived an existence that was designed to draw attention away from their Catholic beliefs. "Church papist" was the term used by the Church of England to describe a group of people whom the Catholic Church called "schismatics." A schismatic, according to the sixteenth-century Jesuit John Gerard, was a "Catholic by conviction but conforming externally to the state religion." Those who conformed "externally" usually did so by attending Anglican worship services, sometimes in addition to Catholic services, but more often in lieu of them. Many members of the Society of Jesus condemned schismatics as heretical hypocrites. Henry Garnet, however—a Jesuit who was ultimately executed in 1606 for attempting to blow up Parliament—believed that the Catholic-minded men and women who went to hear Anglican Masses did so not out of a sense of disloyalty or ambivalence toward their true Church, but out of a "fear of being a hollow and dissembling [English] subject."[14]

In the middle of the sixteenth century, the Catholic character of a church papist's religious commitment to Rome was vague and various. By the turn of the seventeenth century, however, many church papists were keeping Catholic clergy and schoolmasters in their homes, sending their sons—and sometimes their daughters—away to Continental Europe to be educated at Catholic schools, and carefully arranging for their daughters to marry into well-known, Catholic recusant families, even as they were attending Anglican services every Sunday. Although officials in Rome considered them to be outside the Catholic Church, many schismatics were able to receive Communion from Roman Catholic priests, because the secular clergy tended to be sympathetic to the delicate religio-political situation their laity found themselves in.[15]

To not count schismatics as part of the English Catholic community would be to underestimate the degree of lay Catholic commitment in early modern England. To count them, however, is difficult, since schismatics very consciously lived their lives below the radar of most of the people who would have been keeping the records. Nevertheless, in spite of the difficulties, historians have tried to come up with a number that reflects the level of Catholic commitment in early modern England, and the most respected estimates put the Catholic population at somewhere between 40,000 and 120,000 during the first half of the seventeenth century. The overall population fell somewhere between 2.5 and 3 million. Catholics, in other words, made up as little as 1 percent, and at most just 5 percent of the entire population in Stuart England. In contrast, the earliest surviving census from colonial Maryland reveals that nearly 10 percent of the colony's white population was Catholic—explaining why Lord Baltimore's experiment along the Chesapeake was considered to be a "Catholic colony," even though Catholics never came close to approaching a majority in Maryland.[16] English Protestants who migrated to the colony had to deal with many more Catholic neighbors than they had ever encountered in mid-seventeenth-century England—and in Maryland, these Catholics also served in government.

There was no dearth of priests willing to serve England's tiny Catholic community. However, because the Jesuits tended to cluster in the southeast, rather than the north and west, Catholics in Wales and the Scottish Borderlands often had to go for weeks without the benefit of clerical council, while priests in and around London were sometimes left with little or nothing to do. Technically speaking, after 1585, it was a capital offense for any Roman Catholic priest to set foot on English soil—and of the 800 priests who came from seminaries on the Continent to serve secretly in England between 1574 and 1603, 123 were executed, while countless others were forced to spend time in Catholic concentration camps in East Anglia.[17]

The Jesuits were the largest, single group of Catholic clergy serving in England, but many of England's priests in the first half of the seventeenth century were not tied to any particular order. These so-called "secular" clergy comprised the core of the itinerancy movement within English Catholicism that helped to keep the faith from dying out completely in the northern and western regions of the country, where many Jesuits did not serve. Secular priests would travel between and among the households in an assigned region, hearing confessions and distributing the Eucharist in the privacy of the laity's homes. In Yorkshire, for example, two secular priests traveled among more than a dozen Catholic households in the county, often disguising themselves as peddlers, so as not to attract the attention of local, Anglican authorities. The priests' efforts at subtlety were not always successful, however, and in 1592, authorities in Yorkshire discovered that a local schoolmaster was using a "popish primer" he had received from a secular circuit rider to "indoctrinate" the boys in his classroom. Among the parents called to task for letting their sons be tutored by this schoolmaster was Leonard Calvert, whose sons Christopher and George—the future Lord Baltimore—were forced to convert to the Church of England and study with a Protestant tutor in nearby Bilton.[18]

The seculars' experiences with the challenges of itinerant mission work exacerbated tensions that already existed between secular clergy and the Society of Jesus in the seventeenth century. Although the south and east were home to barely a quarter of England's Catholics, 42 percent of the Jesuits serving in England in 1635 lived and worked in this region, prompting one priest in Oxfordshire to complain that "there are so many priests in this country it is difficult to find shelter for them all." While working-class Catholics in Yorkshire were receiving Communion from an Anglican parson because the overworked secular priest who served their circuit could not be with them each week, Jesuits like William Freeman and John Gerard were enjoying quiet, domestic chaplaincies, free of the "sundry perils" that confronted any Roman Catholic priest traveling around the English countryside in the early modern period, and living in East Anglia, where, by Gerard's own account, "Catholics were very few" and "mostly from the better classes."[19]

The maldistribution of priests, however, was the least of the gripes that the secular clergy had with their Jesuit colleagues. More than half of the Jesuits in England were not in the southeast, after all, and a report commissioned by the Society in 1616 found that many of the Society's members were, like the seculars, "travelling in different localities, either on foot or on horseback . . . and had for the most part at least one house in which they could remain for some days to recruit [recoup?] themselves."[20]

The real reason the seculars were upset with the Jesuits is that the Society of Jesus tended to make the lives of all the priests in England difficult whenever its members on the Continent encouraged Spanish acts of aggression against England and called for the assassination of Queen Elizabeth as a heretic. Although the secular clergy understood the delicate circumstances under which they worked in England—many of them signing a proclamation in 1603 in which they declared that the Queen had "full authority, power and sovereignty over us"—the Jesuits adamantly rejected the notion that the Pope's power could be diminished in any way. This made the Jesuits unpopular not just with the secular clergy but also with many of the working-class laypeople who were trying to navigate the increasingly difficult religious waters in England without the benefit of a title or a healthy purse to protect them.[21]

Among those Catholics who were titled and/or wealthy, relations with the Jesuits tended to be a bit more agreeable—although the gentry, too, found reasons to disagree with their Jesuit advisors. Members of the Society of Jesus actually targeted the wealthiest and most influential Catholics in England when they arrived from seminaries on the Continent, facilitating the development of a mindset among some of the Catholic gentry that saw the secular clergy as culturally and intellectually inferior—and encouraging the seculars, in turn, to resent the Jesuits even more than they already did.[22] Whether the Jesuits deliberately cultivated this impression of the secular clergy is unclear; what is clear, however, is that they purposefully built a domestic framework for Catholicism—one that historians have come to call "seigneurial"—that stood in stark contrast not only to the congregational, or "parish," model that had characterized Catholicism in England prior to the Reformation but also to the itinerant model that the secular clergy in the north had worked so hard to develop in the years following the Elizabethan Settlement.

William Allen, founder of the English Jesuit college at Douai, laid the groundwork for this seigneurial approach to Catholicism in 1575, when he wrote that the priests serving in England should do their work "in private houses after the old example of the Apostles of their days."[23] This was, of course, precisely what the itinerant secular clergy working in the north and west had been doing, and as mentioned earlier, some of the Jesuits Allen advised did follow their example and move between and among families, never actually joining any of the households they served. But because the Society of Jesus chose to focus on the southeast, where the distance between Catholic families could be quite large, and where many families were wealthy enough to support a priest—or even two—entirely on their own, the peripatetic lifestyle of the northern itinerants ended up being neither practical nor necessary for a sizeable portion of the Jesuits working in England. For these men, Allen's instructions were an injunction to live with the families they served.

Getting England's wealthy Catholics to agree to the "domestic chaplaincy" scenario the Jesuits envisioned, however, seems to have taken some doing. In an effort to market this unusual living situation to the laity, Jesuits like John Gerard took the interesting—and historically significant—tack of pointing out that domestic chaplaincies gave laypeople the power to choose who their clerical leaders would be.[24] No longer would a rigid, episcopal framework and the accident of geography force laypeople—or at least those who were wealthy enough to feed, clothe, and hide a clergyman—to accept the services of an incompetent or ill-tempered priest, simply because Rome had assigned the man to serve the parish in which the laypeople lived. Under the Jesuits' plan, people would have a choice.

Indeed, the Jesuits' decision to focus disproportionately on the southeast created a glut in the "market" for priests in that region, such that Gerard's words about choice were more than just clever marketing. The wealthy laity were able to pick and choose their clerical leaders, and because the priests they chose were utterly dependent upon them for their subsistence, the laity also began to feel entitled to tell their priests what to do. This unintended side effect of the domestic chaplaincy model the Jesuits created took on a life of its own in the seventeenth century, and by the 1640s, Catholic clergy serving in England were complaining to each other and to the laity about laywomen who felt entitled to teach priests how to clean their chalices or even how say the Mass.[25]

The right to instruction, however, did not seem to go both ways. Priests who deigned to tell the laity how they should conduct their business or family affairs were often told by the laity to stay away from such "tender points," because they were encroaching upon their patrons' "temporals," an area that—in the minds of a growing number of laypeople—was beyond clerical concern. Not even Richard Smith, the Bishop of Chalcedon, was immune to this kind of treatment from the laity. In 1627, after Smith created a Church tribunal that was supposed to approve all Catholic wills and oversee the settlement of all Catholic estates, a group calling themselves "The Lay Catholics of England" sent him a letter, in which they informed him that "to set up any new tribunal with certain forms for the administration of justice, differing from or foreign to what is already established by law ... is the crime of high treason."[26] Domestic chaplaincies had, perhaps unavoidably, become "seigneurial Catholicism;" that is, a relationship in which laypeople viewed their priests as performing services in exchange for subsistence and protection—much like servants.

The reason the Jesuits focused on the southern regions where England's wealthiest Catholics lived was that their founder, St. Ignatius of Loyola, had believed his priests would be able to spread the Catholic faith more effectively if they devoted a considerable amount of personal attention to the spiritual and intellectual formation of the elites in any given society. The best way to "go about making converts," the Jesuit missioner John Gerard wrote during his time in England in the 1580s, was to "bring the gentry over first and then their servants, for Catholic gentlefolk must have Catholic servants."[27] This strategy proved to be successful in some families. The Babthorpes in Yorkshire and the Abingtons in Worcestershire, for example, encouraged the priests living in their homes to minister not just to their family members but also to their servants and to the tenants living on their property. Magdalen Browne, the Viscountess of Montagu, even went so far as to invite tenants and servants into her home in Sussex on Sunday mornings to hear the Masses that were said by her domestic priests.[28]

Many of the Jesuits who had domestic chaplaincies, however, "lived as remote as possible from the observation of [non-Catholic] domestics and visitors," because their sponsors did not want to generate controversy within a religiously mixed household and risk being charged with recusancy—or worse yet, treason. Not only were these priests not able to follow John Gerard's lead and cultivate the Catholic faith among their sponsoring families' servants, but they also did not conform to some modern-day historians' descriptions of England's Jesuits as sitting in the lap of aristocratic luxury, re-creating the discourse of their student days. There could be no late-night discussions over sherry when priests were hiding in so-called "priest holes" in "the upper stories or attic of the house" like "sparrows upon the housetop." Such circumstances prompted at least one Jesuit serving in Continental Europe and contemplating an assignment in England to remark on "how oppressive this constant solitude" must have been "to those accustomed to habits of conversation and reading."[29]

Still, the Jesuits in England remained committed throughout the seventeenth century to the Ignatian strategy of focusing on elites and cultivating personal relationships with them—even if that meant that the laity occasionally got uppity. Many of the "gentlefolk" the Jesuits focused on were titled peers—men like Anthony Browne, the Viscount Montague; Emmanuel Scrope, the Earl of Sunderland; and Thomas Arundel, the Baron Arundel of Wardour. As the years progressed, these men and their wives came to form the core of the Catholic community in early modern England. No more than 5 percent of the English population overall was Catholic, but more than 20 percent of the peers—and 25 percent of the middle-income landed gentry—subscribed to the Catholic faith in the mid-seventeenth century.[30]

Certainly the special attention that wealthy families received from the Jesuits played a significant role in the gentrification of English Catholicism. The political protections that came with membership in the English peerage also helped, as did the ability to afford the various recusancy fines—which, under James I, could be as high as £20. Literacy rates among the gentry, which in some areas were ten times higher than what they were among common farmers, also played a role. Beginning in the last few decades of the sixteenth century, Catholics and evangelical reformers alike relied on an extensive collection of polemical "tract" literature to strengthen the resolve of those who already subscribed to a particular faith, while encouraging those who were on the religious fence to commit one way or the other.[31]

Catholic writers like Richard Smith, Anthony Champney, and James Gordon took great pains to ensure that the tracts they authored in the early seventeenth century were short, concise, and unencumbered by theological details that would not have mattered to or been understood by most laymen. Their arguments consisted of simple recitations of the differences between Catholics and Protestants, unnuanced claims that "only the Catholick Romaine Religion is truth," and pervasive "persuasives" against "frequenting Protestant Churches." The tracts referred to Scripture only when biblical passages could be used to emphasize that God's "true" church was an unbroken one that—unlike any Protestant church—could point to a continuous line of clergy from the time of Christ to the present day. Still, no matter how intellectually accessible the polemical tract literature may have been, one had to be able to read in order to experience the tracts' unmediated influence, and in a country where it was illegal for Catholic priests to preach openly, the unmediated potential of these tracts was—ironically, perhaps, given the Catholic context—their chief asset.[32]

By the time James I assumed the British crown in 1603, then, Catholicism in England was thoroughly gentrified. This development meant that Catholics in seventeenth-century England were not only disproportionately wealthy, they were also disproportionately educated, as compared not just to their Protestant contemporaries, but also to their Catholic ancestors in England and their Catholic contemporaries in Continental Europe.[33]

Some of these gentry were educated at English Catholic colleges like the ones in Douai, Rome, Lisbon, and Valladolid, all of which were founded specifically to train Catholic clergy. At the start of the seventeenth century, slightly less than half of the young men who were studying to become priests in the College at Valladolid were from landed gentry families; by 1610, two-thirds of the clerical students fell into this category, and by the 1650s, nearly 75 percent of the English men studying to be priests in Valladolid and Rome were of "gentle" birth.[34]

Not all of the Catholic gentry whose parents sent them to the Continent to be educated intended to become clergy, however. Girls were often sent to school in convents like the one the Benedictines ran for English students in Pontoise, France, or the one that belonged to the Order of the Immaculate Conception of Our Lady—a.k.a. the "Blue Nuns"—in Paris. While many of the young women who attended these schools did become sisters, some did not. The number of students who left the Blue Nuns to marry was significantly greater in the eighteenth century than it was in the seventeenth, but young women like Henrietta FitzJames do testify to the fact that even in the seventeenth century, not all of the English Catholic girls who were educated at convents on the Continent wished to become nuns. FitzJames was the illegitimate daughter of the Catholic Duke of York and his mistress, Arabella Churchill. She spent three years at the school the Blue Nuns ran in Paris before leaving in 1683 to marry Henry Waldegrave, a prominent English Catholic peer. Henry and Henrietta, then, had two children—a boy and a girl—each named after Henrietta's parents.[35]

Boys who did not wish to enter the clergy had the option of attending St. Omer's College, which the Jesuits founded in the 1590s specifically to provide a Catholic education to young Englishmen who had no intention of becoming priests. In the 1630s, then, officials at the Jesuit College in Douai, which was facing a "crushing debt amounting to nine times the annual revenues," opened their doors to wealthy students who did not wish to be ordained, but who were in a position to pay. There is no evidence, however, that the curriculum at Douai was changed to accommodate these non-clerically oriented students, or that the curriculum at St. Omer's was radically different from what the Jesuits were offering at their clerical colleges. As late as 1761, Charles Carroll of Carrollton was writing home to his father in Maryland that the curriculum at St. Omer's "is only fit for priests."[36]

In the words of one historian, the young people who attended the Jesuits' schools on the Continent were subjected to "a diet of austerely monastic devotional manuals" by "a scrupulous clergy who abominated modern life." Indeed, the lecture notes of Nicholas Middleton, who taught astronomy at Douai in 1638, do seem to suggest a certain degree of hostility toward modernity that is, perhaps, not surprising, given the Catholic Church's antagonistic history with heliocentrism.

The notes feature a diagram of the universe in which Earth is clearly depicted at the center—this, nearly 100 years after Nicolaus Copernicus had first published *On the Revolutions of the Heavenly Spheres* and challenged the idea of geocentrism.[37]

In contrast, at Oxford and Cambridge, the seventeenth century saw the development of a new relationship between modernity and the course of study that was provided to the Protestant students attending school there. A growing number of these students were—like their Catholic counterparts—not interested in joining the clergy upon their graduation. Indeed, by 1640, roughly half of the students at "Oxbridge" schools had no intention of entering a profession at all—a freedom available to them, as members of the gentry class. Of the remaining half who did intend to assume a vocation, nearly 45 percent were not looking to join the clergy. Just 28 percent of the entire student body, in other words, wished to take on the responsibility of leading a Protestant congregation.[38]

These secular students, by virtue of their numbers, altered the kind of education that was available at Oxford and Cambridge. As university-wide lectures declined in importance throughout the early decades of the seventeenth century, and one-on-one instruction within the colleges themselves became increasingly common, students were free to seek out tutors who had modern approaches to history, science, and mathematics—the kind of approach that would benefit those looking to enter not the Church, but the increasingly globalized world of commerce. Because secular students wanted modern tutors, and because these students were far more numerous than their clerical peers, the first half of the seventeenth century saw the cultivation of a modern intellectual mindset among many of the tutors serving the Oxbridge population.[39]

Inventories of the books that belonged to students at Oxford and Cambridge—inventories like the one Joseph Mead compiled on more than 100 students while he was a tutor at Christ's College between 1613 and 1638—reveal that secular students gravitated toward tutors who emphasized History, Arithmetic, Latin, and Geography, rather than the Ethics, Hebrew, and increasingly outdated Aristotelian Physics that were taught to students looking to enter the clergy. Secular students wanted tutors who could provide them with insight into the ideas put forth by people like Francis Bacon and Walter Raleigh. Bacon's inductive reasoning—the foundation of what became the Scientific Method—was a repudiation of the Aristotelian logic that still dominated the clerical curriculum at Oxford and Cambridge and the entire curriculum—clerical or otherwise—at Catholic colleges throughout Europe. Raleigh's endorsement of Copernican physics—derived from his experience with using the skies to navigate his Atlantic crossings—might have generated controversy in Protestant circles, had he issued the endorsement seventy years earlier. Martin Luther, himself, after all, had spoken out against Copernicus in 1539, saying that the idea that the sun remained stationary belied the Book of Joshua, in which God temporarily alters the sun and makes it stand still. By 1614, however, when Raleigh published his *Historie of the World*, Protestant leaders were fairly comfortable with heliocentrism, and it was the Catholic Church that expressed the most ardent opposition to heliocentric theory, condemning—and then eventually banning—all books that endorsed Copernicus' ideas until 1757.[40]

Much has been written about the connection between the Scientific Revolution—and the work of Francis Bacon, in particular—and the birth of enlightened liberalism in the western world.[41] "The general spread of the light of science," Thomas Jefferson wrote in 1826, just days before he died, "has already laid open to every view the palpable truth, that the mass of mankind has not been born with saddles upon their backs, nor a favored few booted and spurred, ready to ride them legitimately by the grace of God."[42] America's third president understood that the challenge to traditional authority first posed by modern science—together with the discovery that everything in God's universe was bound by a set of permanent and discernible laws—had radically changed people's understanding of themselves and their government. He also realized that this change had been a long time coming and that men like Francis Bacon, writing and experimenting a century and a half before America was founded, were vital to the process. Indeed, Jefferson's musings on religious freedom were strongly influenced by Bacon's *New Atlantis*, a story first published in 1627 about a religiously pluralistic community in which the pursuit of knowledge is the foundation of all custom and law.

One needs to be careful, of course, not to exaggerate the changes that were made to the education Protestant students received at Oxford and Cambridge in the first half of the seventeenth century. As the late historian Christopher Hill was quick to point out, if we relied simply upon a list of the books and papers that were owned by a few students and dons in the 1930s, "it would be easy to argue that Marxism was being taught to undergraduates at Oxford and Cambridge" during that period. We know, of course, that Marxism never did become a pervasive or entrenched part of the curricula at these two universities, and we know this because we are fortunate enough not to have to rely upon just the scarce and incomplete inventories of a few students and teachers when it comes to the history of education in the twentieth century. We also know, however, that Marxist ideas, while not dominant, were salient enough at Oxford in the 1930s to produce some pretty influential Communists—including, ironically enough, Professor Christopher Hill, who concealed his membership in the Communist Party in 1940 so that he could work for British Military Intelligence and who—the world was shocked to discover in 2003, upon his death at the age of 91—may also have been a Soviet spy.[43]

The challenge to traditional knowledge and authority represented by scientists like Copernicus and Bacon—and the emphasis on "the glorious name of liberty" that Thomas Hobbes insisted, much to his dismay, was the unavoidable consequence of the growing popularity of Latin in Oxford and Cambridge (Tacitus and Livy, after all, liked to write histories in which "Kings abuse their places, tyrannize over their Subjects, and wink at all outrages and abuses")—did not coalesce into a full-scale, liberal movement in the first half of the seventeenth century. The seed of what would eventually blossom into an "enlightened" liberal mentality, however, whereby individuals came to think of themselves as having inherent rights, and governments were thought to be the servants, rather than the masters of the people, was planted by the educational changes that began, slowly, to take place at Oxford and

Cambridge in the first half of the seventeenth century. John Locke, after all, graduated from Christ Church, Oxford, in 1656, suggesting that Thomas Hobbes may have been on to something when he called the universities "the core of rebellion" and insisted that they were "to this nation what the wooden horse was to Troy."[44]

But what does any of this have to do with the relationship between Catholicism and Enlightenment liberalism? What implications did the education that a bunch of Protestants received at Oxford and Cambridge in the seventeenth century have for the gentrified Catholic community in England at the time—or for the Catholic community in British America a century later? To answer these questions, we must first understand that a significant number of gentry Catholics in England were actually educated at Oxford and Cambridge—often because they had officially been raised as Protestants. This was the case with George and Cecilius Calvert, the first and second Lords Baltimore and the founders of the colony of Maryland. It was also the case with John Lewger, who received his bachelor's degree from Trinity College, Oxford, in 1626 and was deeply involved with the Church of England until 1635, when he converted to Catholicism and subsequently migrated to Maryland, where he became Secretary of the colony. Indeed, at least 60 percent of the Catholic men who served as the governor's appointees to Maryland's Proprietary Assembly in 1639 were educated at schools in Oxford or Cambridge.[45]

It is not clear how many English men and women who were raised as Protestants chose to convert to Catholicism as adults. We do know, however, that conversion became almost trendy in the 1620s and 1630s, thanks to the efforts of Charles I's French Catholic wife, Henrietta Maria, for whom the colony of Maryland was ultimately named. The Queen had a habit of choosing converted Catholic women to serve in her household, in the hopes that these Catholic ladies-in-waiting might be able to proselytize among her husband's courtiers. Olivia Porter, for example, who converted to Catholicism after marrying a Spanish art dealer, belonged to a prominent Protestant family that included George Villiers, the Duke of Buckingham. Porter helped bring the noted intellectual Kenelm Digby back into the Catholic fold and was linked to the conversions of Lady Margaret Fielding, wife to the first Duke of Hamilton; John Villiers, younger brother to the Duke of Buckingham; and Robert and Charles Howard, sons of the first Earl of Berkshire.[46]

The playwright James Shirley was among a number of well-known Catholic converts who had had the benefit of an Oxbridge education. A 1618 graduate of St. Catherine's College, Cambridge, Shirley had converted by 1625, the year he was forced to leave his post as master of the St. Alban's School because of his Catholic faith. Undaunted, the young man went on to become the house dramatist for an acting company that Queen Henrietta Maria founded the year she married Charles I.[47]

Other noted converts who were educated at Oxford or Cambridge included Andrew Marvell, the poet and parliamentarian; Thomas Farnaby, the soldier and Latin scholar; and Christopher Milton, an attorney and jurist whose older brother, John, was really far more famous. A significant number of priests working in England were also converts who possessed Oxbridge degrees. For some, the decision to become priests had actually been a result of the negative reaction their families had had to their conversions. Herbert Croft, William Roos, Robert Venner, and John Campion, for instance, all cited lost inheritances or a "want of maintenance" as their reason for joining the clerical community.[48]

The personal and financial sacrifices that people like Croft, Roos, Venner, and Campion made when they converted to Catholicism are an important reminder that in seventeenth-century England, the decision to live as a Catholic was—almost paradoxically—an act of individual will, directed against a myriad of traditional authority figures not just within the state, but often within the family as well. No one understood this better than Elizabeth Tanfield Cary, the Viscountess Falkland. An extremely intelligent and well-read woman, Tanfield was married at the age of 16 to Sir Henry Cary, a member of the Privy Council who was an early supporter of British colonization in North America. Fluent in seven languages, Elizabeth Tanfield was entirely self-taught and had grown up hording candles, so that she could read at night against her mother's wishes. At the age of thirteen, she translated Abraham Ortelius' *Le Mirroir du Monde* into English, and in 1613, she became the first woman in England to write and publish a full-length, original play.[49]

When she was 20, the Viscountess Falkland secretly converted to Catholicism after reading and privately critiquing the works of great theologians like John Calvin and Richard Hooker. She bore her husband eleven children and kept her conversion secret from him for more than twenty years, until 1626, when she revealed her religious identity to members of King Charles I's court in a fit of anger over her husband's efforts as Lord Deputy of Ireland to force the Catholics living there to join the Anglican Church.[50]

Elizabeth Cary announced her Catholic identity by attending Mass with England's new Catholic queen. Henrietta Maria proved unable to protect the Viscountess Falkland from her husband, however. Sir Henry abandoned his Catholic wife upon hearing of her conversion. He refused to give Elizabeth the yearly sum of £500 that the Privy Council he served on had instructed him to give her, and contemporary accounts of the domestic dispute described Elizabeth as living in a state of poverty so abject that it included bouts of hunger. Sir Henry also denied his wife access to her children, as he was legally permitted to do under a 1593 law that allowed for all children over the age of seven to be taken from recusant parents. Elizabeth eventually kidnapped two of her sons and smuggled them to France. By the time she died in 1639, six of her ten surviving children had converted to Catholicism.[51]

By 1633, then, when a religiously mixed group of men and women set sail from Gravesend to help found a new British colony along the Chesapeake—one that was to have a Catholic proprietor and no established church—the Catholic population in England had become smaller, wealthier, better educated, and more invested in its religious identity than it had been a hundred years earlier when King Henry VIII initially broke with Rome. Whether it was that they had chosen to remain committed to the marginalized faith of their birth, or that they had chosen to convert, these people were Catholic not because they were required to be, or because it was the way things had always been done, but because they were genuinely moved by the idea that salvation was not an individualistic exercise. It required more than just an understanding of Scripture, as the Protestants insisted. "How can it appear unto me that I may be assured that this Book is the word of God," one young Catholic convert asked his Protestant father in a letter that was published in London in 1623. "I have ever found Protestants to be extremely puzzled in this point. . . . Their answers were so weak, different, disjointed, and uncertain, that at the last they have no refuge but to depend upon the tradition of the Roman Church, from whence they have their Scriptures."[52]

Salvation, for this convert and others like him, was a communal exercise—something that could happen only within the corporate body and tradition of the Catholic Church. *Sola Scriptura* did not "carry credit sufficient whereupon to build an infallible Faith," because Scripture had been translated countless times over the centuries, and "Luther himself differeth in about 30 places . . . in several translations of St. Matthews Gospel." Additionally, the Scriptures were not as "easy and plain" as Protestants liked to think they were. "The Trinity, Unity in God, the Incarnation, Resurrection and Ascension of Christ, our most B[lessed] Savior . . . do involve great and hidden mysteries and profound difficulties," the convert told his father. Only with the help of the "great Clerks and Holy Fathers" of the Catholic Church could the fullness of the Word of God be understood.[53]

Yet, though converts such as this writer saw themselves as dependent upon the wisdom and authority of the Catholic Church for their salvation, circumstance had forced them to assert themselves and challenge a vast collection of other authority figures in order find their salvation in the community of Catholicism. To be Catholic in England—even secretly Catholic—was to challenge authority on some level. The stakes associated with this challenge had always been high, as the countless Catholics who were imprisoned and hanged throughout the sixteenth century could attest. But after 1606, when James I convinced Parliament to enact an oath requirement that essentially defined English identity as being synonymous with loyalty to the king, Catholics were faced with more than just the threat of death when they chose to embrace and defer to the wisdom of the Catholic Church. Their sense of themselves as Englishmen was also at stake.

The early decades of the seventeenth century were marked, therefore, by an effort among some of England's Catholics to defend and reconcile their English and Catholic identities. As they did this, Jacobean Catholics found themselves privately embracing and sometimes even publicly endorsing a distinction between the "spiritual" and "temporal" realms that was not recognized by Catholic authorities in Europe. This distinction would one day become a key tenet of enlightened liberalism, articulated most forcefully by John Locke in 1689—the same year, ironically enough, that the Glorious Revolution firmly established that to be English was to be Protestant.[54]

The oath that raised the question of whether it was possible to be a loyal Catholic and a loyal Englishman at the same time was part of a greater act passed in the wake of the infamous Gunpowder Plot of 1605. That failed attempt by a small group of Catholics to blow up the houses of Parliament and restore Catholicism by force had been authorized by Henry Garnet, the leader of the Society of Jesus in England. Following the plot's discovery, Parliament became obsessed with the "better discovering and repressing of Popish Recusants." The MPs passed a law that required churchwardens and constables to compile a yearly list of people who had been absent from Anglican worship services for at least a month, so that these recusants could be identified and given the opportunity to start receiving Communion in the Church of England without penalty. If they refused, the recusants were fined £20 for the first year of their refusal, and £40 for the next. Because so many of England's Catholics were quite wealthy, Parliament also reserved the right to seize two-thirds of a recusant's lands if the king determined that the annual fines were not arduous enough, and to imprison violators without charge until the next session of the Court of Assize.[55]

The greater issue for church papists, however—who often did attend Anglican worship services and receive Communion from Anglican priests—was that anyone suspected of having Catholic sympathies could be required to swear an oath in which he asserted that the Protestant King James was the "lawful and rightful King of this Realm," and that the Pope had no authority to "depose the King... or to authorize any Foreign Prince to invade or annoy him." Takers of the oath also swore that even if they were threatened with papal excommunication, they would "bear Faith and true Allegiance" to the king and his successors, and that they renounced as "impious and heretical" the notion that the Pope could call for princes to be "deposed or murdered by their Subjects."[56]

The oath touched off old antagonisms between the Jesuits and their secular counterparts, as the Jesuit Robert Parsons accused the seculars of more or less writing the loyalty oath for the king. In a letter to Cardinal Robert Bellarmine in Rome, Parsons insisted that the language of the oath was taken straight out of a proclamation that thirteen prominent seculars had written and signed three years earlier. That proclamation asserted that Queen Elizabeth had "full authority, power, and sovereignty over us." Even though two of the seculars who signed the proclamation were subsequently executed for refusing to swear James's oath of allegiance because it used the word "heretical" in reference to the Pope, Robert Parsons still insisted that there was a direct connection between the seculars' proclamation and the king's oath.[57]

Within particular orders, there was dissension as well. The Jesuits Thomas Lister and Nicholas Smith were accused by the Society of Jesus of telling certain laypeople that it was possible to swear the oath as a matter of temporal loyalty. Benedictines who lived and worked in England often counseled their laypeople that it was permissible to swear the oath of allegiance, while Benedictines on the Continent like William Rudesind Barlow condemned the oath and everyone who took it as enemies of the Church.[58]

Even the seculars had dissension—or at the very least, inconsistency—in their ranks. The leader of the seculars, Archpriest George Blackwell, initially condemned the oath, claiming that it was "unlawful," but then backed away from that position a few months later, saying that although the Pope retained the power to depose any ruler whom he had excommunicated, he could exercise that power only if doing so would benefit the Church—which was not the case with King James. After Pope Paul V issued a breve against the oath in September 1606, however, Blackwell reverted to his original position, instructing his priests to refuse to swear the oath—until he was taken into custody by Protestant authorities in the summer of 1607. After several lengthy "interrogation" sessions, then, Blackwell swore the Oath of Allegiance and agreed to write a letter in which he instructed the priests in his charge both to take the oath and to ensure that their laity did the same.[59]

Blackwell's letter made no mention of the spiritual–temporal bifurcation that would one day serve as a foundation for the Enlightenment's ideal of government. Blackwell simply told the priests that he had changed his position on the oath after being informed that Parliament did not wish to challenge the Pope's right to excommunicate, but wanted only to "prevent the dangers which might ensue" if Catholics did not reiterate their loyalty to the king.[60]

Some of the Catholics who came forward to support the oath, however, did confront the spiritual–temporal bifurcation head on, and because their thoughts on the subject mirrored those of the king, these Catholic supporters of the loyalty oath often had their writings published and distributed at royal expense, while the responses of their opponents were formally banned from the kingdom. The ban did not mean, of course, that the responses against the oath did not make their way into the English Catholic community; after all, the tract literature that helped Catholics sustain their religious identity was illegal as well, but Protestant commentaries written against these tracts suggest that they were readily, if not widely available in England.[61] The ban on treatises against the oath, however, when combined with the royal support that treatises written by Catholics in support of the oath received, meant that England's lay Catholics were exposed to a disproportionate amount of literature that told them they could take the oath and still be good Catholics. And the title of one of the most popular of these pro-oath treatises suggests that the message was one that England's lay Catholics wanted to hear.

Thomas Preston's *New-Yeares Gift for English Catholikes* was published in 1620, and it was one of several books Preston wrote between

1611 and 1634 in defense of the king's oath—not because he felt a particular sense of loyalty to King James, but because he was fiercely opposed to the Jesuits, who had widely condemned the oath. Preston was a Benedictine monk who had actually studied at the Jesuits' English college in Rome before leaving to join the Benedictines in 1590.[62] His goal in publishing the book was the "appeasement of the Consciences of English Catholikes," suggesting that many Catholics in England had already taken the oath, or else wanted to take the oath and were just looking for a way to reconcile that action with their religious identity.

Thomas Preston gave them that way. He told them that they could be loyal Catholics and loyal Englishmen at the same time, so long as they had a firm understanding of "what authority is Spiritual and due to the *Pope* or *Church*, and what authority is temporal and due to temporal *Princes*." Catholics were obliged to obey the Pope when it came to matters affecting their salvation. When it came to matters affecting their country, however, their duty was to obey the king.

Catholics, according to Preston, were not only free to take the oath, they actually had an obligation to do so—because by not taking it, they did nothing to better their relationship with God, but they did risk bringing a great deal of temporal hardship to the families God had given them to protect. "If you have a charge of Wife and Children, for whom in nature you are obliged to provide," Preston told his readers, you were not at liberty "willfully to cast away" the resources that allowed you to take care of them. To follow Pope Paul V's breve and refuse to take the oath was, in many respects, to abandon the familial responsibilities that God had given you. English Catholics who were tremulous about ignoring the papal breve should remember that "the *Pope* is not the *Church*, but only the chief member thereof; and that the *Popes* [sic] opinion, and consequently his declarative *Breves*, when they are grounded either upon false suppositions, or else only upon his opinion, are not the *Rock* on which Catholikes ought to build their eternal salv ation."[63]

Preston's words were stunningly radical, given that they had been written not just by a Catholic, but by a priest. But such were the notions, attitudes, and experiences that characterized the community that British colonial America's first Catholics came from. Theirs was not a typical Catholic community for the early modern period. By the time King Charles I placed his seal on the charter that granted Cecilius Calvert proprietary rights to a colony that would ultimately stretch from the Chesapeake Bay to the Monocacy Valley, England's Catholics had become both self-consciously English and self-consciously Catholic. They had been required to take responsibility for both identities and to find a way of reconciling the differences between the two—differences that had been created and sustained not by them, but by their government and their church.

To achieve this reconciliation, England's lay Catholics drew upon their wealth, their education, the personal experiences many of them had with Protestantism, and the empowered, seigneurial relationship they had with their clergy, thanks to the illegal status priests were forced to endure in England. Lay and clerical Catholics alike became comfortable with a certain degree of rebelliousness because rebellion was a necessary and unavoidable component of the reconciliation they sought. Some Catholics, such as the Jesuits, rebelled more strongly against the government; others, such as the lay schismatics and church papists, rebelled more strongly against the Catholic Church. Most, however, pushed back against both with equal weight, telling their king that he could not have dominion over their religious consciences, and telling their church that it could not dictate their civil loyalties or behavior.

None of this is to suggest that Catholics, more so than Protestants, were the ones who bent the arch of English history toward Enlightenment liberalism. While it was a Catholic—Cecilius Calvert, the second Lord Baltimore—who created the first act of religious toleration in the British world, the fact remains that without the rise of "the individual" that resulted from the Protestant Reformation, liberalism, quite simply, would not have happened. It also goes without saying that the influence John Locke had on the development of liberalism was foundational, while that of the second Lord Baltimore was minimal—except within the Catholic community in colonial Maryland, where Baltimore's understanding of the relationship between religion and the state had a profound influence on what generations of Catholics understood to be the proper relationship between their colony and England. This, of course, is the subject of the rest of this book.

The experiences of the early modern English Catholic community force us to recognize that Catholics in British colonial America were never the blindly obsequious automatons that their Protestant countrymen often made them out to be. These early experiences also help us begin to understand why, when they were asked to take the radical step of accepting a new national identity that was to be defined according the basic tenets of Enlightenment liberalism, colonial Catholics were up to the challenge.

2

Prescience, Pluralism, and Profit

George Calvert was a truly remarkable figure. Born in England more than a century before John Locke published his "Letter Concerning Toleration," the first Lord Baltimore was a social visionary who believed it was possible for men and women of different religious persuasions to live in harmony with one another under the aegis of one common, national identity. Decades before the architects of modern liberalism put forward the idea that lawmakers should, in Locke's words, "distinguish exactly the business of civil government from that of religion," George Calvert invested his family's fortune in a colonial experiment that aimed to make money by doing just that.[1] Calvert, it turns out, was too prescient to be profitable. His colonial enterprise in Canada was a failure, and the colony he envisioned along the Chesapeake proved to be a financial black hole for his son and grandson. Calvert's vision of a profitable, pluralistic society, however, and of the church–state separation that would make pluralism possible, had a profound influence on the Catholic character that developed in British North America, even if the vision itself did not become a reality until hundreds of years after Calvert's death.

The contributions that George and Cecilius Calvert made to the history of liberalism in America have not attracted the mainstream attention they deserve. While the prolific Calvinist founders of a colony that hanged Quakers and held onto its state-supported church until well into the nineteenth century have been widely depicted as having come to North America in the name of "religious freedom," the men whose ideas and actions inspired the first act of real religious toleration in the British world have been relegated to a footnote—or at best a few casual sentences—in the traditional national narrative.² James Wilson, one of the nine men from Pennsylvania who signed the Declaration of Independence, recognized the injustice of this development when he commented in 1790 on the "ungracious silence" that characterized historians' treatment of George and Cecilius Calvert. "Before the doctrine of toleration was published in Europe, the practice of it was established in America," Wilson told an audience of lawyers at the College of Philadelphia. Pointing specifically to Cecilius Calvert and the Act Concerning Religion that Calvert pushed through Maryland's General Assembly in 1649, Wilson lamented that "the character of this excellent man has been too little known," before predicting that the Lords Baltimore would one day be hailed by students of History because "to their memories justice should be done ... by a just and grateful country."³

Alas, James Wilson may have underestimated the extent to which religious toleration has been more of an ideal than a reality in the United States—and the power, therefore, of religious bias to corrupt and mislead even scholarly minds. Countless Protestant historians in the decades that followed Wilson's lecture failed to appreciate the contribution that the Catholic Lords Baltimore made to the history of liberalism in America, and their indifference was rooted, almost certainly, in a general antipathy toward all things Catholic. To be fair, their biases may also have reflected a more contemporary understanding of the relationship between Catholicism and liberalism—which, as we saw in Newark, New Jersey, in 1903, was far from friendly.⁴

Many early Catholic historians were also persuaded by self-defensiveness and religious bias to inflate the Calverts' contributions to the history of religious toleration in America by ascribing to Maryland's founders a degree of altruism that cannot, in truth, be verified by the surviving evidence. This Catholic scholarship failed to alter the Protestant-dominated narrative on toleration that developed in the nineteenth and early twentieth centuries, and it may have pushed the Calverts farther toward the margins, by associating them with scholars whom many saw as Catholic apologists. There was, for example, "no room for doubt," according to the great, but parochial Catholic historian, John Gilmary Shea, "that Calvert's design in founding Maryland was to give his fellow-believers a place of refuge."[5] While such a conclusion was not without its reasoned merits, the fact remains that we have no documentation on what either the first or second Lord Baltimore's motives were, other than the fact that they both hoped to make money. To what degree, then, the Act Concerning Religion was a genuine move to create a refuge for Catholics, and to what degree it was a marketing ploy—designed to attract and protect an English population that was disproportionately wealthy—cannot be fully determined.

And this brings us, then, to the biggest reason the First and Second Lords Baltimore have not garnered the kind of mainstream attention they deserve: Very little documentary evidence exists about their lives or their motivations, leaving the historians who draft the scholarly narratives that ultimately determine the characters in America's story with little to go on, as far as the Calverts' personal investment in the idea of religious toleration is concerned. We know much about the philosophical and theological underpinnings of William Penn's and Roger Williams's commitment to religious toleration, for instance. "Liberty of Conscience," according to the founder of Pennsylvania, was a "Divine Prerogative," because only God "is the Object, as well as Author both of our Faith, Worship, and Service." The founder of Rhode Island had more practical reasons for promoting toleration. "To batter down idolatry, false worship, [and] heresy," Roger Williams wrote, "it is vain, improper, and unsuitable to bring those weapons that are used by persecutors." After all, "the sufferings of false and antichristian teachers harden their followers" and encourage them to "tumble into the ditch of hell after their blind leaders with more inflamed zeal."[6]

The First and Second Lords Baltimore, however, made no "Great Case of Liberty of Conscience," the way William Penn did. Unlike Penn, Cecilius Calvert had to fight the opposition of a group of Virginians who claimed he would "bring in the [Catholic] Spaniards" to Maryland once he had enticed unsuspecting English Protestants to settle along the Chesapeake. The second Lord Baltimore, therefore, could not afford to make a great case for liberty of conscience before sending the first group of colonists off to his colony in 1634. Consequently, scholars are left with a very limited understanding of the beliefs and strategies that motivated some of the earliest architects of religious toleration in the British world.[7]

We know that both the first and second Lords Baltimore were converts to Catholicism. George Calvert, the father, was born into a prominent Catholic family in Yorkshire in 1580, but by 1592, he had converted to Anglicanism, a denomination he seems to have remained faithful to until 1624 when, in his mid-forties, he made the decision to leave court politics and convert back to the faith of his childhood. George's oldest son, Cecil, converted at around the same time as his father, as did Calvert's second-oldest son, Leonard, who ultimately became the first governor of Maryland. Cecil Calvert actually changed his name to the more Roman-sounding "Cecilius" to announce and forever highlight his conversion to the Church of Rome.[8]

We also know that the colony George Calvert pushed for—and Cecilius Calvert brought into being—was the epicenter of British colonial, and then American Catholicism for more than two hundred years, giving Maryland a special place in the history of American Catholicism.[9] The attitudes and ideas that developed out of the experiences that early colonial Catholics had in Maryland reverberated into the eighteenth and nineteenth centuries, shaping the understanding that later colonial Catholics would have of their colony's relationship with the parent country and influencing the character that Catholicism would ultimately develop in the early republic.

―――◈―――

The spiritual circumstances that led George Calvert to revert to the faith of his childhood are—and probably always will be—shrouded in mystery. Undoubtedly, his return to Catholicism was something Calvert had been considering for months, and possibly even years before he finally took the step of converting in November 1624.[10] Conversion to Catholicism, after all, is not something one generally decides to do at the spur of the moment, even today—and in seventeenth-century England, the political ramifications of such a conversion gave anyone considering a switch to Catholicism an extra layer of rumination to work through.

Indeed, Calvert's conversion back to the Roman Catholic faith almost certainly would have ended his career as a Member of Parliament and King James's Secretary of State had he not already decided to resign from public life before announcing his return to Catholicism. The six years he spent as James's principal secretary were difficult ones for Calvert. During his tenure in that office, he became strongly associated with what ended up being a failed diplomatic endeavor known as the "Spanish Match." The match was an effort to marry Prince Charles, heir to the British throne, to Maria Anna, the youngest daughter of King Philip III of Spain. King James I coveted the Infanta's impressive dowry, because he resented having to go to Parliament to fill the royal coffers. He had also been searching for a long-term guarantee of peace with Spain ever since 1604, when he had negotiated a stable, but fragile end to England's nineteen-year-old conflict with that country.[11]

George Calvert and a few of the other, more ecumenically minded Protestant members of the king's court strongly endorsed the match. In addition to campaigning for it in the House of Commons, Calvert also played a role in the negotiations, wining and dining Spain's ambassador to London in an effort to get him to recommend the match to Philip, and defending the ambassador whenever prominent MPs inconveniently claimed that the ambassador harbored traitors by allowing English Catholics to worship in his home. In spite of Calvert's efforts, however, the proposed match encountered problems when Parliament balked at the idea of an alliance with Catholic Spain. Rather than endorsing the match, the House of Commons sent a petition to the king, asking him to declare war on Spain and to require that his son, Charles, marry a Protestant. James responded by imprisoning the MPs who wrote the petition, on the grounds that they had spoken disrespectfully about the king's "fellow Sovereign and ally, the king of Spain."[12]

As one of James's advisors and a vocal supporter of the Spanish Match, George Calvert was ridiculed by his colleagues in the House of

Commons, who expressed their anger at the king's imprisonment of the MPs in a time-honored, parliamentary fashion: They ignored and insulted Calvert whenever he raised his voice in the Chamber, even when the issue he was speaking on had nothing to do with the Spanish Match. Just three weeks after the MPs were arrested, for instance, Calvert challenged Parliament's right to legislate over England's North American colonies. His arguments were mocked, and the protest, itself, only confirmed in the minds of Calvert's colleagues that he was nothing more than the king's lackey.[13]

At issue was a bill that would have encroached upon the proprietary fishing rights in Renews (present-day Newfoundland) that King James had given to William Vaughn in 1617. According to Calvert, "the plantations," as the colonies were called, "are not yet annexed to the Crown of England, but are the King's as gotten him by Conquest."[14] As the personal property of the king, Calvert insisted, Jamestown, Henricopolis, St. George's, Renews, New Cabriol, St. John's, and Plymouth were all beyond Parliament's jurisdiction. Any laws passed by the Lords and Commons, therefore, could not be implemented in the North American colonies.[15] It was an argument that proved to be no more popular with Parliament in 1621 when George Calvert made it, than it would be a century and a half later, when the Sons of Liberty made it in response to Parliament's passage of the despised and notorious Stamp Act in 1765.[16]

Although his colleagues in the Commons saw his opposition to the bill as proof of his obsequiousness, George Calvert did have his own reasons for insisting that James could assign autonomous proprietary rights to colonial investors like William Vaughan. By 1621, Calvert had developed an interest in the revenue-generating potential of New World colonization. He had been an early investor in the Virginia Company of London, and just a few months before he made his defense of the king's prerogative, Calvert had purchased nearly 3,500 acres from William Vaughan and financed a small expedition to Caplin Bay, to see if the climate and topography there were conducive to settlement.[17]

These colonial plans were accelerated by the continued deterioration of Calvert's influence and reputation, not just in the Commons but also in James's court. The negotiations over the Spanish Match fell apart in 1623. The teen-aged Infanta, it turns out, did not care that George Calvert had staked his career on her matrimonial future. When Prince Charles traveled to Spain to secure the marriage, she announced that she was unwilling to marry anyone who was not a Catholic. The conversion of England's heir-apparent was out of the question at that point in time, and so Prince Charles and his advisors returned to London empty-handed and proceeded to shun everyone who, like Calvert, had led them down what turned out to be a diplomatic dead-end. Prince Charles immediately set out to build an alliance with another strong, Catholic monarch—this one involving a woman who would not insist that he convert. Less than two years after the negotiations over the Spanish Match collapsed, Charles wed Henrietta Maria, the younger sister of King Louis XIII of France.[18]

George Calvert was now seen by his colleagues both in the Commons and in the court of King James as the ardent advocate of a failed diplomatic initiative. This reputation only exacerbated the substantial degree of stress that Calvert was already feeling. A few months before the young Infanta decided to undo all of his diplomatic hard work, George Calvert had lost his wife of eighteen years, Anne Mynne. Her death had touched him deeply and left him a little less prepared than he might otherwise have been to handle the blow to his career brought on by the failed Spanish Match. Calvert wrote to his friend, William Cecil, that he was haunted by sorrowful images of Anne, "who was the dear companion and only comfort of my life." His wife had died giving birth to the couple's tenth child. Their oldest child, Cecil, had left for Oxford less than one year before his mother died, but Cecil's siblings—all nine of them—were still at home with their widower father, a man whom friends described as being prone to bouts of "melancholy" and having a tendency to dwell on "sad thoughts of his past" that sometimes "devour him."[19]

Heartbroken by his wife's death, embarrassed by the failure of the Spanish Match, saddled with the obligation of caring for nine, motherless and minor children, marginalized by court officials, and tired of the invective that was regularly directed against him by his colleagues in the House of Commons, George Calvert resigned as Secretary of State in February 1625. Three months earlier, he had secretly converted to Catholicism. Although there was much discussion in James's court about whether Calvert's claims to be resigning for health reasons were, in fact, legitimate, no one speculated that the reason he was resigning was that he had converted back to Popish faith. Very few people knew of his conversion, which suggests that his return to Catholicism was not the reason he resigned. In fact, his career may have been the only thing preventing his return to the faith of his birth, and once he made the decision to leave public life, George Calvert saw no reason to pretend that he still saw the Church of England as his path to salvation.[20]

Following his resignation and the public announcement of his conversion, Calvert was rewarded for his years of service to the king by being elevated to the peerage of Ireland. He became the first Baron of Baltimore when James gave him a patent to 2,300 acres of pastured land in the Irish Midlands. This was not unusual, even in light of Calvert's conversion. During his two decades as king, James I actually elevated ten Catholic men to the peerage, more than doubling the number of Catholic nobles who had lived in England under his predecessor, Elizabeth I. James's more tolerant attitude toward Catholics may have been the result of a personal connection to Catholicism through his wife, Anne. Some historians believe Anne converted to Catholicism from Lutheranism shortly after her arrival in England from Denmark, and that the king grudgingly accepted the conversion, so long as she practiced her faith quietly.[21]

Delighted though he was by the financial prospects of his barony in County Longford, the new Lord Baltimore was focused primarily on Newfoundland. His scout—failing, perhaps, to appreciate the difference between being a scout and being a booster—had assured him that the weather in Canada was "better, and not so cold as England" and that the land was "most commodious." On the basis of this information, Calvert had secured a royal charter in 1623 for a colony that he called "Avalon," named for the place in Somersetshire where many believed the Catholic Church had gained its foothold in England. The name suggests that Catholicism was something Calvert had been thinking about long before he actually converted.[22]

It took just one winter in Avalon for George Calvert to realize that his scout had duped him and that the weather in Canada was, in his own words, "so intolerable cold" it "could hardly be endured." He arrived in the colony in June 1628, in the midst of a three-hundred-year period that twentieth-century climatologists would eventually identify as a "little ice age." He had his second wife, Joan, seven of his children, two secular priests, and a religiously mixed group of artisans and craftsmen in tow. Calvert's intention was to stay in Avalon for good. By August 1629, however, he had sent his children back to England and announced that he was ready to "quit" his "dear bought experience" in Newfoundland and move to a more hospitable climate.[23]

The year that George Calvert spent in Canada, while short, is historically significant, because it provides scholars with a glimpse of Calvert's too prescient plan to turn a profit through religious pluralism. The first Lord Baltimore did not care what a settler's religious affiliation was, so long as that settler was skilled and willing to do the work necessary to make the colony thrive. Calvert had brought two priests along with him to serve his family, following the model of seigneurial Catholicism that characterized the English Catholic community in the early seventeenth century. His home, however, was a nondenominational place of worship. Not only did Calvert invite Avalon's Catholics to worship with him in his home whenever his priests said Mass or heard Confessions, but he also invited Anglican ministers to have their services in his house, and he encouraged Avalon's Protestants to worship there, as well.[24] It was an attempt to reach out to Avalon's non-Catholics and make them feel comfortable in an English colony that had a Catholic proprietor and no established church. The effort, alas, backfired.

Although it was not his intention, Calvert's gesture afforded Anglicans the opportunity to witness Catholic ceremonies freely taking place on what everyone (except, of course, the native Beothuk and Micmac Indians) thought of at the time as English soil. The whole point of a charter like the one James I had given to Calvert, after all, was the expansion of the king's dominion into areas that previously had not benefited from his governance. There was no difference between "England" and the colony of "Avalon" in the minds of the colonists, the king, or even George Calvert, himself—and at least one Protestant in Avalon did not like seeing papist rituals' performed on English soil.

Erasmus Stourton was an Anglican clergyman who arrived in Avalon in 1627 and returned to England a year and a half later, so that he could testify to the Privy Council that Catholics were worshipping as openly and freely in Avalon as they did in Spain. Stourton claimed that George Calvert had had the child of one of Avalon's Protestant settlers baptized by a Catholic priest against the will of the child's father. Calvert vehemently denied the charge, calling Stourton "wicked and lewd" for making it. In a move that suggests he did not grasp the extent to which Stourton's complaints might have represented a pervasive threat to his pluralistic experiment, Lord Baltimore also banished Stourton from the colony, as if keeping the man out of Avalon were enough to maintain the religious stability that the proprietor sought.[25]

The threat that Stourton posed to Avalon's success was never realized, because shortly after the angry Anglican testified to the Privy Council, George Calvert decided that Canada was not the place where he would make his fortune. Stourton's testimony, however, revealed a weakness in Calvert's plan to turn a profit through religious pluralism—and that weakness was that many English Protestants just were not "there" yet. Catholics, too, had their issues with pluralism. An official in Rome who was in contact with the two priests living in Calvert's home complained in 1630 that in Avalon, "the heretics held their services in another part" of Calvert's house.[26] Years later, when George Calvert's son, Cecilius, was attempting to realize his father's plan in a different colony—this one along the banks of the Chesapeake Bay—the flaws in that plan would manifest themselves in two violent civil wars, the second of which would ultimately lead to the conversion of the Calvert family back to Protestantism in the eighteenth century.

The harsh realities of life along the Avalon Peninsula were something "which other men for their private interests always concealed from me," George Calvert wrote to King Charles I in August 1629. While he still believed he was destined to find glory for himself and England in the New World, Lord Baltimore was convinced that he needed to be in a place "where the winter be shorter and less rigorous." The place he had his eye on lay just south of the colony of Virginia.[27]

George Calvert had been familiar with Virginia for quite some time. He had invested with the Virginia Company of London in 1609, and in 1624, when the company's charter was revoked after years of mismanagement, Calvert, who had not yet resigned from his position as Secretary of State, was among the men appointed by the king to manage the colony's business on behalf of the Crown. When he left Avalon for good in September 1629, Calvert traveled to Virginia "with an intention," according to the colony's governor, John Potts, "to plant himself to the southward . . . to make his residence therein with his whole family." Calvert did, indeed, leave his wife and servants on an estate in southern Virginia before returning to London in November, but his intention was to do more than simply "make his residence" in the colony. As he told King Charles before he had even left Avalon, he wanted a "precinct of land" south of the James River "with such provisions as the king, your father, my most gracious master, was pleased to grant me here."[28] George Calvert, in other words, wanted another proprietary colony.

Calvert had not abandoned his colonial endeavor in Newfoundland simply because he, personally, could not handle the cold weather (though certainly there was that). The fact of the matter was that the colony had failed to attract the settlers Calvert needed to turn a profit. He needed farmers, and in a land where "no plant or vegetable thing appear[ed] out of the earth until the beginning of May," it was unlikely that anyone looking for a life in agriculture would ever come to Canada. Newfoundland was the sort of place where only "fishermen that are able to encounter storms and harsh winters" could make a living—and fishing alone was not going to generate the kind of revenue Calvert needed to make a profit off of Avalon. "I . . . may yet do the King and my Country more service," he wrote to a friend in August 1629, linking his own fortunes to that of England, "by planting of Tobacco."[29]

By the time he left Avalon, Lord Baltimore was nearly broke, having lost more than £20,000 of his own money on his colonial experiment in Canada. A shipping accident along the Irish coast in 1630 only exacerbated his difficult financial situation. In addition to losing his second wife, Joan, who was returning from Virginia, in that accident, Calvert also lost all of the possessions he had originally brought over to North America with him when, in 1628, he had set sail for Avalon, planning to stay there for good.[30]

Still, in spite of the bad luck he had had with New World colonization—investing first in a joint stock company that was disbanded because of poor management, and then in a proprietary colony that made him miserable, ate up his personal wealth, and, in a roundabout way, killed his wife—George Calvert continued to pursue the idea of a proprietary colony in the New World. This dogged and seemingly irrational determination to have his own colony may be one of the strongest bits of evidence we have that George Calvert was motivated by more than just a desire to make money. Although the nineteenth-century Catholic historian John Gilmary Shea was a little too eager to say it, George Calvert may, indeed, have wanted to "give his fellow-believers a place of refuge."

Calvert campaigned for a proprietary charter in spite of his own poor and declining health—which never fully recovered from the winter he had spent in Avalon—his inadequate financial resources, and the vehement opposition he faced from anti-Catholic members of Parliament and from officials in Virginia, who were extremely vexed by his intention to encroach upon territory that they considered to be theirs. Even though the Virginia Company's charter had been dissolved in 1624, officials there still considered the boundaries of the original grant from 1606 to be in their jurisdiction. Those boundaries extended from present-day Kennesaw, Georgia, to Yonkers, New York. Baltimore sought a patent only for lands that had not yet been surveyed by officials in Virginia, but in anticipation of this move, Governor John Potts commissioned William Claiborne, a Calvinist surveyor who lived on a 20,000-acre island in the middle of the Chesapeake, to chart as much of the territory south of the James River as he could. Claiborne sailed to England in 1630, then, to oppose Baltimore's petition for a charter on the basis of these surveys.[31]

Baltimore's efforts to secure the charter relied heavily on the connections he still had within the court of King Charles, and especially on his long-standing friendship with Thomas Wentworth, the Earl of

Strafford. Calvert's friendship with Wentworth went back many years, and surprisingly, it seems not to have been adversely affected by Calvert's conversion. Wentworth was no friend to the Catholics, however. In 1632, just shortly before George Calvert died, he was made Lord Deputy of Ireland precisely because he had a reputation in Parliament for dealing harshly with English and Irish Catholics.[32]

While Wentworth did what he could to help Calvert secure the charter, Calvert did what he could to ensure that the new colony he fully believed he would soon be founding would have an adequate supply of Roman Catholic priests. Before sailing to Avalon, George Calvert had tried to secure the support of the Propaganda Fide, the Vatican office that, to this day, coordinates worldwide Catholic missionary efforts. The Propaganda, however, had not been interested in assigning priests to Avalon, and the two secular priests who ended up serving in the colony were there at Calvert's own expense.[33] When considering a new colony, therefore, Lord Baltimore turned to the Society of Jesus—an organization that was viewed with suspicion in England by Catholics and Protestants alike, but one that had made a financial commitment to mission work in the untamed corners of the world.

The bad reputation that the Jesuits had, particularly after the discovery of the Gunpowder Plot in 1605, may have been the reason George Calvert did not turn to them immediately after the Propaganda rejected his request for priests for Avalon. The last thing Calvert needed, after all, was for his loyalty to the king to be questioned by an association with the Jesuits. Additionally, Calvert wanted to attract as many Catholics as possible to Avalon, and the Jesuits had alienated a whole lot of laypeople with their uncompromising attitude toward the delicate situation English Catholics found themselves in during the reign of James I.

By 1629, however, Calvert had determined that the Society of Jesus was safe. His courtship of the Jesuits began before he had even left Newfoundland. Huddled in front of his hearth, imagining a new colony in a warmer climate, Lord Baltimore wrote to Andrew White, an English Jesuit whom he may have first become familiar with in 1622, when, in his capacity as Secretary of State, he had kept track of all of the priests who illegally entered the country. The text of Calvert's letter has not survived, but Andrew White referred to it many years later, in correspondences he had with George Calvert's son, Cecilius.[34] The dialogue that the first Lord Baltimore started with the English Province of the Society of Jesus in 1629 ultimately had a profound impact on the history of Catholicism in British North America. Thanks to that dialogue, the Jesuits would dominate the clerical landscape in the English-speaking New World for nearly two hundred years.

In February 1632, Lord Baltimore learned that he would be receiving the charter he and his friends had worked for more than two years to get. The arguments against the grant that the Calvinist surveyor William Claiborne had presented on behalf of Virginia's governor had held no sway with the Privy Council, which ordered the attorney general to draw up a patent that gave Baltimore jurisdiction over a relatively small parcel of the land south of the James River and north of what was then called the "Passamagnus" River. Today, that river is known as the Chowan, and it begins just north of the border between Virginia and North Carolina and runs south to the Albemarle Sound along the Outer Banks.

A group of businessmen from London who had spent some time in Barbados, however, were not happy to hear of the impending grant. They had been hoping to draw upon their Caribbean experiences to create a sugar colony in the territory that Baltimore was about to receive. Rather than risk having this new source of opposition delay the grant any longer, Baltimore suggested that the patent be modified, so that the land he received was well north of Jamestown, in a less desirable, somewhat swampy area north and east of the Potomac River and along the Chesapeake Bay.[35] The Privy Council agreed to the change, and a new patent was drawn up in March 1632. A few weeks later, however, before the charter for what was to be called *Terra Mariae*, or "Maryland," could formally receive its seal, George Calvert, Baron of Baltimore and Lord Proprietor of Avalon, died. He was fifty-two years old.

The illness that killed George Calvert was swift. He died just one day after updating his will to reflect the fact that his second son, Leonard, was now over the age of twenty-one.[36] It had been nearly five years since Leonard Calvert first reached the age of adulthood, but not until April 1632 did George Calvert feel it was necessary to reflect that milestone in his will. The fact that he died the next day indicates that Calvert's death was quick; the fact that he updated his will at all—after five years of not being concerned that it was out-of-date—indicates that he knew he was dying and would never see Maryland.

George's death, while untimely, did not undermine his efforts to secure the charter for a colony along the Chesapeake, and in June 1632, five weeks after George Calvert died, his oldest son, Cecilius, became the first proprietor of Maryland. When he accepted the charter, Cecilius was not yet twenty-seven years old. He had been married for five years by that point—and had officially been Catholic for only a couple of years longer. His wife, Anne Arundel, came from a long line of English Catholics and was the daughter of Thomas Arundel, a prominent Catholic peer. Anne Arundel was just thirteen years old when she married Cecilius, which is probably the reason the couple had only one child after five years of marriage. That daughter, Mary, was one of three Calvert children who would survive to adulthood—and the only one born before her father became the second Lord Baltimore.

Technically speaking, Cecilius Calvert did not have to assume ownership of the colony his father had worked so hard to realize. Because the proprietary charter for Maryland had not actually been given to George Calvert before he died, the colony was not formally a part of Cecilius' inheritance. The second Lord Baltimore clearly wanted it, though—and King Charles I had no reason to deny George's son the inheritance that certainly would have been his, had the first Lord Baltimore lived just a few weeks longer.

Why Cecilius Calvert wanted Maryland remains a mystery, however, since neither he nor his father left any surviving correspondence on the subject. On the one hand, it seems reasonable to conclude that Cecilius Calvert wanted to make money—many people do, after all—and that a proprietary colony in the New World looked like a good way to go about doing that. On the other hand, though, the second Lord Baltimore had little actual reason to believe that Maryland would be anything other than a colossal money pit; his father, after all, had lost

£20,000 on the colonial experiment in Canada, and the colony of Virginia, while plagued with bureaucratic and demographic problems that could easily have been avoided with just a little bit of planning, still stood as a testament to the fact that moving a colony to the warmer climes of the South was in no way a guarantee of its success.

Much like his father, though, Cecilius Calvert wanted to live in the New World, not just make money off of it, and this desire offers us an important clue into his motivation for seeking the charter. The second Lord Baltimore would never actually make it to Maryland, tied to England as he was by financial and political obligations that forced him to govern the colony from the other side of the Atlantic Ocean until his death in 1675. He told a number of his friends, however, that he wished to leave England and live with his wife and children on an estate in North America—where his status as Lord Proprietor would allow him to create a climate that welcomed, or at the very least accepted the Catholic faith he had embraced in his early twenties.[37]

Cecilius Calvert's intention when he accepted the charter to Maryland, then, may have been to create a kind of seigneurial Catholicism writ large. The society he attempted to build along the Chesapeake certainly mirrored many of the mixed households that England's Catholic peers lived in at the turn of the seventeenth century. In these households, resident priests served the Catholic members openly, but quietly—like "sparrows upon the housetop"—so as not to offend the Protestant servants who were a necessary and important part of the household.[38] This scenario, on a much grander scale, was the vision that Cecilius Calvert had for Maryland.

Maryland's residents, alas, did not always share this vision. Throughout the first fifty years or so of the colony's existence, Protestants seemed determined to be offended by their Catholic neighbors, and Catholic priests seemed determined to be anything but quiet. These attitudes complicated the vision Cecilius Calvert had for his colony, and those complications, ultimately, caused the Catholic Calverts to lose Maryland—but not until after Cecilius Calvert had formulated the first act of religious toleration in the British world and, in so doing, provided a foundation for the making of an American Catholic identity.

The charter that Cecilius Calvert received from King Charles I was pretty special. In the history of British colonial involvement in North America, England's king handed out just three charters that provided the recipients with the kind of authority and autonomy that the second Lord Baltimore enjoyed in Maryland. Cecilius Calvert's was the second of the three charters. The third was issued to the eight proprietors of Carolina nearly thirty years after the first English settlers had arrived in Maryland. The first was issued to George Calvert, so that he could found the colony of Avalon.[39]

What made the charters for Avalon, Maryland, and Carolina so generous is that they granted the recipients every privilege that the "Bishops of Durham . . . ever heretofore hath had, held, or enjoyed." Durham was a remote and sparsely populated province, far removed from the centers of power in London. The local authorities there had possessed a great deal of autonomy in relation to the Crown since at least the fourteenth century, if not earlier. The Durham bishops could create circuit courts and appoint judges to them. All writs and indictments that came out of those courts were issued in the name of the bishops, rather than the king or queen, and because of that, the rulers of Durham had the power to indict or pardon anyone for anything—even the capital offense of treason. The Durham bishops also had the authority to declare war and raise an army whenever they deemed it was necessary.[40]

The reason the Durham bishops had so much autonomy was that the territory's precarious position along the Scottish borderlands required that the authorities there have the flexibility to respond quickly and successfully to the tenuous and often volatile local conditions. The Bishops of Durham, in other words, were rulers of a unique community within England that the king recognized could not always be governed by the principles animating life in the rest of the country. The rulers of Durham, therefore, were allowed to construct a legal system that reflected the unique needs of the population living in their province.

Decades after he left Durham, where he had lived as a boy after the Yorkshire High Commission mandated that he and his brother, Christopher, be educated by an Anglican tutor, George Calvert must have remembered the special privileges that the bishops of Durham had. Tellingly, the charter that he helped to secure for what he knew was going to be a religiously mixed colony—in an area already populated with angry, Protestant Virginians—gave Maryland's Catholic proprietor the same privileges that Durham's bishops used to control their unusual population.[41]

Why, exactly, the Protestant king of England was willing to give a Catholic nobleman so much power is a bit of a historical puzzle, and the Maryland charter may actually serve as proof of what some scholars (and certainly many of Charles's own contemporaries) have alleged—namely, that Charles I, if not an actual church papist, was at the very least someone who had Catholic sympathies. Not only were his wife and mother Catholic, but throughout his reign—which was cut short in 1649 by his execution—Charles I actually worked privately to reconcile the Anglican and Roman Catholic Churches. He expressed regret that the Reformation had happened, and at one point, he even outlined a "middle way" between Anglicanism and Catholicism that included having the Catholic Mass said in the vernacular. Charles felt that Catholic priests should be allowed to marry, provided that they were not bishops, but he believed that bishops in both the Anglican and the Catholic Churches ought to be prohibited from marrying, since the marriage bed could compromise the code of clerical silence that gave the Sacrament of Penance its integrity.[42] Penance, of course, was not technically "sacramental" in the Church of England, and so when he placed so much moral weight on the power of the Confession, Charles I revealed his openness to certain elements of Catholic doctrine.

While Catholic sympathies may explain why King Charles was willing to give Lord Baltimore so much power in Maryland, they do not explain why he felt it was necessary to place the colony's proprietor on an even level with the bishops of Durham. To understand that, we need to consider the goals that George and Cecilius Calvert must have had for Maryland and their strategies for achieving those goals.

The Durham clause makes sense only if we assume that the Calverts intended to target Catholics for colonization, and that King Charles knew this was their intention and supported them in the endeavor.

Cecilius Calvert, like his father before him in Avalon, had no plans to formally establish the Anglican Church in Maryland; the lack of establishment, in all likelihood, would make the colony attractive to Catholics. Although it would not have been realistic for Lord Baltimore to expect that Maryland could ever have been populated exclusively, or even primarily with English Catholics, it was reasonable for him to assume that the absence of an established, Protestant church would convince many Catholics to make the hazardous journey across the Atlantic. Perhaps Cecilius Calvert wanted large numbers of Catholics to come to his colony because he wished to provide a free religious environment to as many of his coreligionists as possible. Or maybe he targeted Catholics because he had inherited a substantial amount of debt from his father, and England's Catholics were disproportionately wealthy and nicely poised to bring the bodies to the colony that Calvert needed to turn a profit. Either way, Cecilius Calvert clearly planned to have a whole lot of Catholics living in his colony.

Catholics, however, would not be the only people to make the journey to Maryland. Many Protestants, the king and Calvert undoubtedly knew, would also want to travel to the Chesapeake Bay, seeking not religious freedom, per se, but the modicum of independence that the vast acreage of the New World promised. Indeed, many of the servants that Maryland's early Catholic settlers brought over with them were Protestants who had agreed to give up several years' worth of freedom in exchange for passage to the New World. Lord Baltimore wanted them to come; Maryland, after all, was an investment that could pay off only so long as it was populated. These Protestants, however, were going to find themselves surrounded by more Catholics than they had ever been exposed to before in England—and not only that, but many of these Catholics were also going to be in leadership roles. Maryland's charter, after all—like many of the colonial charters issued by the king of England before it—called for the creation of a local legislative assembly. Cecilius Calvert had every intention of allowing Catholics to serve in that assembly. Indeed, Maryland's first resident governor was the proprietor's own brother, Leonard, who, like Cecilius, was a convert to Catholicism.

King Charles knew, then, that Protestants in Maryland were going to have to do something they had never had to do while they were in England, and that is answer to the authority of Catholic political leaders. Those Catholic leaders, in turn, were going to have to find a way of legitimizing their leadership in the minds of Maryland's Protestants, and they were going to have to do this in a way that still allowed them to protect themselves from the anti-Catholic biases that most of those Protestants carried with them—biases that would never completely disappear, no matter how much legitimacy the Protestants might be willing to grant to their Catholic governor and proprietor.

Hence, King Charles I included a provision in the charter that allowed Lord Baltimore to do what he needed to do to keep the peace in Maryland. This is what the Durham clause was all about. Interestingly, Calvert did not actually make use of the Durham clause during the first fifteen years of Maryland's existence. The tactics he employed initially for keeping the peace did not depend upon the extra-special privileges the king had given him. To keep his colony's Catholics in line, Calvert relied simply upon "the dependency which the Government of Maryland hath upon the State of England," reminding lay and clerical Catholics alike that it was British law, not canon law, to which he was bound as an English proprietor.[43] To keep Maryland's Protestants in line, he relied on good old-fashioned nepotism, constructing a government in his colony that was made up primarily of Catholics and sympathetic Protestants who either had Catholic mothers, or else had married into prominent Catholic families and were willing to work hard, therefore, to protect the political status of their relations.

It was only when these tactics failed, and Maryland's government was briefly taken over by a gang of angry Protestants who stole from Catholic landowners and forced the proprietor's Catholic governor to flee to Virginia, that the second Lord Baltimore took advantage of the Durham clause. Following what is known as the Ingle-Claiborne Rebellion of 1645, Cecilius Calvert used his vast amount of proprietary autonomy to push a law through the colonial assembly that demanded a degree of religious toleration from Maryland's residents that no person living in England at the time was obliged to respect. This law, Catholics would correctly insist decades later, marked the beginning of a constitutional separation between England and Maryland—one that would ultimately have enormous consequences in the 1760s and 1770s.

In his bid to rapidly populate Maryland, Cecilius Calvert focused on England's losers in the game of primogeniture. His charter gave him the right to "confer favors, rewards, and honors" upon the inhabitants of his colony and "invest them with what titles and dignities soever he shall see fit." The titles could "be not such as now used in *England*"—a baron in Maryland, in other words, would not be recognized as a baron in the parent country.[44] Nevertheless, Cecilius Calvert hoped that the opportunity to receive a title like the one that he had inherited in Ireland would prove to be very attractive to the second and third sons of England's noblemen, since these young men were barred by law from inheriting their fathers' titles and estates.

Any individual who transported five "able men between the ages of 16 and 50" to Maryland would receive one thousand acres "which shall be erected into a Manor, and be conveyed to him, his heirs, and assigns for ever, with all such royalties and privileges as usually belong to Manors in *England*." For every five additional men that a newly minted, New World baron brought over, another one thousand acres would be added to his grant. Calvert's only stipulation was that each man brought to Maryland had to be completely provided for, "which, together with their transportation, will amount to about 20 £ a man." The new barons also had to pay an annual quit-rent to the proprietor of 20 shillings for every one thousand acres.[45]

To publicize his colonial endeavor, Baltimore relied upon a few, key partners—all of them Catholic. Some of these Catholics quietly, but deliberately targeted the English Catholic community when extolling the advantages that immigration to Maryland presented. Robert Wintour, for instance, wrote to his friend and coreligionist, Captain John Reade, in September 1635 and told Reade that in Maryland, Catholics had "nothing to doe but to be merry and grow fat, eat, drink & recreate, and give God thanks." Wintour had spent the early part of his maritime career illegally ferrying Benedictine nuns from England to Brussels. No doubt he found recreating and growing fat to be a less dangerous—and more enjoyable—expression of his faith.[46]

Other Catholics who worked to populate Maryland were more ecumenical in their approach, writing for a general, unnamed audience and staying away from the issue of religion for the most part, focusing instead on the colony's climate and on "the commodities that may be procured in Maryland by industry." Jerome Hawley and John Lewger, for instance, were two Catholic converts who chose not to sign their names to the *Relation of the Lord Baltemore's Plantation in Maryland* that they composed in 1635, lest their known Catholic identities detract from the message they wanted to convey.[47] That message was surprisingly honest, lacking the hyperbole and bombast that typically characterized colonization tracts from the period. Their honesty, however, did not diminish their enthusiasm; Hawley and Lewger made it clear that Maryland was a place of "great abundance" where Englishmen with a sense of adventure could thrive. The soil there was "very rich," the pork was "not inferior to the bacon of *Westphalia*," and the summers, while not exactly pleasant, were tolerable—about as "hot as in *Spain*."[48]

Hawley was among the original group of settlers who sailed from Gravesend in November 1633, landing on the southern tip of Maryland's western shore in March 1634. The tract he published in the spring of 1635, therefore, contained information that he had experienced firsthand, even if only for a short time. John Lewger, however, did not arrive in Maryland until November 1637, two and a half years after the *Relation* had been published. His contributions to the pamphlet, therefore, were merely literary.

Like Jerome Hawley, Fr. Andrew White was one of the first settlers to come to Maryland. He published one colonization tract for Lord Baltimore in 1633, before he set sail for the New World. Everything else he wrote about the colony, however, was derived either from his own experiences or from conversations he had had with the English people he lived with until 1645, when, in the midst of the Ingle-Claiborne Rebellion, he was arrested for being a Catholic priest and shipped back to England.[49] White, too, chose not to identify himself (or his religious leanings) to most of the colonists he hoped to attract. His *Realtio Itineris in Marylandiam,* written in 1634, was directed to the Jesuit community in Rome—as the Latin title might suggest. The other four tracts he authored, however, were all written in English, for an English audience—and all of them were welcoming to Protestants.

White focused primarily on the weather and soil in Maryland. Like many colonial boosters at the time, he did list the opportunity to bring the Native Indians to Christ as a reason to make the hazardous journey across the Atlantic. The "Christ" White insisted the Indians should be brought to, however, was always a generic one, a nondenominational savior that Protestants of any stripe could feel comfortable with. Although White did mention in one of his tracts that the first group of settlers constructed a cross upon their arrival in the Chesapeake and "kneeled down and said certain Prayers" in front of it, he carefully said nothing about the denominational character of those prayers or about the Catholic faith of the "Governor and Commissioners who put . . . their hands first onto [the cross]."[50]

In spite of the promotional literature, the European peopling of Maryland was slow. By 1681, nearly fifty years after the *Ark* and the *Dove* had landed at Point Comfort in Virginia and sailed up the Potomac to what would eventually become St. Mary's City, the white population in Maryland was just 19,000. In contrast, New England had more than 25,000 white people living in the region by 1660. New England's settlers had arrived after the founding of Plymouth in 1620 and the Massachusetts Bay colony in 1630. The Puritans had had a head start, in other words—but only just barely.[51]

The slow population growth in Maryland was not the consequence of a lack of interest. More than 30,000 Europeans came to Cecilius Calvert's colony between 1634 and 1684. Their mortality rates, however, were quite high. Death came more frequently to the muggy, mosquito-infested Chesapeake than it did to the shores of New England, where the summers were short, cool, and considerably less humid. Mortality rates in seventeenth-century Massachusetts, for example, were lower than what they were at that same time in England. The average man in seventeenth-century England, however, lived fifteen years longer than did his contemporary in Maryland. Indeed, 17 percent of the men who either came to Maryland when they were in their early twenties, or else reached that age during the time that they spent in the colony, were dead before the age of 30. And because most of the people who came to Maryland during these early decades were men who had been raised in a culture that scorned miscegenation with the native North American Indians, the early immigrants to Lord Baltimore's colony were not only dying, but they also were not replacing themselves.[52]

The first crop of settlers was small. Although some clerical leaders in the English Catholic community claimed that as many as 800 people were on the *Ark* and the *Dove* when the ships set sail for Maryland—and that the passengers were, for the most part, Catholic—Baltimore, himself, estimated that no more than 325 people were among the first group of settlers, and the actual number may have been as low as 140. Before the two ships departed, 128 passengers swore the Oath of Allegiance—an oath that many, but not all English Catholics had reconciled with their faith.[53] It is possible that some of the people who swore the oath were Catholic; if we assume, however, that a majority of them were Protestant—and that the admittedly conservative estimate of 140 total passengers is correct—that means that the majority of Maryland's first settlers did not share a faith with the colony's proprietor, its governor, or its two commissioners.

Much to his dismay, Cecilius Calvert was not among his colony's first group of settlers. The proprietor fully intended to move to Maryland along with his family, but difficult financial matters that he had inherited from his father, combined with a series of political battles that he had to fight, not just with anti-Catholic MPs but also with the English Province of the Society of Jesus, kept him in England and Ireland. Consequently, Cecilius Calvert, like his father before him, never actually got to see Maryland.[54]

That did not mean, however, that the second Lord Baltimore did not exert a personal influence over the lives—and specifically, the religious lives—of the people who chose to live in his colony. As an absentee proprietor, Cecilius Calvert needed to instruct his representatives on a wide variety of difficult matters involved with colonial settlement. The topic that he chose to begin with was the matter of religion—that is, how English Catholics were to behave while they were in Maryland, and how Protestants there were to be treated by their Catholic neighbors and by the proprietor's representatives in the colony's government.

Calvert started with religion, because the issue was inextricably linked to many of the other matters that he needed to instruct his brother on—especially the two most pressing matters of concern: (1) the question of how Leonard Calvert was going to build a trading relationship with his neighbors in Virginia, when those neighbors had tried to prevent the settling of Maryland by spreading rumors that the *Ark* and the *Dove* would be "carry[ing] over Nuns into Spain and Soldiers to the King [of Spain]"; and (2) the question of how Leonard Calvert was going to approach the Calvinist surveyor, William Claiborne, whose hatred for Catholics was well known, but who lived in territory that was now, technically, a part of Maryland.[55] Claiborne had worked hard in 1629 to chart the land south of the James River so that George Calvert could not include it in the grant he was seeking from Charles I. One can only begin to imagine the disappointment and consternation that William Claiborne must have felt, then, in 1632, when he learned that the grant Cecilius Calvert had received from the king included Kent Island, the large landmass in the middle of the Chesapeake Bay where Claiborne had been living for more than five years!

In a letter that he wrote just a few days before the *Ark* and the *Dove* left Gravesend, Cecilius Calvert informed his brother and the two Catholic commissioners he would be working with, Jerome Hawley and Thomas Cornwallis, that it was their responsibility to "preserve unity and peace amongst all the Passengers ... at Land as well as at Sea." To accomplish this, Calvert insisted, the governor and his men were going to have to make sure that the Catholics in their group did not become too bold in their new, more religiously tolerant environment—that they did not get "carried away," so to speak, with the "spirit of freedom" that was going to characterize life for them in Cecilius Calvert's New World.[56]

Yes, there would be no tax to support the Anglican Church in Maryland or law requiring that the people living there attend Anglican worship services; and yes, the priests there would be able to live openly as priests, without the fear of being arrested simply because they ministered to people who were already Catholic. But there was still the matter of nearby Virginia and its angry Protestants to be considered. There was also the reality that Catholics would only ever be a minority in Maryland, and that the proprietor owed his allegiance to the Protestant king of England. Lord Baltimore, therefore, demanded that his co-religionists be discreet.

All "Acts of the Roman Catholique Religion," Calvert told his brother, would have to be "done as privately as they may be," and Catholics were going to have to be "silent upon all occasions of discourse concerning matters of Religion." Being the governor of Maryland meant that Leonard Calvert would have to ensure that "no scandal nor offense" was "given to any of the Protestants" in the colony, and that Protestants there were treated "with as much mildness and favor as Justice will permit," so that no "just complaint may hereafter be made, by them, in Virginia or England."[57] Lord Baltimore was determined to have Maryland be a colony where Catholics had the freedom to be Catholic. In order to do that, however, he needed to know that the colony would not be a place where Catholics had the freedom to be impolitic.

Cecilius Calvert wanted Maryland to be a haven for English Catholics. His instructions to his brother make it clear, however, that he did not expect the Catholicism that thrived in his colony to be anything like the religion that thrived in the great, Catholic countries of Continental Europe. Unlike French or Spanish Catholics, Maryland's Catholics were going to have to at least pretend that they believed there could be more than one way to know God, and they were going to have to accept that the responsibility for maintaining their faith would lie with them, and not with their government. Religion in Maryland was to be a private affair, subject to neither the support nor the opposition of the state. The priests who served in the colony were to be treated just like the other, nonclerical gentlemen who chose to come to Maryland. They would not be thrown in jail because of their vocation; they would, however, be responsible for their own passage to the colony and rewarded with land grants under the same terms that applied to the other gentlemen adventurers. The Catholic laymen who governed Maryland would do so as the subjects of the king of England and the Lord Proprietor of Maryland; they would not govern the colony as the subjects of Pope Urban VIII in Rome.

By all accounts, most of the Catholics in early Maryland understood and respected Baltimore's instructions. They accepted that they would have to be discreet—maybe not as discreet as they had been in England, but "quiet" Catholics, nonetheless. A few of Cecilius Calvert's coreligionists did need to be "encouraged" to accept the obligations that came with their new freedom, however, and—perhaps not surprisingly, given the uncompromising attitude that the Jesuits had shown toward James I's Oath of Allegiance in 1606—the most dramatic of these cases often involved priests and/or lay Catholics who worked closely with the Society of Jesus. Indeed, the initial unwillingness of the Jesuits to accept the notion that Catholic identity in Maryland was necessarily different from the Catholic identity that predominated in Continental Europe provoked the first, major crisis that the second Lord Baltimore had to deal with as the proprietor of his father's dream. It was a crisis that some of his contemporaries suggested could have a negative impact on Catholic immigration to Maryland.

There were three Jesuits in the first crop of settlers who came to the colony: Andrew White, John Altham, and Thomas Gervase. Others did follow, but Maryland's Catholics never had more than five priests serving them at any given point throughout the seventeenth century, largely because mortality rates among the clergy were even higher than what they were among the laity. Eight of the first twelve Jesuits who came to Maryland were killed in the colony, either by violence or disease, and five of those eight men, including Thomas Gervase, were dead before the second anniversary of their arrival in Maryland. The Jesuits were teachers—not laborers, and not soldiers. In this sense, historians' descriptions of them as pampered and aristocratic, while exaggerated, are nevertheless useful. The men who belonged to the Society of Jesus had spent the bulk of their lives in the best universities of Europe, studying rhetoric, music, and language, rather than the martial arts or animal husbandry. They were, in many respects, the least prepared Europeans to assume the rigors of life in the New World.[58]

And yet, the Jesuits did come to the New World willingly—and not just to Maryland. As historian James Axtell has revealed in delightful and remarkable detail, the Society of Jesus was more successful than any other missionary group at converting North America's Indians to Christianity in the sixteenth and seventeenth centuries. The Jesuits practiced a form of cultural relativism that entailed living with the Native American tribes, adopting their dress, learning their languages, and studying the various elements of their faith, so that those elements could be twisted into something that coincided with Catholic doctrine. It was an approach to conversion that was anathema not just to the English Calvinists in Massachusetts, who believed that the Indians needed to be "civilized" before they could be saved, but also to the Spanish Dominicans and Franciscans who worked in what is now Mexico and Florida, and to the French Recollects and Ursulines who, like the Jesuits, focused primarily on the Indians who lived in present-day Quebec. As abhorrent as the Jesuits' cultural relativism was to their European contemporaries, it was a tactic that yielded more Indian converts than any other.[59]

George Calvert had first approached the Jesuits about serving in Maryland, not because he was particularly enamored with the Society, but because his experience with Avalon had taught him that the Vatican was unwilling to provide priests to serve the English Catholics living in his colony. On top of that, very few secular priests in England were willing to risk the hazards and assume the hardships that came with life on the other side of the Atlantic. The Jesuits, however—as controversial as they were in England—had a solid commitment to missionary work. The risks involved with life in the New World were something the Jesuits actually embraced, as evidenced by Christopher Morris's confession in 1640 that a "desire of Martyrdome" lay behind his application to go to Maryland.[60]

The Society of Jesus also had a great deal of experience serving English Catholics outside England, and this was an important consideration.

They had been operating what were, technically, foreign missions for the English Catholic laity ever since 1576, when the Society had been forced to close its schools in England and move their English-language books and English-speaking faculty and students to France and Belgium.[61] George Calvert knew, after spending just a little bit of time in Avalon, that the mission to Maryland, much like these schools on the Continent, would be both "foreign" and "English," and it may have been with that fact in mind that he first approached Andrew White, head of the Jesuits' English Province, about providing priests for Maryland.

The Jesuits eagerly responded to Calvert's solicitation, though they do not seem to have understood his vision for Maryland and the place of Catholicism within that vision. As early as 1637, we find evidence that the Jesuits did not accept Cecilius Calvert's understanding of them as mere gentlemen, possessing the same rights as every other gentleman in the colony, but also being burdened with the same responsibilities and enjoying no special, legal privileges by virtue of their clerical status. We also find evidence that the Jesuits may not have understood how important it was that Maryland's Catholics not engage in any behavior that could be interpreted as confrontational by Protestants, despite the warning that had been issued to all of the colonists about this very subject by their Catholic proprietor, through their Catholic governor.

Frs. White, Altham, and Gervase brought enough servants with them in 1634 to qualify for a 6,000-acre manorial grant from the proprietor. There is no evidence, however, that the men ever applied for such a grant, and not until 1636, when Fr. Thomas Copley arrived in the colony to replace the recently deceased Gervase, did the Jesuits set up a manor for themselves, as all of the gentlemen in Maryland were expected to do. Rather than claim the land that the Jesuits were entitled to under Lord Baltimore's Conditions of Plantation, Copley chose to purchase a prime piece of real estate about four miles south of St. Mary's City, near where the Potomac empties into the Chesapeake. The manor, which the Jesuits purchased from one of the original lay Catholics to come over on the *Ark*, consisted of around 2,000 acres.[62] They chose to call their new estate "St. Inigoes," named for the Spanish saint on whose day the Jesuits purchased the land.

As freemen and now landowners, the priests were required, under Lord Baltimore's Conditions of Plantation, to serve in the colonial assembly that the proprietor, himself, was required by the charter to create. Thomas Copley and his clerical colleagues, however, had no interest in accepting the inconveniences of time, travel, and expense that were involved with service in the General Assembly. At that body's first meeting in January 1638, it was noted that all but three of the freemen in the colony had shown up for the gathering. The three men who were absent were Andrew White, John Altham, and Thomas Copley, the only priests serving in Maryland at the time.

The assembly issued a writ requiring the priests to appear in St. Mary's City a few weeks later to explain their absence. Only John Altham made the trip, further suggesting that the clergy wished to avoid traveling to the capital. According to Altham, the priests had been sick—an excuse that might have been legitimate, given that at least two of them, Altham and Copley, were living in the same household. The fact that the Assembly felt the need to order the men to explain their absence, however, indicates that someone in the Assembly had reason to believe that the priests were missing the official gathering on purpose.[63]

That person may have been John Lewger, who seems to have quickly caught on to the fact that the Jesuits were reluctant to accept the responsibilities that came with landownership in the colony. In April 1638, Fr. Thomas Copley wrote to Lord Baltimore to complain that Lewger had not been allowing the Jesuits to vote by proxy at the General Assembly's meetings. The priests, it seems, wanted to be able to send their manor's lay overseer to vote in the Assembly for them; John Lewger, however, in his capacity as the colony's Secretary, adamantly refused to allow them to do this.

Not only that, but Lewger had also had the poor manners to demand that the Jesuits do as all other landowners in the colony were being required to do, and that is relinquish "fifteen hundred weight in Tobacco toward the building of a fort." This, to Copley's way of thinking, was completely unacceptable, and the reason he gave to Baltimore for why he, White, and Altham should not have to pay the tax was that they were all priests. "One would think that even out of gratitude, they might free us of such kind of taxation," Copley wrote to the proprietor, "especially seeing we put no tax on them, but help them gratis."[64] If the priests in Maryland were not going to enjoy the kind of support from the state that their contemporaries in Continental Europe enjoyed, Copley insisted, then at the very least they should be freed from the responsibilities that all laymen in the colony were expected to meet.

It was not an argument that Lord Baltimore was willing to accept. He did, however, agree to release the priests from their legal obligation to attend the meetings of the General Assembly, following the execution of Thomas Smith, a rogue who was convicted of piracy in March 1638 by eighteen of the twenty-one assemblymen present on the day of his trial. The Assembly voted to deny Smith's request to see a clergyman before he died, insisting that "clergy could not be allowed in this crime." It was a judgment that offended a number of the Catholic assemblymen who had actually voted to execute Smith. Following the decision to deny the pirate the benefit of clergy, these Catholic assemblymen stormed out of the room in anger. Smith was not Catholic, and it is possible that the Assembly voted to deny him access to clerical council because they would have had to send to Virginia for an Anglican priest, there being no clergy from the Church of England in Maryland at the time.[65] Nevertheless, the decision to deny Smith the right to see a clergyman before his death offended Catholics' understanding of the Last Rites as sacramental.

Lord Baltimore recognized that this was not a situation he could ask the priests serving in Maryland to participate in, should it arise again in the future—particularly since St. Ignatius of Loyola's *Constitutions* condemned all forms of capital punishment. The proprietor therefore instructed his representatives in Maryland to excuse the Jesuits from their obligation to serve in the General Assembly. In doing so, however, Cecilius Calvert was careful to stipulate that the exemption should not be interpreted in any way as a recognition of an all-encompassing clerical immunity for the Jesuits.[66] Copley's complaints about taxation were unfounded. The Jesuits would pay taxes, just like everyone else.

Throughout the 1630s, the Society of Jesus brought approximately sixty servants to Maryland to work at St. Inigoes—which, by the close of the decade, had become a rather substantial operation consisting of an orchard, a garden, at least one stable, a chicken coop, a gristmill, a store, and a blacksmith shop. The Jesuits also had a number of tenant farmers living and working on their land, and to oversee the manor's operations, they hired a layman by the name of William Lewis.[67] Very little is known about Lewis, except that he was an ardent Catholic, which would explain why the Jesuits felt comfortable hiring him to oversee their plantation. Lewis's zeal for his faith, however—and his employers' inability or unwillingness to rein that zeal in—nearly provoked the very situation that Cecilius Calvert was hoping to avoid when he sent his last-minute instructions to Governor Leonard Calvert and Commissioners Jerome Hawley and Thomas Cornwallis.

Some of the servants who were brought over by the Jesuits to work for them were not Catholic. Just how many of them were Protestant is not known, nor is it known what variety of Protestant—Anglican or Calvinist—each of the Jesuits' non-Catholic servants was. Regardless of their theology, though, the Protestants working at St. Inigoes could not have been pleased to discover that their masters were not only Catholics, but priests to boot. No doubt the men who agreed to indenture themselves to those early Jesuit settlers held their noses while doing so, figuring that they could put up with the humiliation of being made to work for a pack of priests in exchange for the freedom and opportunity that life in the New World offered.

Life under the direction of a zealous Catholic overseer like William Lewis, however, proved to be insufferable for more than a few of these Protestant servants. In July 1638, a small, but literate group of men working at St. Inigoes drew up a petition that they planned to give to the governor of Virginia, in which they claimed they had suffered "abuses and scandalous reproaches" from William Lewis on account of their Protestant faith. Lewis, according to the servants, had told them that "our books are made by the instruments of the devil." He had ordered them to get rid of any books that "doth appertain to our religion," an action that the servants claimed caused them "great discomfort," since they lived in a "heathen country where no godly minister is to teach and instruct ignorant people on the grounds of religion."[68] Without their books, the servants would not be able to maintain their Protestant faith—and the petitioners believed that was precisely their overseer's objective.

Lewis wanted to do more than just keep the Protestant servants he oversaw from maintaining their faith, though. According to the petition, he was also working to convert people, inviting anyone who happened to pass by Smith Creek into his home, where he would "laboreth with all vehemency, craft and subtlety to delude ignorant persons." The servants appealed to the authorities in Virginia to invade Maryland and save the colony's Protestant residents from such "absurd abuses and herediculous crimes." Such an action, they believed, would be "recompensed with eternal joy and felicity to reign in that eternal kingdom with Jesus Christ, under whose banner we fight for evermore."[69] Virginians, the Protestant servants at St. Inigoes Manor insisted, would receive an everlasting reward in Heaven in exchange for their willingness to commit acts of violence against Maryland's Catholic leaders.

It was an assertion that, as we have seen in our own times, had powerful and dangerous implications. Fortunately for the Catholics in Maryland, Commissioner Thomas Cornwallis managed to intercept the petition before it could reach its destination, and because the allegations—and the petition's intended consequences—were so serious, he ordered an immediate investigation. The servants' allegations, after all, were precisely the sort of complaint that Cecilius Calvert had told Cornwallis he needed to prevent, and Cornwallis, a life-long Catholic who had pointed to "Security of Conscience" as the "First Condition" he expected from Maryland's government, fully intended to take the Protestants' claims of religious persecution seriously.[70]

Three Catholics led the investigation: Cornwallis, Governor Leonard Calvert, and Secretary John Lewger. William Lewis told his coreligionists that his actions had been entirely provoked—that the Calvinist servants at St. Inigoes had been taunting him for weeks, reading the sermons of Henry Smith out loud in his presence. Smith was widely considered to be one of the most popular Puritan preachers in Elizabethan England, and his "silver-tongued" sermons often spoke of Catholics and atheists as if they were one and the same. Smith was also fond of referring to the Pope as the Antichrist.[71] Such ideas were, understandably, offensive to the Catholic overseer, and so Lewis forbade Francis Gray, a layman who sometimes conducted services for the Calvinists at St. Inigoes, from reading Smith's sermons at any of his gatherings.

Gray testified to the Catholic judges that he had spoken to Fr. Thomas Copley about the situation before resorting to writing the petition to Virginia's governor. Copley, according to Gray, had agreed with the Calvinist lay preacher that Lewis had a tendency to exhibit "ill-governed zeal" for which "he should be punished." The Jesuits did nothing to rein Lewis in, however, and so the servants decided to turn to authorities in Virginia instead.[72]

The Catholic governor and his two Catholic commissioners found William Lewis guilty of disturbing the peace and violating a "publique proclamation set forth to prohibit all such disputes." That proclamation was probably Cecilius Calvert's letter to his brother, which may have been read out loud to the residents of Maryland, as a way of assuaging Protestant fears about what life would be like for them in a colony that had so many Catholics. Such a public reading would also have reminded the colony's Catholics that although the proprietor and his governor shared their faith, Catholics were still a minority—and Maryland was still an English colony.

The officials who convicted William Lewis felt it was important to emphasize to him that he had made a mistake when he assumed that because the proprietor, governor, and commissioners of Maryland were all Catholic, religious intolerance toward Protestants would therefore be allowed in the colony. To that end, the officials stipulated that they were punishing Lewis because he had kept the Protestants at St. Inigoes from reading "a book otherwise allowed & lawful to be read in the state of England." What made Maryland different from England was not that the colony had outlawed religious practices that were perfectly legal in England, but that it had permitted religious practices that were outlawed in the parent country. Lewis was fined 1,000 pounds of tobacco and told he would forfeit another 3,000 pounds if he ever again engaged in behavior that violated "the peace of this colony or the inhabitants thereof by injurious & unnecessary arguments or disputations in matters of religion." Pointedly, the commissioners also warned Lewis not to utter any more "ignominious words or speeches touching the books or ministers authorized by the State of England."[73]

The investigation into the servants' complaints did not determine the truth or accuracy of Francis Gray's story about how he had spoken with Fr. Thomas Copley before writing the petition. We do not know, therefore, if the leader of the Maryland Mission did, in fact, believe that William Lewis's behavior was unacceptable, as Gray reported—and if he did, why the Jesuits never did anything to control their overseer. Gray's story is plausible, however, and it may be that the priests did not act on their servants' complaints because they were not particularly focused on the goings-on at St. Inigoes Manor. Indeed, this lack of interest in the plantation may have been the reason the clergymen hired William Lewis in the first place.

Cecilius Calvert had asked the Jesuits to come to Maryland so that they could serve the English Catholic community—which, presumably, meant that the priests would either build a church that all of the English Catholics in the region could travel to, or else they would travel between and among the various Catholic households in Maryland. Either way, it was the English whom Calvert was most concerned about. To sweeten his invitation, however, the proprietor had also emphasized to the Society of Jesus that settlement in Maryland would provide the Jesuits with an excellent opportunity to convert the native Indians to Christianity—and conversion, then, seems to have become the primary objective of the first priests in Maryland.

"Your Reverences exhoratory letter towards Marylands Mission caused such comfort and joy in my heart," a young John Cooper wrote in 1640 to England's Jesuit Provincial, Edward Knott. Upon learning of the Jesuits' mission to Maryland, Cooper was overjoyed to learn "that there was now hope of compassing my desires in helping to reduce such barbarous people to the knowledge of one God and the true faith of Christ." Similarly, Lawrence Worsley wrote of the "no small joy and comfort" that he felt when he learned that "not any one [Jesuit] in particular, but all in general" had been invited to "employ their lives and labors in the undertaking of so glorious an enterprise, of converting souls to God by means of that [Maryland] mission." For Christopher Morris, "the inconveniences of diet, apparel, and lodging" that came with "the teaching of Christ's cross in all senses in Maryland" was to be preferred over the "most honorable chair" at any university in Catholic Europe.[74] Morris, who was English, had never once volunteered to give up his academic position in Liege so that he could return to his native country and minister to his marginalized coreligionists there. When presented the opportunity to travel to the wilderness of North America and convert the Patuxent Indians, however, he jumped at the chance.

Indeed, the evidence suggests that the early Jesuits had no interest in living among the English once they arrived in Maryland. They wanted to live among the Indians. Andrew White actually did take up residence, briefly, in what the Jesuits called the "palace" of the Piscataway "king." He wrote proudly to Lord Baltimore of the progress he was making in learning the Piscataway language, eventually translating the Catholic catechism and several prayers into that language and creating a manuscript that survives today as the only extant example of an eastern Algonquian language.[75] White also arranged for the Piscataway chief's seven-year-old daughter to live and be educated among the English in St. Mary's City. At the age of eleven, that girl—who was given the Christian name of Mary Kitamaquund—was married to Giles Brent, a Catholic convert who held a number of prominent positions in Maryland's government and was in his forties when he took his child bride.[76]

White did not stay long with the Indians. In March 1639, at the urging of Cecilius Calvert, the colonial assembly made the "withdrawing of ones Self out of an English Plantation to inhabit or reside among any Indians" a crime, punishable by imprisonment. No reason was given for why the assembly and the proprietor felt it was inappropriate for members of Maryland's English community to be leaving their European settlements and living among the Indians.⁷⁷ Given that Fr. Andrew White was the only person whom we know to have done this, however, it is possible that the act criminalizing White's behavior was a deliberate attempt by Maryland's Catholics to force the small number of priests working in the colony to serve their spiritual needs, rather than the spiritual needs of the Natives.

Eighteen of the twenty-eight people serving in the Assembly of 1639 whose religious identities are known were Catholic. Membership in the Assembly, after all, was contingent upon landownership, and the Catholic population in Maryland, much like its counterpart in England, was disproportionately wealthy.⁷⁸ The theory that these Catholic assemblymen wanted their priests to start paying more attention to them is bolstered by the fact that shortly before the Assembly called Andrew White back into the English fold, it unanimously passed a law requiring all clergy in the colony to undertake the obligation of being "pastors." The language used in the legislation was not unimportant. Being a "pastor" was very different from being a "missionary." Pastors were settled in known locations. They served well-defined congregations, conducted regular services, and were readily available to perform baptisms, marriages, and burials. Fr. Thomas Copley called the law "inconvenient" and complained that it prevented the priests in Maryland from meeting the missionary obligations that Ignatius of Loyola had given to all of them as Jesuits. This was not the first time that English lay Catholics felt entitled to instruct their priests on how to do their jobs, however—nor would it be the last.⁷⁹

Now, it is possible—and even likely—that Cecilius Calvert did not want Maryland's settlers living among the Indians because the practice made it difficult for him to realize a profit from his colony. Lord Baltimore wanted the settlers to be paying rents and producing tobacco for sale in Europe, after all; he did not want them withdrawing from European society, taking only what they needed from the land, and contributing nothing to his coffers.

Such financial interests, however, would not have precluded his being concerned about the extent to which the Jesuits were making the English Catholics in Maryland a priority, as well. Indeed, whether he was ordering Fr. White back to St. Inigoes out of a concern for his pocketbook, a concern for the spiritual welfare of his coreligionists, or both, the fact remains that Cecilius Calvert—an English Catholic convert who had been raised in a Protestant family and educated at a Protestant college that cultivated the kind of critical thinking skills that empowered students to challenge the traditional sources of authority that governed their lives—did not hesitate to push a bill through the General Assembly that defined the Jesuits' pastoral agenda in Maryland for them.

The Jesuits were not happy about this. They were also not happy about other pieces of legislation that restricted their activities and, in so doing, constrained their vocation. The same assembly that approved the law defining White's domestic activities with the Piscataway as criminal, for example, also passed an "Act for Trade with the Indians," which outlined the penalties that would be inflicted upon anyone in the province who deigned to trade with the Natives without first receiving a license from the Lieutenant Governor or Secretary of the colony. This Act was not necessarily directed specifically against the Jesuits; the clergy were certainly not the only Europeans in Maryland who had been trading with the Indians. The trades the Jesuits had orchestrated, however, were far more obvious—and encroached far more extensively on Baltimore's proprietary rights—than anything their nonclerical neighbors had been able to negotiate with the Natives.

Shortly before the Act was passed, the Patuxent Indians had given the Jesuits a tract of land near the mouth of the Patuxent River—a token of their gratitude, the Jesuits insisted, for the work Andrew White had done in bringing Christianity to their chief, Macquacomen. According to the new Act, however, the land transaction between the Jesuits and the Patuxent was completely and utterly illegal, and to make that point even more clear, Lord Baltimore reissued his Conditions of Plantation in 1641, declaring specifically that the "possessing or enjoying [of] any lands" in the colony required a "special license first, had and obtained for this end under the hand and seal of his Lordship."[80]

Thanks to this legislation, not only would Andrew White have to return to St. Inigoes from his post among the Piscataway more than one hundred miles away, but John Brooke and Walter Morely, the church officials who had recently begun a new mission, known as Mattapany, on the land given to the Jesuits by the Patuxent Indians, would now have to remove themselves to St. Inigoes, as well.[81] The situation was deplorable, according to Thomas Copley, and a complete violation of the clerical immunities that the priest insisted ought to be extended to the Jesuits. He wrote to Maryland's proprietor to complain about the way the Catholic governor, his Catholic secretary, and all of the members of the General Assembly, many of whom were also Catholic, had been running the colony.

"First, there is not any care given to promote the conversion of the Indians," Copley complained. More to the point, however, no effort had been made to "provide or show any favor to Ecclesiastical persons, or to preserve for the Church the Immunity and privileges which she enjoyeth every where else."[82] It was a weighty charge—and one that revealed just how unaware Thomas Copley was of both the delicate situation that Lord Baltimore found himself in as the Catholic proprietor of an English colony, and the radical and unique means by which Cecilius Calvert unabashedly planned to achieve the balance that his situation demanded.

Copley clearly believed that in the Catholic Lord Baltimore's Maryland, the clergy would enjoy the same financial privileges and lay deference that the clergy in all of the various Catholic countries of Continental Europe enjoyed. The situation that Baltimore had constructed in Maryland, whereby the Church was neither supported nor opposed by the state, was completely beyond Copley's realm of comprehension—and perhaps understandably, given just how novel and untested the idea really was. In Copley's mind, the state either supported the Church, or else it worked against it. There were no other options. And because the government in Maryland was clearly not supporting the Catholic Church when it denied the Church's representatives tax and trade exemptions and told them that they could not "freely go and abide and live among the Savages," the state—and its Catholic proprietor—must have been working against the Catholic Church, at least according to Thomas Copley's understanding of the situation.[83]

Copley made his charge clear to Baltimore. The proprietor was obliged—as a Catholic—to review the existing laws in Maryland and change them, so that the priests would be exempt from the taxes, duties, and restrictions that applied to all other landowners in the colony. "I beseech your Lordship," Copley warned, "Before you do anything about these laws, that you would be pleased to read over and ponder well the *Bulla Coenae*." It was a thoroughly unveiled reference to the authority of the Pope, a reminder to Lord Baltimore that in 1627, Pope Urban VIII had issued a bull that prohibited Catholic rulers from imposing taxes on Church properties without first receiving the Pope's permission. The decree also threatened those who encroached upon ecclesiastical liberties with excommunication, an action that Thomas Copley not so subtly hinted might be taken against Lord Baltimore if he did not do something about the legislation that had been passed in Maryland.[84]

Cecilius Calvert was furious and ready to take the Jesuits on. Not every Catholic in Maryland was as combative as he was, however, and some were actually quite uncomfortable with their proprietor's antagonistic posture toward the clergy. Thomas Cornwallis, for instance, was a cradle-to-grave Catholic who would rather "sacrifice myself and all I have in the defense of God's Honor and his Churches [sic] right, than willingly consent to anything that may not stand with the Good Conscience of a Real Catholick." The commissioner who had led the investigation of William Lewis actually wanted all of Maryland's laws to be subject to ecclesiastical review. "Wise Learned and Religious Divines" should evaluate the laws, he wrote to Maryland's proprietor, and make sure they were in "no ways prejudicial to the Immunities and Privileges of that Church which is the only true Guide to Eternal Happiness."

Cornwallis warned Calvert that he would leave Maryland if the proprietor's dispute with the Jesuits were not resolved peaceably. "I shall with as much Convenient speed as I can with draw myself, and what is left of that which I brought with me," he wrote to the proprietor, "out of Danger of being involved in the spiritual ruin" that Lord Baltimore was courting.[85] Cecilius Calvert needed to be careful. If he did not strike the right balance with Copley, not only would Catholics like Cornwallis choose to go home, but Catholics who were contemplating colonization might decide not to come. In England, after all, the fields had been cleared for centuries, the summers were less muggy, and Indians, for the most part, were just parlor attractions in the court of King Charles.

Copley was convinced that he had the proprietor backed up against a wall. "I am sure none have done near so much as we, nor indeed are likely to do so much, in [the] peopling and planting [of] this place," he wrote ominously to Lord Baltimore. The priest warned Calvert that his Conditions of Plantation were not nearly as enticing as the proprietor thought they were. Copley noted that none of the landowners in Maryland liked having to pay a twenty-shilling quit-rent on land that they had secured for themselves by paying for men to come to the colony. More than a few settlers were also not pleased to discover that when their servants died or ran away, they were required to pay for or forfeit the acreage they had received in exchange for the servants' passage. These "hidden restrictions," so to speak, in Baltimore's Conditions of Plantation were onerous and alienating—and word of their existence was starting to get out. Without the recruitment help of the Jesuits, Copley informed the proprietor, "I doubt very much, whether many will be found in England that will be able and willing to venture" to Maryland.[86]

Copley's estimation of the Jesuits' importance to colonial recruitment was slightly inflated. While it is true that Baltimore had relied heavily on the Society of Jesus in his effort to target Catholics, those efforts had not been as successful as Calvert had hoped they would be. By the 1630s, Catholicism in England had become thoroughly self-contained, such that most of the country's small number of Catholics now lived on the estates of powerful Catholic noblemen, enjoying the political protection and clerical services of seigneurial Catholicism. The Catholic community, therefore, was fragmented, and while this fragmentation facilitated the faith's survival in England, it also tended to make New World recruitment difficult, regardless of whether that recruitment was being orchestrated by laymen or clergy.[87]

Still, Lord Baltimore did not take Thomas Copley's threat lightly. The proprietor fired off a letter to Edward Knott, the English Provincial for the Society of Jesus, telling the Provincial to rein his Jesuits in. Calvert demanded that the Society relinquish all claims to "directly or indirectly trade or traffic with any Indian or Salvage [sic]" and that the Jesuits in Maryland "disavow and disannul all purchase whatsoever of any such land made by any of the Community or Society." Asserting that the laws of Maryland "do bind all persons whatsoever as well spiritual and lay," Baltimore reminded the Provincial that although the colony's proprietor was Catholic, and although the free practice of Catholicism was certainly to be maintained in Maryland, the colony was still English, and its laws, therefore, had to conform as near as possible to the laws of England. Baltimore and his colonial officers, "although they be Roman Catholics," were not "obliged in conscience" to give any special consideration to the Catholic clergy or to the mandates of the Pope. The same laws that applied to the laity in Maryland would apply to the Jesuits, and Baltimore insisted to Knott that he could enforce these laws "without committing any sin or incurring the censure of Bulla Coenae for so doing."[88]

Knott was taken aback. Determining that parts of Calvert's letter were "derogatory in no slight degree to the dignity and authority of his Holiness," the Provincial appealed to the nearest Papal Nuncio, Monsignor Rosetti in Cologne, for guidance before responding.[89] In the mean time, Baltimore refused to allow any more Jesuits into the colony, and he tried, unsuccessfully, to replace all of the remaining Jesuits in Maryland with secular clergy. His disagreement with Fr. Thomas Copley was now a full-blown and very public imbroglio, one that made a number of Catholics, some even within the proprietor's own family, uncomfortable. While English Catholics had, over the course of the previous century, become far more assertive and self-defining than their coreligionists in Continental Europe, the secularism that Cecilius Calvert was mandating in Maryland and the priority that he was giving to civil over clerical authorities there were something many English Catholics still did not know how to navigate or receive.

The proprietor's sister, brother, and brother-in-law all appealed to him to make good with the Society of Jesus. Cecilius Calvert, however, would not budge. "Whatsoever you may conceive of [the Jesuits]," he wrote to his brother, Leonard, from London in 1642, "you have no reason upon my knowledge to love them very much if you knew as much as I do concerning their speeches and actions here towards you." Baltimore did not elaborate on what the Jesuits in England had been saying about the governor of Maryland; he did make it clear, however, that he could not, as an Englishman, bow to their wishes simply because he was Catholic.

In a letter that is truly remarkable, given that it was written by an English Catholic more than forty years before John Locke articulated our modern understanding of government, natural rights, and church–state separation—and more than three centuries before the Catholic Church finally sanctioned that understanding of church–state relations in Vatican II's *Dignitatis Humanae*—Cecilius Calvert told his brother that laymen would be "the basest Slaves and most wretched creatures upon the earth" if they allowed themselves to believe that "all things that Clergy men should do should be accounted just and should proceed from God." There had to be a separate sphere for the temporal affairs of a man's life—a place where the authority of the Church did not apply and where lay deference was never required. "If the greatest saint on earth should intrude himself into my house against my will . . . with intention to save the souls of my family," Calvert told his brother, "but give me just cause to suspect that he likewise designs my temporal destruction . . . although with all he may do many spiritual goods, yet certainly I may and ought to preserve myself." In words that might have warmed John Locke's heart, in spite of the philosopher's well-documented dislike of Catholicism, Cecilius Calvert told his brother that such preservation was natural. "The Law of nature," he wrote, "teacheth this."[90]

In the end, outside forces, rather than any internal, Catholic negotiations were responsible for the détente that Cecilius Calvert and the Jesuits eventually achieved. A civil war, motivated in part by religious differences, broke out between King Charles I and the Puritan-dominated Long Parliament in 1642. In a pattern that would repeat itself later in the century, political unrest in England spilled over into Maryland, to the detriment of the colony's Catholics. The proprietor and the Jesuits put their disagreements aside, therefore, so that they could work together to save Lord Baltimore's colony.

Cecilius Calvert had been obliged to support the king in the English Civil War. Charles I had not only provided Calvert with the charter to Maryland, but he had also provided Catholics in England with a relatively peaceful existence throughout his time on the throne. Indeed, Charles's overtures to the English Catholic community were among the many problems that the Calvinists in Parliament had had with his reign. His crypto-Catholicism was one of the "high crimes" Parliament convicted him of in 1648. That trial, rather infamously, ended in the king's execution in January 1649.[91]

The support that the proprietary government had given to the king exacerbated tensions between Catholics and the growing Calvinist community in Maryland. In addition to harboring a great deal of theological animosity toward all things Catholic, these Calvinists also tended not to be as well-off as their Catholic neighbors. Indeed, many of the Calvinists in Maryland had come to the colony as the indentured servants of Catholic landowners. Although each man received 50 acres from the proprietor once his term of indenture was over, most of these former servants could never hope to own a manor, the way their former masters did.[92]

Four years prior to the outbreak of civil war in England, Governor Leonard Calvert had sent a force of thirty men up to Kent Island, where the irascible Calvinist, William Claiborne, was living with a gang of approximately 100 landless fur traders. The men had been attacking boats from St. Mary's County and preventing anyone from lower Maryland from trapping and trading in the Eastern Bay. The governor's forces subdued Claiborne and his men, but the men continued to insist that they were Virginians who owed no allegiance to Maryland's proprietary government.

In 1645, when Richard Ingle sailed into St. Mary's City, claiming to have a commission from Parliament that allowed him to plunder papist properties and seize anything that belonged to supporters of King Charles I, Claiborne and his Calvinist cronies were eager to join the fight. Ingle was a ship captain from England who had done a lot of business in

Maryland prior to declaring war on Governor Leonard Calvert. He was also a Puritan who had named his ship the *Reformation* and was heard on more than one occasion to claim that Charles I was not a legitimate king.

The rebels targeted Catholic properties. The estate that Giles Brent shared with his sister, Margaret, on Kent Island was plundered and destroyed by William Claiborne's forces. The rebels slaughtered the Brent family's cattle and sheep, stole their tobacco, and burned their fields and library. In all, Margaret Brent claimed that more than £1,200 in damage had been done to her property by Claiborne's men, who seemed particularly interested in destroying all of the Catholic reading material they could get their hands on. Fr. Thomas Copley reported that the rebels had burned the Jesuits' entire library at St. Inigoes—a collection of books that, at £150, was worth more than three-quarters of the estates in St. Mary's County.[93]

The rebellion was finally crushed in November 1646, after nearly two years of intermittent fighting. Leonard Calvert had retreated to Virginia shortly after Richard Ingle launched his initial assault. He raised an army there by gathering together a group of displaced Marylanders and promising about a dozen Virginians an ample reward for their help. The promise may actually have been one that the governor was not in a position to make. In the months that followed his successful recapture of St. Mary's City, Leonard Calvert found himself facing a series of lawsuits filed by soldiers from Virginia who claimed they had not been paid for their services.

The governor did not have to deal with these lawsuits for very long, however. In June 1647, just seven months after he had regained control of Maryland, Leonard Calvert was bitten by a snake and died.[94] His brother, Cecilius—who had remained frustratingly silent throughout the Ingle-Claiborne Rebellion (at least in the surviving historical record)—was now faced with the problem of having to find a new governor for Maryland, along with a new method for achieving peace in his colony.

The Ingle-Claiborne Rebellion forced Lord Baltimore to realize that his system for achieving religious stability in Maryland had not worked. He had tried to achieve that stability without going to extraordinary lengths. First, he had encouraged Catholics to be discreet, warning them to worship quietly so as not to antagonize the Protestants in their midst. William Lewis and Thomas Copley, however, had shown that a mere mandate from the proprietor was not enough to keep Maryland's Catholics quiet.

Then, Lord Baltimore had built a government in his colony that was dominated by Catholics. He appointed Catholics to serve as the colony's governor and commissioners, and the property requirements he placed on officeholding guaranteed that Catholics would enjoy a disproportionate share of the seats in the General Assembly. This tactic, however, proved to be an inadequate means of keeping the colony's Protestants in check. The Ingle-Claiborne Rebellion showed that even without a strong presence in the government, anti-Catholic Protestants could still have a devastating impact on the colony. Indeed, their lack of representation may have made the effects of their anti-Catholicism even worse.

It was time therefore, for Cecilius Calvert to make use of the Durham clause. That clause allowed him to do whatever was necessary to keep the peace in Maryland, and Calvert understood what needed to be done. The Jesuits were no longer a problem for him. After St. Inigoes was burned, Thomas Copley backed away from his demands in exchange for the proprietor's protection; from 1650 on, then, the Jesuits in Maryland worked in partnership with the laity to maintain the Catholic faith in British colonial America.[95] The main problem facing Calvert now was plain, old, run-of-the-mill religious bigotry—from Catholics and Protestants alike. While that bigotry could not be legislated out of existence, it might be pushed underground with the help of the Durham clause. Civility became Cecilius Calvert's goal.

The first fifteen years of Maryland's existence had been defining ones for Catholics. First, lay Catholics had learned that they had a right and an obligation to tell their priests how to do their jobs. The laity developed a sense of ownership over their clergy, and this ownership empowered them to legally define their clerical leaders' pastoral agenda for them. The clergy rejected this new model of Catholicism at first. But just as the New World environment had taught the laity that they needed to assume a more active role in the maintenance of their faith, that same environment also—eventually—taught the clergy that Catholicism could survive in Maryland only if the faith became a lay–clerical partnership. Without such a partnership, Catholicism became vulnerable to religious bigotry.

Second, Catholics in Maryland learned a lesson that would be reiterated to them numerous times over the course of the next 126 years, and that was that their colony's connection to England was doing them no favors. The events in London in the 1640s did not create the antagonism that became the Ingle-Claiborne Rebellion, of course. But without the English Civil War, it is possible that the anger felt by Calvinists in Maryland might not have manifested itself in the way that it did. It is unlikely that the Catholics living in Maryland in the 1640s saw the Ingle-Claiborne Rebellion in quite this way, but certainly by the end of the century, when the Glorious Revolution in England spilled over into Maryland, and the rule of the Catholic Lords Baltimore was brought to an end, Maryland's Catholics were able to look back on the history of their colony's connection to England and see that connection as a source of corruption.

Finally, those first fifteen years gave Maryland's Catholics something that the colony's connection to England could corrupt—a cultural and legal tradition of limited, but real religious toleration. In the wake of the Ingle-Claiborne Rebellion, Lord Baltimore decided it was time to formalize and legislate the religious pluralism that he had hoped, naively, could be achieved in Maryland simply through the lack of an established church and a few, well-placed words of caution. Capitalizing on the Durham clause, Lord Baltimore pushed the first act of religious toleration in the English-speaking world through his colony's assembly. That law did not survive without some fight, but it did, ultimately, govern the lives of Maryland's residents until 1689, when it was forced to go the way of the Catholic Calverts.

3

Inconsistencies and Consequences

One of the frustrations faced by anyone looking to understand the past is the reality that human beings are not and never have been consistent. Like many of history's most prominent figures, Cecilius Calvert was out of sync with his times. He was not out of sync in a dependable, logical, or historically "neat" sort of way, however. When it came to the issue of religion—and specifically to the relationship between the church and the state—Calvert was far ahead of his times in his attempt to construct a society along the Chesapeake that had no state-supported church and mandated an atmosphere of religious civility and legal tolerance for all Christians. In the seventeenth century, when wars between and among the various Christian denominations were taking place in Austria, Bohemia, Denmark, England, France, Germany, Ireland, Scotland, and Switzerland, Calvert's ideas about church–state separation and the need for formal religious toleration in Maryland, even if only for the sake of fiscal prosperity, were progressive—even radical—and a little too avant-garde to work.

When it came to government, however—and specifically to the relationship between governors and those they governed—Cecilius Calvert was behind the times, or at the very least unappreciative of the reality that the times were changing, and that his philosophies of government were failing to keep up. Calvert ruled Maryland the way James and Charles Stuart ruled England; like those early Stuarts, he believed he was "beholden to no elective power." John Milton's radical idea that "the king or magistrate holds his authority of the people, both originally and naturally for their good" was not a notion that Cecilius Calvert felt compelled to entertain in 1650, when Milton first articulated it. Lord Baltimore tolerated Maryland's General Assembly, because his charter required him to create such a legislative body. His proprietary authority did not emanate from the people, however; it emanated from the charter. And whenever the Assembly passed legislation that did not mesh with Calvert's understanding of what was good for himself and his colony, the proprietor did not hesitate to veto it.[1]

This absolutist approach to authority—while understandable, perhaps, given the hostility that many of Maryland's Protestant residents had toward their Catholic proprietor—was at odds with the new, "contractarian" philosophy of government that was gaining adherents in England in the seventeenth century, particularly after the execution of Charles I in 1649. By 1690, Englishmen in the Old World and the New no longer believed their leaders had a "divine right" to rule over them. That year, John Locke proclaimed that everyone in a properly organized political society, even the king, was obliged to "submit to the determination of the majority." The year before, the majority of England's MPs had determined that they no longer wished to submit to the rule of the Catholic King James II. The majority of Maryland's Protestants had also determined that they did not want to submit to the rule of a Catholic proprietor who vetoed the decisions of their elected representatives.[2] 1689, then, was not just the year of the Glorious Revolution in England. It was also the year the Calvert family lost control of the colony of Maryland.

In an effort to ensure that his plan to push religious bigotry underground would work, Cecilius Calvert reached out to the Protestant community in Maryland after the Ingle-Claiborne Rebellion. In a show of bipartisanship, he appointed a new governor's council in 1648, this one made up of five men, only two of whom, John Pile and Thomas Greene, were Catholic. The other three councilmen were still closely tied to the proprietor, however, even if they did not attend the same church. Robert Vaughan was an Anglican who had led the contingent that Governor Calvert sent to Kent Island in 1638 to stop William Claiborne's sacking of licensed boats in the upper Chesapeake. John Price was the captain of a fort in St. Mary's County that the proprietor had had built shortly after the Ingle-Claiborne Rebellion was over, and the third Anglican, Thomas Hatton, was a personal friend of Lord Baltimore who had arrived in the colony from England just a few months before assuming his position on the governor's council.[3]

All five men were landowners. None of them, however, had brought the required number of men to Maryland to qualify for a manor grant. This reality was another change to the composition of the governor's council that followed the rebellion. Not only would the council no longer be dominated by Catholics, but it also would not be dominated by Maryland's nobility.

As important as Calvert's overtures to the Anglican community were, the anger that had fueled the Ingle-Claiborne Rebellion in Maryland was not Anglican. It was Calvinist—just like the government that Cecilius Calvert had to deal with in England, now that Parliament had arrested King Charles I. The proprietor therefore reached out to the Puritans in Maryland, as well, and in an extremely risky move, he had his council ask William Stone to replace Leonard Calvert as the colony's governor. Stone was a Calvinist. He had been living in Virginia, along what is now known as the Delmarva Peninsula, since the 1620s, and his wife, Verlinda Cotton, was related to John Cotton, the Puritan minister from Massachusetts who famously helped to banish Roger Williams in 1635.[4]

Stone was an unusual choice for governor. He had no residence in Maryland at the time of his appointment; he had done an extensive amount of business on the eastern shore with Richard Ingle; and his brother-in-law, William Cotton, was William Claiborne's minister on Kent Island. The only real connection William Stone had to Maryland, in other words, was through two men who had just tried to overthrow the proprietary government.

William Stone, however, had promised Lord Baltimore that if the proprietor made him governor, he would bring 500 settlers from Virginia to

Maryland with him. These settlers would not have to go through the "seasoning process" that killed so many European immigrants shortly after they arrived in the New World, and Stone insisted that the settlers would be eager to come, because they were Puritans living in a colony that had formally established the Anglican Church and refused to recognize the legitimacy of the Puritans' takeover of the English government.[5]

It was an offer that Cecilius Calvert felt he was not in a position to refuse. The Ingle-Claiborne Rebellion had done a great deal of damage to Maryland. By some estimates, 80 percent of the settlers in St. Mary's County had either left or been killed during the two-year period that constituted the rebellion, and the value of the property damage done to the colony was close to £10,000.[6] Years later, the second Lord Baltimore and his son, Charles, who succeeded him as proprietor, would learn that it was a mistake to invite so many Calvinists into the colony; Calvinists, after all, had an almost endemic propensity for religious intolerance. In 1648, however, it seemed like a good idea.

Baltimore felt he could safely invite the Puritans in, because he intended to capitalize on the Durham clause in his charter. Before he appointed William Stone as governor, Cecilius Calvert sent his friend Thomas Hatton to Maryland with a draft of what eventually became the Act Concerning Religion. Although the law that the General Assembly and Governor Stone ultimately approved in April 1649 was not an exact replica of Baltimore's proposal, the new law did accomplish the proprietor's objective, at least on paper. It also received the approval of Catholic and Protestant lawmakers alike, which was not an unremarkable achievement.

Baltimore's objective when he proposed the law was to force Maryland's residents to extend a modicum of civility toward one another.[7] The Act Concerning Religion did more than simply guarantee that the government would not interfere in matters of religious (or at the very least Christian) conscience. It also required the colony's residents to keep their religious bigotry to themselves. It forbade the use of a long list of terms, some of them perfectly innocuous today: "heretic"; "schismatic"; "idolator"; "Puritan"; "Independent"; "Presbyterian"; "Popish Priest";

"Jesuited Priest"; "Lutheran"; "Calvinist"; "Anabaptist"; "Antinomian"; "Roundhead"; "Separatist"; the list went on. Under the Act, anyone in Maryland who used a "name or term in a reproachful manner relating to matter[s] of Religion" was subject to a fine that escalated with each incident. If the fine got to a point where the guilty party could no longer afford to pay, imprisonment and/or a public flogging would become the new penalty.[8]

Yes, it was important that the government not meddle in the private religious affairs of the individual; this very un-Catholic notion was enshrined in the Act's promise that no Christian in Maryland would "henceforth be . . . compelled to the belief or exercise of any religion against his or her consent."[9] But before making that promise and placing that obligation on the government's shoulders, the Act Concerning Religion placed an obligation on the shoulders of every private citizen in Maryland: Behave yourself. Use your manners. Play nice.

Cecilius Calvert and his allies in Maryland's colonial assembly recognized the important role that civility played in the achievement of religious pluralism—and the vital role, then, that pluralism played in the achievement of peace and its consequent prosperity. Ideally, the civility that Lord Baltimore knew Maryland needed would be voluntary. Until that day came, however, he was determined to force it. Every time another generation grew up in Maryland not hearing words like "Puritan" and "Papist," or else seeing the people who used such offensive language flogged and fined for doing so, the goal of achieving genuine civility and real religious pluralism would get a little closer. The process would be slow, but in the meantime, Calvert hoped that the Act Concerning Religion would at the very least shut people up long enough that they could start working together in the colony and making money for themselves—and, of course, for him.

The years that followed the Ingle-Claiborne Rebellion were far from peaceful in Maryland, in spite of Lord Baltimore's efforts to reach out to the Protestants in his colony. The Act Concerning Religion was tested several times during the remaining twenty-five years of Cecilius Calvert's life, and in each case, what was tested was not just the law but also the commitment of Maryland's residents to the extraordinarily novel idea of religious pluralism. This commitment, which seemed strong at first, waned quickly. Indeed, by the tenth anniversary of the passage of the Act Concerning Religion, even Cecilius Calvert's commitment to the spirit of the Act had become somewhat selective. The law continued to be an important component of his plan for turning a profit in Maryland, but by 1659, Lord Baltimore had determined that not everyone in the colony could be trusted with the responsibilities of religious pluralism. During the last seventeen years of his proprietorship, therefore, Cecilius Calvert refused to extend religious liberty to anyone whom he believed might be a threat to his authority.

The first two tests happened very early in the 1650s, and in each case, it seems that the Act Concerning Religion functioned exactly as Lord Baltimore had hoped that it would. This may have been because both cases involved Thomas Hatton, the Anglican whom Cecilius Calvert had sent to Maryland in 1648 to deliver the proprietor's proposed act of religious toleration to the General Assembly. If anyone knew what Calvert wanted the Act Concerning Religion to accomplish, it was Thomas Hatton, Maryland's secretary and attorney general.

In the first instance, a Roman Catholic assemblyman by the name of Walter Pakes accused Hatton of making several ignominious comments about the Catholic faith—comments that were prohibited under the Act Concerning Religion. As required by the law, the General Assembly launched an investigation, and ultimately, Hatton was found to be innocent. Walter Pakes's legislative colleagues, however, did not allow the incident to end there. In language that revealed just how important they believed an atmosphere of religious civility was, Maryland's assemblymen ordered Governor Stone to ensure that Hatton's "reputation" was "fully vindicated from the foul imputation which the said Pakes endeavored to lay upon him."[10] Hatton's reputation in Lord Baltimore's colony, in other words, was to be judged according to how tolerant he was of his Catholic neighbors. Had the Protestant secretary actually uttered the disparaging words about Catholicism that Pakes accused him of having said, his reputation in St. Mary's County would have been justifiably sullied. Because he had not, however—and a formal investigation had proven as much—it was the government's responsibility to ensure that Hatton's good reputation was restored.

In the second instance, Thomas Hatton—who clearly did not have an axe to grind against Catholics, as evidenced by his willingness to travel to Maryland at Cecilius Calvert's request—convinced the governor to issue an arrest warrant for Luke Gardiner, who had hired Hatton's niece to serve in his household and who, Hatton alleged, was attempting to "train her up in the Roman Catholick religion contrary to the mind and will of her said mother." Elinor Hatton was just twelve years old when she joined Gardiner's household; her nineteen-year-old sister, Elizabeth, had married Gardiner five years earlier, shortly after arriving in Maryland with her mother and uncle. Elizabeth and Luke would have had to have published banns before they could be married, and so Luke Gardiner's Catholicism must not have been troubling to Thomas Hatton when Luke and Elizabeth wed. What was troubling to him, however, was that Gardiner was attempting to convert twelve-year-old Elinor Hatton—and doing so, apparently, against her widowed mother's wishes.

The Act Concerning Religion was a law that protected liberty of conscience. It was not a guarantor of free speech, and in fact, it was quite the opposite, as evidenced by the list of terms that were explicitly forbidden in Maryland. Gardiner's proselytizing, while religious, was not essential to the maintenance of his personal faith; it did intrude, however, upon Margaret Hatton's faith, which, legally, was the same as her daughter's, so long as that daughter was a minor. Determining, then, that Luke Gardiner may have violated the Act Concerning Religion and was, at the very least, engaging in behavior "of very dangerous and destructive consequence in relation to the peace and welfare of this province," Governor William Stone ordered his lieutenant to take Elinor Hatton and Luke Gardiner into custody. Hatton was sent home to her family, then, and Gardiner was put on trial. The prosecution was conducted by Maryland's attorney general, Thomas Hatton.[11]

The surviving records do not indicate what happened to Luke Gardiner in the weeks that followed his arrest. In all likelihood, however, Thomas Hatton went easy on him in court. Gardiner was family, after all, and once the young girl was returned to her mother, there was no personal reason for Hatton to pursue the case. Politically, Gardiner's arrest would have served its purpose—that is to say, Protestants and Catholics alike would have learned that Cecilius Calvert's government intended to take liberty of conscience seriously. Margaret Hatton did not want her twelve-year-old daughter practicing the Catholic faith, and the governor whom Lord Baltimore had chosen for his colony had every intention of ensuring that Mrs. Hatton's right to have that wish was protected. In the end, however, the wish seems to have been for naught. In 1658, twenty-year-old Elinor Hatton married Thomas Brooke, and together the couple converted to Catholicism.[12]

It was an interesting choice for the Brookes to make, given that just a few years before they converted, the wager that Lord Baltimore had staked in 1649 when he invited William Stone to come to Maryland and bring 500 disenfranchised Calvinists with him had fallen short. Governor Stone remained loyal to Calvert and paid the price for that loyalty. The Calvinists he brought with him, however, revealed themselves to be intolerant, fundamentalist ingrates who refused to respect any part of the Act Concerning Religion that did not specifically apply to them. These Calvinists also showed that much like their coreligionists in England, they were not above using violence to undermine any Catholic influence in their society and promote their religious agenda.

A little more than a year before the first Calvinists arrived from Virginia, Cecilius Calvert ordered his representatives to create a new county in Maryland just for the Puritans. That county, Anne Arundel, was named for Calvert's wife, who had died at the age of thirty-four earlier that year. The proprietor insisted that Anne Arundel County's capital, Providence (which was later renamed "Annapolis"), would have its own representatives in the colonial assembly and be home to the county's own courts, so that the Puritans living along the Severn River would not have to travel nearly seventy miles south to St. Mary's City just to have their disputes arbitrated. Pointedly, Calvert also wrote the Act Concerning Religion for the Calvinists' benefit, as evidenced by the long list of prohibited insults that specifically applied to adherents of John Calvin's theology: Puritan, Independent, Presbyterian, Brownist, Roundhead, and Separatist.[13]

Cecilius Calvert's hospitality, alas, was not enough to make the new Calvinist residents of Maryland forget that their proprietor was a Catholic—and therefore a minion of the anti-Christ. They refused to patent their land and pay the required quit-rents to the proprietor. They also refused to swear their fealty to him, an action that Lord Baltimore had initially required only of officeholders, but which he started requiring of all landholding residents in the colony after the Ingle-Claiborne Rebellion in 1645.

By the mid-1650s, nearly half of Maryland's white residents were Puritans who had come up from Virginia. The simple fact of the matter was that they did not have to abide by the proprietor's wishes. They were nearing a majority in the colony; their faction had successfully taken over the government back home in England; and in the summer of 1654, these Puritans realized they had the manpower to do the same in Maryland.[14]

In July of that year, William Claiborne—that old, familiar "pestilent enemy to the welfare of [Maryland] and the Lord Proprietor"—arrived in St. Mary's City with a parliamentary order to take over Maryland's government on behalf of the Commonwealth of England.[15] "The Commonwealth" was the name used by the Puritan-dominated, loosely republican government that ruled in England for approximately ten years between the execution of King Charles I in 1649 and the coronation of his son, Charles II, in 1660. During the Commonwealth period, Parliament and Oliver Cromwell, the so-called "Lord Protector of England, Scotland, and Ireland," were particularly keen to secure the loyalty of Virginia and Maryland, since unlike their counterparts in New England, neither colony had been founded by English Calvinists. Both also had strong ties to the recently deceased King Charles. Virginia had been a royal colony with an established Anglican Church, and Maryland, of course, was the result of a charter that Charles I had given to Cecilius Calvert. It was with that background in mind that Parliament had empowered William Claiborne to take over Maryland's assembly.

Calvert's hand-picked governor, William Stone, did not have the resources to oppose Claiborne and the forces he brought with him when he arrived in St. Mary's City, and so the governor resigned without a fight—wishing, perhaps, that he had executed the disruptive surveyor from Kent Island, as he had Richard Ingle just the year before. Acting on his commission, then, William Claiborne and the other man listed on the parliamentary order—Richard Bennett, Virginia's new Calvinist governor—appointed ten men, all of them Calvinists, to form a committee "for the well Ordering, direction, and Governing [of] the affairs of Maryland." This committee summoned the General Assembly to a special meeting—but not before barring those officeholders who had "borne Arms against the Parliament or do profess the Roman Catholick religion."[16]

In October 1654, the reconstituted assembly passed a reconstituted Act Concerning Religion "in the Name of his Highness, the Lord Protector." This Act restated the old Act's mandate that those who "profess faith in God by Jesus Christ" would be "protected in the profession of the faith." The new Act denied the legitimacy of Cecilius Calvert's charter, however—and specifically the Durham clause that was so important to the maintenance of religious pluralism—when it asserted that "none who profess and Exercise the popish religion . . . can be protected in this Province by the Laws of England." Maryland's laws, the Calvinist assemblymen insisted, were just an extension of the laws of England. Neither the assembly nor the proprietor could give rights to the residents of Maryland that had not already been given to the residents of England. The religious liberty provided by the new Act Concerning Religion, therefore, could "be not Extended to popery or prelacy nor to such as under the profession of Christ hold forth and practice Licentiousness."[17]

When news of the revised Act reached Cecilius Calvert in London, he flew into a rage and, according to one anonymous observer who was far from sympathetic to the proprietor's cause, fired off a letter to William Stone, accusing him of cowardice and ordering him to raise a force and take back the government from the Puritans. The governor did as he was told, and in March 1655, a battle ensued along the Severn

River, just a stone's throw away from where the U.S. Naval Academy sits today. Thirty-two people were injured and nineteen were killed—including Maryland's secretary, Thomas Hatton, the man responsible for bringing the text of the original Act Concerning Religion to the colony in the first place. The effort was a resounding defeat for William Stone, who was among ten men arrested and immediately put on trial by the Committee of Ten. Perhaps because the former governor of Maryland was also a Calvinist, Stone was one of six prisoners who avoided execution.[18]

Lord Baltimore understood now that he had made a tremendous mistake when he had decided to deal with Maryland's depopulation by inviting a passel of Puritans into his colony. That mistake could not be corrected by force, however, as the Battle of the Severn had shown, and so the proprietor turned to the softer tactic of diplomacy. He knew that following the controversial execution of King Charles I, England's Lord Protector was anxious to ensure that everything Parliament did was legal and above-board. The parliamentary commission that William Claiborne and Richard Bennett possessed, however—that is, the one that they had used to change the makeup of Maryland's assembly according to rules that did not meet with Lord Baltimore's Conditions of Plantation—usurped Calvert's proprietary authority and undermined his charter without due process. Legally, there were grounds on which to challenge the commission.

The only problem was that Oliver Cromwell hated Catholicism. While it is true that he often called liberty of conscience a "natural right," and that he even broke ranks with the English and Scottish Presbyterians who shared his Calvinist theology when he insisted that Protestant radicals like the Anabaptists ought to be included in a nondenominational, national church, the Lord Protector never had any intention of allowing Catholics in England, Scotland, or Ireland to practice their faith freely. "I meddle not with any man's conscience," Cromwell wrote to Lucas Taaffe, the Catholic governor of New Ross, shortly after the Puritan army had seized County Wexford in a brutal takeover of Ireland in October 1649. "But if by liberty of conscience, you mean liberty to exercise the mass, I judge it best to use plain dealing and let you know that where the Parliament of England have power that will not be allowed of."[19]

Of course, in making that statement, Oliver Cromwell had inadvertently hit upon the big, unresolved question with regard to the North American colonies. Did Parliament have any power in those territories? Cecilius Calvert's father, George, had insisted that the answer was "no" back in 1624, when several members of Parliament had attempted to encroach upon the proprietary fishing rights that King James I had given to William Vaughan in Newfoundland. Parliament's effort in that instance had failed precisely because, in George Calvert's words, "the plantations ... are not yet annexed to the Crown of England, but are the King's, as gotten him by conquest."[20] Now that there was no longer any king in England, what did that mean for proprietary colonies like the one Cecilius Calvert owned in North America? If Baltimore played his cards right, he might be able to convince Cromwell—in spite of the Protector's hatred of Catholicism—that it meant the commission Parliament had given to William Claiborne and Richard Bennett was illegal.

The task before Calvert was formidable. Seventy-eight Calvinists had published a series of lies and exaggerations about what life had been like for them under the Catholic Lord Baltimore's rule. Steeped in the language of Miltonian contractarianism, they told their coreligionists in England that Calvert behaved like "an absolute prince and hereditary Monarch" and that the laws of Maryland were determined by "the Arbitrariness of his own will." Government officials in the colony were "bound by Oath to countenance and defend the Roman Popish Religion" and Calvert had arranged for "an establishment of the Romish Religion only" in his colony along the Chesapeake. In what may have been their most insulting lie of all, the Calvinists ungratefully claimed that Baltimore had forced the Assembly to accept a law that was meant "to protect chiefly the Roman Catholick Religion in the free exercise thereof." No mention at all was made of the freedom that that law had also guaranteed Calvinists—who, until they succeeded in taking over Parliament, had been discriminated against in England in many of the same ways Catholics were.[21]

Cecilius Calvert was tempted, no doubt, to defend himself against these spurious allegations of religious intolerance. Nevertheless, he steered clear of religion for the most part when making his case for why Oliver Cromwell needed to intervene on his behalf. He began by noting that he had received a legal patent to Maryland, and that the colony had "always been in the Name of the Lord Proprietary." Unlike Virginia, which began its life as a proprietary colony, but then had that claim rescinded by King James I because of poor management, Maryland was a place where "the king's name was never used" when it came to discussions of ownership. The colony belonged exclusively to Cecilius Calvert, and—in an argument that may have been designed to appeal to the contractarian leanings of Oliver Cromwell's personal secretary, John Milton—Baltimore wrote that as he understood it, property rights were to be respected by the government in the new English Commonwealth.[22] All patents issued by the former king were to be honored, and the "Keepers of Liberty" in Parliament, Calvert obsequiously observed, "could not without breach of trust, concur to any such alteration" of a legal patent.

The proprietor went on to highlight the great personal sacrifices he and his partners had made in founding Maryland, and he pointed out that the colony had served the English nation well by preventing "the Dutch and Swedes from encroaching any nearer to Virginia." He claimed that investors had spent more than £40,000 on the colonial endeavor, and that he himself was responsible for half of that amount. Baltimore also noted that he had paid the ultimate price, losing two of his brothers in the settlement of Maryland. Leonard Calvert had died in 1647, after spending thirteen years as the colony's first governor. George Calvert, the proprietor's second-oldest brother, had died at the age of twenty-one shortly after his arrival in Maryland, a victim, in all likelihood, of the "seasoning process" that all immigrants had to go through when they first encountered the New World's viruses.

Not until the end of his plea did Cecilius Calvert touch upon the issue of religion, and then, when he did, his approach was thoroughly passive-aggressive. It was "advantageous to the interest and honor of this Commonwealth," Baltimore wrote to the Lord Protector from his home in London, "that an Englishman (although a Recusant, for the Lord Baltimore knows of no Laws here against Recusants which reach into America) should possess some part of that great Continent of America." Yes, Calvert conceded to Cromwell, he was a Catholic. And yes, he seemed willing to imply, that made him a second-class citizen—in England. In words that would not realize their full potential, however, until many decades later, Baltimore insisted that America was a very different world, one where England's anti-Catholic laws did not need to reach.[23]

The argument was strong enough to convince Cromwell to write to Richard Bennett, William Claiborne's partner in crime, and order him in January 1655 to "forbear disturbing the Lord Baltamore or his Officers and people in Maryland" and to "permit all things to remain as they were there, before any disturbance or alteration made by you."[24] The instructions were issued without any threat of penalty, however, and so their effect was minimal. The Committee of Ten that Claiborne and Bennett set up in 1654 continued to control Maryland's assembly, and that control continued to include a prohibition on Catholic membership. Cecilius Calvert kept pressing the Protector, however, and eventually, after more than two-and-a-half years of negotiations, Maryland's proprietor finally regained control of his colony.[25] In March 1658, the original conditions that determined membership in the Assembly were restored, and Calvert's Act Concerning Religion, complete with the protections it afforded Roman Catholics, once again directed the religious conversation in Maryland.

Cecilius Calvert, however, was no longer naïve. He was unwilling to assume, as he had before, that loyalty would necessarily follow in the wake of the Act Concerning Religion. From now on, loyalty to Maryland's Lord Proprietor would need to be exhibited before any religious protections were extended to the colony's residents. Once a resident had sworn his fealty to the proprietor, Baltimore showed that he was willing to apply the spirit of the Act generously—even more generously than he had originally intended, before the Puritan Uprising. Until that fealty was sworn, however, the fullness of the Act's protections would not be realized.

Jacob Lumbrozo reaped the benefits of Calvert's generous application of the Act Concerning Religion when he swore his fealty to the proprietor shortly after his arrival in Maryland in 1656. Lumbrozo was a physician who had come to the colony from Portugal, where officially (and perhaps not surprisingly), he had lived as a Catholic.[26] Upon his arrival in Maryland, however, the doctor chose to live openly as a Jew—a decision that, ironically, may have been prompted by the fact that Cecilius Calvert's Act Concerning Religion was not in force at the time of Lumbrozo's arrival in the colony. The Puritans' Act Concerning Religion, like the one Calvert had helped to write, guaranteed religious liberty only to those who had accepted Christ as their savior. The Puritans, however, prescribed no punishments—other than disenfranchisement—for individuals who failed to comply with the Protestant faith. In contrast, Calvert's Act Concerning Religion ominously stipulated that anyone in Maryland who deigned to "deny our Savior Jesus Christ to be the Son of God" would be "punished with death and confiscation or forfeiture of all his or her lands."[27] The threat, as it turns out, was not one that the proprietor was willing to act on. In 1656, however, it was the Puritans' Act, not Cecilius Calvert's, that seemed to offer Jews a better life than what they had had in Continental Europe.

During his first two years in the colony, Jacob Lumbrozo was not molested on account of his faith. Then, in the summer of 1658, a Quaker named Josias Cole, who had actually joined the Society of Friends just a few years earlier after spending the bulk of his life as a Calvinist, asked the physician in front of a roomful of people "what he was that was crucified at Jerusalem." Lumbrozo—who had undoubtedly faced far more clever interlocutors when he had lived in Portugal—replied simply that Jesus had been "a man." The veracity of such a statement was, of course, something that no Protestant or Catholic would deny—the whole point of Christianity, after all, was that God's son had, in fact, been a man—and so the Quaker convert pushed the Jewish doctor further. Eventually, Cole got Lumbrozo to admit that he believed Christ's miracles were works of "magic," and that the Resurrection was probably just a rumor that had been started when several of Jesus' disciples removed his body from the tomb. The statements were enough to get Jacob Lumbrozo arrested and charged with blasphemy.

Lumbrozo claimed that it had not been his intention to offend anyone, and that he never would have said anything at all about "him [that] Christians acknowledge for their Messiah," except that he had been asked—and when asked, he had answered honestly, "being by profession a Jew." In spite of his defense, Lumbrozo was required to post a bond in order to get out of jail. Ten days later, however, while he was awaiting his trial, the doctor was pardoned by Josias Fendall, the man Lord Baltimore had chosen to replace William Stone as governor. Fendall claimed to be acting on behalf of Cecilius Calvert. Jacob Lumbrozo went on to enjoy a lucrative career as one of Maryland's few physicians—even being offered the opportunity to lay with one patient's wife in exchange for his services (a proposal that the doctor tactfully refused, insisting on payment in tobacco instead). In 1663, Cecilius Calvert issued Lumbrozo letters of denization, which gave the Portuguese-born doctor many of the same rights that were afforded to natural-born English subjects. His status as a denizen allowed Lumbrozo to become a landowner under the proprietor's Conditions of Plantation, a right that he promptly acted upon in the months that followed the receipt of his denizen papers.[28]

Dr. Lumbrozo was afforded these opportunities, in spite of his identity as a Jew, because even though the Act Concerning Religion did not technically apply to Jews, he had proven himself to be loyal to the proprietor. Loyalty was precisely what Calvert had been hoping to engender when he had had Thomas Hatton present the Act to the Assembly back in 1649. Loyalty, however, was not what the residents of Anne Arundel County had shown the proprietor in the years leading up to the Puritan Uprising, and so Lord Baltimore was very keen to make sure that an oath of fidelity had been sworn by all of the landowning residents of that county before any discussion of religious liberty could take place there.

Surprisingly, Governor Josias Fendall had little trouble getting the Puritans in Providence to swear the oath. Fendall was a Protestant, and although his precise brand of Protestantism is unknown, it is possible—and even likely—that he shared a Calvinist orientation with the majority of residents in Anne Arundel County.[29] Fendall may have drawn upon this shared theology, then, to convince the Puritans that Parliament was not going to support another bid to take over the government from Calvert. Cooperation with the proprietor, therefore, was their best bet for a peaceful existence in Maryland.

In spite of Fendall's success, there were a few holdouts—Calvinists like Josias Cole who had converted to the Quaker faith in the midst of the Puritan Uprising and were refusing to take the oath of fidelity, because the Society of Friends taught that oath-taking created multiple standards for truth-telling and, in so doing, undermined the obligation to be honest at all times. Friends also believed that Jesus had specifically advised his followers to avoid oaths when, in his Sermon on the Mount, he had instructed them to "swear not at all; neither by Heaven, for it is God's throne; nor by the earth, for it is his footstool.... But let your communication be yea, yea, nay, nay: For whatever is more of these cometh of evil."[30]

Christ's communications from Mount Zion aside, Baltimore's representatives on the governor's council were disinclined to trust the Quaker converts who refused to swear their fealty to the proprietor. Had the converts not been raised in a theological tradition that equated the Pope with the anti-Christ, perhaps the reaction of the governor's council would have been different. As it was, though, Baltimore's men advised Governor Fendall that the Friends' unwillingness to take the oath of fidelity had the potential to "set our wounds even then scarcely healed fresh on bleeding & to embroil the county in worse & more dangerous distempers." It mattered not that the converts were refusing to swear the oath because their new religious faith had a well-established, theological antipathy toward oath-taking. The Act Concerning Religion simply did not protect the religious beliefs of anyone who was not willing to swear his allegiance to the proprietor.

The governor's council issued a proclamation in July 1658, demanding that all Quakers in the colony subscribe to the oath of fidelity by March 1659, or else leave the colony forever. Quakers who stayed in

Maryland but did not swear the oath were warned that they would be considered "Rebels & Traitors" and dealt with accordingly. The threat was a genuine one, and surviving records indicate that four months after the deadline had passed, several Quakers were, in fact, sitting in prison in Cecilius Calvert's religiously pluralist colony, having been convicted of treason because of behavior that they considered to be religiously motivated.[31]

Oath-taking was an important component of Cecilius Calvert's overall approach to government. The fealty that tenants swore to their manor lords, and the fealty that those lords, then—and, indeed, all landowners in the colony—swore to Lord Baltimore were meant to bring stability to Maryland through the creation of an easily identifiable network of hierarchy and obligation. Robert Wintour had called this network the "Maryland Designe" back in 1635, when he wrote to John Reade, encouraging him to immigrate to Cecilius Calvert's colony. By accepting the Maryland Designe and pledging their loyalty to the proprietor before both society and God, the Catholic and Protestant residents of Maryland would, according to Baltimore's philosophy of government, secure a peaceful and predictable existence for themselves, their children, and their neighbors.[32]

In an earlier age, such a political philosophy might have achieved Calvert's desired result, even in spite of the religious disconnect between the proprietor and the majority of his colony's residents. The Maryland Designe, after all, was similar to the philosophy of government that had animated Elizabethan and Jacobean England. In the late sixteenth and early seventeenth centuries, it had been possible for the Church of England to teach that individuals were obliged to "patiently suffer and obey" their leaders—even those leaders whom the subjects may have believed were incompetent—because "kings, queens, and other princes . . . are ordained by God," and "such subjects as are disobedient or rebellious against their princes disobey God and procure their own damnation."[33]

The times, however, were changing, and by the mid-seventeenth century, English thinkers had begun to challenge the traditional, hierarchical, and absolutist understanding of obligation that lay at the core of Cecilius Calvert's Maryland Designe. Following the execution of Charles I in 1649, many English people understood that perceived incompetence in a leader nullified any obligation they might have had to obey him. "To depose bad princes," John Milton wrote in 1651, was an obligation just as real and powerful "as to honour and obey good ones." Oaths of allegiance such as the one Lord Baltimore required in Maryland might still be taken by the English people. But "a People obliged to Obedience by such an Oath," Milton wrote, "is discharged of that Obligation, when a lawful Prince becomes a Tyrant."[34]

In Maryland, it seems that a majority of the property-holding residents did swear the oath of fidelity to the proprietor—if not before the Puritan Uprising of the mid-1650s, then certainly after.[35] Swearing that oath, however, did not prevent the colony's residents from criticizing Lord Baltimore's actions and decisions, or from chafing under the collar of what they perceived to be his increasingly autocratic rule.

Even before the Ingle-Claiborne Rebellion and the Puritan Uprising that followed, Maryland's assemblymen—Catholics and Protestants alike—had established a tradition of rejecting the proprietor's proposals whenever those proposals did not meet with the settlers' expectations for the colony. In 1639, for example, sixteen of the eighteen men serving in the Assembly—at least eight of whom were Catholic—rejected seven proposals that Lord Baltimore placed before them; only Leonard Calvert, the governor, and John Lewger, the secretary, voted in favor of the proposals. The following year, in 1640, when at least half of the men serving in the Assembly were Catholic, lawmakers voted overwhelmingly to reject ten bills that had been proposed by the proprietor. One request that was rejected unanimously—an effort to impose a tax that would have funded a military campaign involving the Susquehannock Indians—was denied by the assemblies of 1641, 1642, and 1643, as well.[36]

So long as Cecilius Calvert respected the Assembly's decision to reject his proposals, most of the men who served in that body—and who had sworn their fealty to him—continued to demonstrate their loyalty to the proprietor, regardless of their religious affiliation or their views on the legislation he proposed. After the Puritan Uprising of the 1650s, however, and the temporary loss of his proprietary control in Maryland, Lord Baltimore became less willing to accept the decisions of the colonial assembly when those decisions clashed with his own agenda. With each veto that the proprietor exercised, then, his hold on the loyalties of the assemblymen who had sworn their fealty to him became more tenuous.

In 1650, Cecilius Calvert divided Maryland's assembly into two houses as part of his effort to ensure that the kind of rebellion Richard Ingle and William Claiborne had launched in 1645 would never happen again. It was the proprietor's hope that a bicameral legislature would allow Maryland's less wealthy, predominantly Protestant residents to feel that they had a voice in their government—while at the same time ensuring that that voice did not become so loud that it dominated the legislative conversation.[37]

The Upper House, which included the governor, consisted of twelve men, all of whom were appointed by the proprietor for life. The Lower House was made up of landholders who had been elected by the freemen in each county to serve for a term of two years. The number of delegates assigned to each county ranged from one to four. Although the number was, in theory, determined by the county's population, the allotment of delegates was technically at the discretion of the proprietor—a prerogative that offended many people in the predominantly Protestant counties of Anne Arundel, Calvert, and Kent.[38]

This new, bicameral form of government had hardly gotten off of the ground when William Claiborne moved in with his parliamentary commission in 1654 and kicked anyone who was Catholic and/or supportive of the proprietor out of Maryland's assembly. It was not until the restoration of proprietary control in 1658, therefore, that Calvert's bicameral assembly really had a chance to develop, and by the late 1660s, it was apparent that his scheme was not going to placate the Protestants in his colony.

In 1669, the Lower House of the Assembly presented the Upper House with a list of "Public Grievances" against Cecilius Calvert. The twenty-seven delegates, at least nineteen of whom were Protestant, were unhappy that none of the legislation passed by the General Assembly was official until the proprietor had signed off on it. They were particularly dismayed that Lord Baltimore had insisted on literally being the one to approve the legislation, refusing to designate anyone in the colony to make the required approvals for him. Because Cecilius Calvert lived in England, it was often several months before any of the legislative changes that the men living in Maryland clearly believed were necessary could actually be implemented. On top of this delay, there was also the reality that the proprietor sometimes chose not to approve the legislation that had been passed by the colonial assembly—as he had done two years earlier in 1667, when he vetoed a bill that was meant to limit the fees county clerks could charge residents for writs and licenses, along with one that would have eliminated the twelve-pence poll tax that ship captains had to pay on servants they brought into Maryland.[39]

The Upper House of the Assembly—which was there to represent the proprietor's interests—responded to the grievances by reminding delegates in the Lower House of the violence and mayhem that the colony had experienced in recent years, thanks to the efforts of men who sought to destroy Cecilius Calvert's hold on the colony. The final approval of legislation, therefore, was "not a power fit to be entrusted with any person but ought to be reserved to himself [i.e., Calvert] alone ... for the good of the people of this Province."

The power to approve was real only so long as there was also the power to disapprove, and so the vetoes exercised by Calvert that delegates in the Lower House complained about were part and parcel of the "rules given him [i.e., the Proprietor] by his Majesty in his patent."[40] To challenge the right of the proprietor to veto colonial legislation was to challenge the wisdom of the king, who had given Baltimore that right in Maryland's charter—and while the contractarian philosophies of people like John Milton may have enjoyed some powerful popularity during the eleven years of the Interregnum, England's monarchy had been fully and unequivocally restored in 1660. In 1669, therefore, Lord Baltimore's representatives in the Upper House assumed that the hierarchical principles of the Maryland Designe were thoroughly back in play.

They were wrong. And because many of the men who had been appointed to the Upper House were, like the proprietor himself, Roman Catholic, their outdated political philosophy served to confirm the increasingly virulent association in the English-speaking world between Catholicism and tyranny.[41] It mattered not to the Protestant majority in Maryland that Cecilius Calvert had never had the freedom to consider whether a contractarian approach to government might have been a better "designe" for Maryland, consumed as he was with the task of defending his interests against Calvinists who relentlessly attacked his claim to the colony on the basis of his faith. It was irrelevant, and indeed forgotten by many of Maryland's Protestants that in the early years of the colony's existence, before Richard Ingle and William Claiborne had launched their rebellion, Catholics in Maryland had been just as willing as Protestants to push back against the proprietor's wishes whenever his wishes did not meet the colonists' needs. No, by the mid-1670s, as the people back home in England were starting to fret about the fact that King Charles II had no legitimate heirs—and that his Catholic-convert brother James, therefore, was next in line for the throne—all that mattered to the Protestant majority in Maryland was that the colony's popish proprietor and his popish minions in the Upper House of the Assembly were, in the words of Virginia's Anglican governor, Thomas Culpeper, woefully "unsuited to this age."[42]

It was unfortunate, then, that Cecilius Calvert should have died in 1675, and that his oldest son, Charles—who was thoroughly ungifted in matters of diplomacy—should have taken over as the second Catholic proprietor at such a delicate time in Maryland's colonial history. One of the first edicts Charles Calvert issued as the colony's new proprietor was a writ that cut the number of Lower House delegates representing Anne Arundel and Kent Counties in half. Both counties were sparsely populated, but both were also Calvinist strongholds. When the third Lord Baltimore reduced the number of representatives from Anne Arundel and Kent to just two delegates each, all the while allowing St. Mary's and Charles Counties, which were home to about 95 percent of Maryland's Catholics, to continue to have four, he revealed himself to be naïve, impolitic and—at least in the minds of his Protestant critics—religiously corrupt.[43]

Unlike his father, Charles Calvert lived in Maryland. He had arrived in the colony in 1661 at the age of twenty-four and served as Maryland's governor until his father's death fourteen years later. Even after he became the proprietor, Calvert continued to reside in St. Mary's County, returning to England just two times during his proprietorship—once, shortly after Cecilius Calvert's death, to settle his father's estate; and a second time in 1684, in an attempt to settle a boundary dispute that he was having with William Penn, who had founded the colony of Pennsylvania two years earlier. That dispute would not actually be resolved until eighty-three years later, when Charles Mason and Jeremiah Dixon were jointly hired by the Calvert and Penn families to fix the boundary between the two colonies.[44]

The fact that he lived in Maryland—and had personal interactions with the colony's residents, Catholics and Protestants alike—may have been the reason Charles Calvert constructed a government that seems, even today, to have been deliberately designed to protect Catholics' interests. At the height of the third Lord Baltimore's proprietary rule, for instance, Catholics made up just 14 percent of the white population in Maryland; yet, they were 67 percent of the men whom Charles Calvert appointed to serve in the Upper House of the Assembly, at least among those whose religious identities are known. Even the disproportionately small number of Protestants who served in the Upper House reflected a policy of nepotism. Benjamin Rozer and William Digges, for example, both of whom were Anglican, were married to Charles Calvert's Catholic stepdaughters, Ann and Elizabeth Sewall. William Burgess's daughter, Susanna, who, like her father, had been raised in the Church of England, was married to Ann and Elizabeth's older brother, Nicholas, who, like his sisters, had been raised in the Church of Rome.[45]

In addition to stacking the Upper House with people who were sympathetic to the Catholic cause, the third Lord Baltimore also changed the property requirements on voting, so that only men who had at least fifty acres of land or £40 sterling in moveable property could vote. To actually hold office under Calvert's new rules, a man would need to own at least 1,000 acres. This requirement had a minimal impact on the lives of the Catholics living in Maryland, since more than 40 percent of them owned estates that were worth more than £100, and nearly a fifth had estates that were in excess of £500. In contrast, just one-quarter of the people in Maryland overall owned enough property to easily clear the hurdle that Charles Calvert had placed in front of the voting franchise—and that one-quarter included the 40 percent of Catholics whose estates were worth more than £100.[46] Under the third Lord Baltimore's rule, then, many Protestants who had recently been freed from indentured servitude and had managed to acquire small, but sustainable tracts of land for themselves were not allowed to cast a ballot.

As Governor William Berkeley of Virginia discovered during the notorious "Bacon's Rebellion" in 1676, the late seventeenth century was not a good time to have a bunch of angry freeman running around a colony with no mechanism for expressing themselves politically. Just a few months before Nathaniel Bacon and his gang of 500 yeoman farmers and former servants turned their guns against the House of Burgesses, claiming that the elite members of that body had been ignoring their interests and leaving them vulnerable to Indian attacks, a group of men from Maryland, "a great many" of whom had "come [to North America] as servants," joined their counterparts across the Potomac in sending King Charles II a "Complaint from Heaven with a Huy and Crye and a petition out of Maryland and Virginia."[47]

In addition to griping about Governor Berkeley's Indian policies and his recent marriage to a young woman who was, apparently, distracting him from his duties and encouraging him to act like a "fool," the petitioners complained about the nepotism in Charles Calvert's government and the favoritism that he was showing toward Catholics. Maryland's proprietor had, according to the petitioners, filled the Upper House of the Assembly with "papists, [his] own creatures, and ignoramuses" who assisted him in his campaign to "overturn England" and "drive us Protestants to Purgatory within ourselves in America." The petitioners claimed that "the Lord Baltemore puts himself in equal computation with ... the King's Majesty" and "holds forth that he is an absolute Prince in Maryland." Among the proofs the petitioners offered of Calvert's absolutism and his inappropriately monarchical tendencies were the oaths of fidelity that all landowners were required to swear to the proprietor and the recent disenfranchisement that Calvert had affected when he changed the property requirements on voting and reduced the number of delegates from primarily Protestant counties.[48]

In spite of the anger that was apparent in the petition, Maryland did not erupt into rebellion in 1676 the way Virginia did. The storm, however, continued to gather, and five years later, in October 1681, the Lords of Trade in London—who represented the king's interests in North America—determined that it was time to intervene. They wrote to Charles Calvert, offering him their "hearty Commendation" for the work he had done in Maryland before telling him of the concerns that a number of the colony's residents had expressed to them. The Lords had heard that "there are very few of his Majesty's Protestant subjects admitted to be of the Council of the Colony of Maryland," and that "there is partiality and favour showed on all occasions towards those of the Popish religion." They told Baltimore that they thought the information they had received might have been a "misrepresentation." Nevertheless, the allegations were serious and needed to be "speedily addressed," and the Lords told Charles Calvert that they thought he could go a long way toward assuaging the anger of certain Protestants in his colony if he simply expressed his "Trust and Confidence in his Majesty's Protestant Subjects" by providing them with the "arms and ammunition" that the Lords of Trade had recently sent to Maryland at the proprietor's request.[49]

It was an incredibly bizarre note. Its tone was unusually solicitous—almost obsequious—and the Lords' suggestion that Calvert consider dealing with the rising tide of Protestant anger in Maryland by giving those angry Protestants guns is curious, to say the least. Whether the letter was a genuine effort to address Protestants' concerns about discrimination, while at the same time respecting the authority of Maryland's Catholic proprietor—or a manipulative effort to arm Maryland's

Protestants in anticipation of the revolution that many people in England were working hard to foment—will never be known. What is known, though, is that Charles Calvert chose not to heed the Lords' advice about the need to "speedily address" the discontent in his colony. Instead, he responded to the note by simply sending the Lords of Trade a signed testimony in which thirteen high-ranking Protestant assemblymen denied that there was any religious discrimination in the colony against non-Catholics. At least five of the Protestant men mentioned in the testimony were related to the proprietary family, and at least six—William Burgess, Henry Coursey, William Digges, Benjamin Rozer, William Stevens, and Thomas Taylor—were titled in Maryland, thanks to the manorial system that the second Lord Baltimore had set up.[50] Indeed, all of the signers of the testimony would have had to have owned at least 1,000 acres; they could not have served in the Assembly under Calvert's new rules otherwise. Their testimony, therefore, did little to address the allegations of nepotism that the authors of the "Huy and Crye" had made five years earlier—or the class resentment that was implicit, if burgeoning, in their complaint.

The decision to ignore the growing discontent in Maryland would ultimately lead to the third Lord Baltimore's downfall. In seven years' time, Protestant resentment, inflamed by Charles Calvert's clumsy, outdated approach to government and stoked by the anti-Catholic rhetoric of the Glorious Revolution in England, would explode into a rebellion in Maryland that was far more extensive than anything Governor Berkeley had had to deal with in Virginia thirteen years earlier. The colony's charter would be suspended, and Charles Calvert would watch his son and grandson abandon the faith of his father and grandfather in an attempt to get the charter back. But first, England's Anglican majority would have to rise up in rebellion against their Catholic king and accept a Calvinist prince as the leader of their church and their nation.

To be fair, the Glorious Revolution was about more than just a hatred of Catholicism. Far more so than Cecilius and Charles Calvert, King James II had an absolutist approach to government that was entirely incompatible with the direction English political philosophy had taken in the years following the execution of James's father, Charles I. In the brief, three-and-a-half-year period that constituted his reign, James II managed to suspend Parliament indefinitely and disband the local assemblies of every British American colony north of Pennsylvania.[51] Such actions did not mix well with the spirit of contractarianism that had taken flight in the English-speaking world. Additionally, King James quadrupled the size of England's standing army, from 8,865 troops at the time of his brother's death in February 1685, to more than 34,000 by November 1688, when his son-in-law, William, invaded from Holland. This peacetime expansion violated long-standing traditions on the role of the army in English society and was one of the first five violations of the "laws and liberties of this kingdom" that Parliament (or what was technically called the "Convention," since only the king could convene Parliament) pointed to when inviting William and Mary to assume the throne in 1689.[52]

Still, the first violation that Parliament listed in its Declaration of Right was the charge that James "did endeavour to subvert and extirpate the Protestant religion" with the policies he had implemented throughout his tenure as king. Sure, the growing army in what was technically a time of peace was problematic—but primarily because it represented a threat to England's Protestant identity. The Declaration of Right mentioned James's military expansion only in the context of his decision to order "several good subjects being Protestants to be disarmed at the same time when papists were both armed and employed contrary to law." James had used his royal dispensing power in 1687 not just to expand the army but also to replace several Protestant lieutenants with Roman Catholics. These armed Catholics in positions of authority were, according to Parliament, dangerous to the Protestant integrity of the English nation.[53]

By the time the Declaration of Right was passed in December 1689, Parliament had been clambering for a fight with Catholicism for quite some time. More to the point, English society was well prepared to receive the anti-Catholic propaganda that the Calvinist Prince of Orange made sure was widely circulated throughout England and the colonies before he landed with his troops on Devonshire's shores. William understood that the Puritan–Anglican antagonisms that had animated English politics throughout much of the seventeenth century would need to be eclipsed by a hatred and fear of Catholicism before a prince whose theology mirrored that of Oliver Cromwell could successfully take over as the head of the Church of England. His agents made sure that eclipse took place.

"Never before in England or on the Continent," according to one scholar, had tracts, broadsides, medals, and prints been "utilized together in such large number for a single purpose" as they were during the months leading up to and following the Glorious Revolution. William's advisors in London wrote to him in April 1688, telling him that he would need to put the country "in good humor" about the prospect of an invasion from Holland if that invasion were to succeed. To win the English over, William should "entertain them by papers." To that end, officials at The Hague published an English-language broadside in October 1688 and distributed it to several prominent MPs. Entitled simply *Character*, the broadside described William as "benign" and "affable." He had the "Courage and Valiancy of Joshua" and the "meekness of Moses," and the "charming dispositions of his Mind" were attributes any legislator would be happy to encounter, since William, unlike King James II, had "never violated the personal rights or abridged the municipal privileges" of his subjects.[54]

Although William's advisors agreed that a propaganda campaign was necessary, they did not always agree about the elements that needed to be in that campaign. During the weeks that followed the invasion, while Parliament debated whether James's retreat to Ireland constituted an abdication and, if so, whether an invitation to William and Mary to assume the throne might be appropriate, William's advisors bickered about whether to include a criticism of the king's dispensing power in their media blitz. Some felt such a criticism was important, since James's use of the dispensing power to relax the penal laws against Catholics had been a source of concern for "the body of the whole nation." Other advisors believed, however, that the dispensing power, in and of itself, was not a problem, and that William should not allow himself to get dragged into a debate about whether the sovereign of England, regardless of who he or she was, should ever be allowed to disregard the decisions of Parliament.

Another point of contention among William's advisors was the question of whether the literature should address the highly controversial arrest of seven Anglican bishops the year before. The bishops had been arrested because they opposed James's suspension of the penal laws against Catholics. Some of William's advisors wanted to point to the mass arrest as a motivating factor in the stadtholder's decision to invade. Others knew, however, that five of the seven bishops remained loyal to King James, in spite of their arrest—largely because they had sworn an oath to God that they would remain faithful to the king. These bishops could not be relied upon to support a coup by William and Mary. It was questionable, therefore, whether the bishops' arrest should, or even could, be used successfully in William's propaganda campaign.[55]

One point the stadtholder's advisors did not disagree on, however, was that anti-Catholicism had the power to provide William's invasion with the legitimacy it needed. The link between English and Protestant identity that the advisors planned on exploiting had a long history— one that went back at least to 1563 and the publication of John Foxe's religiously charged tome, the "Book of Martyrs." That work was fundamental to the creation of a distinctly "English" national identity, because it told readers that they had been graced by God with a special mission to protect the One, True Church—identified almost always as the "Protestant Church"—from the evil effects of "popery."

John Foxe used the word "popery" to describe the Catholic belief system because that word, which was not yet common in the 1560s, reminded readers that Catholics owed their allegiance not to England's Queen, but to a religious leader on the other side of the Alps. By associating Catholicism with a foreign power and declaring England's Protestant mission to be blessed, Foxe helped to establish the inherently "alien" nature of Catholicism and, in so doing, paved the way for the Dutch Calvinist William of Orange to take over England 166 years later.[56]

The road that Foxe had paved, however, had developed some potholes by the late seventeenth century, thanks to the English Civil War. William's advisors sought to patch those holes, therefore, with well-distributed anti-Catholic iconography that was both entertaining and easily accessible to even the most illiterate of England's Protestant residents.

The printed word continued to play an important role in the stadtholder's propaganda campaign, but it was the iconography that had the most far-reaching effect in an age when only about 40 percent of the adult males in England could read. At least forty-nine prints, two sets of playing cards, and thirty-one medals, all of them supporting William's invasion, were distributed in England, Scotland, Ireland, and the North American colonies between October 1688 and January 1690.[57] Many of the prints did contain text, indicating that they were designed, at least in part, to appeal to the king's literate subjects. But the humorous, even ribald character of the images suggests that the prints were also meant to appeal to a broader audience, one that may not have been equipped to read about "England's . . . Wonderful deliverance from French tyranny and Popish oppression," but one that could easily recognize the Devil and a Jesuit—and could understand that a conference between the two and King James II spelled trouble for England.

Figure 3.1 is representative of the way in which the iconography that William's agents distributed made use of the "foreign" status that Catholicism had in the English-speaking world. The orange tree in the center of the print was a well-known symbol in 1688 of the House of Orange. To the right of the orange tree, there stands a chapel that has been erected under the benevolent eye of Providence. Providence soothes the chapel, telling it that "with this Balsamick Plant I heale Thye Wounds," to which the chapel gratefully replies, "Under the blessed shade [of this tree], I breathe againe."

A council of Satan and Jesuit priests is situated in the opposite corner from Providence—the opposite corner from Providence being the only place where the Devil and his Catholic minions could gather. Satan complains that "this curssed plant has Sav'd the Heretick Church," while a Jesuit laments that "just one Beast more & the Work

Figure 3.1 England's Memorial of its Wonderful Deliverance from French Tyranny and Popish. Oppression, c. 1688. Bridgeman Art Library International.

was done." Beneath the Jesuit council, there is an image of a king, identified as "The French King, murthering his owne Subjects." As he whacks away at three helpless men with a sword and a crucifix, King Louis XIV advises James II, who stands next to the orange tree with his Catholic wife and son, to "tread on my Stepps and be great." James's crown teeters on his head and is clearly about to fall off, thanks to an orange that has dropped from one of the tree's flourishing branches and landed directly on the king's head.[58]

The message conveyed by this print is clear: England's identity is inextricably linked to the Protestant Church, and the salvation of both the Church and the country lies with the Protestant William of Orange. England and her Church, together, are the embodiment of freedom; this is a partnership ordained by God, and God has given William of Orange to the people of England in an effort to protect that partnership from Satan's arm on earth, the Roman Catholic Church.

The decidedly un-English future that England and her colonies had to look forward to under the reign of King James II is made apparent in another print released shortly before William's invasion. This print (figure 3.2) was particularly popular in the colonies, and it features a bed-ridden James, vomiting serpents. The snakes wear the four-cornered hat typically associated with the Jesuit order—as does James—and each of the snakes announces the developments that England has to look forward to under the reign of a Catholic king: "Jesuit Colleges," a "French Alliance," and "No Free Parliament." All three developments stand in absolute opposition to the Protestant freedom that English identity was thought to embody. In the upper right-hand corner of the print, surrounded by the eternal light and glory of the sun, William of Orange and his fleet stand ready to enter the scene and rescue England from the un-English future that awaits the country so long as James remains king.[59]

No doubt the print's message resonated with particular force in Maryland, where the Jesuits were already operating schools (not colleges, but classrooms, nonetheless), and where traditional, English anti-Catholicism was mixed with growing class antagonism, anti-proprietary

Figure 3.2 "Qualis vir Talis Oratio." © The Trustees of the British Museum.

politics, and Protestant disenfranchisement. Added to this mixture was the reality that while Catholics and Quakers were thriving in the colony, many Anglicans had been left with literally no religious leadership. The Act Concerning Religion had meant that no church in Maryland received funding from the government, and Anglicans had been slow to provide private support for their ministers. The Anglican clergy, unlike their Catholic counterparts, did not have a burning desire to endure hardship for the sake of bringing Christ to the Indians, and so priests from the Church of England had refused to come to Maryland without a guarantee that they would be taken care of. Protestants in the colony did not hesitate to blame the Catholic proprietor and his political servants for this situation, and when they rebelled in 1689, Protestant leaders insisted that as an English colony, Maryland was obliged to provide financial support to the Church of England.[60]

In 1683, Charles Calvert ended the headright system. No longer would men be given land on the basis of how many people they brought to the colony. Instead, land would be given to them in exchange for a fee.[61] The surviving records do not indicate why Lord Baltimore decided to make this change, but his action may have been an attempt to limit the number of Protestant servants coming into the colony. Although he had refused to heed the advice given to him by the Lords of Trade about the discontent in Maryland, Calvert must have known that things were heating up on the religious landscape—not just in his colony, but in England, as well. He still needed to get his colony populated in order to turn a profit, but he was not going to make the same mistake his father had made when, in an effort to repopulate Maryland after the Ingle-Claiborne Rebellion, Cecilius Calvert had been willing to accept anyone into the colony. For now, at least, the flow of Protestants into Maryland would have to be slowed.

The headright system had long been a means by which financially secure, but far-from-wealthy residents in Baltimore's colony could get ahead. Financial success in the New World—particularly in tobacco economies like the one that dominated Maryland and Virginia—required more than just the possession of large tracts of land. It also required control of a labor force that could cultivate that land. The headright system had been a way for ambitious men in Maryland to kill the proverbially two birds with one stone. By paying for the passage of several men to come to the colony, a middling-planter could acquire both the labor of those men for a period of four to nine years and the land that Cecilius Calvert's Conditions of Plantation promised to any settlers who brought able-bodied men into the colony.[62]

Under Charles Calvert's new conditions, however, planters would have to pay the proprietor for the land, and then pay the ship captains—or, increasingly in the 1660s and 1670s, the slave traders—for the labor. It was a change in policy that destroyed the system that Protestant planters like John Coode and Nehemiah Blakiston had used to make their livings (or in the case of Blakiston, their fortunes). Thanks to the second Lord Baltimore's generous Conditions of Plantation, Coode had managed to accumulate a personal estate that was worth nearly £260 sterling at the time of his death in 1709. While that amount paled in comparison to the estate value of £1,500 that Blakiston's executors recorded after his death in 1693, Coode's estate was still considered to be quite substantial at the turn of the eighteenth century.[63]

Cecilius Calvert's Conditions of Plantation had helped Blakiston and Coode acquire their wealth; his son's policies on voting, office-holding, and landownership, however, had led to an erosion of the power and prestige that might otherwise have come with that wealth. Throughout Charles Calvert's tenure as proprietor, wealthy Protestants increasingly found that their situation in Maryland mirrored that of wealthy Catholics in England, at least before the reign of King James II. Neither group was able to achieve the degree of political prominence that would have accompanied its financial strength and social standing, had religious circumstances been different. Wealthy Protestants found that a "glass ceiling" of sorts prevented their full ascension into the ranks of the politically powerful in Maryland, and Coode and Blakiston were great examples of this fact. Neither man was able to get much beyond the level of county leadership while Charles Calvert was in possession of the colony. In fact, by 1689, there was just one Protestant sitting on the governor's council, and that man was William Digges, who was married to the proprietor's Catholic stepdaughter and was raising his children as Catholics.[64]

Into this situation sauntered William Joseph, a Roman Catholic from Ireland who arrived in Maryland in October 1688, knowing little or nothing about the religious and political climate in the colony. Joseph came to Maryland to assume the governorship, since George Talbot, the deputy Charles Calvert had appointed to assist his infant son in that position, had fled the colony following a drunken argument with the king's tax collector, Christopher Rousby. That argument had ended with Talbot's knife in Rousby's chest. Charles Calvert was in England at the time of the murder, attempting to resolve the boundary dispute that he was having with William Penn. It is not clear how or when he met William Joseph, or why he chose Joseph, specifically, to take over the governorship from his infant son. It does seem, however, that Charles

Calvert did not adequately brief the Irishman on the delicacy of the situation he was about to walk into.[65]

Joseph alienated the Protestants in the Lower House of the Assembly almost immediately after his arrival in the colony. In his first speech before that body, delivered within days of William of Orange's assault on Devonshire, Joseph claimed that a "Divine Sentence" was the basis of the Catholic King James's authority. He then insisted that the delegates swear oaths of allegiance to the proprietor. On that same day, Joseph also revealed just how oblivious he was to the religious and political dynamics in Maryland when he asked the assembly to make June 10th an annual day of thanksgiving. That day was the birthday of James's first and only son—who, unlike his older half-sisters Mary and Anne, would be raised as a Catholic, just like his mother, Mary of Modena.[66]

It was in January 1689, however, that William Joseph made his biggest blunder. Transatlantic communication being what it was in the seventeenth century, it took several weeks for word of William's invasion of England to reach North America. When it did, it was in the form of instructions that King James's advisors had sent to the governors of Maryland and Virginia. William Joseph and Francis Howard were both told that they needed to put their colonies in a "posture of defense," so that each could respond appropriately should the Dutch decide to bring their invasion to North America. Such a posture of defense, the governors were told, would require an accurate count of how many guns were in each colony and who was in possession of them.[67]

Joseph and the governor's council in Maryland responded to the order by calling in all of the public arms, saying they needed to be repaired by gunsmiths in Patuxent, Mattapany, and St. Mary's City. Since all of these towns were located in St. Mary's County, the order essentially mandated that every gun in Maryland be sent to the county where the majority of the colony's Catholics lived. This left Protestants in Anne Arundel and Kent Counties, far to the north, vulnerable to attacks by Indians and the French—who, like William Joseph, Charles Calvert, and many of the residents of St. Mary's County, subscribed to the Roman Catholic faith. Needless to say, it did not take long for rumors to spread that Maryland's Catholics were plotting with the French and Indians to "cut off all the protestants in the province."[68] English Catholics, after all, were just as "foreign" and dangerous to English identity as the French and Indians were. The propaganda that William of Orange had arranged to have circulated in the colonies made that clear.

In February 1689, William and Mary accepted an invitation from Parliament to jointly rule over England. Word of their coronation reached the Chesapeake in April of that year, and Virginia's government wasted no time in proclaiming the legitimacy of the succession. Realizing how tenuous his proprietary status was, Charles Calvert, who was still in England, sent instructions to William Joseph, telling him to endorse the change in government, as well. Calvert's messenger died in Plymouth, however, before he could reach Maryland, and lacking any instructions, Governor Joseph chose to do nothing.[69] By July of that year, Protestants in the colony decided that they had had enough. John Coode and Nehemiah Blakiston, the self-proclaimed leaders of the Protestant interest in Maryland, declared the failure of the governor's council to endorse the succession of William and Mary to be treasonous, and they took up arms against the proprietary government.

The "Protestant Associators," as the rebels called themselves, published a list of grievances, explaining the reasons for their rebellion to anyone in England or the colonies who might not have been familiar with the circumstances they had been forced to endure. They accused Lord Baltimore—with some degree of justification—of allowing Catholics in the colony to monopolize all of the truly powerful leadership positions. They condemned his attempts to limit Protestant power by restricting the number of representatives from predominantly Protestant counties, and they alleged that under the Catholic proprietor's leadership, "several children of protestants have been committed to the tutelage of papists, and brought up in the Romish Superstition." The Associators also challenged the English loyalties of Maryland's Catholics when they accused "Jesuits, Priests, and lay papists" of publically calling for the "prosperous success of the popish forces in Ireland, and the French designs against England."[70]

On July 25th, a crowd of more than 700 angry Protestants surrounded the proprietor's manor, which lay about eight miles outside St. Mary's City. The governor's council had been meeting in Charles Calvert's home, Mattapany House, during the proprietor's absence. They surrendered to the Protestant Associators without a fight and agreed that Catholics would no longer be allowed to hold civil or military office in the colony.

The Protestant Associators were not satisfied simply to strip Catholics and their sympathizers of their political power, however. According to Charles Carroll, a wealthy Catholic Irishman who had arrived in Maryland just six weeks before William of Orange invaded England, "neither Cathlolique nor honest Protestant" could "well call his life or estate his own," during the months that constituted the Associators' rebellion. "Daily their cattle are killed, their horses pressed and all the injury imaginable [is] done to them," Carroll wrote to Charles Calvert in England. James Heath, a Catholic from England who was living in Cecil County, near the Pennsylvania border, charged in 1690 that Coode's men had confiscated his property and "applied [it] to their own private uses." Eleven Protestants from Baltimore County also complained that the Associators had "arbitrarily seized and plundered" the estates of anyone who deigned to question their authority. These men were among sixty-seven Protestants who had had the temerity to suggest that the Associators ought not to hold an election for a new General Assembly until a "Lawful Power from England" could come to Maryland to verify the election results. [71]

The fighting lasted for more than a year, but by the summer of 1691, tempers in Maryland had cooled. There were still a few incidents that indicated that some people in the colony were not happy with what the Protestant Associators had done, but the property damage involved was minimal. In January 1692, for example, a group of Anglicans and Catholics in Talbot County got drunk and openly mocked the Protestant Associators. These men apparently "rid their Horses into the court House"—and then, presumably, allowed the animals to wreak all manner of havoc once inside. Also, in 1693, Randolph Brandt of Charles County and Peter Sayer of Talbot County were arrested for separate acts of "Contempt and misbehavior toward the Government." Sayer, a Catholic, stood accused of having called Parliament a "parcel of Rogues" and the Anglican bishops in England a "Company of heretick Dogs."[72]

By the time Lionel Copley arrived in Maryland in April 1692 to assume the governorship, however, there was little resistance to the changed political landscape that the Protestant Associators had created. In the summer of 1691, the Lords of Trade decided to strip Charles Calvert of his right to appoint a governor to the colony. They chose to send Copley to Maryland because he had gotten into some mail-tampering trouble while he was serving as the lieutenant governor of Hull, and the people in that region were demanding his removal. Lionel Copley had also established his anti-Catholic bona fides during his time in the army, and the Lords felt that his authority would therefore be respected by the Protestant Associators.[73]

Baltimore's hold on his charter had been tenuous ever since William's assumption of the English crown, and the loss of his right to appoint a governor to Maryland effectively amounted to a suspension of his charter. Charles Calvert was allowed to maintain his ownership of the colony, which meant that he could continue to collect quitrents and make money off his father's investment. He would no longer be allowed to issue directives with regard to voting and office-holding in the colony, however. Those directives would instead come from the governor, who was working not for Calvert, but for the Lords of Trade.[74]

Under the Lords' direction, Copley announced that the Book of Common Prayer was "established" in Maryland, and that it would have to be "read each Sunday and holiday" under penalty of a fine. The Sacrament would be administered "according to the Rights [sic] of the Church of England," and the government of Maryland would provide for the "competent maintenance" of Anglican ministers in the colony. To pay for the ministers' upkeep, Copley proposed a poll tax of 40 pounds of tobacco. In the four years that followed his arrival in the colony, twenty-five Anglican churches were built, and eighteen Anglican priests were brought to Maryland.[75]

In June 1692, the General Assembly passed a resolution that established the Church of England in Maryland. That resolution, interestingly enough, was rejected by King William III, even though William and his advisors were very interested in using the Anglican Church to shore up Maryland's English identity. England's attorney general worried that the resolution, which called for the extension of English liberties to Maryland, implied that Parliament had some form of direct authority over the colony. Because all of the North American colonies were considered to be the "king's, as gotten him by conquest," the wording of the resolution needed to be changed.[76]

An acceptable resolution establishing the Church of England in Maryland would not be passed until 1702, by which point William and Mary were both dead, and Mary's younger sister, Anne, had assumed the throne.[77] The ten-year delay did not mean that Cecilius Calvert's Act Concerning Religion was in force in the mean time, however. That Act had depended upon the Durham clause in Maryland's charter, and when the charter was suspended, everything that depended upon it was suspended, as well.

From June 1692 until November 1776, when the provisional government that had been set up after Maryland declared its independence from England passed a new state constitution, the Anglican Church was effectively the established Church of Maryland. The descendents of George and Cecilius Calvert accepted this reality and abandoned the Roman Catholic Church in an effort to regain their family's proprietary control of the colony. In the years that followed, then, the fifth and sixth Lords Baltimore would endorse legislation that made life inconvenient, and at times even onerous for Roman Catholics in Maryland.

It is unlikely that the seventeenth century would have ended much differently in Maryland, even if Cecilius and Charles Calvert had been more willing (and able) to extend some of the liberalism that characterized their religious policies to the political sphere.

Even if the relationship between the proprietor and the General Assembly had been more contractarian, Protestants in the colony still would have rebelled in the wake of the Glorious Revolution. That revolution, after all, firmly established that to be English was to be Protestant—and for Englishmen who were trying to eke out an existence 3,600 miles away from London, the rule of a Catholic proprietor constituted a grave threat to their national identity, regardless of that proprietor's political proclivities.

Still, it is important to understand what the rule of the second and third Lords Baltimore looked like in seventeenth-century Maryland, because in the decades that followed, the liberal nature of that rule—both real and imagined—became an anchor to which eighteenth-century Catholics in Maryland tied their religious and national identities. As the century progressed, Maryland's Catholics became more and more invested in an understanding of the colony's early history that emphasized the liberal environment the Catholic Calverts had created and stressed the striking degree of independence from England that the colony's early settlers had been allowed to enjoy. The settlers had had this independence because of the colony's charter, which Maryland's Catholics increasingly thought of in constitutional terms. This mentality not only sustained the Catholic community throughout a difficult period in Maryland's history, it also prepared Catholics to accept the ideology of the independence movement.

4

Catholic Commitment in an Inhospitable Climate

The eighty-four years that followed the temporary, but significant revocation of Maryland's charter are often referred to as the "Penal Period" in the colony's history.[1] Between 1692 and 1776, the General Assembly took up numerous pieces of legislation as part of a collective effort to restrict the civil, military, educational, economic, religious, and even parental rights and behavior of Maryland's "papists." Even when these bills were not actually turned into laws—and they were, frequently, turned into laws—the discussions and debates that the bills engendered made it decidedly inconvenient, at times even onerous to be Catholic in Maryland.

In spite of the antagonistic cultural and legislative environment, Catholicism survived in Maryland—and the Catholic population itself grew more than fivefold throughout the Penal Period—because the people who made up the Catholic community refused not to be Catholic. They did not always attend Mass as frequently as they or their priests would have liked, and they did not always approach their fasting obligations with the reverence and consistency that were required of them by their Church. Very few of Maryland's Catholics ever took the step of renouncing their Catholic baptism and joining a Protestant denomination, however—even though the gains to be gotten from such a move were substantial—and the fact that many Catholics requested dispensations from their priests before failing to observe a religious obligation testifies to the respect that they still had for the idea of religious obligations, and to the depth with which they identified themselves as Catholics.

This commitment among Catholics in eighteenth-century Maryland was apparent at a time when western Europeans were becoming increasingly indifferent toward institutional Christianity. At the dawn of the eighteenth century, fewer than half of the villagers in Essex County, England, for example, were attending weekly Anglican services. In Yorkshire, the attendance rates were slightly better, but most of the people who went to services there chose not to receive Communion. Across the Channel in France, the situation was even more depressing. Fewer than 25 percent of the Catholics in Paris and Rouen were regularly receiving Communion in the 1730s. Not even the Easter holiday could affect a bump in those statistics.[2]

In contrast, a Church-sponsored survey of the Catholic population in British North America in the 1760s found that more than half of the Catholics living in Maryland were "approaching the Sacrament... on a regular basis," in spite of the legal restrictions on public worship and the severe dearth of priests that characterized Catholic life in the colony at the time. In the uncultivated environment of the New World, where most of the landscape was still wilderness and the number of priests serving in Maryland typically hovered between five and seven, the physical challenges involved in getting to a priest, giving one's Confession, and then receiving the Eucharist could be quite great. Yet, the Communion rates in Maryland were two times higher than what they were in France, where the landscape had been conquered for centuries and the Catholic Church enjoyed the support of the State.[3]

More so than their participation in the Sacrament, however, Catholics' refusal to apostatize in an environment that was politically and culturally hostile and institutionally and clerically poor was what spoke volumes about their religiosity in eighteenth-century Maryland. Catholics had numerous reasons to convert, but they did not. Even when they were not able to make it to a Mass, Maryland's Catholics were naming their children after Catholic saints and sending their children to Catholic schools. They settled in predominantly Catholic enclaves—or what were called "hundreds"–so that their friends and neighbors could remind them of what it meant to be Catholic and help them sustain their sense of themselves as members of an ancient, if unjustly vilified faith.

Throughout the eighteenth century, Maryland's Catholics fashioned a version of Catholicism for themselves that reflected both the adverse political circumstances under which they lived and the New World contingencies with which they were forced to grapple as colonists on a daily basis. Their priests, for the most part, supported and assisted them in this endeavor. The difficult lay–clerical relations that had characterized the early years of the colony, when priests like Thomas Copley had insisted that they were entitled to the same privileges and lay deference that their clerical colleagues in Continental Europe enjoyed, were a thing of the past. The survival of Catholicism in Maryland now required the kind of cooperation that characterized seigneurial Catholicism in England. It also required the clergy and the laity to make compromises that set them apart from their religious brethren in Europe and, in so doing, laid the foundation for a distinctly "American" Catholic identity.

Even after the founding of Pennsylvania in 1682—with its generous Quaker extension of religious liberty to all "who shall confess and acknowledge One Almighty God"—the vast majority of Catholics in British colonial America continued to live in Maryland. In 1708, the Lords of Trade commissioned a census that revealed there were roughly 3,000 Catholics living in the colony that Cecilius Calvert had founded. Fifty-five years later, when the Roman Catholic Bishop of England, Richard Challoner, arranged for all of the Catholics in British North America to be counted, the number of Catholics in Maryland had grown to more than 16,000. Across the border in Pennsylvania, where the only other significant concentration of British colonial Catholics lived, the census takers reported just 8,000 Catholic souls—and given that the boundary between Maryland and Pennsylvania was still contested at that time, it is possible that some of those Catholics may have thought of themselves as living in Maryland.[4]

Challoner's census noted that approximately 8,500 of Maryland's 16,000 Catholics were regularly receiving Communion—an impressive feat, given that the year the census was taken, there were just eighteen priests working in Maryland. The priests' average age was fifty-one, and three of the men—Benedict Neale, Thomas Digges, and John Lewis—were in their seventies. In 1763, Maryland had just one priest for every 940 lay Catholics living in the colony. It was a less-than-ideal ratio for a faith that put so much emphasis on the guidance of its clergy in a colony that was exceedingly rural and had virtually no transportation infrastructure.[5]

Fortunately for these priests, the Catholic population tended to be concentrated in Charles and St. Mary's Counties, on the southern tip of the Chesapeake's western shore. Sixty-five percent of the Catholics living in Maryland in 1708 resided in these two counties. The remaining 35 percent were divided among nine counties, only two of which had a Catholic population that reached into the triple digits. While Catholics were only about 10 percent of the white population overall in Maryland, they made up 32 percent of the people in St. Mary's County and 22 percent of the people in Charles County, making those two counties the epicenter, really, of British colonial Catholicism.[6]

Several family names dominated the early eighteenth-century Catholic records from the region. The Boarmans, Carrolls, Darnalls, Diggeses, Greenes, Neales, Rozers, Sewalls, Slyes, and Van Sweringens were all large families with significant landholdings. Many of them traced their roots in Maryland back to the initial European settlement in the seventeenth century and—like many of the colony's early Catholic settlers—these families tended to be quite wealthy. In 1758, when Maryland's governor Horatio Sharpe remarked that just "one Thirteenth of the Inhabitants" of his colony were Roman Catholics, ten of Maryland's twenty largest estates belonged to members of the Catholic faith. The situation was hardly new. In 1698, for example, when Garrett Van Sweringen died, his estate had a value of £300, putting him in the top 5 percent of the colony's population, financially. When William Boarman died in 1709, he owned 3,300 acres in Charles County. His Catholic grandson, George Slye, owned 284 slaves at the time of his death in 1733, making him a "great planter" according to the standards used by historians.[7]

Many of the same families that were prominent in Charles and St. Mary's Counties in 1708 continued to dominate the landscape on the western shore seventy years later when the colony was in the throes of a revolution against England. Not all of the descendents of these early Catholic families were still Catholic, however. Indeed, by the turn of the eighteenth century, several prominent Catholic families had well-known Protestants living among them. One such Protestant was Philemon Lloyd, Jr., an Anglican who served as Deputy Secretary of Maryland in the 1720s and 1730s and whose mother, Henrietta Maria, was a member of the wealthy Neale family that would eventually produce Leonard Neale, the second Catholic archbishop of the United States.

Henrietta Maria Neale Bennett Lloyd was born in Spain to English Catholic parents. Her father, Captain James Neale, had been among the earliest English Catholics to come to Cecilius Calvert's colony. He returned to Europe in 1647, however, to work in Spain and Portugal on behalf of England's future Catholic king, the Duke of York. Henrietta Maria Neale was born during her parents' time on the Continent, and she did not come to Maryland, then, until she was nearly thirteen years old. She remained loyal to the Catholic Church until the day she died in 1697, and during the Maryland Revolution, she worked hard to defend Charles Calvert's proprietary claim to the colony, secretly stockpiling arms and ammunition in her home, in a failed effort to ensure that Catholics did not lose their control of Maryland's government.[8]

Henrietta Maria Neale, however, did not let her faith determine her marital matches. Her first husband, Richard Bennett, was the son of the Calvinist governor of Virginia who, together with William Claiborne, had ousted all of the Catholics from Maryland's General Assembly during the Puritan Uprising of 1654. Her second husband, Philemon Lloyd, Sr., was a Calvinist who specifically demanded that the children he had with her be "brought up in the Protestant religion." To that end, Henrietta Maria Neale raised the six children she had with Philemon

Lloyd, Sr. in the Church of England, where the theology was sufficiently "Protestant," but not nearly as offensive to her Catholic sensibilities as the ideas put forth by her husband's spiritual benefactor, John Calvin. The son and daughter she had had with her previous Calvinist husband, Richard Bennett, Jr., Henrietta Maria Neale raised as Catholics following their father's drowning in 1676.[9]

Five of Henrietta Maria Neale's six Protestant children eventually married. Philemon Lloyd, Jr., married Margaretta Freeman and had one daughter, Henrietta Maria Lloyd, whom he raised as a Protestant. Edward, James, and Anna Maria Lloyd married Protestants and raised their children in the Church of England, as well. Their one sister, Henrietta Maria, married a Catholic, however, and their other sister, Margaret, never married at all.[10]

It is possible—and in the case of Henrietta Maria, even likely—that Margaret and Henrietta Maria Lloyd converted to Catholicism. Margaret's failure to marry was most unusual among women in the Chesapeake region, where the unbalanced ratio between men and women made marriageable women a hot commodity and single women an aberration. If Margaret joined a convent in Europe—as we know at least thirty-one women from Maryland did in the generation that came after her—that would explain both her failure to take a husband and her apparent disappearance from the historical record in the colony.[11]

Henrietta Maria Lloyd's husband, Charles Henry Blake, was the grand-nephew of one of the original Catholic settlers who came over on the *Ark* and the *Dove*. The couple had a chapel in their home that the Jesuits in Maryland sometimes referred to as "Blakes on Chester," and they raised their four children, John, Philemon, Henrietta Maria, and Dorothy, as Catholics. Dorothy Blake married Dr. Charles Carroll, first-cousin-once-removed to the Catholic Charles Carroll of Carrollton who eventually signed the Declaration of Independence. Dorothy's nephew, Philemon Lloyd Blake, son to her older brother John, was among the first class of students to enroll at the college the Jesuits founded in Georgetown in 1791.[12]

The Neale-Lloyd-Carroll-Blake family was fairly typical of those families in eighteenth-century Maryland that could trace their roots back to the colony's early Catholic settlers in that the family was not comprised exclusively of Roman Catholics. In the eighteenth century, very few of Maryland's original Catholic families could say that there were no Protestants among them. Religiously mixed marriages had become quite common, in spite of the heroic efforts that some Catholics, such as William Boarman, had gone through to avoid them. After his first wife, Sarah Linle, died in 1674, the forty-nine-year-old Boarman refused to settle for any of the women his own age who were available to him in the colony because all of those women were Protestants. He chose instead to marry fourteen-year-old Mary Matthews because she was a Catholic. Mary's older brother, Thomas, had married William Boarman's daughter, Sarah, six years earlier. That meant that William Boarman became Thomas Matthews' father-in-law and his brother-in-law when he married Mary Matthews—all so that the family's religious identity could remain unadulterated.[13]

Most Catholic families did not go to such lengths to avoid being infiltrated by Protestants, and—much like the Neale-Lloyd-Carroll-Blake family—most Catholic families that had Protestants among them did not have those Protestants among them because someone in the family had converted. For the most part, religiously mixed families were mixed because someone had married a Protestant—be it an Anglican, a Quaker, or a Calvinist—and agreed to raise the children in that Protestant's faith. The willingness of Catholic parents to raise their children as Protestants was undoubtedly frowned upon by the Jesuits who served in Maryland; yet, their surviving sermons and correspondence do not mention the practice as having become a problem. This suggests that the majority of Catholics who married outside their faith may actually have raised their children in the Catholic fold.

The number of Catholics who married Protestants was not insubstantial in the eighteenth century; indeed, in just one year, 70 percent of the marriages that Frs. Joseph Mosley and John Bolton performed for Catholics in Queen Anne's and Cecil Counties involved Anglican or Calvinist partners. Granted, this extremely high rate of out-marriage was not typical for the community that Bolton and Mosley served, and the following year, just 14 percent of the marriages they performed involved Protestant partners.[14] Queen Anne's and Cecil Counties also did not enjoy the high concentration of Catholics that St. Mary's and Charles Counties did. In an age when most of the people a person met in his or her life lived within a few miles of the place where he or she had been born, the likelihood that an eighteenth-century Catholic in Queen Anne's County was going to grow up to marry a Protestant was quite high.

Still, the point remains that mixed marriages were not uncommon in colonial Maryland; and yet, the Jesuits never complained in any of their sermons that the children who were conceived in these mixed marriages were not being raised as Catholics. Not only did the Jesuits serving in Maryland not work to discourage mixed marriages, some of them actually defended such marriages to their clerical colleagues in Europe. In 1715, for example, Fr. William Hunter, who lived in Maryland from 1692 to 1723, wrote to the English faculty at the College of St. Omer, telling them that "disparity of Cult" was not a "diriment impediment," that is, grounds for annulment, "to Matrimony in Maryland." In words that might have surprised a Protestant, given that they were coming from a Roman Catholic priest, Fr. Hunter told his colleagues that to deny the laity in Maryland the right to marry outside their faith would be "odious to the liberty of men." Decades later, Fr. John Carroll, the first Catholic bishop in the United States, echoed these sentiments when he wrote to his friend and fellow Jesuit in England, Charles Plowden, that Catholics in America were "so mixed with Protestants in all the intercourse of civil Society & business" that to confine them just to Catholic marriage partners would be to "reduce many of the faithful to live in a state of celibacy."

To be fair, Carroll's letter was a not exactly a whole-hearted defense of mixed marriages. Writing in 1803, more than a dozen years after an episcopal structure had been created for the Catholic Church in the United States, Bishop Carroll referred to the practice of marrying outside the Catholic faith as an "abuse" of the Sacrament, and he acquiesced to it only because "it surpasses my ability to devise any effectual bar against it." William Hunter's letter, however, was an all out defense of not just the practice of marrying outside the Catholic faith but also of the need to recognize that America was different from continental Europe. "For more than six hundred years now," Hunter told the Jesuits at St. Omer's, "the custom has prevailed in Europe of holding the marriage of one of the faithful with a nonbaptized infidel to be invalid." Such a custom, Hunter insisted, could not be allowed to take on the authority of "law" in Maryland as it had in Europe because the custom was "morally impossible" for Catholics in British North America to maintain.

Hunter was interested primarily in defending the marriages of two groups of colonial Catholics: Those who were enslaved and had chosen (or been forced) to take non-Christian partners, and white Catholics who had elected to marry Quakers, who did not believe in baptism. Because marriages between Catholics and baptized Anglicans and Calvinists did not make the Jesuit hierarchy in Europe very happy either, Fr. Hunter included a defense of those marriages in his letter as well.

Pointing to the work of the Italian Cardinal Roberto Bellarmine for support, Hunter insisted that "a custom ought not to be transferred from place to place, v[erbi] gr[atia] from Europe to Maryland, especially where there is not the same or equal reason for introducing it." Not only were there not enough Catholics in Maryland to insist that the members of the Catholic community there marry only each other, but the custom, Hunter informed his colleagues, was "never received by Protestants and Quakers, who constitute more than 9/10 of this province." A "law," the priest seemed to be saying—even an ecclesiastical one—was ineffective and pointless if it were not acknowledged by the majority of people who made up the community where the law was to be lived out. When it came to marriage, the "community" Maryland's tiny Catholic minority was living in necessarily included baptized Protestants and unbaptized Quakers and "infidels." Catholics could avoid mixed marriages in religiously homogeneous countries like France or Spain perhaps, but it was an "error" to think that they could be avoided in a religiously pluralist climate like Maryland.[15]

Mixed marriages and the religious identities of the children who were conceived within them were not the only topics that the Jesuits might have complained about, but did not. Maryland's priests also never complained that Catholics in the colony were leaving the Church to join the Anglican faith. This does not mean that such conversions did not happen, of course; in fact, we know that they did. It does suggest, however, that the phenomenon of apostasy never escalated to a point where the Jesuits believed it represented a problem.

The careers of the men who did convert to Anglicanism testify to the advantages that came with apostasy in eighteenth-century Maryland. Thomas Brooke, Jr. converted to the Church of England in 1692, shortly after William and Mary revoked the third Lord Baltimore's charter. Brooke was the oldest son of Thomas and Elinor Hatton Brooke, both of whom had converted to Catholicism shortly after they were married in 1658. Governor Lionel Copley appointed Brooke to the Upper House of the Assembly immediately after his conversion. He served there until 1708, when Maryland's new royal governor, John Seymour, dismissed him because of his strong family ties to the Catholic Church. Inconveniently, three of Thomas Brooke's five brothers were Jesuits. When Queen Anne returned Maryland's charter to the Calvert family in 1715, the recently Anglican fifth Lord Baltimore, Charles Calvert, reappointed Thomas Brooke to the Upper House. In 1720, his colleagues selected him to serve as that body's president.[16]

Dr. Charles Carroll, who married Henrietta Maria Neale Bennett Lloyd's Catholic granddaughter, Dorothy Blake, was raised as a Catholic in England and Ireland and migrated to Maryland in 1715. He settled in Annapolis, practiced medicine, and had three children: Mary Clare, John Henry, and Charles—who is often referred to by historians as "the Barrister," in an effort to differentiate him from his father, the medical doctor, his second cousin, the signer of the Declaration of Independence, and his first-cousin-once-removed, the father of the signer of the Declaration. All four men were named Charles Carroll, and all four men played prominent roles in Maryland's eighteenth-century history.

The four Charles Carrolls were not all Catholic, however—at least not for the entirety of their lives. Around 1738, Dr. Charles Carroll converted to the Church of England. There is no evidence that his wife joined him, but shortly after he converted, Dr. Carroll did remove his son—the eventual "Barrister"—from the English Catholic school he had been attending in Portugal. He enrolled the sixteen-year-old boy in Eton College, a school outside of London that only Protestants could attend. In a letter that he wrote to his son in 1739, Dr. Carroll advised the boy not to mourn his conversion to the Church of England. "In points of Religion, be not too much attached to any [beliefs] grown up with you," the elder Charles Carroll advised. "Bigotry and Superstition in Religion is a grand error . . . [and] the Church of England as by Law Established is worthy of your consideration."[17]

Other than this letter, there is no concrete, surviving evidence that might explain why Dr. Charles Carroll chose to leave the Catholic faith. It is noteworthy, however, that the Catholic school in Lisbon he had been sending his son to was not operated by the Jesuits. Among those prominent Catholics in Maryland who elected to send their children to Europe to be educated, Dr. Carroll seems to have been the only one who did not send his son to St. Omer's, the school the Jesuits ran in French Flanders. It is possible, therefore, that Dr. Carroll may have had a falling out with the Society of Jesus—the only order ministering to Catholics in British North America at the time—and that this breach played a role in his decision to convert. If so, such an explanation would not preclude the possibility that Dr. Carroll also wanted to participate more freely in the political climate that governed his colony. Voters in Anne Arundel County sent him to the Lower House of the Assembly shortly after he converted. He served in that body, then, until his death in 1755.[18]

The fact that he sent his son to Eton and forced the boy to convert indicates that Dr. Carroll took his conversion seriously. It is unlikely, however, that Henry and John Darnall were serious about the conversions that they affected in the 1730s. Both men seem to have joined the Church of England just so that they could practice law, and in Henry's case, the bargain paid off considerably in that it afforded him the opportunity to become Maryland's Attorney General in 1751. The two brothers continued to send their sons to St. Omer's, however, in spite of their public conversions, and they also had Catholic Masses said in their homes each week.

In a report presented to Maryland's General Assembly in June 1752, the Committee of Grievances and Courts of Justice complained that even though a number of prominent Catholics had sworn that the Masses said in Henry Darnall's home were for his Catholic wife and children only—and that the Attorney General had never attended any the services—the people who lived in the area also "never saw Mr. Darnall at any Protestant Church," suggesting that his conversion to the Church of England may have been insincere. The Committee noted that the same could also be said of Henry's brother John, who was serving as one of the judges of the Provincial Court in Frederick County. If the Darnall brothers were still Catholic, the Committee suggested, it was possible that they could have been showing favoritism toward the "papists" who came before them in court. If so, such favoritism was one of the "many and dangerous Innovations against Law, made by the Popish Interest within this Province."[19]

Other than Thomas Brooke, Dr. Charles Carroll, and the two Darnall brothers, only one other Catholic convert to Anglicanism figures prominently in the surviving records from eighteenth-century Maryland—and his behavior suggests that his soul's salvation was not a top priority, regardless of which denomination he officially belonged to. Thomas Macnamara was born and raised in County Clare, Ireland. He came to Maryland in the late 1690s as an indentured servant, performing services for Charles Carroll, the Irish grandfather of the Charles Carroll who would one day sign the Declaration of Independence. Shortly after his term of indenture expired in 1703, Macnamara converted to Anglicanism so that he could practice law. That same year, he also married Margaret Carroll, Charles Carroll's niece, whom he had had the poor manners to impregnate while working as a servant in the Carroll household.

Four years later, in October 1707, a Chancery court granted a legal separation to Margaret Macnamara because she had appeared before the court "so battered, bruised, and inhumanely beaten . . . that had she not been of a constitution more than ordinarily strong, she could hardly have recovered." In spite of the obvious abuse, the court allowed for the possibility that the Macnamaras might one day get back together. In the mean time, the judges ordered Thomas to pay his wife nearly £4 sterling every three months for however long Margaret wished to remain separated.

Thomas refused—and went on to accumulate a whole host of other criminal charges, among them assault, sodomy, and murder. The authorities in Maryland eventually branded Thomas Macnamara in an effort to warn the colony's citizens about his violent temper. Their efforts to have him barred from practicing law, however, seem to have been unsuccessful for reasons that are not clear.[20]

These five prominent converts are the exceptions that proved the rule—that rule being that in spite of the obvious advantages that came with Protestant identity, most of the people in eighteenth-century Maryland who were born into the Catholic faith remained in that faith, suggesting that their Catholicism was vital to their understandings of themselves. Historian Ronald Hoffman has noted that in the case of the Catholic Carrolls, much of their loyalty to Catholicism was rooted in an uncompromising attachment to the family's "Irish past." While this was undoubtedly true for the Carrolls, many—if not most—of colonial Maryland's Catholics traced their ancestry to Protestant England, rather than to Catholic Ireland. Yet, even English Catholics like Charles Digges spoke proudly of "the religion of our forefathers" when explaining that they were unwilling to leave the Catholic fold.

Of course, by the early 1770s, when Digges was writing to Maryland's Anglican proprietor to protest the anti-Catholic legislation that characterized life in his colony, the "forefathers" he was referring to were the Neales, Darnalls, and Sewalls he was descended from, all of whom had come to Maryland from England nearly a century-and-a-half before. It was an uncompromising attachment to a "Marylandian past," therefore, rather than an "English past" that underpinned Digges's commitment to his Catholicism.[21]

Still, an attachment to one's heritage was only part of the story, as the 189 people whom Fr. Joseph Mosley claimed to have converted between 1766 and 1786 make clear. Catholic proselytizing was technically illegal in Maryland, thanks to a law that was signed by Governor Francis Nicholson in 1698 and reiterated at various points throughout the proceeding decades. As a consequence, Fr. Mosley said very little about the people he converted, recording just their names in a private diary that he kept in his home on the eastern shore of the Chesapeake. The forces that compelled these people to convert, therefore, are unknown; it seems reasonable, however, to assume that many of them would have understood the words of the young English convert who wrote to his Protestant father in 1623 about his conversion to Catholicism. The "great and hidden mysteries and profound difficulties" that characterized the Christian Scriptures, this convert wrote, were the reason he had chosen to turn to the "tradition of the Roman Church" and the "great Clerks and Holy Fathers" for help.[22]

One hundred sixty of the people Joseph Mosley claimed to have converted were white, and the evidence suggests that some (if not all) of these people were eager to keep their conversions quiet—and not simply because Fr. Mosley could have been fined, thrown in jail, or even executed for converting them. In order to hold office in eighteenth-century Maryland, a man had to swear the Oath of Abjuration, which denied the authority of not just the Pope but also the Catholic Doctrine of Transubstantiation. Once sworn, the oath would never have be taken again, so long as the man continued to hold the same office and gave the authorities in Maryland no reason to doubt his commitment to a Protestant faith.[23] In becoming a Catholic, one accepted the authority of the Pope and the viability of Transubstantiation automatically. No public renunciation of the oath was therefore necessary, because conversion in and of itself was a renunciation.

Catholic converts could not, of course, take the Oath of Abjuration again and still remain true to their newly adopted faith. Unlike the Oath of Supremacy that King James I had asked English Catholics to take at the turn of the seventeenth century, the Oath of Abjuration did more than simply insist that temporal loyalties could be separated from spiritual ones. It actually denied a fundamental Catholic doctrine. The Oath of Abjuration could not, therefore, be reconciled with Catholic identity—not even a flexible understanding of that identity like the one that had taken root among many of England's Catholics in the seventeenth century. So long as converts checked their ambition at the door and kept their Catholic faith quiet, however, there was no reason for them to have to swear the oath again or leave their posts—as the career of Benjamin Young attests.

Young lived in St. Mary's County, where he worked as the county clerk from April 1765 until November 1770, when he moved to an estate that he owned in Cecil County on the eastern shore and transferred his clerkship there. In 1755—ten years before he assumed the clerkship of St. Mary's County and two years after he had sworn the Oath of Abjuration—Young became the Surveyor General for the entire eastern shore of the Chesapeake, a job he held onto until 1776, when the position was eliminated because of Maryland's proclaimed independence from England. The job required Young to spend a significant amount of time getting to know the people in Queen Anne's, Talbot, and Dorchester Counties, where the majority of Fr. Joseph Mosley's 500 congregants lived.[24] It was probably during one of his surveying trips that Young first came into contact with Joseph Mosley, who started a mission in Dorchester County in 1757.

Benjamin Young's mother, Ann Rozer, was a Catholic, and his brother, Notley Young, had converted to Catholicism some time in the late 1750s or early 1760s after marrying Jane Digges, his second cousin and a member of one of the more prominent Catholic families in Maryland. It may have been Notley's conversion that prompted Benjamin Young to start chatting with Joseph Mosley about theological matters. In any event, Mosley recorded Young's conversion to Catholicism in his diary in 1768. Benjamin Young continued to hold his posts as county clerk and Surveyor General for the eastern shore, however, in spite of the conversion.[25]

Joseph Mosley could not have been the first Catholic priest Benjamin Young ever met. His mother's uncle, Henry Whetenhall, was a Jesuit who served in Maryland between 1724 and 1733. Although Whetenhall left to teach at the College of St. Ignatius in Barcelona, Spain, before Benjamin Young was born, the familial connections that Young's mother had to the clerical community in Maryland surely would have brought Benjamin into contact with some of the colony's priests while he was growing up. A number of those priests were still serving in Maryland at the time that Benjamin Young converted. Indeed, Fr. John Lewis, who began serving the Catholics in Prince

George's County in 1750, often preached at the estate of Benjamin's brother, Notley.²⁶

Benjamin could easily have asked Fr. Lewis to guide him through his conversion. He also could have asked Fr. James Framback, who lived on one of the Jesuits' estates in St. Mary's County, where Benjamin Young lived and worked as the county clerk. Of course, Framback was German, and it is possible that his English may have been limited or highly accented, which would have made the personal conversations that are a necessary part of any conversion experience difficult. Young had another priest in St. Mary's County whom he could have gone to, however—and this one, Thomas Digges, had actually been born in Maryland. Not only that, but Fr. Digges was a relative; his father, William, was the brother of Jane Digges, Ann Rozer's mother and Benjamin Young's grandmother.²⁷

Benjamin Young did not choose to convert with any of the priests he knew in St. Mary's and Prince George's Counties, two of the most populous counties in all of Maryland. Instead, he chose to convert with Joseph Mosley, who was running an isolated Catholic mission on the sparsely populated eastern shore. Even today, the eastern shore of the Chesapeake is quite rural and remote in comparison to the western shore; in the eighteenth century, the contrast was far more stark.

Joseph Mosley often wrote to his sister in England about the loneliness he experienced in Dorchester County. "I've lived entirely alone these 9 years past, not one white person with me," he wrote in July 1773. Admitting that the isolation could be oppressive and stultifying, he told his sister that he sometimes felt "banished" to an existence that was "lonesome & solitary." On the rare occasions when Mosley did have visitors, his guests were almost always struck by the "miserable" conditions of his life. Mosley lived in "a cell such as the woman of Sumanite prepared for the prophet Elisus [probably Elisha]," John Carroll reported in the late 1760s. There was "just space enough for a bed, a table and a stool." Given the circumstances, it is doubtful that Fr. Mosley's visitors ever chose to spend the night.²⁸

The remoteness of the mission that Joseph Mosley ran along the Wye River must have been the reason Benjamin Young chose to convert with him, rather than with the priests he knew on the western shore. Had Young converted with Thomas Digges or John Lewis, word of the conversion might have gotten out, and Young would have been forced to relinquish the tiny bit of legal authority he had in Maryland. Yet, Young was able to hide his conversion so well that his contemporaries were not the only ones who remained ignorant of his religious proclivities. Even modern-day historians have missed his conversion, raising the question of how many other secret Catholics may have been serving in Maryland's colonial government—and how many other Jesuits may have been willing to forgive these converts for the Protestant charade they insisted on playing.[29] In England, such compromises were anathema to the Jesuits. In America, however, the rules of the game were different.

More than two dozen of the people Joseph Mosley claimed to have converted were enslaved, and one convert—Isaac—was described as a "free Negro."[30] Race-based slavery had been legally recognized in Maryland for nearly 100 years by the time Joseph Mosley started keeping his diary in the 1760s. The black population along the Chesapeake had been self-sustaining since the early 1720s.[31] Many of Fr. Mosley's enslaved converts, therefore, had probably been born in the western hemisphere, rather than in Africa, and some of them may even have been born in Virginia or Maryland.

Protestant slave owners were still very hesitant in the eighteenth century to bring Christianity into the slave quarters, fearing that it might be immoral to hold a fellow Christian in bondage, or that the themes of liberation that were woven throughout the Judeo-Christian narrative might empower slaves to rebel. Not until the early nineteenth century, when evangelical Christianity began to take root in the South, were large numbers of African-Americans exposed to the Christian faith. In the hands of evangelical ministers, Christianity became a faith capable of "reducing men to habits of cheerful industry . . . [and] submission to authority and law."[32]

If colonial Catholics feared that Christianity would make their slaves insubordinate, they kept those fears to themselves. They certainly did not fear that it was immoral to keep a fellow Christian in bondage.

Indeed, the founder of the Jesuit order that served Maryland's Catholic community believed that slavery could be a powerful tool in the Church's fight against the spread of Protestantism. Unlike their Protestant counterparts in the eighteenth century, Catholic priests had an unambivalent understanding of slavery as part of God's plan. For them, the debate was not whether slaves should be brought to Christ; without question, they should. Rather, the debate for Catholic theologians was whether slavery was humanity's punishment for Original Sin, as St. Augustine had asserted in the fifth century, or a relationship of reciprocal obligation that allowed the strong and weak elements of human nature and society to complement one another, as Thomas Aquinas had argued in the thirteenth century.[33] Either way, Catholics were obliged to bring their bondsmen to Catholicism.

Many—if not most—of the enslaved people Fr. Mosley baptized were the property of Catholic men and women, suggesting that one of the ways colonial Catholics expressed their commitment to their faith was by exposing their slaves to Catholicism. Denis Carey was a Catholic from Queen Anne's County who saw to it that Joseph Mosley baptized two of his slaves, Daphnis and Isaac. We know that Carey was Catholic, because he served as a godfather to Lucy Sexton, Anne Burke, Anne Rennells, and John Seth's daughter, Rachel. Fr. Mosley baptized Seth's slave, Charles, four months before Rachel Seth was born. Henry Meekins, whose Catholicism is revealed by his decision to serve as a godfather to Agnes Thomson and George Leddle Blake, had two of his slaves baptized in the 1760s. The first of the two slaves, Sarah, went on to serve as a godmother to George Sleakam's slave, Francis. Between December 1766 and December 1767, eleven of the people who belonged to the families of John and Philemon Blake—the sons of Charles and Henrietta Maria Lloyd Blake—became Catholic under the direction of Fr. Joseph Mosley.[34]

Still, not all Catholics accepted that it was their duty to expose their slaves to Catholicism. Charles Carroll of Annapolis went to the expense of keeping a priest in his home—first, Fr. John Ashton, whom he brought over from Ireland in 1767, and then Fr. Bernard Diderich, who was born in Luxembourg and served the Carroll family after John Ashton left to live on the Jesuits' plantation in Prince George's County. Despite the fact that he had a priest at his beck and call, Charles Carroll never encouraged Ashton or Diderich to cater to the spiritual needs of the 386 enslaved people who lived and worked on his plantations in Anne Arundel and Frederick Counties. Their salvation was simply not a priority for the wealthy Catholic Carroll.

Indeed, the unwillingness of Charles Carroll of Annapolis to let his resident priests serve the needs of the slave community may have been the reason John Ashton decided to leave in November 1773. Four years earlier, Ashton had complained about an adulterous relationship that Charles Carroll's overseer, William Sears, was having with a slave named Henny. "I really wish we never had sent for a priest," Charles Carroll of Carrollton wrote to his father when he learned that Ashton was insisting Henny needed to be removed from Sears's purview. "They are troublesome animals in a family." The older Carroll conceded that John Ashton was a "silly Peevish disagreeable man," but he did not believe the family could do without a resident priest.[35] Of course, the priest Carroll replaced Ashton with was not a native English-speaker—and that decision almost certainly cut down on the ferocity of any clerical thrashings the Carrolls received.

Charles Carroll of Annapolis had the freedom to ignore the Jesuits' mandate that slaveholding Catholics teach their slaves about Christianity and "bring them to do their duty to God." Carroll, after all, did not need to express his commitment to Catholicism by having his slaves baptized. His commitment was evident in other ways—such as the £33, 6s, 8d that he paid every year to his resident priest.[36]

For more modest Catholic families like the Meekins, however, who lived in rural Dorchester County and owned on average just 283 acres per household, it was important that the small number of slaves they owned be exposed to the Catholic faith that the Meekins, themselves, were only just clinging to during the weeks and months when Fr. Joseph Mosley could not be there to serve them. Abraham Meekins and his wife, Mary, therefore, became the godparents of their slave, Thomas, when Fr. Mosley visited their home in May 1767. One year later, Matthew Meekins entered into a spiritual partnership with a "negro" named

Catherine, when the pair agreed to serve as godparents to a slave named Sarah. Such racial ecumenism was rare among Catholics in Maryland, but it was not unheard of—nor was it confined to the Meekins family. Robert Jarboe, an officer in the St. Mary's County militia who joined the Continental Army in 1781, allowed a pair of unnamed "negroes" to serve as godparents to his oldest daughter, Rachel, when she was baptized after the war was over.[37]

Throughout the Penal Period, Maryland's Catholics devised several ways to express—and, in so expressing, maintain—their Catholic identity. Some of these ways were adopted by all Catholics, regardless of whether they were wealthy or poor. Other ways, such as slave baptisms or the keeping of household priests, required Catholics to have access to a modicum of wealth. Not everyone could afford to own a slave, after all—and even fewer people could afford to feed and house a priest, whose contributions to the household, unlike those of a slave, would never generate income.

Many Catholics, regardless of their financial circumstances, expressed their Catholic identity by giving their children Catholic, or sometimes "Roman" sounding names. Some overtly Catholic names—such as "Henrietta Maria," the name of King Charles I's Catholic wife and the woman the colony of Maryland had been named for—were not confined to Catholics. Protestant parents, too, sometimes gave their daughters this name, not because they wished to express some latent Catholic sympathies, but because someone in their family had had the name, and the parents wished to honor that person or her memory. Other Catholic names, however—all of them male—do seem to have been passed on to subsequent generations primarily or exclusively by parents who were Catholic.

Philemon Lloyd, it will be recalled, chose to name his daughter Henrietta Maria, because his mother, Henrietta Maria Neale, had been given that name by her Catholic parents. Henrietta Maria Lloyd was raised in the Church of England by her Protestant father, and she raised her own children—one of whom was named Henrietta Maria Chew—as Protestants, as well. Henrietta Maria Chew, in turn, had a Protestant niece with the very same name, since her older brother, Samuel Chew, chose to name his daughter after his mother and sister. By 1759, then, there were at least three generations of Protestant "Henrietta Marias" in the Lloyd-Chew family, all of them bearing a Catholic name not as an expression of their parents' devotion to the Church of Rome, but as an expression of their parents' commitment to the family's history. That history did include the Catholic faith at one point, but by the time the third Protestant Henrietta Maria was born, the original, Catholic Henrietta Maria had been dead for more than fifty years.[38]

Family tradition undoubtedly played a role in the prevalence of names like "Ignatius" and "Francis Xavier" among the residents of eighteenth-century Maryland, as well. "Athanasius," "Justinian," and "Rudolphus" were also quite common. Whenever the religious identities of men who had these names can be determined, however, the records almost always reveal that the men were Catholic. They indicated as much in their wills, or they were married by Catholic priests, or they belonged to Catholic congregations, or they had parents or siblings who did any and all of the above. This suggests that something more than just a respect for one's family history may have been at work when parents chose to give their sons Catholic names.[39]

Rhody (i.e., Rudolphus) Posey, for example, resided in the Port Tobacco Hundred of Charles County, where Francis and Thomas Posey—likely brothers—also lived. Francis Posey was a member of the Catholic congregation at Newtown in 1773, and Thomas Posey agreed to be Bennet Vann's godfather when one of the priests at St. Inigoes baptized Bennett in 1768. Elizabeth Posey—possibly the wife of one of the three Posey brothers—belonged to a Catholic sodality that had been organized by the priests serving in Port Tobacco.[40]

Nine men with the first name "Ignatius" belonged to the Catholic congregation at St. Inigoes in 1768. Their last names were Brown, Clark, Fenwick, Hagden (probably Hagan), Kelly, Mattingly, Moore, Sims, and Wathan. The congregation also included two men with the name Rudolphus—Manly and Jarber (probably Jarboe). Francis Xavier Wheeler and Francis Xavier Wheatley were both married by Jesuits at the appropriately named Francis Xavier Church in St. Mary's

County. Wheeler married Ann Birchmore in December 1775, and Wheatley married Anastasia Cecil in June 1771.[41]

In 1795, Joseph Greenwell and his four brothers—Justinian, Ignatius, Nicholas, and Bennett—were all sued by Raphael Neale, who insisted that the Greenwells' father, George, had left a parcel of land to him. Twenty-one years earlier, Joseph Greenwell had married Elizabeth Newton in a ceremony that was conducted by a Jesuit, indicating that he and his four brothers were probably all Catholic.[42] Athanasius Ford's sister, Monica, married John Fenwick, who came from a prominent Catholic family in Maryland; Fenwick married Mary Thomson at St. Francis Xavier Church after Monica Ford died in 1751. John and Monica Ford Fenwick had a daughter, Mary, who grew up to marry Ignatius Combs; Combs's mother, Mary Manning, belonged to a Catholic sodality in St. Mary's County. John Fenwick's brother, James, also got married at St. Francis Xavier Church; he and his wife, Catherine, had a son named Athanasius, whom they sent to Europe to be educated by the Jesuits. Athanasius Fenwick seems not to have gotten along with the European priests he encountered in France, however. The Maryland-born Jesuit Joseph Mobberly noted in his diary in 1826 that Athanasius Fenwick had delivered an Independence Day speech in St. Mary's City a few years earlier, in which he railed against the European priests he had encountered in his youth because they "opposed the high pretentions of Liberty."[43]

When a Catholic couple chose to give their son an overtly Catholic name like "Ignatius" or "Francis Xavier," they were permanently marking the boy as a Catholic in a society that was suspicious of anything that smacked of Catholicism. Ignatius of Loyola was the founder of the Jesuit order that served the Catholic community in Maryland, and Francis Xavier was one of the Society's first seven members. Even if Ignatius Fenwick or Francis Xavier Wheeler had grown up to convert to Anglicanism—which they did not—a cloud of suspicion would have followed them into whatever career they chose to adopt after their conversions because it was simply impossible not to know that the men had strong ties to the Catholic Church. As Thomas Brooke learned in 1708 when Governor Seymour removed him from the Upper House because his brothers were priests, sometimes a mere association with Catholicism was enough to cost a man his job.

But the Fenwicks and the Wheelers were not concerned that they might be damaging their sons' career prospects by giving them Catholic names. They intended to raise strong Catholic men who would never consider leaving the Catholic fold. If Ignatius Fenwick and Francis Xavier Wheeler were going to have public careers—as the men ultimately did, when Fenwick represented St. Mary's County at Maryland's Constitutional Convention in 1776, and Wheeler served in the St. Mary's County Militia in 1777—it was going to have to be in a religiously tolerant society like the one the Catholic Lords Baltimore had tried to build during the previous century.[44] Fortunately for Fenwick and Wheeler, that society was reclaimed in Maryland during their lifetimes.

Naming was a mode of religious expression that was open to all Catholics, regardless of how much wealth they had at their disposal. Books, crucifixes, pictures, and rosaries also helped Catholics all along the financial spectrum maintain their faith. Bearing in mind that colonial American literacy—and particularly the degree of literacy that was required to do more than simply sign one's name—may have been greater among the upper classes than it was among the lower, the fact remains that low- and middle-income Catholics still had access to a lot of the same religious literature and material culture that wealthy Catholics had access to.[45] Lay Catholics asked their priests to provide them with this access, and their priests obliged, understanding that material culture was vital to the maintenance of the Catholic faith in an environment where the clergy could not always be there to serve the laity's spiritual needs.

"A crowd of people came to my church to see the new monstrance which I received through your generosity," Fr. Ferdinand Farmer wrote to his brother in Europe in 1755, praising the "increased devotion" that "our simple folk here are deeply stirred to" by the accoutrements of Catholicism. Farmer, whose real name was Steinmeyer (he changed it upon his arrival in the British colonies), served the Maryland Mission from 1752 to 1786, spending most of his time in Philadelphia, which was a part of the mission the Jesuits ran out of Maryland. Farmer wrote that the lay Catholics he worked with "adored with tender devotion our dear savior on his throne," describing the Eucharist in a way that would have seemed bizarre—and perhaps even funny—to any Christian who did not subscribe to the Doctrine of Transubstantiation and could not imagine, therefore, how a full-grown man like Jesus Christ might have been able to sit on a monstrance that was just twenty-five inches tall and six inches across at the base.

In spite of his gratefulness, Fr. Farmer could not help but observe that his brother might have been more generous. "O would I had also been presented with a censer and a cope," the priest lamented, before informing his brother that Catholics in Maryland and Pennsylvania were hoping to receive "a supply of pictures, rosaries, one or the other Gospel Book and some spiritual history and sermon books" from sympathetic Catholics abroad.[46] This material culture was what sustained colonial Catholics during the weeks when they could not receive the Eucharist.

In August 1716, James Carroll, Charles Carroll of Annapolis's cousin, asked Fr. Peter Atwood for some advice on the titles he should select for the "Widow Jones," who had asked Carroll to purchase a few religious texts for her during his impending trip to England. Atwood recommended titles that were a part of the Jesuits' library at St. Inigoes Manor—books that the priests frequently lent out to the men and women they served. He advised Carroll to purchase a copy of the Rhemish Testament, which was the only English-language version of the Bible authorized by the Catholic Church. Atwood also felt that *The Three Conversions of England* (1604), by the English Jesuit, Robert Parsons, would be a good book for the Widow Jones to have, as would Matthew Kellison's *The Touchstone of the Reformed Gospel* (1675), "wherein sundry chief heads and tenets of the Protestant doctrine ... are briefly refuted by the express texts of the Protestants own Bible."[47]

Other books that the Jesuits kept in the lending libraries at their St. Inigoes, Newtown, and White Marsh plantations included Joseph Mumford's *The Plea of the Roman Catholics* (1686), Robert Manning's *The Shortest Way to End Disputes about Religion* (1716), and Richard

Challoner's *The Catholic Christian Instructed* (1737). Manning's book was a response to Charles Leslie's *The Case Stated*, which had been published three years earlier and accused the Catholic Church of claiming an infallibility for itself that could only be claimed by God. Manning insisted that Protestants like Leslie could not possibly understand how a church might be infallible, since "their pastors were established by the people, in whom they place the source of authority and vocation." Challoner's book was a reader-friendly series of questions and answers about the Sacraments, ceremonies, and observances of the Catholic Church. It and his *Garden of the Soul*, published in 1740, were wildly popular with Catholics in the British colonies. Indeed, Challoner's works were still popular with English-speaking Catholics well into the twentieth century.[48]

The Garden of the Soul was a book of devotion. Written by the Vicar Apostolic of London, who oversaw all Catholic activities in England and British North America, it opened with a summary of Catholic doctrine and then prescribed a series of morning prayers and exercises for Catholics to engage in: the Lord's Prayer, the Hail Mary, the Apostle's Creed, and the *Confiteor*, which is a general confession of sin. Challoner's book, as it was first published in 1740, did not contain many of the Jesus- and Mary-centered devotionals that are common among English-speaking Catholics today. There were no Devotions to the Sacred Heart or the Blessed Sacrament, for instance, and no Stations of the Cross or Devotions to Our Blessed Lady—exercises that, in the words of one nineteenth-century editor of *The Garden of the Soul*, "now form a necessary part of every Catholic prayer-book."[49]

These devotions did not become common among English Catholics until the middle of the nineteenth century. It makes sense, then, that they would not have been included in Richard Challoner's original book. "Certain manifestations of devotion like plaster statues of the Virgin Mary, pictures of the Sacred Heart, or bottles of the Lourdes water," one historian has observed, "were invented or popularized in the nineteenth century" as a part of the ultramontane Catholic revival that culminated in the First Vatican Council. This material culture was a "strategy carefully managed by Rome," so that the Church could exercise greater control over the lives of English Catholics in the Victorian period. By stressing those aspects of Catholic doctrine that were most different—and often most abhorrent—to Protestants, the Church hierarchy shepherded Catholics who lived in secular and/or predominantly Protestant cultures to the margins of their societies and reinforced a "church-centered" understanding of Catholicism in the minds of all of the faithful.[50]

In the United States, devotional practices and Catholic material culture played a similarly controlling role. Priests cultivated a "fascination with the miraculous" in the nineteenth century as part of their effort to convince parishioners that only a "close adhesion to the hierarchical church protected believers in a sinful environment." It became common in the 1840s and 1850s for American Catholics to recite devotions to the Sacred Heart or complete the Stations of the Cross, a ritual that entails moving through a chapel and stopping at fourteen predetermined points to contemplate Christ's suffering in the hours before his death. These spiritual exercises utilized images of the bleeding heart of Jesus and the grief of his mother Mary, and they were viewed by priests as a way to protect Catholics from the "cold egoism and materialism" of the modern era.[51]

But if devotional exercises and Catholic material culture were used by the Church to reassert its control over the lives of Catholics in the nineteenth century, the same could not be said of these trappings of Catholicism in the eighteenth century—at least not in colonial Maryland. Leaving aside the reality that the ultramontane Catholic revival was a reaction against the secularism and anti-clericism that grew out of the French Revolution of 1789 (and would not, therefore, have strongly influenced Catholic devotionalism in the years prior to the war), the reality is that devotional exercises and material culture could not have exercised a consolidating and controlling influence over the Catholic laity in eighteenth-century Maryland because the Church, quite simply, did not have the clerical, educational, or ecclesiastical infrastructure in colonial America to shape Catholic devotionalism in that way.

Catholic material culture and devotional exercises were not about Church control in eighteenth-century Maryland. They were about the partnership that had developed between the clergy—and specifically the Jesuits—and the laity, as each group worked in its own way to maintain the Catholic faith under difficult circumstances. Long before the Vatican seized on devotions to the Sacred Heart and the Blessed Sacrament as a way of reasserting its authority in an increasingly secular world, the Jesuits had identified these exercises as an important mechanism for sustaining faith. As a mission-oriented order that placed great emphasis on the mystical power of prayer, the Society of Jesus recognized early on that devotional exercises had tremendous potential to facilitate the survival of Catholicism in areas where the Church's infrastructure was weak or sometimes nonexistent.

Sodalities—or what were sometimes called "confraternities"—embodied the Jesuit approach to mission work. They were Church-sanctioned groups of laypeople who came together to promote charity and/or piety through devotional exercises. The Society of Jesus promoted and organized these groups as a way of sustaining a commitment to Catholicism among peasants in seventeenth-century Italy, slaves in eighteenth-century Brazil, and Native Americans in nineteenth-century North Dakota.[52]

Indeed, by the end of the sixteenth century, lay sodalities had become "a primary element of Jesuit ministerial strategy," according one scholar. These lay sodalities were deliberately independent and "frequently became detached from any significant Jesuit connection within a few years" of their founding.[53] This independence was the sodalities' great strength. The reason these devotional confraternities could sustain Catholicism in places where priests were scarce and ecclesiastical structures were nonexistent was that once they had been founded by a priest, the sodalities—and the lay piety that was expressed within them—became self-sustaining.

Clearly, when speaking of sodalities that were made up of enslaved African prisoners or conquered Native Americans, control is an undeniable layer to the story—if not the control of the Church hierarchy, then certainly the control of the white, European Christians who were seeking to dominate North and South America. When speaking of sodalities that were made up of English and Irish colonists, however—that is, cradle-to-grave Catholics who were living in an English colony where Protestants dominated the population and Catholicism was legally and politically marginalized—the "control" issue is necessarily more complicated and complex.

A comparison with modern-day Judaism, while imperfect, is nevertheless useful. American Jews today are swimming in a sea of religious pluralism. Anti-Semitism is still an ugly reality, of course, but in general, Jews have the freedom to surf, ski, and play chicken with a wide variety of people in an ocean that is lined in many directions with public access beaches. The danger for these Jews is that they might forget their Jewish identity while they are cavorting. The rules of Kashrut remind them, therefore, to get out of the water on a regular basis and give their puckered skin a break on an island that is uniquely theirs.

Similarly, devotional sodalities reminded Catholics in eighteenth-century Maryland of their unique, Catholic identity. For them, the issue was not that they might forget that they were Catholic while they were playing in the ocean with their Protestant friends. For them, the issue was that they were on a barge that was being tossed around by some angry Protestant currents. They had very little guidance from their captain about how stable or sturdy the barge was, and it was tempting, therefore, to throw on a life-vest and hop off the boat, rather than wait for it to sink and go down with it. Devotional exercises reminded these Catholics, however, of why they were on that barge—and gave them a reason to keep fighting to stay on.[54]

The voluntary nature of Kashrut allows the Reformed and Reconstructionist Jews who choose to keep kosher to develop a sense of ownership over their religious identity. Jews today cannot keep kosher without the assistance of a mashgiach, whose expertise on the rules of Kashrut helps him (or rarely her) determine if a food item meets the faith's dietary mandates. In this complicated world of corn syrup and monosodium glutamate, rabbis are also occasionally called in to rule on whether a modern ingredient is in accord with Judaism's ancient standards.[55] "Keeping Kosher," then, is a partnership between lay and clerical Jews. The clergy certify a food item as kosher, and the laity bring that food into their homes, cooking it according to the rules of Kashrut, as those rules have been explained to them by their clergy. No rabbi or mashgiach stands behind the laity, however, looking over their shoulders to make sure they are cooking the food correctly—or even that they are keeping kosher at all. This final step in the expression of Jewish identity is one that the laity take on their own.

The voluntary nature of Catholic devotionalism also allowed the colonial Catholics who chose to express their faith in this way to develop a sense of ownership over their religious identity. Although many Catholics in colonial Maryland chose to complete their devotional exercises in private—using "pictures" such as the ones Ferdinand Farmer wrote to his brother about in 1755 to guide their prayers—others chose to express their devotion to God, Jesus, Mary, and the doctrines of the Church in a more public and communal, but no less individualistic and voluntary manner. These communal expressions of devotion through sodality membership, like keeping kosher, required the assistance of the clergy. No civil or ecclesiastical law compelled Catholics to join a sodality, however. Their commitment was entirely their own.

In 1776, for instance, fifty-five lay Catholics came together in St. Mary's County and, with the help of Fr. James Walton, formed the Sodality of the Sacred Heart of Jesus. Nine years earlier, thirty lay Catholics who were served by the priests at St. Inigoes Manor formed the Sodality for the Adoration of the Blessed Sacrament. Several members of this earlier sodality were not listed as belonging to the congregation at St. Inigoes when the Jesuits recorded the names of their congregants one year after the sodality was formed. This was probably because people like Ann Oad, Janice Wimsatt, Eleanor Dugings (probably Duggins), and Frances Melhorn lived too far away from St. Inigoes to attend weekly worship services at the chapel the Jesuits had on their plantation.[56]

The priests did not consider these women to be members of the St. Inigoes congregation. The nice thing about the lay sodality the women belonged to, however, was that the piety and religious identity that the confraternity promoted—much like kosher cooking—could be expressed and perpetuated at home, without the assistance of a priest.

Oad, Wimsatt, Duggins, and Melhorn, therefore, could see themselves as "good Catholics," even though they were unable to attend Mass and give their Confessions each week.

In 1768, nearly 200 Catholics joined a sodality in Charles County. While the other two sodalities in eighteenth-century Maryland for which we have records were composed entirely of women (an interesting fact, given that the Catholic Church had only started allowing women to join sodalities in 1751), the Sodality for the Perpetual Adoration of the Blessed Sacrament was made up of men and women both. Entire families joined this sodality, signing up for blocks of time on particular days throughout the month, during which they agreed to be "on their knees, in honour of the B[lessed] Sacrament, by meditating or saying of vocal prayers."

Martha Matthews, for instance, agreed to be on her knees for half an hour on the 1st, 15th, and 29th day of each month. Her son, Jesse, and her nephew, William, joined her on the 1st and the 15th. Her daughter Jane joined her on the 29th. William Matthews was a particularly ardent Catholic, signing up to be on his knees, contemplating the miracle of the Blessed Sacrament on the 5th, 6th, 19th, and 20th days of each month, in addition to the days when he would be praying with his aunt. His cousin Jane's commitment was not quite so zealous—though in addition to the 29th, she also agreed to be on her knees for half an hour on the 2nd and the 16th of the month. Mary Ann Doyne, who was probably related to Martha Matthews through Martha's mother, Mary Doyne, signed up for the 2nd and the 16th of the month, along with Jane Matthews. Mary Ann's sisters, Sarah and Jane, were on their knees on the 1st and the 15th, and the 3rd and the 17th, respectively. Meanwhile, Marmaduke Semmes (whose relation to Martha Matthews is really far too complicated to explain in just a few words), made sure he and his daughter, Violetta, had the 7th and the 21st days of each month covered.[57]

Not only did these Catholics sign up for particular days, but they also signed up for specific time blocks—10:00–10:30, say, or 5:30–6:00—during which time they promised themselves and each other that they would stop whatever it was they were doing—feeding the chickens, greasing a wagon wheel, distributing slave rations, darning a stocking—and contemplate the gift that was the transubstantiated Host. "When hindered by sickness or otherways," the members of the sodality vowed, they would "apply to some other, to supply their place." In this way, no hour of any day in any month of any year would ever pass without some Catholic somewhere in Charles County on his or her knees, thinking deeply or praying out loud in gratitude for the sacrifice that Christ had made, so that humanity might live.

By joining sodalities, Catholics created for themselves their own religious obligations. These obligations were, of course, intimately connected to the sacramental obligations that the Church had placed upon the laity through its doctrines. The obligations that were assumed through sodality membership were different, however, because laypeople were in control of them. Laypeople were the ones who made the decision to accept these obligations, and in all likelihood, they were also the ones who verified that the obligations were being met. No priest was going to check up on William Matthews to make sure he was on his knees on a Tuesday morning, after all. If anyone were going make sure William met the obligation he had freely accepted, it was going to be his aunt, Mary Matthews.

The Church told Catholics that the Eucharist was a Sacrament and that as such, it must be venerated. The veneration that the Church obliged lay Catholics to engage in, however, was not the kind of veneration that William Matthews was engaged in when he was kneeling in his barn or field, or Jane Doyne was engaged in when she was kneeling in her mother's kitchen, thinking about the Eucharist. The veneration that the Church demanded involved receiving the Eucharist from the hands of a priest during a consecrated Mass, and Catholics in Maryland did not deny that this was, indeed, the best way to venerate the Sacrament. It was not the only way, however, and in an environment where the services of a priest could not always be available, Catholics embraced sodalities as a mechanism whereby their religious obligations could be molded to fit the contingencies of their lives in the New World.

Devotionalism that was done in one's home did not excuse a Catholic who failed to attend Mass whenever a Catholic Mass was available. The

Sacrament of Penance that was a prerequisite to taking Communion was a fundamental component of Jesuit spirituality, and the Jesuits serving in Maryland wanted their laity to participate in the two, related sacramental rituals as frequently as possible. To that end, the priests who served in Maryland traveled extensively throughout the boundaries of their mission. Fr. Joseph Mosley claimed to cover as many as 300 miles per week. According to Hugh Neill, an Anglican priest who served the three counties that eventually became the state of Delaware, the five Catholic families who lived within the boundaries of his parish were "attended Once a Month from Maryland" by a Catholic priest.[58]

The priest who traveled to Delaware probably lived on the Jesuits' plantation in neighboring Cecil County. Bohemia Manor had been founded in 1706, after Thomas Mansell, a Jesuit who first began serving in the colony six years earlier, inherited 300 acres from a devout Catholic woman named Mary Ann O'Daniel. Several years later, Mansell purchased two adjoining estates from James Heath, who was also Catholic, bringing the total size of Bohemia to nearly 900 acres.[59]

One of the priests who lived at Bohemia was James Beadnall, an English Jesuit who arrived in Maryland in 1749 and was stationed in a number of eastern shore locations, including Bohemia Manor, until 1766, when he moved to the Jesuits' plantation at Newtown, in St. Mary's County. Beadnall must have understood that weekly Mass attendance was not a possibility for those Catholics who lived far away from a priest; it was the reason he endured the inconvenience of traveling throughout the northern regions of the eastern shore, even in the wintertime. Whenever a Jesuit such as himself made the effort to travel to a community where Catholics were living, however, Beadnall fully expected every Catholic in the vicinity to be there at Mass. Alas, this was not always the case.[60]

In a sermon that he delivered in 1768, James Beadnall complained that not even the "thunderclaps of excommunication" were enough to compel some Catholics to attend Mass and receive the Eucharist. "'My family must be looked after... I've a plantation that demands all my care... my horses are reduced and I cant come in time to perform my devotion,'" Beadnall mocked, before telling the laypeople in his audience that "every excuse you allege will be your own condemnation." This sentiment was echoed a few years later in sermons that were delivered by Frs. Charles Sewall and Bennett Neale. "Some of you think nothing to absent yourselves upon such days of obligation, as if you could be saved without complying with the commandments of the Church," Sewall alleged in 1774. "There is no temporal affair ever so pressing," Bennett Neale warned, "which almighty God . . . prefer[s] to the care of your soul."[61]

Clearly, some Catholics in Maryland felt that the operations of their farms were more important than the obligations of their faith. The clerical harangues that Beadnall, Sewall, and Neale delivered, however, were not being heard by those Catholics. The laypeople hearing their sermons were the ones who were actually fulfilling their sacramental obligations—raising the question, then, of what, exactly, the Jesuits were up to when they delivered these homilies. Was the purpose to condemn those individuals who had not come to Mass and to lament a decline in Catholic orthodoxy? Or were the homilies more like the Puritan jeremiads that the literary critic Sacvan Bercovitch has written about—that is, rhetorical rituals that were "designed to join . . . the shifting 'signs of the times' to certain traditional metaphors, themes, and symbols"?

For many years, the sermons that Calvinist ministers like Increase Mather and John Norton delivered in colonial New England suggested to historians that there was a decline in piety in late seventeenth-century Massachusetts. The grandchildren of the original Puritan settlers, it was assumed, were not replicating the pious orthodoxy that had compelled their grandparents to sail to the other side of the Atlantic Ocean. Demographic research done in the 1970s on colonial church membership, however, did not necessarily support this assumption about a declension in Puritan piety. As a consequence, historians started looking for a more subtle explanation of what Increase Mather had been trying to accomplish when he delivered a thirty-one-page sermon in 1674, warning that the "Day of Trouble" was "near" in New England, thanks to the "sin and corruptions in the hearts of the best."[62]

The explanation offered by Bercovitch is that the jeremiads were not an expression of disappointment or a lament that the next generation of Puritans was failing to "get" what their parents' and grandparents' "errand into the wilderness" had been all about. Rather, the American jeremiad was a "realistic way to deal with crisis and change," a reminder to New England's early Calvinist settlers that although the circumstances under which they were living their faith were markedly different from those of their religious brethren in England, they were all still God's newly chosen people, sharing the same destiny and the same obligations.[63]

Seen through this lens, the Jesuits' "jeremiads" become much more than just rants about attendance at Mass. They become statements about the unusual circumstances under which lay and clerical Catholics alike were forced to live their faith in Maryland. Beadnall's words about the "thunderclaps of excommunication"—while certainly designed to get more people participating in the Sacraments—were also a reminder to the lay Catholics who did make their Confessions and receive the Eucharist that although circumstances in the New World had forced their priests to compromise on some religious obligations, the priests were willing to bend only so far.

"You must not imagine that every trifle, as a little ache or such like pain ... is case sufficient to be exempted [from your Catholic duties]," Fr. Leonard Neale advised his parishioners before excusing them from a Lenten fast that came at the end of what had been a particularly harsh winter. Fr. Arnold Livers reported in 1745 that he had, under some duress, granted a "great many" fasting dispensations that year. According to Livers, parishioners who were not given formal exemptions from their fasting obligations would often compensate for the lack of food by "drinking betwixt meals as much, if not more, as upon other Days." In a world where hard cider was drunk more commonly than tea or water, Fr. Livers felt he could not allow his parishioners to drink excessively on empty stomachs.[64]

The Catholic obligation to fast, then, was something the laity occasionally demanded that they be excused from—and their priests obliged. Work dispensations, too, were not unheard of in Maryland. In 1722, the priests who were serving in the colony applied to the Vicar Apostolic in London for a large-scale work dispensation that covered all of the Sundays and most of the English Catholic Holy Days that fell between May and September. The dispensation was to apply only to those Catholics who worked in the fields; house servants were still expected to refrain from work, as were merchants and other businessmen. Four of the most important Holy Days on the Catholic calendar were also excluded from the request, even though they fell during the spring and summer. Those days were Ascension Day, Whitsun Monday, Corpus Christi Day, and the Feast of the Assumption.[65]

The petition to the Vicar Apostolic is important in spite of its limited reach, because it illustrates that the Jesuits understood and appreciated the unusual circumstances under which their laity lived. As environmental historians have shown, establishing a new farm in North America was no easy endeavor.[66] Immigrants who came from a land where the forests had been cleared for generations faced dense wilderness when they arrived in Maryland—forests that were thick with trees, vines, and underbrush, all of which needed to be cut down and burned in a multiyear process before any ploughing or planting could begin to take place. In such a world, the fifty-odd Sundays and thirty-six Holy Days that peppered the English Catholic calendar and demanded a total abstinence from work could be an incredible hindrance to the survival of one's family.

Catholic farmers in Maryland simply refused not to work—but some of them, it seems, were rather uncomfortable with having to make this decision. They were, after all, Catholic—in a world where they did not have to be, and where the advantages that came with abandoning their Catholic faith were real. The fact that they had not left the Catholic fold meant that they identified strongly with the tenets and directives of the Church, even if they did not always follow those directives. "The liberty many Catholics take in working generally upon Holydays . . . is in some cases of necessity," the Jesuits told the Vicar Apostolic. Nevertheless, "it is very disedifying & may prove a scandal to the more timorous . . . [unless] something should be settled, by which their consciences may be quieted."[67]

When they requested that Catholic farmers in Maryland be exempted from the Church's proscriptions on work, the Jesuits were seeking out compromises in an effort to maintain the community's Catholic identity. They understood that the Protestant-dominated government in Maryland already made it difficult for Catholics to remain Catholic. They worried that if the Church itself made it difficult for Catholics to maintain their religious identity while addressing their temporal needs in the New World, the result might be that the "more timorous" members of the community would leave the Church, rather than suffer a guilty conscience—or at the very least distance themselves from the Church to such an extent that their children would not develop a strong sense of Catholic identity.

Yet, even as they were being flexible and seeking out compromises, the Jesuits in Maryland had to be careful that they did not bend to the laity's will too much, for sometimes, those trappings of Catholicism that could be decidedly inconvenient in the New World were also the very things that reminded the members of the minority Catholic community that they were Catholic. The inconveniences that were created by fasting, abstaining from work, or having to travel several miles in the cold to receive the Sacraments reminded Catholics of their religious identity. They also set the members of the community apart from the Protestant majority with whom they lived, worked, played, and loved.

Marriage, after all, was not the only medium through which Catholics interacted with Protestants. Many prominent Catholics, such as Charles Carroll of Annapolis and his brother Daniel, were also involved in business partnerships with Protestants. In 1731, the Carroll brothers and their cousin, Dr. Charles Carroll—who was still Catholic at the time—joined forces with Benjamin Tasker, Sr. and Daniel Dulany, Sr., both of whom were Protestant, to found the Baltimore Company, an ironworks that became one of the most ambitious industrial operations in eighteenth-century Maryland. Over the course of several years, the five men ploughed more than £11,000 sterling into the business, which reached the height of its profitability in the 1760s and continued to operate until 1808.[68]

The Catholic Carrolls would not have had the liberty to ignore the affairs of their ironworks on, say, January 1st, the Feast of the Blessed Virgin Mary, or June 29th, the Feast of Saints Peter and Paul, if the company's affairs demanded their attention on those days. Neither feast was recognized as a Holy Day of Obligation by the Anglican Church that Dulany and Tasker belonged to, and the Catholic Carrolls had an obligation to these men that was just as strong as the obligation they had to their Church—and far more immediate. The group dispensation for farm work that the Jesuits requested in 1722 would not have applied to the business dealings of Charles Carroll of Annapolis. Carroll would have had to have applied for an individual dispensation, especially since he had a priest living in his home and would not have been able to address the needs of his ironworks without attracting the notice of either Fr. Ashton or Fr. Diederich. In such instances, Carroll almost certainly got the dispensations he requested. The Jesuits had to be careful that they were not too flexible—but Charles Carroll of Annapolis paid Ashton's and Diederich's salaries and supplied their food and housing. Neither priest was in a position to deny Carroll something he wanted.

The willingness to be flexible on certain Catholic obligations marked the Jesuits in Maryland as different from their clerical brothers in England. In the parent country, the Jesuits insisted that all of the people living in a household headed by a Catholic man had to observe the fasting obligations mandated by the Catholic Church. Catholic gentry who hired Protestant day laborers were not permitted to feed those laborers meat on Fridays or Catholic Holy Days. The gentry could not even serve meat to Protestant guests who happened to be in their homes on Catholic days of Obligation.[69]

In Maryland, however, the Jesuits proved to be less demanding of their parishioners when it came to fasting obligations in mixed households. The priests expected every Catholic adult to observe the fasts unless he or she had qualified for a dispensation. Non-Catholic servants, guests, and family members, however, were never required to participate. Fr. John Carroll defended the American Jesuits' leniency to his friend and Jesuit brother in England, Charles Plowden. He accused the English Jesuits of spending so much time "brooding over undigested scraps of theology" that they were unable to engage "any degree of liberality to enlarge their minds." The Jesuits in England, Carroll declared, threw "indiscriminate censure on every person departing ever so little from the rules of thinking & acting that they have laid down for themselves." Such judgmental behavior would not be applied toward the Catholics who lived in the New World, however. Before sending a priest out to Kentucky to serve several families who had migrated there from Maryland after the Revolutionary War, Carroll warned the missioner that "the necessities of Catholics in that country will justify a deviation from settled rules."[70]

Just as the work dispensations granted by Maryland's priests reflected their willingness to recognize the unique, New World conditions under which their laity lived, so, too, was the Jesuits' refusal to mandate a universal observance of Catholic fasting obligations in mixed households a reflection of the New World environment where the priests served. Whereas the work dispensations had been about the Jesuits' understanding of the natural environment that influenced life in Maryland, however, their unwillingness to demand that Protestant servants observe the religious obligations of their Catholic masters was about the Jesuits' understanding of the political environment that characterized life in Maryland.

William Lewis had learned as early as 1638, after all—more than fifty years before the Maryland Revolution—that Protestant servants in the colony were not to be antagonized by their Catholic masters. Lewis was the lay overseer of the Jesuits' plantation at St. Inigoes, and his Protestant servants accused him of preventing them from reading the "books of our religion." Lewis's actions had nearly resulted in soldiers' being sent from Virginia to Maryland to rescue the Protestants there from "conniving Jesuits," and Lewis, himself, had had to pay a heavy fine before the uproar that his behavior created died down.[71]

Sixty-four years later, Anthony Neale—Henrietta Maria Neale Bennett Lloyd's younger brother—learned that little had changed in the colony regarding Catholic masters and their Protestant servants. In 1702, Neale's servant, John Emory, claimed that Neale had burned some of Emory's religious books. Fortunately for the Catholic landowner, his Protestant servant was not able to offer the court any "Positive Proof" of the offense. Anthony Neale was therefore spared a punishment that—in the year that saw the establishment of the Anglican Church in Maryland—almost certainly would have included imprisonment and could even have meant his death, had the judicial authorities in Charles County determined that his actions were treasonous.[72]

Maryland's priests understood that their laity needed to be careful about how they expressed their Catholicism. It was true that Catholic custom demanded that all of the members of a Catholic household follow the Church's rules on fasting and abstinence, even if not all of the members were Catholic. It was also true, however, that a "custom ought not to be transferred . . . from Europe to Maryland" if circumstances in the New World did not support the practice of that custom.[73] Fr. William Hunter had made that point as early as 1715, with regard to mixed marriages, and Father John Carroll made the point again seventy years later, as he sent a priest off into the wilds of Kentucky to serve the Catholic community that had taken root there.

Through their voluntary membership in sodalities, Catholics affirmed their kinship networks, established connections with other Catholic families in the area, and, in so doing, defined and maintained their religious identity. By exposing their slaves to the Catholic faith and getting those slaves to convert, Catholics exhibited their commitment to the teachings of their Church and to their obligations as Catholic Christians. When they requested fasting or abstinence dispensations from their priests, Catholics verified their commitment to the idea of religious obligations even as they chose not to live up to them. And when Catholic parents in Maryland chose to give their sons names that belonged to Catholic saints, they proclaimed to the communities they lived and worked in that they had every intention of raising the boys as Catholics.

And still, there were other ways for members of the Catholic community—especially the wealthy ones—to express their commitment to their faith. Nearly half of the Catholic gentry living in

Maryland at the turn of the eighteenth century had chapels in their homes—a practice that had begun before the Penal Period among Catholics who lived far away from the Jesuits' plantations, but which took on an added degree of importance after 1704, when Maryland's Assembly outlawed the public celebration of all Catholic Masses. The gentry would often invite their less wealthy religious brethren into their homes to worship with them, and the Jesuits developed the habit of identifying these "congregations" by the names of the families who sponsored them.[74]

Some Catholics kept not just chapels but also priests in their homes, following the tradition of seigneurial Catholicism that had taken root in England in the late sixteenth century. Charles Carroll of Annapolis occasionally loaned his priests out to Clement Hill and William Digges—as he would any other servant. Hill and Digges asked to use the services of Carroll's priests after the Jesuits whom they themselves had been keeping in their homes left. Fr. Robert Harding moved to Philadelphia in 1753 after spending several years in Clement Hill's household in Prince George's County. Fr. Peter Davis began serving the Digges family in 1733. Although it is not clear when, exactly, he left to return to England, it had to have been some time before July 1759, when Davis died in the country of his birth.

Davis may have left the Digges's household shortly after William's son, Thomas, returned to Maryland from Europe. Thomas Digges had entered the Society of Jesus at the age of eighteen, after graduating from St. Omer's College in 1729. He was ordained in 1737 and served in Maryland, then, from 1741 until his death in 1805. He spent most of his career living with the family of his older brother, Ignatius, hearing confessions, saying Mass, and performing baptisms for his nieces and nephews—among them, Mary Digges, who grew up to become the First Lady of the independent state of Maryland. Fr. James Haddock, who, as a Franciscan, was one of the rare priests in Maryland who did not belong to the Society of Jesus, served as the family chaplain for his own half-brother, Marsham Waring. Fr. Thomas Barton lived on Peter Sayer's estate in Talbot County for several years, and John Whetenhall and Notley Rozer, who were half-brothers, shared the expenses and the services of Fr. Henry Whetenhall—who, it will be recalled, was a relation of Ann Rozer, the Catholic mother of Benjamin Young, who secretly converted to Catholicism in 1768.[75]

Priests were not the only people wealthy Catholics brought into their homes as part of their commitment to their faith. In 1747, Justinian Wharton, Edward Digges, and John and Joseph Lancaster were among several "Roman Catholick gentlemen" who turned out for an auction of eighty-eight Jacobite prisoners who arrived in St. Mary's City from England. John Lancaster's Catholic son-in-law, Richard Holmes, was the captain of the ship that had brought the prisoners over, and he had alerted the Catholic community in Maryland of the Jacobites' impending arrival.

The prisoners had been shipped to Maryland as punishment for their involvement in a failed effort to place the deposed King James II's Catholic grandson, Charles, on the English throne. Alexander Stuart was among the convict laborers auctioned off on that day, and he happily recorded in his diary that most of his fellow Jacobites had been purchased by Catholic masters who "would probably give us down two years of our time." As it turns out, Edward Digges released Stuart from his indenture after just a few months of service, and by March 1748, Stuart was in Ireland.

Thirty years earlier, when Donal MacPherson was transported to Maryland because of his involvement in a similar Jacobite uprising in 1715, he, too, reported that he had been purchased by a Catholic who proved to be a very agreeable master. That Catholic was probably Thomas Nichols, who rented his farm from the Jesuits and was not actually as wealthy as many of the other freemen who purchased Jacobite prisoners. "He never makes me work," MacPherson wrote of Nichols to his father, "[unless] I like it myself; the most of my work is watering a Horse, and bringing wine and bread out of the cellar to my Master's table."[76]

Edward Digges's premature voiding of Alexander Stuart's indenture aside, the Catholics who purchased Jacobite prisoners were undoubtedly looking for people to help them on their farms. Tobacco was an extraordinarily labor-intensive commodity, and chronic labor shortages were part of the reason Maryland was the first British colony to legalize race-based slavery.[77] Alexander Stuart's observation that most of the prisoners in his group were bought by Catholics, however—and his confidence that they would all see their terms of indenture reduced by their new masters—suggests that Catholics were deliberately choosing to bring supporters of England's deposed Catholic king into their households when they took action to increase their workforces. By purchasing Jacobite prisoners, Maryland's Catholics were able to express their solidarity with those who denied the legitimacy of the Glorious Revolution and, in so doing, reaffirm their religious identity.

These wealthy Catholics expressed their religious sympathies again in the 1750s when they tried to provide for the hundreds of Acadians who arrived in Maryland, poor and desperate, possessing only that property which they had been able to wear or carry on their backs during their thousand-mile journey down from Canada. The Catholic Acadians were refugees of the Seven Years War. France had formally turned Acadia—which included present-day Nova Scotia, New Brunswick, and Maine—over to the British government in 1713, as a provision of the Treaty of Utrecht. For many years, the French-speaking Catholics who resided in Nova Scotia lived relatively unmolested under British rule, refusing to swear their loyalty to England, but agreeing to remain "neutral" as far conflict between England and France was concerned.

Following the outbreak of hostilities between English and French forces in 1754, however, the high concentration of French neutrals in Nova Scotia became a source of concern for the British government. Between 1755 and 1763, British troops forcibly removed more than 14,000 Acadians from their homes—7,000 of them in the first year alone—in a "scene of terror" that would eventually be immortalized by the American poet Henry Wadsworth Longfellow and which many contemporary historians believe may have been the most brutal and inhumane action taken by the British army in the eighteenth century. Approximately one-third of the Acadians who were removed from Nova Scotia died while they waited on prison ships or marched through the snow toward the English colonies they had been reassigned to.[78]

Around 900 of the original exiles arrived in Maryland in 1756. While much of the correspondence that he kept on the subject is no longer available, Charles Carroll of Annapolis did seem to feel a personal obligation as a Catholic to ensure that the Acadians who came to Maryland were cared for. In one surviving letter that he wrote to his son, Carroll complained that the colonial government had done nothing to provide for the refugees and had, instead, insisted that they be "entirely supported by private charity." This, in and of itself, might not have been a problem, for Carroll believed that the exiles "would have met with very humane treatment from the Roman Catholics here," had the government been willing to let Maryland's Catholics reach out to their religious brethren. Alas, "a real or pretended Jealousy inclined this government not to suffer them to live with the Roman Catholics," and Carroll was not allowed to take in any of the fourteen people he had volunteered to support. Presumably, none of the other wealthy Catholics in Maryland was able to house Acadians, either. The account book that Fr. John Lewis kept at Bohemia Manor, however, indicates that many of Maryland's lay Catholics donated money so that the Acadians could be cared for during their time in Maryland and eventually relocated to Louisiana, where the language, government, and religion would be more familiar.[79]

In addition to keeping priests in their homes, purchasing Jacobite prisoners, and doing what they could to care for the Acadians, the gentry in Maryland also expressed their commitment to the Catholic faith through the artwork they commissioned. Among Maryland's wealthy Catholics, the portrait artist Justus Engelhardt Kühn was particularly popular. A Protestant immigrant who arrived in Maryland from Germany some time around 1708, Kühn was the first person to make a living as a portrait artist in the southern colonies. Only a dozen of his paintings still survive, and of those, all but one are of Catholics. The imagery that Kühn used in these Catholic portraits suggests that the patrons who commissioned them may have wanted their religious identity to be reflected in the paintings—even if the message were clear only to other members of the Catholic faith.

To be sure, the Carrolls, Diggeses, and Darnalls wanted to display their wealth, highlight their lineage, and create a legacy. In this way, they were no different from the Congregationalist Sedgwicks in Massachusetts or the Anglican Lees in Virginia who were also great patrons of portraiture. When crafting a message for future generations, accuracy was not always a priority for any of these families. The portraits that Kühn did of the Darnall and Carroll children, therefore, all feature beautifully manicured estates in the background—gardens that could only have been cultivated over the course of many generations and probably bore very little resemblance to the wooded hills around Woodyard and Doughoregan Manor where the Darnall and Carroll families lived. Indeed, had the house at Woodyard actually featured the marble balustrades that Kühn depicted in his portrait of young Eleanor Darnall (figure 4.1), it is possible that the house might still be occupied today. Instead, Woodyard is a dilapidated archeological site just a few miles away from Andrew's Air Force Base in Prince George's County.[80]

Figure 4.1 Eleanor Darnall (1704–1769). Oil on canvas by Justus Engelhardt Kühn, c. 1710. 1912.1.5, Courtesy of The Maryland Historical Society.

The magnificent fountain in the background of Eleanor Darnall's portrait may have been meant to convey more than just the Darnall family's wealth, however. Enclosed gardens—the so-called "hortus conclusi" frequently mentioned in the Catholic emblem books that the Jesuits put out in the seventeenth century—were classic elements of Marian iconography. Fountains represented the purity of the mother of Christ, who was born without Original Sin, and the walls around the gardens represented her virginity, which she maintained throughout her life, according to Catholic teaching.[81]

The Society of Jesus published more than 1,700 emblem books in the seventeenth century, many of them produced at schools the Jesuits ran in Continental Europe and most of them published in the vernacular, so as to be more effective in the Jesuits' counter-Reformation efforts. The books used images to teach the laity about important elements of Catholic doctrine and to provide them with something to focus on during their devotional exercises. One of the most popular English-language emblem books was Henry Hawkins's *Partheneia Sacra, or The Mysterious and Delicious Garden of the Sacred Parthenes*. Published in 1633 by an English Jesuit who dedicated one of his seven books to Anne Arundel, the wife of Maryland's first proprietor, the *Partheneia Sacra* identified twenty-four images that were associated with the Virgin Mary. Among them were the Garden, the Fountain, the Pearl, the Rose, and the Tulip.[82]

It is probably no coincidence, then, that Eleanor Darnall stands in front of a garden with a fountain, wearing a string of pearls, with a vase full of roses and tulips sitting on a pedestal slightly behind her and to her left. This portrait—which in all likelihood hung in the front hall of the Darnalls' home—would have greeted all visitors who came to Woodyard, Catholics and Protestants alike. Protestant visitors might have interpreted the roses to be a statement about love—an artistic use of the rose that Henry Hawkins himself acknowledged in his emblem book was common in the non-Catholic, English-speaking world. For Catholics, though, the flower was a well-known symbol of the Virgin Mary, "*our rose*, sprung indeed from the thorny stock of the Jewish race, but yet taking nothing of the condition of thorns with her."[83] Catholics visitors to Woodyard, therefore, would have understood that the flowers in the vase were not an expression of Eleanor's love; they were an expression of her faith.

Henry Darnall II, Eleanor's father, may have first encountered the rose's use in Marian iconography during his time at St. Omer's College, the school the Jesuits ran for English-speaking Catholics in French Flanders. Many of the English-language Catholic emblem books that were produced in the seventeenth century were written and/or published at this school. There is no evidence that Darnall actually attended St. Omer's, but we know that the college was quite popular with the Maryland Catholic gentry in the seventeenth and eighteenth centuries, and Darnall did choose to send his two sons there—Henry III, who graduated in 1722, and John, who graduated in 1724. Young Eleanor Darnall joined the English Sepulchrine nuns in Liege shortly after Justus Engelhardt Kühn painted her portrait.[84]

Although they were illegal, Maryland had a handful of Catholic grammar schools that prepared the gentry's sons to tackle the curriculum at St. Omer's. In the 1740s, the Jesuits opened a school on their plantation in Cecil County, and Charles Carroll of Carrollton and his cousin, John Carroll, both studied Latin there. It is possible that the Jesuits may also have run a grammar school at one of their plantations in St. Mary's County, as the account books for Newtown reflect that several Catholic boys were living there in the 1740s.[85]

A St. Omer's education was costly—and the price paid included much more than just the expenses of tuition, room, board, and travel, which could be as high as £130 sterling per student, per year. When Charles Carroll of Carrollton left his mother at the age of eleven in 1748 to travel to Europe, he never saw her again. Elizabeth Brooke Carroll lived for another thirteen years, but "Charley" did not return to Maryland until 1765, after completing two degrees with the Jesuits and then studying law for three years in London, where Catholics could enroll at the Inns of Court—and pay the sizeable tuition—but not practice law.

The separation was hard on Elizabeth Carroll, who had no other surviving children. She often wrote to her son, complaining that "I have not received a letter from you since I wrote to you last . . . (though) your Papa has received two from you since." She wanted Charley to tell her how tall he was and "whether you take care of your teeth as I requested." The lonely mother pleaded with her son to have his portrait done, so that she could see what he looked like and how much he had changed. When she finally received the painting—two years after she had requested it and eight years after her son had left Anne Arundel County—Elizabeth remarked plaintively that "I think it has a great resemblance of you when you were here." Her simple words are heartbreaking, considering their circumstances.[86]

Young Charles Carroll did not have the option of attending Harvard College or the College of William and Mary, the way his contemporaries, John Adams and Thomas Jefferson, did. Those schools were operated by Congregationalists and Anglicans, and Catholics, quite simply, need not apply. Although the Catholic gentry were not the only ones in North America who sent their children abroad to be educated, the need to leave the colonies for the sake of an education did disproportionately affect the Catholic community. According to one historian's estimate, more than half of the boys born into Catholic gentry families after 1740 were sent to Continental Europe to be educated. Indeed, so many of Maryland's native sons were spending their formative years in Catholic Europe that several members of the Lower House of the Assembly tried, unsuccessfully, in the 1750s to get the practice outlawed. These lawmakers warned that if the gentry were not prevented from "sending Youth to Foreign Popish Seminaries for Education," the colony would be infected with a "dangerous intestine Enemy" who was eager to "join French or Indians, who are but too near."[87]

The curriculum at St. Omer's in the early modern period was not designed to encourage the kind of rational thought and critical thinking that formed the foundation of the Enlightenment and eventually led to the American Revolution. The goal of the Society of Jesus' *Ratio Studiorum*, which was formulated in 1599 and guided the curricula at all Jesuit colleges and universities until the suppression of the Society in 1773, was the creation of men who exhibited "eloquent piety," rather than reasoned judgment and independent thought. Unlike the other schools the Jesuits ran for English-speaking Catholics, St. Omer's had been founded specifically to provide an education to boys who were not necessarily looking to enter the clergy. Nevertheless, Charles Carroll of Carrollton may have summed it up best when he remarked to his father eight years after he had left St. Omer's that "that education is only fit for priests" who exhibit an "eagerness to obey without the least enquiry or examination."[88]

Yet, the experience of living abroad at a school that served English-speaking Catholics may have played a role in the making of an American Catholic identity by encouraging the Catholics who made up Maryland's revolutionary generation to see themselves as different from the English. While Charles Carroll of Annapolis's intention in sending his son to St. Omer's was clearly the cultivation the boy's religious identity, it was young Charley's understanding of himself as an American—or more accurately, as a "Marylandian"—that may have received the greatest cultivation during the years he spent studying with the Jesuits in Europe.

The evidence of the experiences that the Catholic gentry had during their years at the Jesuits' schools is sparse. The little that there is, however, suggests that the boys who came from Maryland clustered together when they were at school and saw themselves as different—and maybe even better—than the boys from England with whom they shared their tutors, pews, and dormitories. "Most of our Marylandians do very well, and they are said to be as good as any, if not the best boys in the house," Charles Carroll wrote to his father after he had been at St. Omer's for eighteen months. "I believe Cousin Jack Carroll will make a good scholar, for he is often first."[89]

All of the people James Lawson mentioned in the letters he wrote from the Jesuits' university in Louvain hailed from Maryland. Of particular interest to him were his friend Francis Plunkett's two "very pretty" sisters, who had recently arrived from Baltimore to join a convent. Lawson, who came from Charles County, told his friend, Hugh Matthews, who came from Cecil County and was still studying at St. Omer's, that he had seen the girls before they had entered the English Augustinian convent—and that one of them had had particularly striking eyes. If an "eagerness to obey" were something a Catholic education was meant to instill in a young man, however, James Lawson does not seem to have been a very good student. He complained to Matthews that those "damned rascal Jesuits" were reading his letters before sending them out, so that they could ascertain how much time he was spending at the coffeehouses in town. "I wish they were hanged," Lawson told his friend, as if to challenge the Jesuits to reveal that they had been reading his correspondence.[90]

The boys at St. Omer's who came from Maryland had traveled much farther than their English counterparts for the sake of a Catholic education, and many of them, like Charles Carroll, did not see their homes again until they were fully grown. It was an experience that someone who had come from just across the English Channel could not relate to. On top of that, any differences in accent or dress that had developed between the English and their colonial counterparts by the mid-eighteenth century would have been solidly on display at St. Omer's, especially during that first year at school. Wealthy colonial families made sure they imported the best fabric and china from Europe—but fashions tended to change more quickly than any ship could travel across the Atlantic. England, itself, had a wide variety of accents, as evidenced by the spelling patterns and word usage that dominated certain areas in the eighteenth century. Nevertheless, if we are to believe the essayist Samuel Johnson, "the American dialect" was more grating than anything found in the Old World. It lacked the "elegance" of the English that was spoken in England, and it was marred by a "tract of corruption to which every language widely diffused must always be exposed."[91]

In addition to feeling different from their native-born English peers, the colonial Catholics who studied in Europe also felt extremely homesick during the years that they were away. Charles Carroll wrote to his father at least seven different times between 1759 and 1764, asking that he be allowed to come home. "I am always been and still am as desirous as ever to return," he told his father shortly after he arrived in London to study law. "Of what great advantage will the law be to me? I can't be called to the bar and of course can not practice." Carroll's homesickness became particularly acute after he learned of his mother's death in 1761. "I wish you would permit me to return to Maryland in the next fleet," he wrote. "If I should lose you too, which God forbid, who is there to help me?"[92]

Understanding how difficult the separation could be for the colonial boys, priests who were working in Continental Europe but had some connection to Maryland—either because they had been born there, or else had spent some time serving the community there—would often seek the boys out, offering them guidance and support as they adjusted to their new lives. In so doing, these priests further cemented the boys' attachment to their native Maryland. In addition to his older cousin, John, Charles Carroll had the Jesuit, William Wappeler, to rely upon during those first few awkward years that he spent in Europe. Wappeler lived at the Jesuits' Newtown plantation in St. Mary's County from 1742 until 1748, returning to Europe the same year eleven-year-old Charles Carroll left home. He began teaching at St. Omer's, then, in 1752, and frequently wrote to Charles Carroll of Annapolis about young Charley's progress.[93]

Fr. Leonard Neale was one of eight different Maryland-born Neales who became priests between 1728 and 1773. All of them returned to the colony of their birth after they completed their vows. During his time at Liege, Leonard Neale wrote to his sister, Ann, of the "happiness" he felt upon learning that Joseph Semmes, a native of Charles County, would be his Philosophy tutor. Neale also told his sister that he had sought out the Maryland natives living in Liege—not just the boys who, like himself, were studying at the university there, but also the young women who had immigrated to Europe to become nuns. Neale would have had access to these women in his capacity as a Jesuit novitiate.[94]

One of the women Leonard Neale visited was probably Ann Teresa Matthews. What Charley Carroll melodramatically referred to as his "banishment" was nothing compared to the exile that the daughter of Joseph Matthews and Susanna Craycroft had to endure. One of thirty-one young women who left Maryland between 1747 and 1756 to become nuns, Ann Matthews arrived in Belgium at the age of twenty-two and entered the contemplative order of the Discalced Carmelites. As a cloistered nun, she had very little contact with anyone who lived beyond the boundaries of her monastery.

Unlike Charles Carroll, Matthews wrote no letters home, begging her parents to let her return to her native land. She never seemed to forget her life along the Potomac River, however, and the attachment she felt to Maryland seems to have been just as strong as that of the man who would one day sign the Declaration of Independence. In 1790, after thirty-six years abroad, Mother Bernardina Teresa Xavier of St. Joseph, a.k.a. Ann Teresa Matthews, finally returned to Charles County with her two nieces, who were also Carmelite nuns. Together, with the help of Charles Neale, Leonard Neale's brother, the three nuns founded the first convent in the United States.[95]

The time that the sons—and sometimes even the daughters—of Maryland's Catholic gentry spent at colleges and convents in Europe did much more than just cultivate the young people's loyalties to Catholicism; the time also cemented their loyalties to Maryland. The colonials at St. Omer's saw themselves as different—and possibly even apart—from their native-born English peers. This way of thinking would, of course, have important ramifications in the last third of the eighteenth century when the boys who had been educated at St. Omer's in the 1740s and 1750s came home to assume their positions in Maryland's society and take a stand in the increasingly tense debates between their colony and the parent country.

The Catholic members of Maryland's revolutionary generation were not like their religious brethren in France, Spain, or even England. To begin with, Catholicism was a choice for them. It was not a choice born of the religious "marketplace" that would eventually develop in the United States as the government regulation of religion began to decline.[96] It was still a choice, though, because in eighteenth-century Maryland, Catholicism was not something people could simply fall into. Even individuals who were born into Catholic families and could not conceive of a God that revealed himself *sola scriptura* had to work at being Catholic. They had to take responsibility for their religious identity in a way that was utterly foreign to their contemporaries in predominantly Catholic countries where the faith was supported by the state.

The mechanisms that Catholics adopted for sustaining and maintaining their faith changed the relationship that the laity had with their clergy in Maryland. The Church certainly did not become a democracy in any meaningful sense of the word, but the laity did develop a sense of ownership over their clergy. Priests in the colony became comfortable with being both leaders and servants, listening to their congregants even as they instructed them, and defending compromises that they made with the laity to their clerical colleagues in the Old World. These experiences turned Maryland's Catholics into people who were comfortable with the individualism and republicanism that animated the independence movement and were, ultimately, enshrined in the U.S. Constitution.

Of all of the various mechanisms that Catholics developed for maintaining their faith, however, none was more direct than the efforts they engaged in to fight anti-Catholic legislation. Not only did these efforts help Catholics become comfortable with the challenge to authority that is at the heart of any revolution, they also prepared Catholics to see England as a source of corruption. It is to the role that anti-Catholicism played, then, in the making of an American Catholic identity that we now turn.

5

The Inconsistency of Intolerance

By this point, it should be fairly clear that relations between Catholics and Protestants in the seventeenth and eighteenth centuries were complicated. On the one hand, the violence that characterized early modern Christian sectarianism was as bad, and at times even worse than the violence that plagues relations between Sunni and Shia Muslims in countries like Iraq and Afghanistan today. In 2006, nearly 235,000 people in Iraq fled their homes because of sectarian fighting. As staggering and disturbing as that statistic is, it still represents less than 1 percent of the entire Iraqi population; in contrast, 80 percent of the settlers in St. Mary's County either fled or were killed in the sectarian violence that constituted the Ingle-Claiborne Rebellion of 1644–1645. Maryland also suffered nearly £10,000 in property damage during that revolt, at a time when the median estate value on the western shore was less than £50.[1]

One of the many tragic layers to the sectarian violence in Iraq is that Sunni and Shia Muslims are not strangers to one another. Indeed, 30 percent of the marriages in Iraq involve Sunni and Shia partners.[2] Mixed marriages were common in colonial Maryland, as well, and these marriages were not just between Catholics and their theologically similar Protestant counterparts, the Anglicans. Catholics and Calvinists married one another, too, in spite of the deep theological and political animosity that the two Christian groups had for one another.

Explaining how and why two denominations of Iraqis who know and love one another and worship the same God can also kill and maim one another and destroy each other's property is, of course, far beyond the parameters of this book. Unraveling that same conundrum with regard to Protestants and Catholics in colonial Maryland, however, is crucial to our understanding of why Catholics were willing to embrace the independence movement, why they were willing to join forces with a group of people who spewed anti-Catholicism in their effort to justify a break with Britain, and why those same people who fulminated about the "tyranny of popery" in the run-up to the war were also willing to give Catholics a place at the table when it came time to draft Maryland's new constitution—and to make a Catholic convert their governor before the war was even over.

Anti-Catholicism has always been an unwieldy creature. Institutional or personal, it has meant different things to different people at different times, and its impact has ranged from the merely inconvenient to the downright deadly. When considering anti-Catholicism in an early modern British context, there are at least two constants that students of history can rely upon: (1) that anti-Catholicism, particularly after the Glorious Revolution, was about the nature and meaning of British identity; and (2) that this identity, in turn, was defined against the marginalized and seemingly inconsequential status that the individual had vis-à-vis the Church within the universe of discourse that was the Catholic faith.[3]

To be English in the eighteenth century was to enjoy rights that were given to each individual by God. God did not discriminate when giving rights to humanity; all of God's children, not just the English ones, had the right to property, political representation, personal security, and the rule of law. "The principle aim of society," the eighteenth-century jurist William Blackstone wrote, was to "maintain and regulate these absolute rights of individuals," which were "vested in them by the immutable laws of nature," but "could not be preserved in peace" without the help of "friendly and social communities."

Alas, not all communities recognized the obligation to preserve the rights that God had given to God's children. Early modern Europe, in fact, was full of examples of rulers who trampled on the inalienable rights of humanity: Leopold I of Austria, Louis XIV of France, Peter I of Russia, and John V of Portugal, just to name a few. Indeed, even in England, where personal liberties were seen by all as "our birthright to enjoy entire," individual rights had not always been respected. Before the mid-sixteenth century, William Blackstone reminded his readers, "the particular liberty, the natural equality, and the personal independence of individuals were little regarded or thought of" in England. It was not until the reign of Queen Elizabeth I that things began to change. "Learning ... began to be universally disseminated," thanks to the printing press; the "minds of men" were "enlightened by science and enlarged by observation and travel," thanks to the compass and the "consequent discovery of the Indies"; and England's people "began to entertain a more just opinion of the dignity and rights of mankind," because "the popish clergy, detected in their frauds and abuses ... and stripped of their lands and revenues, stood trembling for their very existence" in the newly Protestant England.[4]

Englishmen believed they were able to enjoy the rights that God meant for them to have because as a group they had embraced the light of technology and turned their backs on the darkness that was the Catholic Church. Even those who could not read (or understand) the voluminous works of William Blackstone knew that they were special because they were English and Protestant. Ministers like Griffith Williams told them as much in sermons that bore wonderful titles like *The Triumph of the Israelites over the Moabites, or Protestants over Papists*. Englishmen could enjoy their God-given rights, Williams's congregants learned, because with God's help they had defeated "their blood thirsty enemies, the Papists."[5] Protecting English rights, therefore, meant continual resistance to the tyrannical forces of Catholicism, because those forces interfered with the individual's relationship with God and, in so doing, subordinated all individual rights to the needs of the Church.

To resist Catholicism, however, an Englishman did not necessarily have to resist individual Catholics. It is a story not often told by scholars (perhaps because the anti-Catholic bombast of the period is so much fun to explore), but the fact is that on a daily basis, relations between

English-speaking Catholics and Protestants were really not that bad. The idea of Catholicism was an undeniable threat—and Catholics could never be allowed to become an actual faction in English politics, lest their reputed deference toward the Pope infect the country's beloved constitution. But on an individual level, Catholics, themselves, could be quite likeable. Thus, Thomas Wentworth could help his friend, George Calvert, secure a charter for Maryland, even as he implemented a plan to deny shelter to Catholic priests in Ireland by confiscating the property of Catholic landowners there. The famous diarist, John Evelyn, could visit Thomas Arundel in his home six days after Arundel was released from prison for his supposed involvement in the "Popish Plot," and he could even bring his nineteen-year-old daughter, Mary, along to sing for the Catholic baron; yet, Evelyn also worried that "secret papists" were teaching among the faculty at University College, Oxford, turning impressionable young men into Innocent XI's minions who would "bring in Popery, which God in Mercy prevent!"[6]

Nowhere was this difference between a fear of Catholicism, on the one hand, and a fear of actual Catholics, on the other, more clearly displayed than in Maryland. The Catholic presence in that colony was greater in size than anywhere else in the British world. Catholics were more familiar to the Protestants in Maryland than they were to the Anglicans in Gloucestershire or the Congregationalists in Massachusetts—where papists, John Adams was relieved to report, were "as rare as a comet or an earthquake." In Maryland, Protestants had the opportunity to discover that Catholics could be trustworthy neighbors, friends, sons-in-law, and business partners. The specter of "papal tyranny," therefore, did not haunt them in quite the same nebulous and incessant way that it did their counterparts in New England, where Guy Fawkes Day was one of the few celebrations the Puritans tolerated, and Harvard University hosted a regular lecture series in which speakers were obliged to "detect," "convict," and "expose" the "Idolatry of the Romish church, their tyranny, usurpations, and other crying wickedness in their high places."[7]

But papal tyranny did, occasionally, haunt Maryland's Protestants—and when it did, the menace seemed more real to them than it did to the Calvinists at Harvard, because in Maryland, Catholics were right down the street. The large Catholic presence along the Chesapeake, combined with Maryland's undeniably Catholic past, made Catholicism more of a threat to Maryland's "English" identity than it was to the English identity of any other colony. This threat, in turn, made anti-Catholicism an extremely effective tool for politically ambitious Protestants in the colony—a more effective tool in Maryland, perhaps, than any place else in North America.

When Jacob Leisler used anti-Catholicism in New York to foment a rebellion and seize political power there in 1689, he quickly learned the limits of his strategy in a colony where the number of Catholics was so small that Jews may actually have outnumbered them. The fear of Catholicism that Leisler stoked was strong enough to force King James II's governor to flee the colony, fearing for his life, but it was not strong enough to protect Leisler once William and Mary had secured the throne and peace had returned to New York. Leisler was arrested, convicted of treason by a jury of New Yorkers, and executed less than two years after his rebellion began.[8]

In contrast, Maryland's General Assembly rewarded Nehemiah Blakiston for his leadership of the Protestant Associators' rebellion by making him governor in 1689. He served in that position until King William appointed Lionel Copley to the post in 1692, and continued, then, to serve as a justice on the Provincial Court until his death by natural causes the following year. The Blakiston name continued to be held in high esteem in Maryland, even after Nehemiah's death. In 1699, Nathaniel Blakiston, Nehemiah's nephew, was appointed to succeed Francis Nicholson—the man Jacob Leisler had run out of New York—as Maryland's governor.

Without a doubt, anti-Catholicism was a powerful political tool in colonial Maryland. But because Catholics were a known—and, for the most part, trusted—quantity there, and because they no longer dominated the government the way they had during the first fifty-five years of the colony's existence, anti-Catholicism in the eighteenth century tended to be effective only when Maryland's Protestants were already feeling particularly insecure about their collective identity as Englishmen.

To be sure, anti-Catholicism was a perpetually popular ingredient in the rhetoric that made its way into Maryland's General Assembly throughout the eighteenth century. Individual Protestants who felt that their political ambitions were being frustrated by Maryland's Anglican proprietor would often lash out at Catholics, because they understood that Maryland's wealthy Catholic families were an important part of the proprietor's financial success in the colony. Their efforts at making life difficult for Catholics, however, did not always result in tangible legislation. It was only when settlers in Maryland felt that their identities as Englishmen were being threatened—either because the colony had been forced to accept Jacobite rebels or Acadian refugees, or because the French had declared war against the English and had brought the fighting dangerously close to Maryland—that the anti-Catholic rhetoric in the Assembly actually transmogrified into bills or laws.

Nehemiah Blakiston's rebellion in Maryland was far more successful for Blakiston than Jacob Leisler's rebellion in New York was for Leisler, because in the early 1690s, the anxiety that the English people in Maryland felt about their "English" identity was at an all-time high. The Glorious Revolution had firmly established that to be English was to be Protestant. Maryland, however, was an English colony with a Catholic governor, a Catholic proprietor, and a General Assembly whose Upper House was dominated by Roman Catholics. That situation, quite simply, needed to change.

The first few years that followed the rebellion of the Protestant Associators saw a flurry of anti-Catholic legislation proposed and passed in Maryland. In November 1689, Catholics were barred from holding office in the colony. In December 1692, they were prohibited from practicing law. In 1699, the Assembly enacted the first of several measures that were designed keep the Catholic population in Maryland from growing any faster than birthrates would dictate. Lawmakers placed a special tax on all "Irish Papist servants" brought into the colony, in an effort to decrease the flow of Catholic immigration. That tax was renewed in 1704, and then doubled in 1717.[9]

Although the passage of anti-Catholic legislation continued into the early years of the eighteenth century, the mania began to die down—albeit temporarily—once it became clear that the era of Catholic hegemony in Maryland was over. Two laws were passed in 1704 that did severely restrict the religious activities of Catholics in Maryland. In September of that year, the Upper House of the Assembly gave Governor John Seymour permission to close the Catholic chapel in St. Mary's City, literally placing a lock on its door and giving the key to the sheriff of St. Mary's County. The reason cited was that the chapel was "both scandalous and offensive to the government." Three weeks later, Seymour signed an "Act to Prevent the Growth of Popery in this Province." The law made it a criminal offense for any priest to say Mass, convert a Protestant, or baptize a baby unless both of the child's parents were Catholics. The first offense was subject to a fine of £50 sterling and six months' prison time; the second offense would get a priest deported to England, where he would be tried under the provisions of England's "Act for the Further Preventing the Growth of Popery," which Parliament and King William had passed four years earlier.[10]

Yet, in spite of these laws, Maryland's Assembly had begun to show some signs of restraint. In 1694, Francis Nicholson arrived in the colony, looking to redeem himself and remove the stain that his association with England's Catholic king had placed on his reputation. Nicholson had served as the Lieutenant Governor of both New York—James II's personal colony—and the ill-fated Dominion of New England, which King James had created in 1687, in an effort to rein in some of the independence the colonies in North America enjoyed and create a relationship between the colonies and the parent country that more closely resembled the relationship France had with Quebec. The measure had not been popular with the residents of the affected colonies, and everyone associated with the Dominion had a great deal of back-peddling to do in the years that followed William III's takeover of England.

Nicholson saw in Maryland an opportunity to re-establish his English bona fides. As governor, he immediately targeted the colony's Catholics, calling them the "professed Enemies" of England and Maryland

and issuing a proclamation in which he warned Catholics not to "seduce, delude, and persuade ... His Majesty's good Protestant Subjects to the Romish faith." Nicholson moved the colony's capital out of St. Mary's County, which was a Catholic stronghold, and up to the predominantly Calvinist Providence—which he then renamed "Annapolis," in honor of Queen Mary's younger sister. He declared that any proselytizing or solicitation by Catholic priests in the colony would be considered a capital offense, and in 1696, he exhorted the Assembly to order all Catholics in the colony to turn in their arms.[11]

The Lower House of the Assembly, however, refused to authorize the governor's request. A year and half earlier, lawmakers in the colony had elected to honor a petition that had been brought to them by a group of men whom the lawmakers tellingly referred to as "Roman Catholique Subjects," implying that the petitioners' religious identity no longer excluded them from the English family. These "subjects" had asked that the arms the Protestant Associators had taken from them during the rebellion be returned. Having just elected to return the arms in question to their Catholic owners, Maryland's assemblymen were not about to authorize Nicholson's order to reconfiscate the arms and risk stirring up the anger of the colony's Catholics. "This province," the assemblymen told Nicholson when rejecting his request, "is God be thanked very peaceable and quiet."[12] By 1696, Maryland was also very Protestant and English—and its government could afford, therefore, to cut the Catholics a little slack, as even the government in England was known to do from time to time.

Not only did the Assembly refuse to reconfiscate the Catholic arms, but it also backed away from one of the harsher restrictions it had enacted against Catholics in 1704 in the Act to Prevent the Growth of Popery in this Province. Queen Anne had succeeded her brother-in-law to the throne two years before the Act was passed, and when word of the measure reached her court in London, she made it known to the Lords of Trade that she felt the law placed too great a hardship on Maryland's Catholics. In April 1707, in response to the queen's concerns, the Assembly modified the law so that priests who performed Masses would no longer be subject to fines or imprisonment, so long as the Masses they performed were in private homes, and not freestanding chapels.[13]

The next ten years or so were quiet ones for Catholics in Maryland. The laws passed in the wake of the Glorious Revolution reminded them every day that the era of religious toleration was over, and Anne's decision in 1715 to restore the colony's charter to the Calvert family after the fifth Lord Baltimore had converted to the Church of England confirmed for Maryland's Catholics that their days in the sun were over. But after 1704, the Assembly left Catholics alone and did not consider additional measures against them until 1716, when two ships carrying nearly 150 Jacobite prisoners arrived in the colony. Not only did Maryland's Catholics respond to the prisoners' arrival by purchasing as many of them as they could, but some prominent Catholics also spent the summer socializing with their new Jacobite servants, celebrating the birthday of the so-called "Pretender," James Stuart, the Catholic son of the deposed King James II.[14]

One of the people who toasted the health of the Pretender was William FitzRedmond, Charles Carroll of Annapolis's cousin and nephew to Charles Carroll the Settler, who had arrived in Maryland from Ireland shortly before the Protestant Associators launched their rebellion. At the time of the Jacobites' arrival, the Settler was already involved in a public dispute with Maryland's governor, John Hart, over the ban on Catholic officeholding. In violation of a direct order from the governor, Carroll had traveled to England a few months earlier, where he had met with the proprietor's representatives and presented a case for why Catholics should once again be allowed to hold office in Maryland. Carroll was unable to secure a proprietary order to restore all rights to the colony's Catholics, but he did return with a commission from Lord Baltimore that allowed him to "Order, Manage and Account for" all of the revenue that was generated for the proprietor in the colony—including fines.

When the Settler tried to use his commission to discharge the fine that William FitzRedmond was assessed for his "Traitorous, Wicked, Audacious & Insolent Action" in the summer of 1716, Maryland's governor appealed to the colonial assembly and accused Charles Carroll the Settler of having tricked the proprietor into giving a powerful commission "to a Papist." Charles Calvert, the fifth Lord Baltimore, was just sixteen years old at the time, and he had spent his first fifteen years of life as a Roman Catholic, making him extremely vulnerable, the governor insisted, to Carroll's "traitorous conspiracies."

Hart argued that no one in Maryland should be allowed to hold any public position without first swearing the Oath of Abjuration, which denied the Doctrine of Transubstantiation. The eight men serving in the Upper House of the Assembly agreed, and by August 1716, the Assembly had passed "An Act for the Better Security of the Peace and Safety of his Lordship's Government and the Protestant Interest within this Province." The Act effectively stripped Charles Carroll the Settler of his proprietary commission by declaring that anyone who had attended "any Popish Assembly, Conventicle or Meeting" was "incapable of taking, holding, or executing any Commission or Place of Trust within this Province."[15]

The Act was the second of three major moves against Maryland's Catholics that reflected lawmakers' fears of Jacobitism. The first move had been made shortly before the passage of the Act requiring the Oath of Abjuration; it restricted the right of Catholic widows and widowers to raise their children as Catholics, if their deceased spouses had been Protestant. The third move came in 1718, a year and a half after the Jacobites' arrival. By then, many of the prisoners had been released from their servitude, and lawmakers were incredibly uneasy about the proliferation of Jacobite sympathies among freemen in the colony.[16] In an effort to shore up and reaffirm Maryland's "English" identity, several members of the Lower House of the Assembly initiated a measure in May 1718 that they hoped would compel Maryland's Catholics to behave themselves by threatening to deport anyone who represented a challenge to the colony's English identity.

The measure did not actually pass. Nevertheless, it played an extremely important role in the making of an American Catholic identity, because when Maryland's Catholics defended themselves against the measure, they not only insisted that they had a claim to the rights of Englishmen—an assertion their own Church might not have supported unconditionally—they also tied their claim inextricably to the colonial context in which they made the claim. Maryland's Catholics insisted that they had the right to property, political representation, personal security, freedom of conscience, and the rule of law not simply because they were Englishmen, but because they were Englishmen who lived in Maryland, where the laws were governed by a constitution that was separate from and superior to the constitution of England.[17]

The measure that several members of the Lower House of the Assembly proposed in 1718 was tricky. It was an all-out repeal of the Act to Prevent the Growth of Popery in this Province that had been signed into law in 1704. The purpose of the proposed repeal, however, was not to make life easier for the Catholics living in Maryland; rather, the assemblymen wanted to throw out Maryland's law, so that they could defer to the recusancy laws of England instead.

Their proposal began by noting that the law passed by Maryland's assembly in 1704 had not worked. The "growth of popery" in the colony had not slowed down, and "professed Papists still multiply and increase in Number." This situation, while troubling, was not a fait accompli. "By one Act of Parliament made in . . . the Reign of His late Majesty, King William the Third," the assemblymen observed, "there is good Provision made to Prevent the Growth of Popery, as well in this Province, as throughout all others his Majesty's Dominions."[18] Protestants, in other words, need not resign themselves to being outnumbered, ultimately, by propagating papists; they simply needed to stop trying to solve the problem on their own. If Maryland's lawmakers repealed their indigenous Act to Prevent the Growth of Popery and instead deferred to the one passed by Parliament in England in 1700, the problem of punishing popery would become the purview of the English courts. Anyone in Maryland who was caught violating the well-codified recusancy laws of the parent country would be subject to deportation, and the colony's Catholic population would consequently be curbed.

The proposal was a flagrant violation of Maryland's separate constitution—at least according to Peter Atwood, an English-born

Jesuit who had begun serving in Maryland six years earlier, in 1712. Atwood was, of course, very concerned about the anti-Catholic goals of the lawmakers' proposal. Knowing that he could not rely upon the religious sympathies of Maryland's assemblymen, however, the priest chose to emphasize the autonomy that Maryland's lawmakers would be giving up if they implemented the plan. "That the Penal Laws of England extend not hither was for seventy years and more the opinion of all in Maryland," Atwood reminded the Assembly, drawing their attention to the distinctive nature of the principles and practices that animated society in colonial Maryland. Criminal laws in the colony had always been drafted by Maryland's assembly, not by Parliament. Any attempt to extend anything to the colony other than those English laws "deemed an Englishman's birthright," therefore, was "highly prejudicial to, if not destructive of our constitution."

The word "constitution" cropped up time and again in an essay that Atwood wrote to defend Maryland's Catholics against the effort to subject them to the laws of Parliament. "Altho our Government is framed... according to the model of that of England," the priest told his readers, Maryland had its own assembly, and the separate and unique nature of the constitution that guided that assembly had made it such that religious toleration was "far from... inconsistent" with the colony's identity. Respect for the collective Catholic right to worship freely may not have been a characteristic of life in England, but in Maryland, it was a "fundamental part of our constitution," according to Atwood. Indeed, "Liberty of Conscience" was the "reason behind the peopling of this province" and the "perpetual and inherent birthright of each Marylandian." Atwood warned the colony's Protestant assemblymen that "to strike [at it] would be to unhinge the Government, destroy our foundation, and reduce this flourishing Colony to ruin and confusion."[19]

The priest's threat was not an entirely idle one. A group of wealthy Catholic men had, in fact, recently considered removing themselves and their families from Maryland—and taking their considerable wealth and labor forces with them. These men sent a representative to London in 1718 to speak with the Spanish ambassador there about the possibility of acquiring some land in the West Indies. By all accounts, the ambassador was quite excited by the prospect of having a group of disgruntled British expatriates living in one of Spain's New World colonies.[20] Nothing ever came of the enquiry, however—possibly because the tobacco planters who contacted the ambassador were, in the end, daunted by the large capital outlays that were necessary to turn a profit in the sugar-producing colonies of the Caribbean.

In any event, it is noteworthy that in his essay, Peter Atwood spoke of both "an Englishman's birthright" and the "birthright of each Marylandian." The distinction was essential to his argument in 1718, and it was one that would ultimately have revolutionary ramifications when Protestant leaders in New England and Virginia articulated it in a different context sixty years later. Even as they insisted that they were good Englishmen, deserving of English rights, Maryland's Catholics did not—and could not—make their argument without appealing to a related, but different birthright: the one that they had as residents of a colony that, unlike England itself, had been founded with their best interests in mind.

To be sure, Peter Atwood was no revolutionary. He and the lay Catholics who utilized his argument in the years that followed were not bold enough during the Penal Period to insist that they were not English subjects. In many respects, Maryland's Catholics did not have the freedom in the first half of the eighteenth century to make such an audacious claim, publicly or even just internally. Many people in North America and England, after all, were arguing that Catholics could not be good Englishmen by virtue of their enslavement to the Pope in Rome. There was much about what it meant to be an Englishman that Maryland's Catholics wanted to see applied to themselves, however, as evidenced by the journey that Charles Carroll the Settler made to England, in an effort to restore voting rights to the colony's Catholics. Catholics were therefore not interested in 1718 in throwing off the mantle of English identity entirely.

But the fact is that long before Protestant colonists recognized that they had evolved into something different from their supposed countrymen in England, Catholic colonists understood that to be English in Maryland meant something different from what it meant to be English in England. When, in the wake of the Stamp Act of 1765, colonial leaders in Anglican Virginia, Congregationalist Massachusetts, and Quaker Pennsylvania started to insist that their rights as Englishmen were being violated by an English government that refused to recognize the separate nature of their colonies' constitutions, Catholics in Maryland heard an argument that was quite familiar to them.

The Lower House of the Assembly approved the proposal to repeal Maryland's indigenous law and defer to the recusancy laws of England, but the Upper House blocked the measure. It seems likely that squabbling between the Assembly's two houses, rather than Peter Atwood's eloquence, was the cause of the resolution's failure. Atwood was called before the Assembly following the publication of his essay, but for unknown reasons he never actually appeared, and there is no further discussion in the Assembly's minutes of his ideas. Atwood's beliefs about the separate nature of colonial constitutions had not yet found a mainstream audience in Maryland. His words, however, do seem to have had an impact on the Catholic community to which he belonged because Catholics in Maryland echoed his sentiments throughout the rest of the eighteenth century.[21]

Catholics used Atwood's belief that England's laws "extend not hither" when they attempted to defend their property from Protestant encroachment. In 1724, for example, the Catholic heirs of Robert Brooke used Atwood's understanding of Maryland's constitution to defend their inheritance against the challenges of Robert's brother, Thomas. Thomas was an Anglican convert, and Robert had been a Catholic priest. Thomas had not challenged his brother's share of their father's estate when the property had been left to them in 1689, but following Robert's death in 1723, Thomas insisted that his brother could not pass the property on to anyone in his will, since the property had never rightfully been his.

Thomas challenged his brother's claim to their father's estate on the grounds that England's "Act for the Further Preventing the Growth of Popery" had made it illegal for Catholic clergy to inherit land. The Maryland native John Darnall—who had been raised as a Catholic, but converted to Anglicanism so that he could practice law—represented Robert Brooke's heirs. He argued that British statutes did not apply to Maryland. The colony, after all, had its own "Act against Popery," and that Act, Darnall pointed out, did not prohibit the clergy from inheriting anything.

After nearly five years of litigation, a British court finally decided on the case. It was determined that Fr. Robert Brooke's claim to the estate was, in fact, legitimate because he had inherited "lands in the Plantations, where our Act against Popery . . . does not extend."[22] It was a seemingly unremarkable decision at the time. In three-and-a-half decades, however, the idea that laws passed by Parliament in England did not "extend" to the "lands in the Plantations" would become an animating argument in the Stamp Act riots, the nonimportation agreements, and the Boston Tea Party.

Although unambiguous, the British court's ruling did not end Protestant efforts to use English law to keep the Catholic clergy in Maryland from inheriting property. In the early 1740s, Dr. Charles Carroll, an Anglican convert, used English law to contest the right of his Jesuit nephew, James, to inherit family property. The estate in question had been that of James's uncle—also named James—and Dr. Charles Carroll was co-executor of that estate with his distant cousin, also named Charles. In this case, the co-executor was Charles Carroll of Annapolis.

At the time of the elder James Carroll's death, the younger James Carroll had not been old enough to claim his inheritance, and so the estate had been put into a trust that was to be managed by both of the Charles Carrolls. Dr. Carroll paid more attention to the estate than did his Catholic cousin; the attention he paid, however, was probably not what the courts had had in mind when they approved the trust. When it came time for James Carroll to claim his inheritance, a good portion of his estate had been spent or sold.

Undaunted by the prospect of an investigation, Dr. Carroll quickly followed Thomas Brooke's example and sought refuge in his nephew's status as a priest. James could not inherit the estate—or what was left of it—according to Dr. Carroll, because the laws of England prohibited Catholic clerical inheritance. The quarrel between James and Charles

Carroll of Annapolis, on the one side, and Dr. Charles Carroll, on the other, was bitter, and it dragged on for years. At one point, Charles Carroll of Annapolis became so despondent that he wrote to his friend, cousin, and fellow-Catholic, Clement Hill, about the case. In words that harkened back to the ideas of Peter Atwood, Carroll complained that "the First Settlers [in Maryland] were chiefly Roman Catholics" who did "not fly from Penal Laws [in England and Ireland] . . . at great personal cost to them, forseeing that their posterity would be subjected to the same here."[23]

Dr. Carroll died before any court in Maryland or England could issue a decree in the case. Because the lawsuit dragged on for many years, though—overlapping with the start of the French and Indian War in 1754—the bitterness that the family disagreement engendered had a long-range impact on Protestant–Catholic relations in the colony. According to Governor Horatio Sharpe, nearly everyone in Maryland was familiar with the squabble, and Dr. Charles Carroll became a veritable crusader against popery after his Catholic relations brought legal action against him. In 1755, shortly before he died, the Protestant Carroll circulated rumors that Catholics in Maryland had shown "Signs of Satisfaction & Joy" following the shocking defeat of England's General Edward Braddock by French forces in Pennsylvania, just a few miles north of the Maryland border. According to Dr. Carroll, Catholics were "Caballing" with "Negroes" on the eastern shore after they heard of the "unhappy Event" that had led to Braddock's death.[24]

It was an extremely serious charge, issued a little more than a year after the start of the French and Indian War and just a few months before the first group of what would eventually be nearly 1,000 French Canadian refugees arrived in Maryland. The *Maryland Gazette* had started fretting about the influx of Catholic exiles long before the first ships had even docked in Annapolis.[25] The Protestants who read the *Gazette* were understandably unnerved, therefore, when Dr. Charles Carroll told them that Maryland was already home to a group of Catholics who celebrated France's victories over the English.

Maryland's governor, Horatio Sharpe, had come over from England just one year before Dr. Carroll levied his charge. Sharpe launched an investigation, and in 1758, he informed Maryland's proprietor, Frederick Calvert—the sixth and final Lord Baltimore—that "none of the county courts ... could upon the strictest Enquiry find that any of the Papists had expressed themselves in an unbecoming manner." In fact, "if I was asked whether the conduct of the Protestants or Papists in this Province hath been most unexceptional," Sharpe wrote, "I should not hesitate to give Answer in favor of the latter."

Significantly, Governor Sharpe implied that if Catholics had expressed themselves in an unbecoming manner, it would not have been without reason. Taking it upon himself to defend Maryland's Catholics—some of whom had clearly become a part of his inner circle and had given him a history lesson on their colony's founding—Sharpe wrote to Frederick Calvert of the "extraordinary burdens" that Protestant lawmakers had placed upon Catholics in the colony. "It might perhaps be unknown," he suggested to the Anglican great-great-grandson of Maryland's original, Catholic proprietor, "that the People who first settled in this Province were for the most part Roman Catholicks & that although every other Sect was tolerated, a Majority of the inhabitants continued Papists till the [Glorious] Revolution."[26]

Sharpe's exegesis on Maryland's history would not have earned him an 'A' on the exam. Although Catholics did comprise a greater portion of the colony's population before the Glorious Revolution than they did in 1758, Catholics had never been a "Majority of the inhabitants" in Maryland, not even during the first year of the colony's founding. The governor's mistaken understanding of Maryland's seventeenth-century demographics must have come from conversations he had had with prominent Catholic property owners, many of whom were quite vocal about the extent to which Maryland's lawmakers violated the colony's constitution whenever they enacted or enforced anti-Catholic legislation.

In the early 1750s, as false rumors spread that "a great Number of French and Indians were within thirty miles of Baltimore Town," the Lower House of the Assembly once again considered a measure that was designed to apply England's recusancy laws directly to Maryland. This time, not only did the lawmakers want to subject Maryland's

Catholics to the laws of Parliament, they also wanted to tap the colony's public treasury to reward anyone "who shall apprehend any Popish bishop, priest, or Jesuit."[27]

The measure passed in the Lower House, and in response, Henry Brooke, Charles Carroll of Annapolis, Daniel Carroll, Henry Darnall II, Philip Darnall, Ignatius Digges, Francis Hall, Clement Hill, Edward Neale, Henry Rozer, and Basil Waring sent a petition to the Upper House. They asked the members of that body not to approve the measure because it would deny Catholics "all those Civil and Religious Rights which they now enjoy." Granted, by the 1750s, Catholics in Maryland had been stripped of most of the rights their ancestors had enjoyed throughout the tenure of the Catholic Calverts. Still, Maryland's penal laws were better than the penal laws of England—where statutes had been passed during the reign of King George I that required Catholics to pay a double-tax on their land and to register their estates, so that royal commissioners could confiscate up to two-thirds of the estates' value.[28]

The petitioners challenged lawmakers to "make some Enquiries into the Conduct and Behavior of the Roman Catholicks of this Province." Any investigation would reveal that "there is not one Man amongst them who does not pay all imaginable Duty to the present Government, and entire Submission to its laws." Maryland's Catholics, the petitioners insisted, were good and reliable Englishmen who could be trusted to defend the colony from its enemies. Not only that, but they were also good and reliable Marylandians—something that could not be said of the lawmakers who seriously considered implementing anti-Catholic legislation. "The free exercise of Religion to all professing to believe in Jesus Christ," after all, "was the fundamental and unchanging law of this country."[29]

In a separate letter that he sent to the Upper House on his own, Charles Carroll of Annapolis reminded the assemblymen that "a Number of Gentlemen of good and ancient Families" were living in Maryland—and contributing significantly to the colony's financial success—because their ancestors, "encouraged by the Faith of a Royal Charter and an Act of Assembly of this Province," had "quit their native

Countries, Friends, and Relations," and "transported themselves into this Province, then a Wilderness, and in the Hands of a barbarous and Savage People, hoping and confiding that by such a Sacrifice they should procure to themselves and their Descendants all the religious and Civil Rights they were deprived of in his Majesty's Dominions in Europe."[30]

The Assembly's efforts to deny Catholics their civil and religious liberties were thoroughly un-Marylandian. This notion became a fundamental component of Catholic identity in eighteenth-century Maryland. In England, the animating force behind the country's constitution may have been the Declaration of Right of 1689, which barred Catholics from the throne and declared them to be a threat to "the safety and welfare of this Protestant Kingdom." In Maryland, however, the animating force behind the constitution was the charter that King Charles I had bestowed upon Cecilius Calvert and his descendants. It was the charter that had determined the "usages and customs" that would govern life in Maryland. It was the charter that had enabled Cecilius Calvert to pass the first Act of religious toleration in the British-speaking world. And it was the charter that had brought Catholics to Maryland in the first place.[31]

In the end, the Upper House of the Assembly once again sided with the Catholics, deciding that the proposal to apply England's recusancy laws to Maryland "contains great Penalties & Incapacities, and ... we are not at Present apprised of their Immediate necessity."[32] Tellingly, however, the lawmakers did not affirm the Catholic assertion that Maryland's constitution was separate from that England. It was ten years before the passage of the Stamp Act, and Protestants in Maryland were still happy to think of themselves as potentially being subject to parliamentary control.

The assault on Catholic liberties that occurred in the 1750s was particularly jarring because it came after a thirty-year period of relatively peaceful relations between Catholics and Protestants in the colony. After the Upper House of the Assembly rejected the Lower House's effort in 1718 to apply England's recusancy laws to Maryland, anxieties over the Jacobite presence in the colony died down. Remarkably, not even a second rebellion in Scotland—and a second round of Jacobite prisoners less than a year later—could provoke the legislative ire of Maryland's assemblymen.

When word of the Jacobite Rising of 1745 reached the colonies, Daniel Hearn of Anne Arundel County supposedly issued a toast in which he called King George II's father a "turnip sewer." Lawrence Robinson and Cornelius Scantling allegedly said they hoped Catholics would soon be able to "wash their hands in the hearts [sic] Blood of the Protestants." In response to these toasts and rumors that Catholics were stockpiling arms in the Monocacy Valley, Governor Thomas Bladen published a proclamation in the *Maryland Gazette*, ordering the Jesuits to "forbear traitorous practices." He also sent a letter to Fr. Richard Molyneaux, Superior of the Maryland Mission, asking the Jesuits to instruct their congregants not to gather in large groups—especially with "Negroes under pretense of Divine Worship"—or to engage in other behavior that might place them in a suspicious light. Yet, no legislative action was taken against Catholics in the wake of The '45, and years later, Catholic leaders would recall that "though deprived of our rights and Privileges ... from the year 1717 or 1718 to the year 1751 ... we enjoyed peace and quiet."[33]

Part of the reason Catholic–Protestant relations were peaceful during this period is that three of the four men who served in the governor's seat between 1720 and 1752 had strong ties to the Catholic Church and were hesitant, therefore, to encourage Maryland's Protestants to act on their fears of popery. Charles Calvert and Benedict Leonard Calvert, cousin and brother to the fifth Lord Baltimore respectively, had both been raised as Catholics and converted to the Church of England under some duress. Thomas Bladen's mother, Anne van Swearingen, was the Catholic daughter of Garret van Swearingen, a wealthy Catholic landowner originally from Holland who had arrived in Maryland via New York following the English takeover of New Amsterdam in 1664.[34] These three governors, Protestant though they were, were all better for Maryland's Catholics than Francis Nicholson, John Seymour, or John Hart had been. Those three men had arrived in the colony looking to use and abuse Catholics to establish their political legitimacy.

Understanding what the Glorious Revolution had been all about, Maryland's Catholics also worked hard during this period to establish and advertise their English loyalties. When George II became the king of England in 1727, they congratulated him on his coronation and affirmed their loyalty to him. In 1732, when the Anglican proprietor and his wife, Mary Janson, arrived in the colony for a visit, Maryland's Catholics presented them with an address, in which they told Charles Calvert of their "constant allegiance to his most sacred Majesty," their "dutiful regard for his royal family," and their "obedience to your Lordship's government." In this same address, the Catholic writers also passive-aggressively welcomed the proprietor to "this your province which your pious and noble ancestors have founded with ... great zeal, hazard, and expense to the enlargement of the British empire." Keenly aware of how far Maryland had strayed from the constitution that those noble ancestors had built, the writers told Calvert they had "undoubted reason to conclude ... that your Lordship's character will be no less conspicuous for carrying on and encouraging what [your ancestors] so nobly began."[35]

In the 1720s, 1730s, and 1740s, Catholics participated in politics to the fullest extent that they were allowed, petitioning local lawmakers to reject a stinting bill that would have limited tobacco production in the colony, and utilizing their marital and familial connections to prominent members of the General Assembly to influence other items of legislation that affected them as businessmen, property owners, farmers, and Catholics. While the editors of the *Maryland Gazette* did report on the political maneuverings of Catholics like Charles Carroll of Annapolis, Henry Darnall II, and Richard Bennett, at no point in this period did the editors suggest that the men's religious identity made their political activity a threat to the colony.[36]

In these halcyon days, Anglican vestrymen commissioned Catholic carpenters to build and repair churches in Anne Arundel and Prince George's Counties. Jesuits distributed pamphlets to Protestants and challenged Anglican ministers to public debates. Catholics attended worship services in Anglican churches, and Anglicans went to hear Catholic priests say Mass in private homes. In 1734, Reverend Samuel Smith, rector of the All Hallow's Parish in Anne Arundel County, confided to his friend, Arthur Holt, that sometimes when he was too sick to hold Anglican services, his parishioners would visit the homes of their Catholic neighbors and attend Mass there. Holt did not condemn Smith for allowing Anglicans to do this; he merely warned the minister to be careful, since the Jesuits were always "seeking to convert the innocent to the lesser ways of Rome."[37]

There is even some evidence that during this period, Catholics may have had limited (albeit it very limited) success in getting Protestants in Maryland to accept that their Catholic identity did not automatically render them unfit to claim the mantle of English identity. In 1740, the Lower House of the Assembly recommended that Dr. Charles Carroll, who had recently converted to Anglicanism, be put in charge of a military expedition that was going to South America. The contingent was part of a greater British effort to combat Spanish influence in what is now Colombia. The members of the Upper House, however—familiar, perhaps, with Dr. Carroll's mismanagement of James Carroll's inheritance—rejected the idea of putting Dr. Carroll in charge of the expedition.

The Lower House assumed that the Upper House was uncomfortable with Carroll's formerly Catholic identity. Several of the doctor's friends and colleagues wrote to the Upper House, therefore, reminding its members that other converts from Catholicism, such and Henry and John Darnall, had been trusted with prominent positions in Maryland's government—and that the Upper House had not expressed concern about those appointments when they had been made. The Upper House responded by pointing out that the Darnalls had come from an English Catholic background, whereas Dr. Charles Carroll was Irish. The distinction was important, the Upper House insisted, because of the well-known "national Antipathy" that existed between the English and the Irish on account of the "Conquest of the latter by the former and the continued Subjection and Restraint the Irish are under to the English."[38] Henry and John Darnell were undoubtedly better men after they had converted to Anglicanism; even before, however, the Upper House was willing to allow that the brothers had been "English."

Of course, the cooperative spirit that characterized Catholic–Protestant relations between 1718 and 1751 did not mean that Protestant fears of popery had completely disappeared. The same people who spoke glowingly of Henry and John Darnall when defending Dr. Charles Carroll also complained about the Darnall brothers' failure to attend Anglican worship services, and they hinted that the brothers' conversions were fake, since Henry and John both continued to send their sons to Catholic schools. Although the *Maryland Gazette* did not suggest that Charles Carroll of Annapolis and Richard Bennett were dangerous when each Catholic man used his money and influence to get the Assembly to reject the tobacco stinting bill, the *Gazette* did deliberately publish stories "from which the Roman Catholics in this Province may learn the unhappy condition of Protestants in France, and the Cruelty with which they are treated in that Country, the least bigoted of any Popish Kingdom in Europe." During King George's War from 1744 to 1748, the *Gazette* also published reports about how the "solicitations and arts practiced by our enemies the French and their Jesuitical Emissaries, have rendered the fidelity of the Six Nations of Indians to be suspected," even though neither the fighting, nor the Iroquois, themselves, were anywhere near Maryland.[39]

Still, the anti-Catholic rhetoric published in the *Gazette* during King George's War paled in comparison to the rhetoric the editors published after General Edward Braddock was killed just a few miles away from Maryland's border. After Braddock's defeat, the newspaper helped launch a campaign to raise money "towards defending our Frontier Inhabitants." The editors warned their "Protestant Reader[s]" that the people living along Maryland's panhandle would be subjected to "Horrid Barbarity" by the "American Allies" of King Louis XV of France, if they did not "give up [their] Religion, Liberty, and every Thing that is dear and valuable, and submit to be his Vassals, and dupes to the Romish clergy, whose most tender Mercies are but hellish cruelties, whenever they have power to exercise them."[40]

The anti-Catholic rhetoric that characterized the 1750s was qualitatively different from the rhetoric that occasionally cropped up in the Assembly or the *Gazette* during the 1720s, 1730s, and 1740s. Both categories of rhetoric equated Catholicism with tyranny and Protestantism with English identity. During the 1750s, however, the rhetoric was more graphic, personal, and inflammatory. Catholics were accused of fixing elections, fraternizing with Indians, and encouraging slaves in the colony to rise up against their Protestant masters. Readers of the *Gazette* learned from a man who claimed to have been taken prisoner by Indians in western Maryland that "a small Party of French, with about 2,000 Indians" had "scalped and plundered" the people living along the Monongahela River in what is now West Virginia. Three months later, readers were told that "French Papists" were wreaking havoc on the frontier. "They frequently commit murders, and laid much of the county waste."[41]

The impact that anti-Catholic rhetoric had on the lives of Maryland's Catholics was also far more severe in the 1750s. Before the French and Indian War, that rhetoric had rarely translated into any legislative proposals. Prompted by an anonymous letter to the *Gazette* in 1754, however, in which the author suggested that Catholic landowners ought to be stripped of their property, so that Catholicism in Maryland would develop the same impoverished and impotent qualities that it had in Ireland, the Lower House of the Assembly proposed a bill that would have required all Catholic priests to swear the Oaths of Allegiance and Abjuration. Those who did not would forfeit all of their property. Since the Church was, technically, outlawed in Maryland, the land held by the Jesuits was held by them individually—not corporately. Because the Oath of Abjuration denied the Doctrine of Transubstantiation, all priests would have had to refuse it; they could not continue to be priests otherwise. Had the Upper House approved the bill, therefore, the Jesuits would have lost thousands of acres of property—and in a colony where the Catholic Church was not established, that property was essential to the Jesuits' survival.

The bill called for the government to sell the land at auction, with the proceeds going toward the colony's defense against the French. The

Upper House of the Assembly remained rigid, however, and its members, many of whom were related to prominent Catholics, rejected the bill in the spring of 1754. It was only a matter of time, though, before that house's delegates realized that they, too, were going to have to sway in the increasingly powerful currents of anti-Catholicism.[42]

That time came after the election of 1754, when Maryland's Protestant voters handed pink slips to 60 percent of the lawmakers in the Lower House who had refused to endorse anti-Catholic legislation. The number of people in the Lower House who exhibited Catholic sympathies had been extremely small to begin with—just twenty out of sixty-nine members. After the election of 1754, however, the number of Lower House delegates whom Catholics could rely upon was reduced to eight.[43]

The times had changed in Maryland. Protestant England was at war with Catholic France, and although that did not represent a great departure from the trajectory of English–French relations throughout the eighteenth century, the fighting was now right next door. The members of the Upper House were not chosen through a general election; the governor appointed them. Nevertheless, the overwhelming defeat of the Catholic-friendly forces in the Lower House made it clear to the men in the Upper House that they no longer had the liberty to protect their Catholic friends and relatives. Even in England, Frederick Calvert, who had inherited the proprietorship upon his father's death in 1751, was feeling pressure from Britain's new Secretary of State, Thomas Robinson, to prove that the Catholics in Maryland were not "too much encouraged."[44]

In 1756, the Lower House passed a supply bill that called for a tax of twelve pence (i.e., one shilling) per one hundred acres on all privately held land, so that Maryland could fund the £40,000 wartime requisition that King George II was demanding from the colony. Under the provisions of the bill, Catholic landowners would have to pay twenty-four pence per one hundred acres because they were prohibited by law from serving in the militia and could not, therefore, contribute to the requisition through military service.[45]

Benedict Calvert, who served in the Upper House of the Assembly and was sympathetic toward Catholics, wrote to Charles Carroll of

Annapolis on May 11, 1756, informing him of the double-tax that had passed in the Lower House. Carroll, Clement Hill, Basil Waring, and Ignatius Digges immediately wrote to Governor Horatio Sharpe, asking him and the members of the Upper House to reject the tax, which Carroll's son, Charles Carroll of Carrolton, would later insist was "subversive of the foundations of the Maryland constitution."[46]

Sharpe, however, had already been backed into a corner by several members of the Lower House who accused him of having exercised his powers "against the British constitution" when he pardoned a criminal who had converted to Catholicism while he was in jail, and then refused to press charges for illegal proselytizing against the priest responsible for the conversion. The Lower House was demanding that Henry Darnall III be removed from his position as Attorney General, since they did not trust that his conversion to the Church of England was sincere, and they were threatening to apply to King George II for "Redress and Protection" if Governor Sharpe did not respond to their grievances. Under these circumstances, the members of Maryland's Upper House felt that they had to approve the double-tax, and Horatio Sharpe signed it into law on May 15, 1756.[47]

The tax was not that much money. At two shillings per 100 acres, Charles Carroll of Annapolis would have had to pay less than £16 per year on the 15,400 acres he had inherited from his father. It was hardly a priestly sum—especially considering that Carroll paid more than £30 a year to the priest who said Mass in his home.[48]

When the Upper House approved the double-tax, however, it was sign of just how powerful the forces of anti-Catholicism had become in the midst of the French and Indian War. The war was like oxygen to the embers of anti-popery that had been quietly—and seemingly harmlessly—burning in Maryland throughout the 1720s, 1730s, and 1740s. The members of the Upper House no longer felt they had the political strength to resist the overwhelming need that Maryland's Protestants had to protect their English identity by incinerating the Catholic presence in their colony. When the Lower House called for the Jesuits to be banished from Maryland, the best response the Upper House could muster was a proposal that would allow the Jesuits to stay, so long as they registered with the government, gave up their land, and swore that they would not help the French.[49] It was hardly a spirited defense of the colony's Catholics.

In a sign of just how bold the fear-mongers in Maryland had become, the sheriff of Talbot County arrested Fr. James Beadnall in September 1756 for saying Mass in a layperson's private home, even though private Masses had been allowed under Maryland law since 1707. The arrest was made on the grounds that England's laws prohibited Catholics from "saying mass, or exercising any other part of the office or function of a popish bishop or priest." Beadnall's friends were eventually able to get the charges against him dropped because of a lack of evidence, but not until after the priest had posted a bond of £1,500 sterling. No officials in Talbot County expressed any concern about the fact that their sheriff was enforcing parliamentary legislation in the colony.[50]

Maryland's Catholics protested that they were not the colony's enemies, that they would "be not only Fools but madmen to entertain any thoughts of disturbing the peace of the Government." Looking again to Maryland's constitution—rather than to the "British constitution" that the Lower House's members had been so concerned about when they strong-armed the governor—lay Catholics argued that their ancestors had "little dreamed that we should be troubled on the score of religion" when they made the arduous journey across the Atlantic. In a display of hyperbole that revealed just how distraught they were, Maryland's Catholics told the proprietor that the double-tax would reduce them "to a level with our Negroes."[51]

In sermons, Maryland's priests encouraged their congregants to "stick steadily to your Faith" and "adhere firm to your Religion" as "you suffer Persecution for Justice sake" and are "deprived of your liberties!" While most of the Catholic clergy counseled patience during this period, Fr. James Carroll—whose inheritance had been stolen several years earlier by Dr. Charles Carroll—actually encouraged Catholics to act. Preaching to a group of laypeople who had gathered in John Crosby's home in 1756, Fr. Carroll exhorted Maryland's Catholics to "manfully defend ourselves and our holy liberties, liberties belonging to the children of God alone."[52] They were words that would have warmed William Blackstone's heart—except that they had been uttered by a Papist.

When he traveled to England to contest the double-tax to anyone who would listen, Fr. George Hunter brought along a copy of Maryland's charter—the document that Catholics insisted was supposed to make Maryland something better than England. The double-tax, Hunter insisted, was "a thing never before practiced in the Province." It was a specific tax on a specific population that had been specifically denied representation in the colony's assembly. As he showed Frederick Calvert a copy of the charter—the charter that Calvert had, in fact, inherited when he became the sixth Lord Baltimore—Fr. Hunter spoke of the "solemn promises" made to Maryland's ancestors, which had "induced them to quit their native soil, in order to settle in that new Colony, and secure to their posterity a peaceable, quiet habitation in the free exercise of their religion."[53] The priest's arguments, alas, did not work.

Frederick Calvert ultimately approved the double-tax. In words that would become meaningless in just twenty years, he also settled the debate about whether England's laws could be applied to the colonies. "The Method on the prosecution of Roman Catholics on Religious Concerns in Maryland," he wrote to Governor Sharpe in reference to Fr. James Beadnall, "is by known Laws not only of the Province But also by Acts of Parliament throughout his Majesty's Realm."[54] Beadnall's arrest, in other words, was valid, even though Maryland's laws had specifically allowed the Catholic clergy to say Mass in private homes. The actions of Parliament had made it so.

Calvert's and Sharpe's endorsement of the double-tax depressed many of Maryland's Catholics and "set others on winding up their affairs in order to quit [the Province.]" Among those who seriously considered looking "for peace & Quiet elsewhere" was Charles Carroll of Annapolis, who actually placed an ad in the *Maryland Gazette* two weeks after the governor signed the supply bill, announcing that he was planning to sell his lands and call in the numerous loans he had made to Catholics and Protestants in Maryland and Pennsylvania. Those loans totaled nearly £24,000 sterling, plus interest.[55]

Carroll wanted to move to Louisiana, where he imagined the French-administered government would be more accepting of his Catholicism. In June 1757, he traveled to France to negotiate a deal for territory along the Mississippi River. The trip was deliberately shrouded in secrecy, and details from it, therefore, are unavailable to historians. Two months before he left, however, Carroll received a letter from his niece, Eleanor, in which she alluded to "the scheme the Roman Catholics were upon and particularly yourself," suggesting that Charles Carroll of Annapolis was not the only Catholic who seriously considered removing his wealth and slave labor from Maryland.[56]

As it turns out, Carroll did not relocate to Louisiana—though he was, apparently, still enamored with the idea two and a half years after his initial trip to France. "By your last, you seem still resolved upon Leaving Maryland," a twenty-three-year-old Charley Carroll wrote to his father from London in February 1760. "I must own you have great reason to be displeased with the people." The younger Carroll understood his father's frustration and, more deeply, his disappointment. Remarking on the love that his mother had for Maryland, Charley Carroll theorized that if she had "been as long absent from it, as I have been, that love so undeservedly bestowed on an ungreatful [sic] country, would be greatly diminished."

Charley admitted that "I cant conceive how any Roman Catholick, especially an Irish Roman Catholick, can consent to Live in England or any the British dominions, if he is able to do otherwise." Nevertheless, he felt that the impulse to move to Louisiana was unwise. "We suffer at present in Maryland for our religion," he acknowledged, but "if you repair to France, there you will only exchange religious for civil Tyranny." Of the two, civil tyranny was by far the worse. "Civil oppression has nothing to console us," Charley Carroll wrote. "Religious persecutions are always attended with this consolation at least, of not going unrewarded."[57]

The fact of the matter was that for a Roman Catholic like Charley Carroll, there was no "otherwise" than living in "any the British dominions." As difficult and frustrating as it was to be English and Catholic, Carroll believed the combination was the best scenario any Catholic in the world could hope for in 1761. At the start of that year, Charley Carroll wrote to his father that he would "choose to live under an English government, rather than any other—Catholic I mean—for I know of no Catholic country where that greatest blessing, civil liberty, is enjoyed." Charles Carroll of Annapolis was justified in being "highly disgusted with Maryland." But after a decade in France and several years more in England, Charley Carroll wrote that he felt "obliged" to settle in his native land because of "our importance there"—and because he felt that in Maryland, there was a "probable" chance of "our enemies [sic] animosity abating."[58]

Charles Carroll of Carrollton was right. In the years that followed the end of the French and Indian War in 1763, the fears of popery that had ignited at the start of that conflict continued to burn in Maryland—but increasingly, Catholics, themselves, were not the primary target of the flames. When anxieties about English identity were the fuel that fed anti-popery, it made sense that Maryland's Catholics should find themselves penned-in by the inferno. So long as the rhetoric equated Catholicism with tyranny and Protestantism with English identity, Catholics in Maryland could do nothing to secure their rights as Englishmen.

But after the passage of the Stamp Act in 1765, the line between tyranny and English identity became blurry. England's colonists continued to use the language of anti-popery to defend their rights and express their fears of tyranny, because that language was evocative, effective, and easily understood. But the language was no longer directed against the Jesuits who lived in Maryland or the wealthy, disenfranchised laypeople those Jesuits served. Rather, the language of anti-popery was directed against the members of Parliament and, eventually, the King of England—all of whom were Protestant.

Maryland's lawmakers were slower than their counterparts in Virginia and Massachusetts to see Parliament as a corrupting influence on England's constitution—and, perhaps not surprisingly, they were also slower to insist that their colony's constitution was separate from that of England. But they did, eventually, reach the conclusion that independence was necessary and unavoidable, and when they did, it was thanks in no small part to the efforts of Charles Carroll of Carrollton, who took ideas that had been sustaining the Catholic community in Maryland for more than half a century by that point, secularized them, and made them applicable to the lives of every free, white person living in Maryland.

6

Papists Become Patriots

In late August 1813, as he and his wife, Abigail, were mourning the death of their daughter, Nabby, John Adams wrote a letter to Thomas McKean, the former governor of Pennsylvania. Looking for an issue that would distract him from his grief, Adams grumbled to McKean about the "apathy" and "antipathy of this nation to their own history." He wondered what, if anything could be done to make Americans more aware of what had happened in the years running up to the Revolutionary War. In a lament that would be echoed by generations of college instructors in the decades to come, the former president observed that "while thousands of frivolous novels are read with eagerness and got by the heart, the history of our own native country is not only neglected, but despised and abhorred."[1]

Adams was being melodramatic—his judgment clouded, perhaps, by his bereavement. The fact was that by the time he wrote to McKean in 1813, several major histories of the American Revolution had already been published. Some, such as Mercy Otis Warren's *History of the Rise, Progress, and Termination of the American Revolution*, were wildly popular with American audiences, while others, such as Jonathan Boucher's *A View to the Causes and Consequences of the American Revolution*, resonated with British readers.[2]

Boucher placed the rebellion's origins squarely in New England, where "their politics, their customs ... their language and their manners" were all derived from the Puritans, a "contrary" lot who "abhorred Monarchy, and approved only of Republican Government." He had been living in Maryland at the time of the revolt, serving as the rector of St. Barnabas Church in Prince George's County (a fact that might have rendered his expertise on the contrary nature of the New England Mind a little suspect to any discerning reader). Boucher considered the Stamp Act to be "oppressive, impolitic, and illegal," and he was highly critical of the Royal Proclamation of 1763, which had prevented many colonists—including his friend James Maury, tutor to Thomas Jefferson—from settling beyond the Appalachian Mountains. Nevertheless, Jonathan Boucher was a Tory, a staunch supporter of the king's prerogative.[3]

In 1796, as he sat in his home in Surrey, England, recalling the events of the 1770s, Reverend Boucher was flummoxed. He was confident that without the rabble-rousing of New Englanders like Sam Adams and John Hancock, the American Revolution never would have happened. Yet, he found it difficult to explain why his former neighbors in Maryland, with their history of "disaffection for New-England," had been willing to "rush into a civil war against a nation they loved" at the instigation of those same New Englanders "for whom they entertained an hereditary national disesteem, confirmed by their own personal dislike." The minister found it "incredible" that a group of Chesapeake tobacco farmers "in full possession and enjoyment of all the peace and . . . security which the best government in the world can give," had joined forces with a coterie of sophistical Yankee merchants to wage war against a country that had given them so much.[4]

In the end, Boucher concluded that the unlikely alliance must have been a consequence of the "old prejudices against Papists" that war hawks in Boston had used to tarnish the king's reputation following the passage of the Quebec Act in August 1774. This New England rhetoric, the Anglican minister insisted, had trickled down the North Atlantic seaboard, thanks to the colonies' well-developed newspaper network. It had found an anxious audience in the Protestant majority of Maryland, where the significant and still growing Catholic population had given added urgency to the Patriots' hyperbolic claims that King George III's decision to let Canadian Catholics practice their faith freely was the first step in his plan to subject everyone in his North American dominions to the "tyrant hand of popish power."⁵

According to Boucher, the anti-Catholic, anti-British rhetoric that had followed the passage of the Quebec Act had left Catholics in Maryland "wavering and undetermined" as to whether they should ally themselves with the Patriots or the Loyalists. "Though dissenters and republicans were their enemies," the minister wrote, the English "could hardly be said to be their friends," either. England's laws against popery, after all, were harsher than the ones that had been governing life in Maryland for more than eighty years.

Following the publication of the Declaration of Independence, it "soon became easy to foresee that neither [Catholics], nor any other, would long be permitted to enjoy a neutrality" in the colony. Jonathan Boucher launched a campaign, therefore, that he hoped would convince Catholics to cast their lots with the Crown. In his capacity as a representative of the Church of England, Reverend Boucher delivered a sermon that called for religious toleration in Maryland, not just for dissenting Protestants, but for Catholics, as well.⁶

Given Maryland's history, it was reasonable for Boucher to expect that his words would resonate positively with the colony's Catholics. Yet, the minister's loyalist tendencies were actually exposed to Annapolis' Committee of Safety when, "soon after the delivery of this sermon . . . a Catholic officiously and eagerly stepped forward as a witness against him . . . [and] preferred a charge, by which it was hoped . . . [his] inimicality to America might have been proved."⁷ Boucher's scheme, quite simply, had not worked. Catholics in Maryland were not "wavering and undetermined" about where their loyalties should lie. Despite the harangues of the Patriots against the "tyrant hand of Popish power," and despite the less antagonistic, even sympathetic stance that Jonathan Boucher had taken in reference to his Catholic neighbors, Catholics in Prince George's County, Maryland, had sided with the Patriots and joined them in excising the contaminant of Loyalism from within their borders.

The Catholic community in Maryland endorsed, contributed to, fought for, and died for an ideology that rested upon republican principles and came wrapped in the rhetoric of anti-Catholicism. On the surface, it was an almost absurd incongruence—one that the British essayist Samuel Johnson seized upon in 1776, when he noted with great sarcasm that all of Maryland's residents "are now become such excellent Protestants," that they "totally forget that their own existence as a Colony is owing to this very religion which [the Sons of Liberty] abhor."[8]

It was true that by 1776, Maryland's leaders had more or less accepted that the king and Parliament had become tyrants and that independence was the only way the colonists could preserve their God-given rights. In comparison to the other twelve colonies that declared their independence from Great Britain, however, Maryland was a little slow to jump on the revolutionary bandwagon. The outrage over Parliament's passage of the Stamp Act in 1765 was palpable in the colony, and Maryland's merchants did eagerly participate in a multi-colony nonimportation agreement that the colonists hoped would hurt England's manufacturers and show Parliament just how dependent the country's economy was on its colonial markets. But two-and-a-half years later, when business and political leaders in Boston, New York, and Philadelphia called for a similar boycott of British goods to protest the Townshend Duties, the merchants in Baltimore and Annapolis were reluctant to participate.

In fact, very few members of Maryland's general assembly expressed concerns about the Revenue Act of 1767, which created the now infamous duties on lead, paper, paint, glass, and tea. Baltimore's merchants did eventually agree to a ban on imports in 1769, but their commitment to the ban was sporadic, and their reasons for agreeing to it do not seem to have been rooted in any genuine anger about parliamentary taxation. Rather, Maryland's merchants were responding to the demands of their colleagues in Philadelphia, who were adamant about the need for a boycott. In an age before dredging, when Baltimore's harbor could not handle any ships that had a draft of more than eight feet, the merchants in Maryland relied heavily upon the port of

Philadelphia to conduct their business. They were in no position to offend the merchants who dominated that port, therefore—at least not overtly.⁹

In Maryland, the concerns about the Stamp Act seem to have been rooted in something other than just the idea that it was an internal tax, collected on business done within the colonies, rather than at the ports; or that it had been imposed on the colonies by lawmakers whose electorate lived in England, rather than in the New World; or that it was a measure designed to generate income for Parliament, rather than simply ensure that the colonies maintained a properly "mercantilist" relationship with the parent country. These were the problems with the Stamp Act that people like James Otis of Massachusetts and Patrick Henry of Virginia articulated. It was one thing for Parliament to do as it had done in 1733, when it passed an act that required the colonists to purchase their molasses from British producers and pay a duty that helped finance the enforcement of that requirement. It was quite another, Otis and Henry insisted, for Parliament to tax any man who wanted to get married or read a newspaper in the colonies, and then use the money generated by the tax to pay off the debts that England's government had incurred because of Parliament's decision to go to war with France.¹⁰

To be sure, Otis's and Henry's ideas did have an audience in Maryland. But the enthusiasm that the people there showed for these ideas tended to be dependent upon the state of the colony's economy. When times were bad, as they were in 1765 thanks to declining tobacco prices, escalating exchange rates, and an overstock of finished goods, the Patriots' complicated polemics about revenue generation and internal taxation found fertile ground in Maryland. When times were good, however, as they were in 1768, after two years in a row of bad tobacco crops in Spain, the arguments about parliamentary taxation had little effect.¹¹

Daniel Dulany's reaction to the imperial crisis is a nice example of Maryland's contradictory combination of passion and ambivalence. In October 1765, six months after Parliament passed the Stamp Act, Dulany published a pamphlet that was extremely popular with his friends and neighbors in Maryland. The pamphlet challenged an opinion commonly held by the members of Prime Minister George Grenville's government—namely, that the colonists were "virtually represented" in Parliament, just as women, children, and people who lived in English boroughs that did not have assigned MPs were virtually represented. Such reasoning, Dulany argued, was specious; the colonists, after all, had no opportunity to interact with the members of Parliament, the way the people who lived in unrepresented boroughs like Leeds or Manchester did. Like Patrick Henry, Dulany accepted "the right of the British Parliament to regulate the trade of the colonies" through "duties on imports and exports." He denied, however, that Parliament had any right to "impose an internal tax on the colonies without their consent for the single purpose of raising revenue."

It was this idea that Parliament was looking to generate income for itself—that is, to tax the colonists, rather than simply regulate them, as it had done with the Molasses Act—that made the Stamp Act so offensive to Daniel Dulany. Yes, free people did pay taxes. But liberty demanded that those taxes be determined only by the people's representatives, and in North America, the people's representatives served in the colonial assemblies, not in Parliament. Not even King George, himself, could tax British citizens. "The levying of money, by Pretense of [Royal] Prerogative," Dulany reminded his readers, "without their Consent who are to Pay it is illegal." This well-established precedent in the "Constitution of England," the former mayor of Annapolis insisted, "effectually establishes the very Principle contended for by the Colonies."[12]

It was a potent argument—and one that gained a loyal following far beyond the boundaries of Maryland. John Joachim Zubly, a Presbyterian minister from Georgia who ultimately opposed the war for independence because of its violence, echoed Dulany's sentiments in 1769 when he wrote that "no member" of any legislative body could "represent any but those by whom he hath been elected." Yet, two years after Daniel Dulany published his pamphlet, when Parliament passed the Revenue Act of 1767 "for the sole purpose of levying money" (in the words of Pennsylvania's "farmer," John Dickinson), nary a peep was heard out of Maryland's lawmakers, not even out of Daniel Dulany, Jr.[13]

By the start of 1768, the colony's economy had recovered. Maryland's merchants had sold off their excess inventories, thanks to the boycott on imports that they had participated in during the Stamp Act crisis, and the demand for Chesapeake tobacco among consumers in Continental Europe was on the rise. That increased demand was destined to continue for the next four and a half years. Maryland's farmers and merchants, in other words, were in a position to pay the tax on lead, paper, paint, glass, and tea; the Townshend Duties did not bother them, therefore, the way the Stamp tax had.

Historians have traditionally concluded that the economy was one of two primary factors influencing the lethargic reaction of Maryland's residents to the growing imperial crisis. The other factor was the political divide between, on the one side, the proprietor and his appointed minions in the Upper House of the Assembly and, on the other side, the popularly elected landowners who made up the Lower House of the Assembly. Throughout the 1750s and 1760s, members of the so-called "Country Party" in Maryland's politics chafed under the collar of proprietary rule and clashed with Lord Baltimore over tobacco inspection, ministerial salaries, officer's fees, and poll taxes. According to the prevailing historical narrative, these Country Party lawmakers were unable, at first, to see Parliament's actions as inappropriate or oppressive because they were too busy interpreting Lord Baltimore's actions in a tyrannical light. It was only when the Country Party's anger at the proprietor merged with the alienation that roughly 30 percent of the colony's freemen were already feeling because they did not own enough property to vote that Maryland found itself, once again, on the verge of a "social revolution."[14]

But a narrative that stresses the synergy between the alienation of Maryland's unenfranchised freemen and the animosity of the Country Party does not fully explain why the people of Maryland finally directed their anger against Parliament or why they were slower than their contemporaries in other colonies to do so. Undoubtedly, historians are right that Lord Baltimore's antics played a role in delaying the anger, as did the healthy economy that Maryland enjoyed between 1766 and 1772. By themselves, however, these explanations are insufficient. William Penn's sons, after all, were also labeled "tyrants" as they clashed with the colonists who lived within the boundaries of their proprietary inheritance, and Virginia's economy was tied to many of the same international forces that determined the health of Maryland's economy; yet Pennsylvania and Virginia were both hotbeds of revolutionary sentiment by the late 1760s, while Maryland's temper was cool.[15]

The reason Maryland's freemen—enfranchised or otherwise—were hesitant to direct their anger against Parliament is that so much of the argument against the Stamp Act and the Townshend Duties rested on the idea that the colonies had constitutions that were separate from those of the parent country. Protests against parliamentary taxation, one anonymous writer to the *New York Journal* insisted, could not be seen as a challenge to the "authority founded ... in the constitution and laws of the government" because the authority the protestors were challenging was Parliament's authority, which had nothing to do with the constitution or laws of New York.[16]

The early leaders of what would eventually become the independence movement did differ with one another over whether Parliament ever had any authority in the colonies. Most allowed that the MPs did have some jurisdiction in North America, but they all drew the line at taxation, and a few prominent leaders, such as Ben Franklin, went so far as to say that Parliament "has a power to make no laws for us."[17]

But regardless of whether the door was left open to some form of parliamentary intrusion, the framing of the debate as one of "separate constitutions" was not going to resonate with the majority of people serving in Maryland's Lower House of the Assembly. That body, after all, had spent the last fifty years or so denying that there was any constitutional separation between their colony and the parent country. These denials were part of the lawmakers' effort to curb the growth of popery in Maryland and, in so doing, preserve the colony's English identity.[18]

Even Daniel Dulany stopped short in 1765 of declaring that Maryland had a constitution that was distinct from that of England. In asserting the "right of the Colonies" to "Exemption from all Taxes without their Consent," Dulany insisted that "they derive this Right from the

Common Law, which their Charters have declared and confirmed." He was careful at all times, however, to ground that common law in "the British Constitution" or the "Constitution of England."[19] Dulany never took the leap that his Protestant contemporaries in Massachusetts and New York—or his Catholic contemporaries in his own native Maryland—took when they declared that their colonies' charters, which were gifts from the king, had actually given birth to constitutions that were indebted to, but separate from the constitution of England.[20]

Before they could embrace the burgeoning independence movement, Maryland's residents needed to hear the "separate constitutions" argument articulated for them in a way that would make them believe their freedom depended upon it. Throughout the eighteenth century, Protestants in Maryland had always believed that to defend their liberty, they needed to preserve their English identity; to preserve their English identity, they needed to curb the growth of popery; and to curb the growth of popery, they needed to elicit the help of Parliament. Until they broke out of that mentality, arguments about parliamentary "usurpations" were not going to gain any traction in Maryland.

The mentality was finally broken in 1773 when a series of editorial letters in the *Maryland Gazette* showed the colony's residents that the only way they could defend their pocketbooks from the sticky hands of the proprietor's stooges was to insist that Maryland had its own constitution and that that constitution trumped any legal custom that had been established in England. Ironically, the stooge at the heart of the controversy was Daniel Dulany—the man who, prior to the 1770s, had brought the people of Maryland closer than they had ever come before to embracing the idea that Parliament's authority in the colony was limited.

Dulany's nemesis in the editorial exchange was Charles Carroll of Carrollton, whose identity as a Catholic rendered him particularly adept at articulating the "separate constitutions" argument and especially invested in its adoption by the Protestant majority of Maryland. That a Roman Catholic was defending their liberty did not go unnoticed by Maryland's Protestants, and Charles Carroll's editorials went a long way toward convincing the people of Maryland that the struggle against tyranny no longer required them to maintain their English identity—or to marginalize their Catholic neighbors, friends, and family.

The event that precipitated the public exchange between Dulany and Carroll actually had nothing to do with parliamentary taxation. Dulany was the commissioner of Maryland's land office, and his brother, Walter, was a probate judge in the colony. Together, the fees these men collected for their services totaled more than £2,000 per year. The fee schedule that gave the Dulany brothers their nice incomes was approved by the General Assembly in 1763. When the schedule came up for renewal in 1769, however, lawmakers in the Lower House wanted to decrease the fees that were paid to officers in the colony, in part because they felt that people like Daniel and Walter Dulany were making far too much money.

The Lower House could not get the Upper House to approve the new fee schedule. Many of the men who had been appointed to the Upper House by the proprietor were also officers in the colony whose incomes would have been adversely affected by the lower schedule. Because the two houses could not reach an agreement, the fee schedule expired in October 1770. It became illegal for any officer in Maryland to perform his job, and that included the officers who inspected the colony's tobacco. The situation had the potential to wreak havoc on Maryland's economy, and so in November 1770, Governor Robert Eden issued a proclamation, reinstating the original fee schedule and completely ignoring the wishes of the Lower House.

The delegates in the Lower House were furious, and several of them accused the governor of "robbery." Because Maryland's economy was running strong, however, the anger at Eden's proclamation quickly dissipated and lay dormant until the fall of 1772, when the international price of tobacco began to drop. By January 1773, Maryland was in a recession, and the colony's residents were once again grumbling about the high fees they were paying to officers in the colony. Many pointed specifically to the governor's proclamation as illegitimate and illegal, because he had circumvented the General Assembly when he made it.[21]

Daniel Dulany miscalculated the anger. On January 7, 1773, he published a fictitious dialogue in the *Maryland Gazette* that he fully expected would convince the colony's residents that Governor Eden's proclamation had been valid. The dialogue was between two "citizens." A "First Citizen," who represented those who questioned the proclamation's legitimacy, and a "Second Citizen," whose knowledge of England's history and political landscape was as extensive as Daniel Dulany's. The First Citizen's opposition to the fee schedule was based upon his paranoid conviction that it was a "monstrous contradiction" to be a "friend both to Government and Liberty." All government officers, the First Citizen insisted, were, pro forma, susceptible to "Court-influence and Corruption." It was dangerous, therefore, for someone like the governor to be allowed to issue proclamations that were not subject to legislative review.

The Second Citizen pounced on this unduly pessimistic argument, insisting that the colony's officers—as men of commerce—could never participate in a "plot against Liberty ... for when Liberty is struck in the heart, Commerce can then put forth her golden fruit no more, but, must per force droop and die." The Second Citizen challenged the First Citizen to present evidence of the court-influence and corruption that he claimed was polluting the colony's government. Faced with such a challenge, the First Citizen vouchsafed that "to these questions I do not choose to give an answer." The Second Citizen chastised him, therefore, to "judge not, lest ye be judged."[22]

Dulany's decision to write and publish the "exchange" was an example of his considerable capacity for cluelessness—a capacity that had led him to request a fee increase in 1770, in the midst of the General Assembly's fight over whether the officers' fee schedule was already too high.[23] Wealthy, cosmopolitan, and well-read, Dulany was not always in touch with the emotional tenor of his fellow Marylandians. He hit a chord in 1765, with his *Considerations on the Propriety of Imposing Taxes in the British Colonies*, but in 1773, his dialogue between the First and Second Citizen fell flat. Not only did the public not like the message that was implicit in the dialogue, but three weeks after the dialogue came out, the doltish "First Citizen" whom Dulany had created mysteriously published an answer to the Second Citizen's arguments—and this time, he came armed with Charles Carroll of Carrollton's impressive knowledge of not just England's constitutional history, but Maryland's constitutional history as well.

Historians (and even some of Carroll's contemporaries) have noted that the future signer of the Declaration of Independence had many personal reasons for responding to the dialogue and attacking Daniel Dulany in public. The Carroll family had a long history with the Dulany family, dating back at least as far as Daniel Dulany, Sr.'s decision in the 1730s to form the Baltimore Ironworks Company with Charles Carroll of Annapolis. The Dulanys and Carrolls often disagreed with one another on the management decisions that needed to be made for that company, and in 1769, Lloyd Dulany, Daniel's younger brother, wrote a nasty letter to Charles Carroll of Carrollton, expressing his frustration and calling Carroll's father "the master of vice and profligacy." This letter only exacerbated the animosity that Carroll was already feeling toward the Dulany family because of an earlier move Daniel Dulany had made. In 1768, Daniel tried to block the passage of an "enabling act" that Carroll needed before his fiancée, who was still a minor, could sign a prenuptial agreement. The effort ultimately failed, but Daniel Dulany did succeed in delaying Carroll's marriage for nearly six months.[24]

His obvious antipathy for Lloyd and Daniel Dulany aside, however, Charles Carroll of Carrollton had another personal investment in the debate over the governor's fee proclamation, and this investment is one that has not been fully recognized by scholars. When he composed his "First Citizen" letters, Carroll did so not just as a husband and a son but also as a native-born Catholic Marylandian. The constitutional arguments that he made against the governor's proclamation subtly reflected his identity as such. Carroll was careful throughout the exchange not to rise to the bigoted challenge that Dulany issued when he reminded the *Gazette's* readers that Carroll had been "disabled" from "interfering" in Maryland's politics because he was a "papist by profession" whose "religious principles" were "inconsistent with the security of British liberty." "Attempts to rouse popular prejudices, and to turn the laugh against an adversary, discover the weakness of a cause," was Carroll's only response to Dulany's "illiberal calumny."[25] But when he argued that Governor Eden's fee proclamation was unconstitutional—in spite of the fact that there was a precedent for it in England—because it reversed a fee-setting custom that had been established and followed in Maryland since the time of the colony's founding, Charles Carroll of Carrollton made an argument about the fee proclamation that mirrored the arguments Catholics had been making about religious intolerance in Maryland since at least 1718.

Dulany's primary defense of the governor's proclamation rested on the idea that the fees paid to judges, tobacco inspectors, deed recorders, and other officers in the colony for the services they performed were not taxes. Their amount, therefore, did not have to be established by the legislature. "No tax can be imposed except by the legislature," Dulany acknowledged, repeating the ideas that he had articulated eight years earlier in his protest against the Stamp Act. "But fees have been lawfully settled by persons not vested with a legislative authority; consequently, the settlement of fees is not the imposition of a tax."[26]

The precedent Dulany relied upon was a case from 1743, in which Philip Lord Hardwicke—the same judge who would one day rule in favor of the Penn family in their decades-long dispute with the Calverts over the boundary between Pennsylvania and Maryland—issued an order that determined the fees of the officers serving in England's Court of Chancery. Lord Hardwicke did this, Daniel Dulany insisted, because the "chief danger of oppression" with regard to officers' fees lay not in the prospect of having non-elected "ministers" determine the fee schedule, but in the prospect of "Officers being left at liberty to set their own rates on their labour." "Judges and others not vested with a *legislative* authority," Dulany wrote, "had settled, and ascertained the fees of officers" in England "for the very purpose of preventing the oppression of the subject."[27] When he issued his officer fee proclamation in 1770, Governor Robert Eden had merely been trying to do something similar for the people in Maryland whom the proprietor had obliged him to protect.

Charles Carroll's response to this argument had two parts. His first and simplest retort was that the governor was not a "minister," the way

Philip Hardwicke was. Lord Hardwicke served as an advisor to the king, whereas Governor Eden was the king's "deputy," or "representative" in Maryland. When he acted in the colony, Eden acted *"in loco Regis,"* that is, in place of the king. "A bill though passed by both houses of assembly, would not be law, if dissented to by [the governor]," Carroll pointed out. Additionally, "in him is lodged the most amiable, the best powers, the power of mercy; the most dreadful also, the power of death. A minister has no such transcendent privileges."[28]

Yet, just as the king was bound by England's constitution to acknowledge the will of Parliament and work with that will, Robert Eden was bound by Maryland's constitution to respect and work with the will of the colonial assembly—especially in areas where the assembly had historically enjoyed a substantial degree of sovereignty.

"Fees in this province have been generally settled by the legislature," Carroll wrote, articulating the second, and most distinctly, if subtly "Catholic" component of his argument. "So far back as 1638, we find a law for the limitation of officers [sic] fees; in 1692, the governor's authority to settle fees was expressly denied by the lower house."

It did not matter, in other words, that custom in England had evolved in such a way as to allow ministers like Philip Hardwicke to set certain officers' fees. In Maryland (where every good Catholic knew that custom had evolved a little differently), the colony's duly elected assemblymen had always been the ones who set the fees. Quoting the Lower House's 1692 decision to deny the governor the right to set officers' fees, Carroll noted that it was "'*the undoubted right of the freemen of this province not to have ANY FEES imposed upon them but by the consent of the freemen in the general assembly.*'" Any action that did not respect that right was, in Carroll's words, "a deviation from the principles of the constitution" and "contrary to the spirit of *our constitution* in particular."[29]

Throughout the entire exchange, the "constitution" Daniel Dulany referred to was always and everywhere the "the constitution of England" or "England's constitution." In contrast, Charles Carroll spoke of two constitutions—England's and Maryland's—and both were equally relevant, as far as the debate over Governor Eden's fee proclamation was concerned. Maryland's constitution was, at all times, indebted to England's constitution, since it had evolved from the customs and usages that were possible under the charter. That charter had been issued to the original settlers in 1632 as a means of guaranteeing that their constitutional rights as Englishmen would be protected, even though they were not actually living in England. But the constitution that Governor Eden was bound to respect in 1770 was "*our constitution* in particular," a collection of precedents and practices that was complementary to, but different from the precedents and practices of England. Regardless of what England's constitution demanded, Maryland's constitution demanded that all officers' fees be subject to legislative oversight.

It was an argument that said nothing about religion; and yet, Charles Carroll of Carrollton's identity as a Catholic was deeply embedded within it. He was telling his neighbors that Maryland was something different—that it had always been something different. During those early years of the colony's settlement, he told them, the men who served in the General Assembly—a body whose very existence had been mandated by Lord Baltimore's charter—had passed a series of laws that gradually turned Maryland into a place where the rights of Englishmen were not only protected, but they were protected more thoroughly than they were in England. In 1773, Charles Carroll of Carrollton pointed to the legislative oversight of officers' fees as a constitutional reality in Maryland that made the colony better. Fifty-five years earlier, Peter Atwood had pointed to the Act Concerning Religion and the seventeenth-century tradition of religious toleration as a constitutional reality that made Maryland better, even if Marylandians, themselves, could not always see it.

Although he was adamant that the precedent set by Lord Hardwicke's fee proclamation in England did not apply to Maryland, Charles Carroll still could not help but comment on that precedent, and on its incompatibility with the spirit of England's own constitution. According to Carroll, the balance between the king and Parliament that had made England's constitution so perfect was being disrupted by self-interested ministers like Philip Lord Hardwicke. These advisors—who, as royal appointees, were not accountable to the people—were influencing the king and Parliament and, in so doing, benefiting themselves at the expense of the British public. "'The King can do no wrong,'" Carroll told Dulany, repeating William Blackstone's articulation of the concept of sovereign immunity. But what could be said of the king in 1773 could not be said of his advisors. "I impute all the blame to his ministers," Carroll wrote, "who if found guilty and *dragged into light*, I hope will be made to feel the resentment of a free people."[30]

George III's only mistake was that he had placed too much trust in the men who advised him. Governor Eden, Carroll hastened to add, had made the same mistake. "The prince, who places an unlimited confidence in a bad minister, runs great hazard of having that confidence abused, his government made odious, and his people wretched," the planter from Carrollton Manor warned.[31] In the case of King George III, men like Philip Hardwicke were among the bad advisors; in the case of Robert Eden, it was men like Daniel Dulany who were the problem.

The key to Carroll's argument was his belief that England's constitution—or any constitution like it, including Maryland's—was not immune to corruption. In Daniel Dulany's estimation, the constitution that had come out of the Glorious Revolution was perfect, because when it denied the throne to James II's Catholic heirs, it guaranteed that the tyranny and abuse the country had suffered under King James would never develop again.[32] While Carroll did not publicly challenge the legitimacy of the Glorious Revolution—for fear that doing so would discredit his arguments and confirm Dulany's assertions that the political opinions of all Catholics were unsafe—the "First Citizen" did insist that the Glorious Revolution was not the vaccination against tyranny and corruption that Daniel Dulany insisted it was.

The perfection of England's constitution lay in its balance—in the checks that each branch of the government provided against the other. But that balance was not unassailable. No matter how perfect the stasis between the king and Parliament may have been immediately following the Glorious Revolution, it was not completely protected from the subtle and insidious corruptions of appointed placemen. These "favorites" of the king, unelected and unaccountable as they were, were in a position to use bribery and intrigue to circumvent the checks that existed between the king and Parliament and, in so doing, corrupt England's constitution.[33]

When Charles Carroll of Carrollton published his letters, the members of the Lower House of the assembly were already poised to accept an argument against Governor Eden's fee proclamation. The argument that Carroll gave them, however, took the colony well beyond the issue of officers' fees. As Bernard Bailyn, Pauline Maier, Edward Countryman, and countless other revolutionary historians have all pointed out, the American Revolution happened only after the colonists recognized and accepted the reality of their own political sovereignty and realized that their ties to England were not only moribund, they were also dangerous. "The leaders of the Revolutionary movement," Bailyn writes, "believed there was nothing less than a deliberate 'design'—a conspiracy—of ministers of state and their underlings to overthrow the ... constitution, both in England and in America."[34] In Maryland, it was Charles Carroll of Carrollton who convinced the residents of this "design."

By the early 1770s, Britain's colonists—even the ones in Maryland—had come to realize that their lives were governed by constitutions that were separate from that of England. By the mid-1770s, they had also come to see that England's constitution was riddled with disease, and they began to fear that that disease would soon spread to their own constitutions. No constitution, after all, no matter how virtuous its origins, was impervious to corruption.

In his "First Citizen" letters, Charles Carroll of Carrollton articulated a secular version of an argument that had, by that point, been animating and sustaining the members of his religious community for more than eighty years. Of course Maryland had its own constitution. Of course that constitution had been founded and built upon virtuous principles. Of course England was corrupt. And of course that corruption was capable of infecting the constitution of Maryland and, in so doing, denying the virtue that was at the core of that constitution. Catholics had learned the truth of these assertions as early as the 1690s, when the Act Concerning Religion, which had guaranteed them a freedom of conscience that was expressly denied to their religious brethren in England, was repealed by bigoted Protestants in Maryland who had been infected with the religious intolerance that fueled the Glorious Revolution in England.

Catholics understood that Maryland's constitution had been contaminated by a bigotry that was distinctly English in origin. Throughout the eighteenth century, they had clung to the idea that anti-Catholicism was foreign and unnatural in their colony, and they believed it was a pathogen that might one day be destroyed. This belief prepared them psychologically to make the break from England. Indeed, in 1776, Maryland's Catholics may well have been the Americans most prepared to embrace independence and accept the mantle of American identity.

At no point in his public letters to Daniel Dulany did Charles Carroll of Carrollton ever blame the king for the corruption that he saw running rampant in England. He denied Dulany's accusations that he had Whiggish tendencies, and his attitude that the king's only mistake was his reliance on unscrupulous advisors was common among proto-revolutionaries in the early 1770s.[35]

Before the colonists could embrace the notion of independence from England, they needed to conclude that George III was just as responsible for the corruption they saw as his royal ministers and the members of Parliament were. Patriot leaders finally reached this conclusion in 1774, when, in the wake of the so-called Boston Tea Party, King George III approved a series of laws that were meant to punish Massachusetts for the destruction of nearly £10,000 sterling in English tea. Known collectively throughout the colonies as the "Intolerable Acts," these measures convinced the colonists that the king was looking to destroy their freedom.[36]

What has always been puzzling about the so-called "Intolerable Acts," however, is that only four of the five pieces of legislation that the colonists grouped into this blatantly propagandistic category had anything to do with Massachusetts or the Boston Tea Party. All five measures were, in fact, passed by the king and Parliament in 1774, but the final measure, passed in August of that year, was neither punitive, nor did it affect the lives of most of the people living in the lower thirteen colonies.

The Boston Port Act, the Massachusetts Government Act, the Impartial Administration of Justice Act, and the amendment to the 1765 Quartering Act that empowered military commanders to lodge their soldiers in people's private homes were all responses to colonial defiance, and they all had an impact on the lives of thousands of people living not just in Massachusetts, but in any colony that relied upon goods from the port of Boston, was occupied by British soldiers, or had a charter that could be revoked. The Quebec Act, however, applied primarily to the people who lived in the Canadian territory that England had acquired from France in 1763 as one of the spoils of the French and Indian War.

To be fair, the Act did extend Quebec's boundaries into territory known as the "Ohio Country," an area that consisted of present-day Ohio, Indiana, and parts of Pennsylvania and West Virginia. A number of land speculators—George Washington among them—had been hoping to make their fortune in the Ohio Country, and so the parts of the Quebec Act that expanded the province's boundaries did have a minor impact on the lives of a small number of men living in the lower thirteen colonies. The Act's main thrust, however, was confined to Canada. King George III issued it so that he could establish his authority in a colony where French-speaking Catholics who had no loyalties to England had been enjoying benign neglect for more than a decade.[37]

The Quebec Act gave legal sanction to the practice of Catholicism in Canada by removing all references to Protestantism in the oaths that officeholders in the colony were required to swear. It did not establish Catholicism in Quebec; the Catholic Church would still receive no funding from England or from Quebec's locally elected assembly. But the residents of the colony would not be taxed to support the Anglican Church in Canada, nor would they be penalized for attending Catholic Mass. As the Act acknowledged, Catholics were a majority of the European residents in Quebec, and they had been attending their church openly throughout the eleven years that had passed since their province became an English colony.[38] When he sanctioned their attendance at Mass, George III was attempting to assume ownership of the Quebecois by laying claim to a matter that, in truth, he really had very little control over.

The reaction to the Quebec Act in the lower thirteen colonies was overwrought. In fact, it was so incredibly hysterical that many revolutionary historians—particularly those who fall into the so-called "Neo-Whig" school—have tried to downplay the Quebec Act when charting the events that led to independence. The cries of "papal tyranny" that the Patriot leadership directed against the Anglican king, after all, do not fit nicely into the "rather old-fashioned paradigm" subscribed to by Neo-Whigs, wherein "real fears, real anxieties, a real sense of danger . . . and not merely a desire to influence [people] by rhetoric and propaganda" are found to have been the animating forces behind the statements of the revolutionaries.[39]

That there was a "real sense of danger" associated with Catholicism in the collective Protestant mind is clear and irrefutable; what is less clear, however, when viewed only through a lens that seeks to soften the propagandistic qualities of the Patriots' rhetoric, is why that sense of danger was associated with the Protestant king of England, almost overnight—or why it was not associated with the Catholics who represented Maryland in the Continental Congress, or helped to write Maryland's new, state constitution, or served in militia units and on committees of safety throughout the state.

In the able hands of the Patriot leadership, the Quebec Act became the proverbial straw that broke the camel's back, the final sign that the king had become irredeemably corrupt. "They have made a law to establish the religion of the Pope in Canada," Samuel Adams announced. Americans up and down the eastern seaboard would soon be forced to "submit to Popery and Slavery." John Adams worried that "the barriers against popery, erected by our ancestors" would be "suffered and destroyed" by the Act, "to the hazard even of the Protestant religion." In Connecticut, Ezra Stiles, the future president of Yale

College, was astonished that "the king and Lords and Commons, a whole Protestant Parliament" had "establish[ed] the Romish Religion and IDOLOTRY" over "nearly Two Thirds of the Territory of English America."[40]

Even outside New England—where the proximity to Canada might have explained some of the fear—the reaction to the Quebec Act was extreme. "Does not your blood run cold, to think an English Parliament should pass an Act for the establishment of Popery and arbitrary power?" Alexander Hamilton asked his colleagues in New York. In South Carolina, Judge William Henry Drayton predicted that a "tyranny under which all Europe groaned for many ages" would sweep the colonies, now that the king had approved the Quebec Act, and a "most cruel tyranny in Church and State" would be "fed with blood by the Roman Catholic doctrines."[41]

In Maryland, the rhetoric surrounding the Quebec Act was equally overblown. On the pages of the *Maryland Journal*, published in Baltimore by William Goddard and his sister, Mary Katherine, the Quebec Act became a sign that George III wished to extend "the medium of French law and popery" across North America, "the one enslaving the body, the other the mind." In Annapolis, where Anne Green and her son, Frederick, published the *Maryland Gazette*, the Quebec Act was "worse in tendency . . . than the Stamp Act" because it "immovably fixed" the "standard of despotism" throughout England's colonies. One contributor to the paper insisted that the king had empowered "a body of popish slaves" to "serve as a curb upon [the Protestants]" in the colonies. It was "high time," another contributor wrote, "for the protestants of all denominations in these kingdoms to take some effectual measures for the safety and security of their civil and religious liberties."[42]

The residents of Britain's lower thirteen colonies were convinced that the Quebec Act amounted to the "establishment" of the Catholic Church in Canada, and that it would only be a matter of time before the "tyrant hand of popish power" took up residence in their own colonies, as well. In point of fact, the Quebec Act did not establish the Catholic Church anywhere in North America, and allegations that it did actually prompted one loyalist in New York to ask "how, and on what Foundation, in the name of common sense, is the Church of Rome *established*?"[43]

Sensical or not, rumors abounded in the colonies that King George III would soon be appointing a "popish bishop" to Canada, and that this bishop would, in turn, spread "wickedness, superstition, and bigotry" across the continent. Colonial newspapers were a reliably unreliable source of these rumors. Their editors often used gossip about the Quebec Act to justify their assertions that the king had "broken his coronation oath" and that the Protestants of North America were therefore "discharged from their allegiance" to him and justified in making "provision for their common safety."[44]

The coverage that the *Journal* in Baltimore and the *Gazette* in Annapolis gave to the Quebec Act made it clear that the threat of popery was still very evocative in Maryland, even though a leading member of the Catholic community there had defended the right of the people to make their own laws. The First Citizen's letters may have been instrumental in getting Marylandians to recognize the corruption in England and the sovereign nature of their colony's constitution, but anti-popery continued to be an incredibly effective rhetorical tool on the eastern and western shores of the Chesapeake.

Yet, the rhetoric in the papers did not always reflect the reality on the ground. When Maryland's leaders convened in Annapolis in the fall of 1774 and the spring of 1775 to discuss their grievances with England and strategize about how best to enforce a nonimportation agreement that the colonies had adopted after the king and Parliament closed the port of Boston, George III's decision to allow the free practice of Catholicism in Canada never came up. The other four "intolerable acts" all made it into the meetings' minutes, but not a word was said about the Quebec Act.[45]

The silence may have been a consequence of the fact that Catholics were actually present at these meetings. Ignatius Fenwick represented St. Mary's County at the Maryland Convention; Thomas Semmes represented Charles County; and Charles Carroll of Carrollton represented Frederick County. Indeed, Carroll was one of seven men selected from within the convention's ranks to serve on the committee of correspondence that would communicate Maryland's ideas and experiences to the Patriot leaders in other colonies. He was not one of the five men selected to travel to Philadelphia in September 1774 to attend the First Continental Congress, but the men who were chosen to represent Maryland asked him to come along with them, so that they could draw upon his extensive legal background when making their decisions.[46]

Fenwick, Semmes, and Carroll could not vote for or serve in Maryland's General Assembly, because their Catholicism was dangerous to the preservation of English identity. They could not own guns or serve in the militia, according to the laws established by that Assembly, because their Catholic faith made them a threat to "His Majesty's Royal Person and Government."[47] Yet, these men could serve in the Maryland Convention—even play a role in the drafting of the new state's constitution—and their coreligionists could enlist in the units that would fight the war for independence on the plains of Brooklyn and in the fields around Germantown. By 1774, Maryland's Protestants were no longer interested in being Englishmen. They believed that "his majesty's royal person and government" had become threats to their liberties, and they stopped being obsessed, therefore, with preserving their English identity—or with marginalizing the Catholics who lived among them.

"Popery," in the minds of America's Protestants, was synonymous with "tyranny," "slavery," "ignorance," and "corruption." For the editors of the *Maryland Gazette* and the *Maryland Journal*, the word was a simple, straightforward, easily recognized, and easily understood way to explain that the king, much like Parliament and the ministers who served him, could no longer be relied upon to protect and nurture the cause of liberty. "Popery" and "arbitrary power" were one and the same. But the editors of Maryland's newspapers and the voters who sent Ignatius Fenwick, Thomas Semmes, and Charles Carroll of Carrollton to represent them at the Maryland Convention understood that "popery" was not what their Catholic neighbors were practicing when they said the rosary or received the Eucharist from the hands of a priest.

Popery was in Spain. Popery was in France. Popery was in Quebec. Popery was not in Maryland—at least not yet. But if the Patriots did not succeed, it would be.

Precise numbers are impossible to determine, but the muster rolls, veteran pension applications, and supply records from St. Mary's County—where the greatest concentration of colonial American Catholics lived—all indicate that support for the Revolutionary War was greater among Catholics than it was among Protestants. An astounding 79 percent of the 145 Catholic men who married in St. Mary's County between 1767 and 1784 swore their allegiance to the free state of Maryland, donated money and supplies to the American war effort, and served in the Continental Army or the St. Mary's County Militia. Fifty-eight percent of the men who belonged to the Jesuits' congregation at St. Inigoes Manor in 1768 did the same, and an analysis of the lives of more than 2,000 men from St. Mary's County who aided the independence movement reveals that more than half of them were probably Catholic—at a time when the Catholic population of St. Mary's County was between 25 and 32 percent.[48]

In contrast, the most generous estimates argue that just 40 to 45 percent of the white population in all thirteen colonies actively supported the independence movement—and that average includes Massachusetts, where support for the Revolution may have been as high as 60 percent. Maryland was home to one of the largest contingents of loyalist soldiers, and, as we saw, Maryland's merchants were among the last to sign onto the colonial nonimportation agreement in the wake of the Stamp Act. Protestants in the colony were ambivalent about independence; that ambivalence, however, was not shared by their Catholic neighbors.[49]

The Catholic population's commitment to the Patriot cause was there from the very beginning. There is no discernible difference between the number of Catholics who joined the independence movement before the solidification of the alliance with France in February 1778 and the number who joined after. Henry Neale enlisted in the 5th Independent Maryland Company in January 1776, fighting in the Battle of Brooklyn six weeks after the Declaration of Independence was signed. Ignatius Mattingly and his brothers, William and Luke, were all privates in the St. Mary's County militia in 1777. Ignatius later joined the Continental Army, where he served until the end of the war. Henry and Ignatius Luckett both joined the Maryland Line in July 1776. That same month, Ignatius and Francis Wathen enlisted in Captain Uriah Forrest's Flying Camp from St. Mary's County. Their cousin, John Baptist, was a sergeant in the 12th Battalion of the Charles County militia in 1777. After the war, John Baptist Wathen joined William and Luke Mattingly in migrating to Kentucky. The men were among the original residents of the Catholic settlement at Cartwright's Creek that eventually became part of the second Catholic diocese in the United States.[50]

The involvement of the world's leading Catholic nation in America's war for independence had little or no impact on the decision of Maryland's Catholics to support the Revolution. These people understood that independence from England was their best shot at eradicating the legislated anti-Catholicism that had been corrupting their colony since the 1690s. For all the talk of the dangers of "popery" in the rhetoric of the revolutionaries, no Patriot ever accused a Catholic from Maryland of being on the wrong side in the war; yet British troops very clearly viewed Maryland's Catholics with suspicion. According to John Carroll, Red Coats "hovered continually near the plantations of the clergy" throughout the war, and they burned down "the priest Hunter's house at the mouth of Tobacco Creek" in 1778.[51] In Maryland, if there were any Catholic Loyalists, they were not active ones.

In Pennsylvania, however, the support for independence among Catholics was not quite so universal. The Catholic population there was a little less than half the size of the Catholic population in Maryland, and because many of its members were Germans who found that they had more in common with German-speaking Protestants than they did with English-speaking Catholics, the community in Pennsylvania was far more fragmented than it was in Maryland. The first Catholic Mass in Pennsylvania was not performed until the late 1720s; Fr. Joseph Greaton, who was stationed at the Jesuits' Bohemia Manor plantation in Cecil County, Maryland, established a mission in 1727 in the home of Thomas Willcox and Elizabeth Cole, who lived in Chester County. Later, in 1733, Greaton founded St. Joseph's Church on Walnut Street in Philadelphia, where a small congregation that was fairly evenly split between Irish and German Catholics began to worship.[52]

In Pennsylvania, Catholics were officially tolerated. Granted, Governor Thomas Penn did announce early in 1734 that he was "under no small concern to hear that a house *lately built* in Walnut Street had been set apart for the exercise of the Roman Catholic religion." Public celebrations of the Catholic Mass were "contrary to the laws of England," and Penn worried that under the colony's charter, lawmakers might be obliged to close the chapel that Fr. Greaton was using (Pennsylvania's charter, after all, did not have a Durham clause). In the end, however, the Quakers who served on the provincial council decided to honor the spirit of Pennsylvania's founding and allow the chapel to remain open. In contrast, the General Assembly in Maryland had forced the Society of Jesus to close its chapel in St. Mary's City thirty years earlier. The building was eventually torn down, its bricks sold for salvage.[53] There would not be another freestanding Catholic chapel in Maryland—at least not one that was legal—until after the Revolution.

The fact that Pennsylvania's Catholic population was solidly German may have been part of the reason that some of the colony's Catholics chose to remain loyal to the Crown. King George, after all, was not only the king of England, he was also the elector of Hanover—and actually, George III was the first British monarch since the Hanoverian succession in 1714 to have been born in England. His grandfather and great-grandfather, George II and George I, were both born in Hanover, and each grew up speaking German, rather than English.[54]

In 1777, during his occupation of Philadelphia, British General William Howe authorized a local Catholic named Alfred Clifton to raise a regiment of Roman Catholic Volunteers, and Clifton managed to find nearly 200 men who were willing to participate. The unit's chaplain was Ferdinand Farmer, the Swabian priest who had written to his brother in the 1750s about his need for a scepter and cope. Farmer's service to the unit suggests strongly that there were a number of Germans among the unnamed men who made up the Roman Catholic Volunteers. The names of the men who served as the unit's leaders, however, indicate that not all of the Volunteers were German. Captains Mathias Hanly and Nicols Wieregan were almost certainly German. But they shared their titles with Kenneth McCullock and Martin McEvoy. John Lynch was the unit's major. John Connell was a lieutenant, and Cornelius Leary was an ensign.[55]

The reluctance of some of Pennsylvania's Catholics to break with the parent country must have involved more that just ethnic loyalty. It is doubtful, after all, that someone named "Cornelius Leary" would have felt any strong, ethnic ties to England's king, regardless of whether that monarch spoke German or English. We will probably never know why Cornelius Leary chose to join the Roman Catholic Volunteers. It is possible, however, that his Loyalist tendencies were sparked—or at the very least sustained—by the words of European Catholic leaders like Fr. Arthur O'Leary, whose condemnation of the independence movement was swift and unequivocal.

In August 1779, around a year after the Catholic king of France had sent soldiers and military advisors to North America to help the overwhelmingly Protestant, English-speaking Americans throw off the mantle of British rule, O'Leary—the so-called "Catholic Swift of Ireland"—published an address to "the common people of the Roman Catholic religion." His words were meant specifically for the Catholics living in his native Ireland. The address, however, had implications for English-speaking Catholics everywhere—even and especially for Catholics in the colonies.

France's decision to send troops to America had gotten some people in Ireland thinking. If the Catholic French had been willing to help the Protestant Americans rebel against English rule, perhaps they would be willing to do the same for their coreligionists in Ireland. It was an intriguing thought—but one that Arthur O'Leary wanted to squelch. "Whatever distinction the laws of this unhappy kingdom may make between Protestant and Papist," he informed his readers, "a conqueror's sword makes none." Ireland's Catholics should not delude themselves into thinking that their salvation could be found on the other side of the English Channel. "If [the French] landed here,"

O'Leary assured them, "it would not be with a design to promote the Catholic cause."

There was another reason, however, that the Irish should not be looking to America for guidance on how things should or could be done in their country. The Americans, after all, were probably going to Hell. "Among the crimes that exclude from the kingdom of Heaven, St. Paul reckons sedition," O'Leary reminded Ireland's Catholics. "And what greater sedition than to rise up against your king and country, and to defile your hands with the blood of your fellow-subjects?"[56] The priest did not deny that England's sovereign had been no friend to Roman Catholics in the Old World or the New. As a Catholic, however, he considered the anti-authoritarianism at the core of the American Revolution to be far more dangerous than the king of England to the stability of the Church and society.

Whether Cornelius Leary ever read and internalized Arthur O'Leary's warning about sedition will never been known. The reason he was even able to consider the possibility that it might have been better if Pennsylvania remained tied to England, however, is clear: Cornelius Leary was not a Catholic from Maryland.[57] His entire experience in Pennsylvania was one of religious toleration. Unlike Henry Neale, Ignatius Mattingly, Thomas Semmes, and Charles Carroll of Carrollton, Cornelius Leary had not grown up hearing about the toleration that his Catholic ancestors had built—and then lost. He did not understand, as his religious brethren in Maryland did, that the colonists were paying a price for their connection to England.

One of the many differences between America's revolution and the one that occurred in France just a few years later was that in America, religious leaders were actively involved in the revolt. In France, the National Assembly confiscated Church lands, closed dozens of monasteries, abolished the tithe, legalized divorce, took control of France's vital records, and deported any clergy who did not swear their allegiance to the new government.[58] In America, however, the revolutionaries did not view the clergy as their enemies. Indeed, some of the most effective advocates of independence were men of the cloth.

Some Anglican ministers did remain loyal to the Crown—and they paid the price for that loyalty. Jonathan Boucher, for example, had to wield a pistol and take a hostage in 1775 in order to leave his church safely after delivering a loyalist sermon. Later that week, he and his wife, Eleanor, sailed for England and never returned to the state where Eleanor had been born.[59]

Dozens of Protestant clergy, however, cast their lots with the Patriots and fulminated freely from the pulpits about British tyranny. Ministers like Abraham Keteltas, Ezra Stiles, and Peter Muhlenberg published sermons in which they insisted that the Patriots fought for "the cause of truth, against error and falsehood." After completing a sermon in the summer of 1776, Muhlenberg rather famously (and perhaps apocryphally) threw off his clerical robes to reveal the uniform of a Virginia militia officer underneath. The following year, Keteltas responded to the Battle of Brooklyn by proclaiming—in the familiar language of anti-popery—that the revolutionaries were defending "pure and undefiled religion, against bigotry, superstition, and human invention."[60]

Maryland's priests were not as vocal about their politics as their Protestant contemporaries. Many of the soldiers in the Continental Army continued to celebrate Pope's Day even after the Continental Congress had cemented an alliance with Catholic France. Maryland's priests, therefore, tended to keep their heads down throughout the conflict. None of the sermons they delivered between 1776 and 1783 even mentioned the war, and during the decade leading up to the fight, the Jesuits' only references to the tensions between England and its colonies were made in private correspondences.[61]

Their silence, however, was prompted by more than just a desire to avoid the limelight. During the years leading up to the war, Maryland's priests were distracted by an issue that had nothing to do with England or its relationship with the colonies. In June 1773, Pope Clement XIV suppressed the Society of Jesus because officials in Spain and Portugal had insisted that the Jesuits were encouraging South America's natives to rebel against colonial authority. Maryland's Jesuits took the news of their society's demise incredibly hard. "I am willing now to retire and quit my post," Joseph Mosley wrote to his sister from his tiny cabin on the eastern shore. "Labor for our neighbor is a Jesuit's pleasure; destroy the Jesuit, and labor is painful." John Carroll was utterly distraught following the suppression. He became a recluse in his family's home in Rock Creek and brooded there for months. "I am not, and perhaps never shall be, fully recovered from the shock of this dreadful intelligence," he wrote in September 1773. "The greatest blessing which in my estimation I could receive from God, would be immediate death."[62]

Depression was not the only distraction the Jesuits were forced to grapple with following the suppression. Rome moved immediately to confiscate their property—and in this situation, Maryland's anti-Catholic laws actually became the Jesuits' best friends. In Maryland, the Church had not been allowed to own any property corporately. The Jesuits' farms, therefore, did not belong to the Society; they belonged individually to each priest serving in the colony. That did not stop Vatican officials from trying to take possession of the Jesuits' farms, however, and in the mid-1770s, while ministers like Peter Muhlenberg were busy donning militia uniforms and delivering flowery speeches about superstition and falsehood, Maryland's priests were citing statues that prevented "foreign prelates" from interfering in the "temporal affairs" of the colony.[63]

The suppression soured Maryland's priests not just on the Vatican's authority, but also on the incestuous relationship that the state had with the Church in predominantly Catholic countries like Spain and Portugal. Catholic Europe was, according to John Carroll, a "scene of iniquity, duplicity, and depredation," a place where the "sinister views of an artful and temporising pontiff" were given free rein to engage in the "free exercise of every act of despotism."[64] Such were the opinions of the man who was destined to become the first Catholic bishop of the United States. It is not surprising, therefore, that America's first Catholics would choose to celebrate the passage of the First Amendment in 1791.

Carroll did eventually snap out of his depression, and in the spring of 1776, he joined his cousin, Charles, their fellow Marylandian, Samuel Chase, and Benjamin Franklin on a diplomatic mission to Montreal.

After avoiding the crisis for months, Maryland's Catholic clergy finally, if quietly, announced their support for independence when their peer left his home in Rock Creek to travel to Quebec so that he could meet with religious leaders there and endeavor to "enlist the Catholic clergy on the side of the United Colonies" and "form an union between the said Colonies and the people of *Canada*."[65]

Chase was one of Maryland's representatives to the Continental Congress, and he specifically recommended Charles Carroll to John Adams when the delegates were trying to decide who among them should be sent to speak with the Canadians. Chase—whose father, Thomas, was a notoriously anti-Catholic Anglican minister—pointed out that Carroll was not only fluent in French, but he also shared a faith with the Quebecois. Entrusting a Catholic with such a sensitive diplomatic mission would, Chase believed, go a long way toward convincing the Canadians that the Americans, rather than the English, were their friends. Carroll then invited his cousin "Jack" to come along, believing that a priest's presence would add to the delegation's legitimacy.[66]

It was an assignment that was doomed to fail, and Ben Franklin and John Carroll realized as much shortly after they arrived in Canada. Less than two weeks after the men spent their first night at Hazen's Inn in the center of Montreal, Franklin left to return to Philadelphia; Father Carroll joined him the following day. According to the journal that Charles Carroll kept throughout the two-month mission, Franklin's "declining state of health, and the bad prospect of our affairs in Canada, made him take this resolution."[67]

Several months before the delegation set out for Quebec, the Continental Army had attempted to secure the support of the Canadians through less diplomatic means when Brigadier-General Richard Montgomery had invaded and captured Montreal. He then moved on to Quebec City, meeting up with the forces of Benedict Arnold, who still enjoyed the Patriots' good graces. Together, Arnold's and Montgomery's men lay siege to Quebec City, only to be staunchly defeated by British forces on the Plains of Abraham in late December 1775.

Franklin, Chase, and the two Carrolls were sent to Montreal, which was still occupied by American troops under the leadership of General

David Wooster, to convince the French Catholics living there that the American occupation was in their best interests. It was a hard sell—and not simply because the residents of Montreal did not like living in an occupied city. The reason the Americans had invaded in the first place was that an earlier, nonmilitary effort to get the Canadians to join them had failed miserably and given the Quebecois reason to mistrust their American neighbors. These earlier efforts at diplomacy are historically significant, not just because their failure occasioned the first act of military aggression by a quasi-independent American republic but also because they reveal much about the incredibly rhetorical role that anti-Catholicism played in the independence movement and the quality of the Patriots' "fear" of Catholics and Catholicism.

In October 1774, about a month after they convened for the very first time, the members of the Continental Congress drafted four different addresses, each designed to justify the colonies' grievances to a different audience. The first two addresses were written on October 21st, and they were directed "To the Inhabitants of the Colonies" and "To the People of Great Britain." The second two addresses were drafted five days later; the first was a "Petition to the King," and the second was "To the Inhabitants of the Province of Quebec."

The address to the Canadians was composed by John Dickinson of Pennsylvania, Thomas Cushing of Massachusetts, and Richard Henry Lee of Virginia, who also penned the letters that the Continental Congress sent to the people of the colonies and Great Britain. The address—which was written in English, and then translated into French and published by Fleury Mesplet, a Catholic printer from Lyon whom Benjamin Franklin had convinced to immigrate to Philadelphia a few months earlier—began by welcoming the Canadians into a brave, new world. Thanks to the "fortunes of war," the letter stated, the residents of Quebec, much like the residents of England's lower thirteen colonies, could claim the rights of trial by jury, freedom of the press, and representation in government, all of which had been entirely unavailable to them while they had lived under the auspices of an absolutist, French government. Quebec's transfer from French to English control, the Americans insisted, had been a good thing.

After articulating the rights that were now available to the Canadians, the letter warned the Quebecois that these rights, while definitely English in origin, were no longer being respected by the British government because that government had forgotten that it had boundaries. As an example of how Parliament had overstepped its bounds, the Americans pointed—with no sense of irony—to the Quebec Act, that is, "that last Act of Parliament wherein Liberty of Conscience was given" to the Canadians. Such liberty, the letter insisted, was never Parliament's to give, for in fact, freedom of conscience was a right granted to all people by God. If Parliament could extend that liberty, Parliament could take it away—and the Canadians should know that Parliament would, indeed, try to take their religious freedom away unless the residents of Quebec "unit[ed] . . . with the other Colonies to the south" in resisting all parliamentary encroachments. This union was most assuredly possible, in spite of the religious differences between Canada and the lower thirteen colonies, because a mutual "devotion to liberty" would elevate Protestants and Catholics alike "above all low-minded infirmities."[68]

How, exactly, America's Protestants were supposed to elevate themselves above low-minded infirmities, when Richard Henry Lee was telling them (in a letter he wrote just five days before he wrote the letter to the Quebecois) that Catholicism was a religion that "disbursed impiety, bigotry, persecution, murder, and rebellions throughout every part of the world," is unclear. The problem with the Quebec Act, according to the letters that were distributed to the people of Great Britain and the colonies, was not that it deigned to extend a right to the Quebecois that had been given to them by God, but that it "established" the Roman Catholic religion in Quebec and, in so doing, ensured that the people there were "deprived of a right to an assembly, trials by jury, and the English laws in civil cases." If it were only French people who lived in Quebec, this act of tyranny might not have been such a problem; the French, after all, as Catholics, were used to having no rights. But when the Treaty of Paris of 1763 was signed, King George III had agreed to extend English law to Quebec, "under the faith of which many English subjects settled in that province." If the people of

Great Britain and the lower thirteen colonies ignored the Quebec Act, they would be abandoning "their affectionate, protestant brethren" in Canada and helping their "enemies; whose intrigues, for several years passed, have been wholly exercised in sapping the foundations of civil and religious liberty."[69]

Had the Canadians only ever read the address that was meant for them, the history of North America might have been very different. According to one anonymous observer in Montreal, the address to the inhabitants of Quebec "attracted the notice of the some of the principal *Canadians*" and "flattered a people fond of compliments," which is, of course, exactly what the Continental Congress wanted to do. Unfortunately for the Patriots, these flattered Canadians soon appealed to a translator "to try his hand at that address to the People of *Great Britain*." The bilingual resident of Montreal did as he was asked and "read his performance to a numerous audience." When he "came to that part which ... draws a picture of the Catholick Religion, and the *Canadian* manners, they could not contain their resentment," the observer wrote. "Oh, the perfidious double-faced Congress," the members of the audience supposedly cried. "Let us bless and obey our benevolent Prince, whose humanity ... extends to all Religions. Let us abhor all who would reduce us from our loyalty ... and whose Addresses, like their Resolves, are destructive of their own objects."[70]

The address that Congress sent to the Canadians was "truly Jesuitical," in the estimation of a Daniel Leonard, a Loyalist whose letters to the *Boston Gazette* irked John Adams to no end. In New York, an opponent of independence declared that "both Boston and Quebec must be blind indeed, if they do not see ... [the Congress'] double dealing at the very first glance." The British essayist Samuel Johnson could not decide "whether our indignation at the Colonies should be more excited by the baseness of their hypocrisy, or the insolence of their presumption." Following the publication in London of all of Congress' letters, Johnson lampooned the Patriots' diplomatic clumsiness. "After representing the Canadians as a nation of blood-thirsty bigots, highly dangerous to the freedom of the Protestant province, we see the Congress flattering those bigots as they call them into rebellion."[71]

Fear, of course, is not always rational, and it can certainly cause people to act in entirely hypocritical ways. It is not clear, however, that the members of the first Continental Congress were as terrified of Catholics as their letters to the people of Great Britain and the colonies suggested they were; after all, there was a Catholic among them when they ordered that the letters be drafted. Charles Carroll could not vote, since he was not an official representative of Maryland to the first Continental Congress. But he was privy to the debates, having been invited to accompany the Maryland delegation and serve as their advisor.

Richard Henry Lee and his colleagues in the Congress were not afraid of Charles Carroll; in fact, shortly after he returned from Canada in June 1776, Carroll was asked to join the Congress and officially represent Maryland's interests there. Fearing Catholics, however, was not the same thing as fearing Catholicism or popery. Samuel Johnson was not quite right when he declared that the Patriots had depicted the Canadians as "a nation of blood-thirsty bigots." The Patriots had depicted the religion practiced by the Canadians as one that encouraged murder and bigotry; the jury was still out, however, on whether Canada's Catholics, themselves, were capable of rising above their religion's legacy. That the Quebecois were accustomed to tyranny by virtue of their Catholicism was certainly implied in the letters to the people of England and the colonies; those letters made it clear that the Quebec Act was intolerable because it inflicted Catholicism's ancillary tyrannies on English Protestants who had no experience with tyrannical religion. But the invitation to unite with the lower colonies through a shared "devotion to liberty" also implied that the Patriots thought the Catholics in Canada might be different from their Old World coreligionists—just like the Catholics in Maryland were.

It is a subtle distinction—the difference between Catholics and Catholicism—and to be sure, not everyone in revolutionary-era America felt that it was an important one. The men who drafted the constitutions of Vermont, New Jersey, Georgia, and North and South Carolina in 1776, for instance, did not believe that Catholics could overcome their faith's hierarchical orientation and develop the sense of virtue and individual responsibility that were essential to republicanism. Rather than engage the possibility, those men simply wrote clauses into their states' constitutions that barred Catholics from ever holding office.

Historians, too, have been reluctant to recognize the difference between a fear of Catholicism on the one hand and a fear of Catholics on the other, sometimes even misidentifying the context of the Revolution's anti-Catholic rhetoric because of a tendency to conflate the two. "The Reverend John Lathrop of the Second Church in Boston said Catholics 'had disgraced humanity' and 'crimsoned a great part of the world with innocent blood,'" Steven Waldman writes in his recent, best-selling book about the origins of religious freedom in America. Except that John Lathrop did not say that—or at least not exactly. "We view it as a calamity," the Congregational minister announced after the passage of the Quebec Act, "that by the Lords Spiritual, that venerable Bench of protestant bishops, a warm opposition was not made to a bill brought in to establish a Religion in the most important colony of his Majesty's dominions which has disgraced humanity, and crimsoned a great part of the world with innocent blood."[72] It was the religion that had disgraced humanity and shed blood, according to Lathrop, not the people.

It may seem unfair to quibble and insist that Waldman got the quote wrong. After all, if it is true that "guns don't kill people, people kill people" (a specious argument, but one that works here), then the same could be said of any religious denomination. Besides, John Lathrop probably did hate Catholics—even and especially since the chances of his actually meeting one in Boston were pretty slim.

But the fact that the Patriot leaders who spewed anti-Catholic rhetoric never accused the Catholics among them of being dangerous, even as they railed against the threat of popery, is important. It is important if we are to understand why Protestant soldiers who hanged the pope in effigy every November 5th were still able to serve side-by-side with Catholics like Basil Brown, who married Anne Mattingly in a ceremony at Bohemia Manor in June 1777, and then joined the St. Mary's County Militia one month later, before moving on to the Continental Army in 1778. It is important if we are to understand why Baker Brook, whose son, Ignatius, was a priest in Charles County, was able to provide the Charles County militia with clothing and the Continental Army with wheat, even though "the real fears of popery ... stimulated many timorous people to send their sons to join the military ranks," according to one revolutionary soldier.[73]

The cries against popery that animated the American Revolution were not about Basil, Brown or Baker Brook. This was especially true in Maryland, where Catholics were such a well-known part of the landscape that in 1779, four years before the Treaty of Paris was signed, voters elected Thomas Sim Lee, a Catholic convert, as their governor. Lee was the son-in-law of Ignatius Digges, a wealthy and prominent planter from Prince George's County who took his Catholicism very seriously. Lee was raised as an Anglican and belonged to the famous Lee family of Virginia and Maryland that would ultimately produce one president, one chief justice, two signers of the Declaration of Independence, and six Confederate generals. Lee had no apparent, spiritual reason to leave the Anglican faith he was born into—but in 1771, he wanted to wed Mary Digges, Ignatius' daughter.

In order to get permission from Mary's father, Thomas Sim Lee had to convert to Catholicism and promise to raise the couple's children as Catholics. He also had to promise that any slaves Mary brought to the union with her would be allowed to practice their Catholic faith.[74] It was not a small requirement. When he agreed to it in 1771, Thomas Sim Lee was essentially giving up what promised to be a very powerful political career. At the time, Maryland was still a proprietary colony, and Catholics were still barred under the laws passed by the General Assembly from voting or holding office.

In just five years time, however, all of that would change. In 1776, Lee joined his fellow Catholics Ignatius Fenwick, John Dent, Thomas Semmes, and Charles Carroll of Carrollton in drafting a written constitution for the newly independent state of Maryland that disestablished the Anglican Church, guaranteed religious freedom for all Christians, and nullified the legislation that three generations of Catholics had insisted was "odious" to Maryland's unwritten, historical constitution. These men were elected to their positions in the Maryland Convention by the freemen in Annapolis and St. Mary's, Prince George's, and

Charles Counties. Twenty years earlier, when Maryland's Protestants were still obsessed with their English identity in the midst of the French and Indian War, the same men who voted for Lee, Fenwick, Dent, Semmes, and Carroll might have accused them of "caballing with Negroes and Indians" and celebrating the victories of England's enemies. In 1776, however, when they declared their independence from England, Maryland's Protestants and Catholics did so together—first as Marylandians, and then eventually as Americans.

Old prejudices, of course, do not disappear overnight, and many Protestants in revolutionary-era Maryland continued to be wary of the idea of Catholicism, even as they elected Catholics to prominent positions in government. It is telling, though, that the same newspapers that warned Maryland's residents of the "tyrant hand of popish power" and used the terms "Popery and arbitrary power" synonymously also congratulated Thomas Sim Lee on his gubernatorial election—and published nary a word about his chosen Catholic faith.[75] If there is one thing history teaches us, it is that humanity is anything but consistent—and Americans have never been an exception to that rule.

In the 1770s, Maryland's Catholics were the colonists most prepared to accept the cultural and psychological implications of independence from England. They had been evolving into Americans ever since the first Catholics set foot on Maryland's western shore in 1634 and began instructing their priests on how to serve their community, having already defied authorities in England in order to remain Catholic. The independence movement's emphasis on liberty and freedom, and its insistence on the separate nature of the colonies' constitutions resonated with a population that had been self-consciously defining itself for several generations and had experienced first-hand the negative consequences of being tied politically to England.

The story of Catholicism's survival in colonial Maryland offers historians a great opportunity to explore how New World experiences facilitated the development of new religious, cultural, and ultimately national identities. It is true that the "American" Catholic identity created by the Maryland colonial experience was muddled and reinvented—and continues to be muddled and reinvented—by Catholic immigration within a few short decades of the country's founding. But we cannot have a full understanding of American Catholicism's various reinventions without an understanding of the forces that made that first American Catholic identity. More important, we cannot fully appreciate just how remarkable (if profoundly flawed) the independence movement that made America was until we have explored why everyone who embraced that movement did so.

NOTES

A Note on Spelling and Dates

1. For more on William Caxton and the Great Vowel Shift, see Seth Lerer, *Inventing English: A Portable History of the Language* (New York, 2007), 101–114.
2. L. P. Hartley, *The Go-Between* (New York, 1953), 17.
3. Jill Lepore, *The Name of War: King Philip's War and the Origins of American Identity* (New York, 1998), pp. xxii–xxiii.

Introduction

1. "Talks on Religious Liberty: Vicar General Fox of Trenton Urges Catholics to Adhere to their Faith," *New York Times*, July 31, 1903.
2. Ibid. Catholic leaders had been feeding American Protestant fears for years by this point. In 1832, Pope Gregory XVI condemned all states that granted liberty of conscience and free speech to their citizens. See Pope Gregory XVI, "Mirari Vos," August 15, 1832, *Papal Encyclicals Online*, April 20, 2009, http://www.papalencyclicals.net/Greg16/g16mirar.htm; John Witte, "Facts and Fictions about the History of Separation of Church and State," *Journal of Church and State* 48 (2006): 35–36.
3. Pope Leo XIII, "Testem Benevolentiae Nostrae," July 22, 1899, *Papal Encyclicals Online*, January 5, 2009, http://www.papalencyclicals.net/Leo13/l13teste.html; H. L. Mencken, "Holy Writ," *Smart Set* (October 1923), rpt. in *H. L. Mencken's Smart Set Criticism*, ed. William H. Nolte (Washington, DC, 1987), 93.
4. The term "Enlightenment liberalism" embodies both classical liberalism's emphasis on the rationality and autonomy of the individual and classical republicanism's insistence on the importance of virtue and the sovereignty of the people. While I realize that liberalism and republicanism are not synonymous with one another—and that some very heated debates have broken out among scholars over which philosophy dominated the independence movement—the fact remains that the philosophies are not mutually exclusive and that elements of each can be found in the independence movement and in the Catholic identity that developed out of the colonial experience. In this book, therefore, I will address the factors that allowed colonial Catholics to develop sympathies toward both liberalism and republicanism—and direct readers who are interested in extricating the one from the other to Joyce Appleby's *Liberalism and Republicanism in the Historical Imagination* (Cambridge, MA, 1992). For more on the term "Enlightenment liberalism," see Amy M. Schmitter et al., "Enlightenment Liberalism," in *A Companion to the Philosophy of Education*, ed. Randall R. Curran (Malden, MA, 2003), 73–93.
5. Philip Gleason, "American Catholics and Liberalism, 1789–1960," in *Catholicism and Liberalism*, ed. R. Bruce Douglass and David Hollenbach (New York, 1994), 51. The United

States scores highest on the "individualism" scale in Geert Hofstede's taxonomy of cultural differences. See his *Culture's Consequences: Comparing Values, Behaviors, Institutions, and Organizations across Nations* (Thousand Oaks, CA, 2001), 209–278, especially 258.
6. See John Courtney Murray, S.J., *We Hold These Truths: Catholic Reflections on the American Proposition* (New York, 1960); Patrick Carey, *People, Priests, and Prelates: Ecclesiastical Democracy and the Tensions of Trusteeism* (Notre Dame, IN, 1987); Jay Dolan, *In Search of an American Catholicism: A History of Religion and Culture in Tension* (New York, 2002); John T. McGreevy, *Catholicism and American Freedom* (New York, 2003); Mark S. Massa, *Catholics and American Culture: Fulton Sheen, Dorothy Day, and the Notre Dame Football Team* (New York, 1999); and James O'Toole, *The Faithful: A History of Catholics in America* (Cambridge, 2008).
7. Murray, *We Hold These Truths*, 42, 17, 31, 32, 36, 41.
8. An anonymous observer at the 1856 graduation ceremony for St. John's College in the Bronx (now Fordham University) reported that Hughes issued this warning before telling the graduates that they should "prepare for days of oppression and persecution" in a country that was dominated by Protestants. See Thomas R. Ryan, *Orestes A. Brownson: A Definitive Biography* (Huntingdon, IN, 1976), 534. Massa, *Catholics and American Culture*, 1–20; Garry Wills, *Bare Ruined Choirs: Doubt, Prophecy, and Radical Religion* (Garden City, NY, 1971), 15.
9. Patricia Byrne, "American Ultramontanism," *Theological Studies* 56 (1995): 301–338; David J. O'Brien, *Isaac Hecker: An American Catholic* (Mahwah, NJ, 1993), 242–320.
10. Michael P. Carroll, *American Catholics in the Protestant Imagination* (Baltimore, 2007), 5–6, 46–48.
11. For a taste of how fascinated historians have been with Americanism, see Philip Gleason, "Coming to Terms with American Catholic History," *Societas* 3 (1973): 305; James J. Hennesey, *American Catholics: A History of the Roman Catholic Community in the United States* (New York, 1983), 117–220; Thomas T. McAvoy, *The Americanist Heresy in Roman Catholicism, 1895–1900* (Notre Dame, IN, 1963); and R. Laurence Moore, "Managing Catholic Success in a Protestant Empire," in Moore, *Religious Outsiders and the Making of Americans* (New York, 1986), 48–71.
12. Murray was featured on the cover of the December 12, 1960, issue of *Time*. Editor Douglas Auchincloss called the feature "the most relentlessly intellectual cover story I've ever done." The quote about how Catholics were an "exotic minority" comes from Mark Noll's "Nineteenth-Century Religion in World Context," in *America on the World Stage*, ed. Gary Reichard and Ted Dickson (Chicago, 2008), 58. The Martineau quote is in Harriet Martineau, *Society in America* (New York, 1837), 2:323.
13. "Letter to Thomas Jefferson and to Congress," December 1818, in Peter Guilday, *The Catholic Church in Virginia, 1815–1822* (New York, 1964), 96, 100. Historian Patrick Carey has written extensively about lay trusteeism. In addition to the book mentioned in n. 6 see his articles: "The Laity's Understanding of the Trustee System, 1785–1855," *Catholic Historical Review* 64 (July 1978): 357–376; and "John F. O. Fernandez: Enlightened Lay Catholic Reformer, 1815–1820," *Review of Politics* (January 1981): 112–129.
14. Murray, *We Hold These Truths*, x.
15. Quoted in Mary Ramona Mattingly, *The Catholic Church on the Kentucky Frontier, 1785–1812* (Washington, DC, 1936), 119–120.
16. John Carroll, quoted in Dolan, *In Search of an American Catholicism*, 23; Pope Leo XIII, "Testem Benevolentiae Nostrae," July 22, 1899.
17. See, for example, Francis D. Cogliano, *No King, No Popery: Anti-Catholicism in Revolutionary New England* (Westport, CT, 1995).
18. Murray, *We Hold These Truths*, 41.
19. In 1805, there were around 500 Catholics in Boston, 15 in Plymouth, 21 in Newburyport, and 3 in Salem. Benedict Joseph Flaget, the first Bishop of Bardstown, estimated there were about 6,000 Catholics in Kentucky when he arrived in 1808 to assume leadership of that diocese. See Thomas Meehan, "P. M. J. Rock," and P. M. J. Rock, "Diocese of Louisville," in *Original Catholic Encyclopedia* (New York, 1907–1912), 2:703, 9:386.

20. Cisalpinism insisted that authority could be found "on this side of the mountain," in England, as opposed to merely on the "other side of the mountain," in Rome. See Joseph Berington, *State and Behaviour of English Catholics from the Reformation to the Year 1781* (London, 1781), 137–140, 152–153, and 185–187; Eamon Duffy, "Ecclesiastical Democracy Detected, II (1787–1796)," *Recusant History* 10 (1969–1970): 317–327; Joseph Chinnici, *The English Catholic Enlightenment: John Lingard and the Cisalpine Movement, 1780–1850* (Sheperdstown, WV, 1980), 93–97. See also Duffy's "Ecclesiastical Democracy Detected: I (1779–1787)," *Recusant History* 10 (1969–1970): 93–207, and "Ecclesiastical Democracy Detected: III (1796–1803)," *Recusant History* 13 (1975): 123–148.
21. Bernard Ward, "Cisalpine Club," *Original Catholic Encyclopedia*, 3:780; Robert Kent Donovan, "Sir John Dalrymple and the Origins of Roman Catholic Relief, 1775–1778," *Recusant History* 17 (1984): 188–196.
22. Thomas O'Gorman, *A History of the Roman Catholic Church in the United States* (Washington, DC, 1895), 247.
23. Maryland Province Archives (MPA), Special Collections, Georgetown University, Box 18, Folder 6; "Official report from the Superior, Father G. Hunter, to the Provincial, Father Dennett, July 23rd, 1765," in *History of the Society of Jesus in North America, Colonial and Federal, from the First Colonization till 1645, Documents*, ed. Thomas Hughes (New York, 1907), 1:337; Tricia T. Pyne, "Ritual and Practice in the Maryland Catholic Community, 1634–1776," *U.S. Catholic Historian* 26 (2008): 24.
24. Fr. James Beadnall lamented that not even the "thunderclaps of excommunication" could compel some colonial Catholics to stop eating meat on days when it was forbidden. American Catholic Sermon Collection (ACSC), Special Collections, Georgetown University, Be-4; "Society for the Perpetual Adoration of the Blessed Sacrament," MPA, Box 57, Folder 2.
25. Tom Paine, "Thoughts on the Present State of American Affairs," in *Common Sense* (1776), USHistory.org, The Independence Hall Association in Philadelphia, April 20, 2009, http://www.ushistory.org/paine/commonsense/sense4.htm.
26. Jack P. Greene, *Pursuits of Happiness: The Social Development of Early Modern British Colonies and the Formation of American Culture* (Chapel Hill, NC, 1988), 70, 175.
27. Patrick Henry to the House of Burgesses, March 23, 1775, *The Avalon Project: Documents in Law, History, and Diplomacy*, Yale University Law School, April 20, 2009, http://avalon.law.yale.edu/18th_century/patrick.asp.
28. *Maryland Gazette*, August 25, 1774. For more of the rhetorical uses of anti-Catholicism in the run-up to the war, see J. C. D. Clark, *The Language of Liberty: Political Discourse and Social Dynamics in the Anglo-American World* (New York, 1994), 147, 168, 214, 270, 344.
29. Murray, *We Hold These Truths*, ix, x.
30. Alexis de Tocqueville, *Democracy in America*, trans. George Lawrence (Garden City, NY, 1969), 295.

Chapter 1

1. Christopher Haigh, "From Monopoly to Minority: Catholicism in Early Modern England," *Transactions of the Royal Historical Society* 31 (1981): 129–147.
2. Until recently, the tendency among historians—both those who write for specialized audiences and those who cater to a more general, Catholic audience—has been to briefly acknowledge the existence of Lord Baltimore, before moving on to a discussion of the Irish, the Italians, the Slavs, and then finally the immigrants from Latin America. Two recent books work against that trend, however. They are John D. Krugler's *English and Catholic: The Lords Baltimore in the Seventeenth Century* (New York, 2004) and Michael Pasquier's *Fathers on the Frontier: French Missionaries and the Roman Catholic Priesthood in the United States, 1789–1870* (New York, 2010).
3. Johann P. Sommerville, "Papalist Political Thought and Controversy over the Jacobean Oath of Allegiance," in *Catholics and the "Protestant Nation": Religious Politics and Identity in Early Modern England*, ed. Ethan Shagan (New York, 2005), 166–167; Thomas Graves

Law, ed., *The Archpriest Controversy: Documents Relating to the Dissensions of the Roman Catholic Clergy, 1597–1602* (New York, 1898).
4. Patrick McGrath, "Elizabethan Catholicism: A Reconsideration," *Journal of Ecclesiastical History* 35 (1984): 424.
5. Haigh, "From Monopoly to Minority," 138–139; 146.
6. Five years after England's Church formally broke with Rome, Henry VIII called upon Parliament to pass an act reaffirming the Roman Catholic doctrine of Transubstantiation. Six years later, four people in Lincolnshire were executed because they denied that the Host was transubstantiated. Concerned that a growing number of his advisors wanted to see a greater degree of "Protestant" reform than he was willing to provide, Henry also pushed the Act for the Advancement of True Religion through Parliament in 1543, restricting the reading of the Bible to clerics, noblemen, and the gentry. While the reality was that these were, for the most part, the only people literate enough to read the Bible, Henry's Act still flew in the face of Protestant efforts on the Continent to translate the Bible into the vernacular and make it available to people in an unmediated form. See Roger Scruton, *A Dictionary of Political Thought* (New York, 1996), 470; Diarmaid MacCulloch, *Thomas Cranmer: A Life* (New Haven, CT, 1996), 241; Doreen Rosman, *The Evolution of the English Churches, 1500–2000* (New York, 2003), 35; A. G. Dickens, *Reformation and Society in Sixteenth-Century Europe* (New York, 1966), 103.
7. Susan Brigden, *New Worlds, Lost Worlds: The Rule of the Tudors* (New York, 2000), 107; Christopher Haigh, *English Reformations: Religion, Politics, and Society under the Tudors* (New York, 1993), 129.
8. F. Procter and W. H. Frere, *A New History of the Book of Common Prayer* (New York, 1965), 94; "Thirty-Nine Articles of Religion," 1571, 1662, and 1801 in *Anglicans Online*, Articles XI and XVIII. July 29, 2011, http://www.anglicansonline.org/basics/thirty-nine_articles.html.
9. Rosman, *Evolution of the English Churches*, 35–54.
10. J. C. H. Aveling, *The Handle and the Axe: The Catholic Recusants in England from Reformation to Emancipation* (London, 1976), 27; 30–31; John Gerard, *The Autobiography of an Elizabethan*, ed. Philip Caraman (London, 1951), 32.
11. Aveling, *The Handle and the Axe*, 24–25; 32. Calvinists, too, benefited from the massive confiscation of land that took place during the first decade after Henry's break with Rome. In 1544, Adam Winthrop, a cloth merchant from London, purchased Groton Monastery from the king, instantly acquiring for his family the prestige and respectability that allowed his son, Adam, Jr., to become the auditor of St. John's and Trinity Colleges in Cambridge, and his grandson, John, to be elected the first governor of the Massachusetts Bay Colony in 1629. See Carole Chandler Waldrup, "Mary Tyndal Winthrop," in *Colonial Women: 23 Europeans Who Helped Build a Nation* (Jefferson, NC, 1999), 26.
12. Aveling, *The Handle and the Axe*, 34–35. Recently, some British historians have come to question whether early modern English Catholicism was as anemic as Aveling and his intellectual contemporary, John Bossy, have argued it was. Bossy insists that Catholicism, as a community of faith, ceased to exist in England until the Jesuit seminary at Douai, in Spanish Flanders, was founded in 1570, and priests who had been trained there returned to England and commenced a reformed and invigorated "mission" in England. In contrast, historians like Alexandra Walsham and Lucy Wooding have argued that at the time of the Henrician Reformation, Catholicism in England was vibrant, if popular, and that this popular Catholicism might have posed more of a challenge to the Reformation had the Jesuits simply been willing to serve and cultivate it. See John Bossy, *The English Catholic Community, 1570–1850* (New York, 1976), 4; Alexandra Walsham, *Church Papists: Catholicism, Conformity and Confessional Polemic in Early Modern England* (Rochester, NY, 1993), 16; Lucy Wooding, *Rethinking Catholicism in Reformation England* (New York, 2000), 6.
13. Bossy, *English Catholic Community*, 7; 49–50; Aveling, *The Handle and the Axe*, 117.
14. Gerard is quoted in Brian Magee, *The English Recusants: A Study of the Post-Reformation Catholic Survival and the Operation of the Recusancy Laws* (London, 1938), 106; Henry Garnet, *An Apology Against the Defence of Schisme* (Douai, 1593), rpt. in *English Recusant Literature, 1558–1640*, ed. D. M. Rogers (London, 1973), 167:143.

15. Bossy, *English Catholic Community*, 4; Walsham, *Church Papists*, 81.
16. For more on the issues involved in calculating the size of the Catholic population in the seventeenth-century, see Bossy, *English Catholic Community*, ch. 8. Of the 29,176 white men, women, and children in Maryland, 2,974 were Catholic. See *Archives of Maryland*, ed. William Hand Brown et al. (Baltimore, 1883–present), 25:258–259.
17. Haigh, "From Monopoly to Minority," 134; Aveling, *The Handle and the Axe*, 59–65; 77; 80–82; Thomas M. McCoog, "The English Jesuit Mission and the French Match, 1579–1581," *Catholic Historical Review* 87 (2001): 185–213.
18. Aveling, *The Handle and the Axe*, 60; James W. Foster, *George Calvert: The Early Years* (Baltimore, 1983), 27.
19. Quoted in Haigh, "From Monopoly to Minority," 134; "The Martyrdom of William Freeman," anonymous, in *Unpublished Documents relating to the English Martyrs*, ed. John Hungerford Pollen (London, 1908), 347; J. C. H. Aveling, *The Catholic Recusants of the West Riding of Yorkshire, 1558–1790* (Leeds, UK, 1963), 210; Gerard, *Autobiography*, 32–33. It should be noted that Freeman did not spend all of his time ensconced in a domestic chaplaincy. He also worked as an itinerate priest in Warwickshire, where he was eventually arrested and executed in 1595. See J. H. Pollen, "William Freeman, Venerable," in *The Original Catholic Encyclopedia* (New York, 1907–1912), 7:258.
20. *Modus Vivendi hominum Societatis*, 1616, rpt. in *Records of the English Province of the Society of Jesus*, ed. Henry Foley (London, 1875), 2:3–6.
21. William Allen, *Cardinal Allen's Defence of Sir William Stanley's Surrender at Deventer, January 29th, 1586–87*, ed. Thomas Heywood (Manchester, 1851), 12–33; "The Protestation of 31 January, 1603," rpt. in *Dodd's Church History of England*, ed. M. A. Tierney (London, 1838–1843), 3:clxxxviii; Sommerville, "Papalist Political Thought," 164; Michael C. Questier, *Catholicism and Community in Early Modern England: Politics, Aristocratic Patronage and Religion, c. 1550–1640* (New York, 2006), 298.
22. Aveling, *The Handle and the Axe*, 131.
23. William Allen, *Some Correspondence of Cardinal Allen*, ed. Patrick Ryan (London, 1965), 9:67.
24. Bossy, *English Catholic Community*, 51; Law, *Archpriest Controversy*, p. i, 54.
25. Richard Lascelles, *Little Way How to Hear Mass* (1644), in Bossy, *English Catholic Community*, 257.
26. John Sergeant, 1667, quoted in ibid., 257–258; "Letter of the Lay Catholics of England to Fr. Richard Smith, Bishop of Chalcedon," July 1627, rpt. in *History of the Society of Jesus in North America, Colonial and Federal, from the First Colonization till 1645, Text*, ed. Thomas Hughes (New York, 1907), 1:205.
27. Thomas M. McCoog, *The Society of Jesus in Ireland, Scotland, and England, 1541–1588* (New York, 1996), 22; Gerard, *Autobiography*, 33.
28. Haigh, "From Monopoly to Minority," 142; Richard Smith, *An Elizabethan Recusant House Comprising the Life of the Lady Magdalen Viscountess Montague (1538–1608)*, ed. A. C. Southern (London, 1954), 44.
29. *Modus Vivendi hominum Societatis*, 5; Henry More, in Ethelred Luke Taunton, *The History of the Jesuits in England, 1580–1773* (London, 1901), 363.
30. Lawrence Stone, *The Crisis of the Aristocracy* (New York, 1965), 742; Aveling, *The Handle and the Axe*, 67.
31. Samuel Rawson Gardiner, *History of England from the Accession of James I to the Disgrace of Chief-Justice Coke* (London, 1863), 1:110. Illiteracy rates among the gentry in Durham at the turn of the seventeenth century were nearly nonexistent, while illiteracy among yeomen was as high as 70 percent, and nearly 90 percent of husbandmen could not sign their names. See David Cressy, *Literacy and the Social Order: Reading and Writing in Tudor and Stuart England* (New York, 1980), 159–163.
32. Richard Smith, *The Prudentiall Balance of Religion* (St. Omer, 1609); Anthony Champney, *A Manual of Controversies* (Paris, 1614); and James Gordon, *A Summary of Controversies* (1618); Robert Persons, *Brief Discoverse Contayning certayne reasons why Catholiques refuse to goe to Church* (1580), 6r 3v; Ralph Buckland, *A Persuasive Against Attending Protestant Churches* (n.d., but had to have been written before 1611, when Buckland died). Also,

Michael C. Questier, *Conversion, Politics, and Religion in England, 1580–1625* (New York, 1996), 15, 19, 25–26; and James Gordon, *A Summary of Controversies* (1618).
33. Bossy, *English Catholic Community*, 75.
34. Ibid., 198–199.
35. Joseph Gillow and Richard Trappes-Lomax, eds., *The Diary of the "Blue Nuns," or Order of the Immaculate Conception of Our Lady at Paris, 1658–1810* (London, 1910), 354.
36. Edwin Burton, quoted in Peter Guilday, *The English Catholic Refugees on the Continent, 1558–1795* (London, 1914), 324; Charles Carroll of Carrollton to Charles Carroll of Annapolis, October 22, 1761, in Ronald Hoffman, Sally D. Mason, and Eleanor S. Darcy, eds., *Dear Papa, Dear Charley: The Peregrinations of a Revolutionary Aristocrat* (Chapel Hill, NC, 2001), 1:231.
37. Aveling, *The Handle and the Axe*, 192; Michael H. Sharratt, "Theology and Philosophy at the English College, Douai: A Handlist of Sources," *History of the Universities* 18 (2003): 200.
38. Lawrence Stone, "The Educational Revolution in England, 1560–1640," *Past and Present* 28 (1964): 41–80; Jefferson H. Looney, "Undergraduate Education in Early Stuart Cambridge," *History of Education* 10 (1981): 9.
39. Mark Curtis, *Oxford and Cambridge in Transition: 1558–1642* (Oxford, 1959), ch. 3. Some scholars disagree with Curtis and insist that the curricula at Oxford and Cambridge remained static and steeped in medieval scholasticism until after the English Civil War in the 1640s. See William Costello, *The Curriculum at Seventeenth Century Cambridge* (Cambridge, 1958) and Christopher Hill, *Intellectual Origins of the English Revolution* (Oxford, 1959). Hill acknowledges that modern ideas about science and history were instrumental in bringing about the English Civil War, but he believes that before the 1640s, it was primarily men of the "middling sort"—merchants and artisans who did not necessarily attend university—who were imbibing the humanist emphasis on the individual that came to characterize modernity.
40. Publishers in Rome were not allowed to print books that relied upon or accepted heliocentric theory until 1822. See Looney, "Undergraduate Education at Early Stuart Cambridge," 11–16; Thomas Kuhn, *The Copernican Revolution: Planetary Astronomy in the Development of Western Thought* (New York, 1997), 191–193, 198; *The Original Catholic Encyclopedia*, 4:350–353.
41. See, for example, John Henry, "Science and the Coming of the Enlightenment," in *The Enlightenment World*, ed. Martin Fitzpatrick et al. (New York, 2004), 10–26; Jerry Weinberger, "Francis Bacon and the Unity of Knowledge: Reason and Revelation," in *Francis Bacon and the Refiguring of Early Modern Thought*, ed. Julie Robin Solomon and Catherine Gimelli Martin (Burlington, VT, 2005); Jonathan Irvine Israel, *Radical Enlightenment: Philosophy and the Making of Modernity, 1650–1750* (New York, 2002).
42. Thomas Jefferson to Roger Weightman, June 24, 1826, in *Jefferson: Writings*, ed. Merrill D. Peterson (New York, 1984), 1517.
43. Hill, *Intellectual Origins of the English Revolution*, 309; *The Times (of London)*, March 5, 2003.
44. Noel B. Reynolds and Arlene W. Saxonhouse, "Hobbes and the Beginnings of Modern Political Thought," in *Thomas Hobbes: A Critical Modern Edition of Newly Identified Work of the Young Hobbes*, ed. Noel B. Reynolds and Arlene W. Saxonhouse (Chicago, 1995), 33, 126–141; Thomas Hobbes, *Behmouth, or the Long Parliament*, ed. Ferdinand Tönnies (Chicago, 1990), 40, 58.
45. Arthur Pierce Middleton and Henry M. Miller, "'Mr. Secretary': John Lewgar, St. John's Freehold, and Early Maryland," *Maryland Historical Magazine* 103 (2008): 132–136; Edward C. Papenfuse, *A Biographical Dictionary of the Maryland Legislature, 1689–1785* (Baltimore, 1989), 1:16.
46. Aveling, *The Handle and the Axe*, 127–128.
47. David Stevens, "The Stagecraft of James Shirley," *Educational Theatre Journal* 29 (1977): 493–516.
48. Ibid., 129, 131; Thomas Fuller, *History of the Worthies of England* (London, 1840), 2:343; John Venn and John Archibald Venn, *Alumni Cantabrigienses: A Biographical*

List of All Known Students, Graduates and Holders of Office at the University of Cambridge, from the Earliest Times to 1900 (1922–1953), 1:122; Questier, *Conversion, Politics, and Religion*, 46.
49. Sean Kelsey, "Henry Cary, first Viscount Falkland," in *Online Oxford Dictionary of National Biography*, January 29, 2009, http://www.oxforddnb.com/public/index.html?url=%2Fview%2Farticle%2F4837 (subscription required); Thomas Longueville, *The Falklands* (New York, 1897), 4.
50. Ibid., 7–29. Longueville mistakenly reports that Tanfield Cary converted in 1626, and this mistake has been repeated by several historians since. Her conversion took place in 1604, however. In 1626, she did briefly consider the idea that the growing strain of Arminianism in the Church of England had rendered that denomination an acceptable alternative to the "true Church" that was Catholicism. In the end, however, she chose to make her conversion to Catholicism a matter of public knowledge. See Bossy, *English Catholic Community*, 159; and Heather Wolfe, *Elizabeth Cary, Lady Falkland: Life and Letters* (Tempe, AZ, 2001), 4–5.
51. Ibid., 1; Longueville, *The Falklands*, 84–94.
52. N.N., An *Epistle of a Catholicke young gentleman, (being for his religion imprisoned.) To his Father a Protestant* (London, 1623), 12–13.
53. Ibid., 19.
54. "The magistrate ought not to forbid the preaching or professing of any speculative opinions in any Church, because they have no manner of relation to the civil rights of the subjects," Locke wrote to his friend, Philip van Limborch, in 1689, the same year Parliament ousted James II because he was Catholic and replaced him with his Calvinist son-in-law, the Dutch Reformed William of Orange. See Locke, *The Works of John Locke in Nine Volumes* (London, 1794), 5:40; Philip Benedict, *Christ's Churches Purely Reformed: A Social History of Calvinism* (New Haven, CT, 2002), 414–422; Tony Claydon, *William III and the Godly Revolution* (New York, 1006), chs. 1 and 4.
55. Sommerville, "Papalist Political Thought," 163; "An Act for the better discovering and repressing of Popish Recusants," Jac. I, c. 3, 4, in *Statutes of the Realm*, ed. T. E. Tomlins et al. (London, 1810–1828), 4:1071–1073.
56. Ibid., 1074.
57. Robert Parsons to Cardinal Bellarmine, May 18, 1606, in *Dodd's Church History of England*, 4:cxxxv–cxxxvi; "The Protestation of 31 January, 1603," 3; Maurus Lunn, "English Benedictines and the Oath of Allegiance, 1606–1647," *Recusant History* 10 (1969): 146.
58. M. C. Questier, "Loyalty, Religion, and State Power in Early Modern England: English Romanism and the Jacobean Oath of Allegiance," *Historical Journal* 40 (1997): 315; Lunn, "English Benedictines," 151–152. Barlow's younger brother, Edward, who was also a Benedictine, was convicted of being a priest in 1641 and hanged, drawn, and quartered near Lancaster. In 1970, Pope Paul VI canonized him. See Bede Camm, "Ven. Edward Ambrose Barlow," *The Original Catholic Encyclopedia*, 2:298.
59. Sommerville, "Papalist Political Thought," 166–167; George Blackwell, "Mr. Blackwels Letter to the Priests his Brethren for the Lawfullness of Taking the Oath of Allegiance, 7 July 1607," in *Mr. George Blackwell (Made by Pope Clement 8. Arch-priest of England) his Answeres upon Sundry his Examinations* (London, 1607).
60. Ibid.
61. Lunn, "English Benedictines," 147, 151; Questier, *Conversion, Politics, and Religion*, 13–23.
62. D. O. Hunter-Blair, "Thomas Preston," *The Original Catholic Encyclopedia*, 12:402.
63. Thomas Preston, *A New-Yeare's Gift for English Catholikes* (1620); Matthew 22:15–22.

Chapter 2

1. John Locke, *A Letter Concerning Toleration* (New York, 2007), 7–8.
2. Roger Williams, who was a contemporary of Cecilius Calvert, was also an ardent advocate of religious toleration. His *Plea for Religious Liberty* actually applied to Jews and Muslims. Although Williams founded the colony of Providence Plantation some thirteen years before Maryland's assembly passed the Act Concerning Religion, religious liberty in

Rhode Island did not become official—that is to say, legal—until 1663, when Rhode Island received a charter from Charles II. Williams's contributions to the history of religious toleration in America have completely eclipsed those of the Calverts. See Edwin Gaustad and Leigh Schmidt, *The Religious History of America: The Heart of the American Story from Colonial Times to Today* (New York, 2004), 67–68.

3. James Wilson, *The Works of James Wilson*, ed. Bird Wilson (Philadelphia, 1804), 1:7–8; John D. Krugler, "An 'Ungracious Silence': Historians and the Calvert Vision," *Maryland Historical Magazine* 99, no. 3 (2004): 374–388.

4. When they were not ignoring the role that Maryland played in the history of religious freedom in America, many early historians sought either to deny the tolerant implications of the 1649 Act Concerning Religion or to deny any connection between the Act and Cecilius Calvert and/or his Catholic faith. William Ewart Gladstone tried to do both. In his *Rome and the Newest Fashions in Religion*, Gladstone both emphasized the fact that the Act Concerning Religion called for the execution of anyone who denied the Trinity—thus emphasizing the Act's intolerant aspects—and claimed, erroneously, that two-thirds of the lawmakers who passed the Act were Protestants. See W. E. Gladstone, *Rome and the Newest Fashions in Religion* (Leipzig, 1875), 15–17, 221. Another good example is B. F. Brown's *Early Religious History of Maryland: Religious Toleration Not an Act of Roman Catholic Legislation* (Baltimore, 1876), 4. Monseignor John Fox's unfriendly posture toward liberalism, which he articulated in Newark in 1903, is mentioned in the opening paragraphs of this book's Introduction.

5. John Gilmary Shea, *History of the Catholic Church in the United States: The Catholic Church in Colonial Days, 1521–1763* (New York, 1886), 37. Bishop William T. Russell also assumed and/or exaggerated the Calverts' religious motivations in his *Maryland: The Land of Sanctuary: A History of Religious Toleration from the First Settlement until the American Revolution* (Baltimore, 1907), as did Archbishop Henry Edward Manning in his *The Vatican Decrees in their Bearing on Civil Allegiance* (New York, 1875). There was a flip side to this tendency to glorify the Catholic Calverts, however—and that was a tendency to downplay the Calverts' position in the history of "true" American Catholicism, because they were not always obedient Catholics. Thomas Hughes, S.J., referred to Lord Baltimore as a "so-called Catholic" when discussing a disagreement that the colony's first proprietor had with Maryland's resident Jesuits. He later used the word "imbecile" to describe the proprietor's understanding of the Jesuits' intentions and insisted that Baltimore's attitudes toward the priests left "no room for debate" about "what kind of Catholic he was." See Thomas Hughes, *History of the Society of Jesus in North America, Colonial and Federal, from the First Colonization till 1645, Text* (New York, 1908), 1:435, 456.

6. William Penn, *Great Case of Liberty of Conscience Once More Briefly Debated and Defended by the Authority of Reason, Scripture and Antiquity: Which may serve the Place of a General Reply to such late Discourses as have Oppos'd a Toleration* (1670); Roger Williams, *A Plea for Religious Liberty* (1644).

7. "Objections Answered Touching Maryland," 1632 or 1633, rpt. in Bradley Tyler Johnson, *The Foundation of Maryland and the Origin of the Act Concerning Religion* (Baltimore, 1883), 28.

8. Krugler, *English and Catholic*, 32; 130–131. Earlier in his career, Krugler did not believe that George Calvert's conversion to Anglicanism was sincere. See "Lord Baltimore, Roman Catholics, and Toleration: Religious Policy in Maryland during the Early Catholic Years, 1634–1649," *Catholic Historical Review* 65 (1979): 51. In *English and Catholic*, however, he points out that Calvert married—and buried—his first wife according to the rites of the Anglican Church. Marriage was not a Sacrament in the eyes of the Church of England, and many church papists, therefore, did not get married in the Church of England because they did not have to. In general, those individuals who chose to be married in the English Church were committed Anglicans.

9. James J. Hennesey, "Roman Catholicism: The Maryland Tradition," *Thought* 51 (1976): 282–295.

10. Krugler, *English and Catholic*, 72.

11. Pauline Croft, "England and the Peace with Spain, 1604," *History Today* 49 (2004): 18–23.
12. Krugler, *English and Catholic*, 52–53; Glyn Redworth, *The Prince and the Infanta: The Cultural Politics of the Spanish Match* (New Haven, CT, 2003), 42; Alexander Samson, *The Spanish Match: Prince Charles' Journey to Madrid, 1623* (Burlington, VT, 2006), 176.
13. Krugler, *English and Catholic*, 57.
14. Wallace Notestein and Helen Frances Relf, eds., *Commons Debates, 1621* (New Haven, CT, 1935), 1:318–319; R. Louis Gentilcore, Geoffrey J. Matthews, and Don Measner, *Historical Atlas of Canada, from the Beginning to 1800* (Toronto, 1993), 48. "The Crown" was a term that referred to the king and his advisors—many of whom also served in the House of Commons. For more on how "the Crown" differed from "the King," see G. E. Aylmer, *The King's Servants: The Civil Service of Charles I, 1625–1642* (New York, 1961), 136–137.
15. Jamestown and Henricopolis were in present-day Virginia; St. George's was in present-day Bermuda; Renews, New Cabriol, and St. John's were in present-day Newfoundland and Labrador; and Plymouth was in present-day Massachusetts. See Nicolas Canny, "England's New World and the Old, 1480s–1630s," in William Roger Louis et al., *The Oxford History of the British Empire*, Volume One: *The Origins of Empire: British Overseas Enterprise to the Close of the Seventeenth Century* (New York, 2001), 148–169.
16. Pauline Maier, *From Resistance to Revolution: Colonial Radicals and the Development of American Opposition to Britain, 1765–1776* (New York, 1972), 100–114; Theodore Draper, *A Struggle for Power: The American Revolution* (New York, 1996), 216–223.
17. Richard A. Preston, "Fishing and Plantation: New England in the Parliament of 1621," *American Historical Review* 45 (1939): 35; Krugler, *English and Catholic*, 79.
18. Pauline Croft, *King James* (New York, 2003), 118.
19. George Calvert to the 2nd Earl of Salisbury, August 12, 1622, in *Calendar of the Manuscripts of the Most Honorable Marquee of Salisbury, Preserved at Hatfield House, Hertfordshire*, ed. Montague Spencer Giuseppi and Geraint Owen (London, 1915), 22:328; William Robinson to William Wentworth, August 27, 1630, in *Wentworth Papers, 1597–1628*, ed. J. P. Cooper (London, 1973), 12:129.
20. Simon Stock, a Carmelite priest whose real name was Thomas Doughty, claimed to have converted George Calvert in November 1624. John Krugler places Calvert's conversion between October 7th and November 14th, based on Calvert's travel itinerary. See Krugler, *English and Catholic*, 66–69, 72; Luca Codignola, *The Coldest Harbour of the Land: Simon Stock and Lord Baltimore's Colony in New Foundland, 1621–1649* (Montreal, 1988), 6.
21. Robert J. Brugger, *Maryland: A Middle Temperament, 1634–1980* (Baltimore, 1988), 4; J. C. H. Aveling, *The Handle and the Axe: The Catholic Recusants in England from Reformation to Emancipation* (London, 1976), 123–125; Croft, *King James*, 24–25; Antonia Fraser, *The Gunpowder Plot: Terror and Faith in 1605* (London, 1997), 15. Simon Stock, the priest who claimed responsibility for George Calvert's conversion, actually insisted that Anne "always put off her conversion, and finally died outside the true Church, although in heart a Catholic." See "Stock's Narrative," in *Carmel in England: A History of the English Mission of the Discalced Carmelites, 1615–1849*, ed. Benedict Zimmerman (New York, 1899), 30.
22. Edward Wynne to George Calvert, August 21, 1621 and August 17, 1622, in *Newfoundland Discovered: English Attempts at Colonisation*, ed. Gillian T. Cell (London, 1982), 253, 255–256; Krugler, *English and Catholic*, 80; Woodrow Wilson, "Colonies and Nation: A Short History of the People of the United States," *Harper's Monthly Magazine*, February 1901, 344.
23. Lord Baltimore to King Charles I, August 19, 1629, in John Thomas Scharf, *History of Maryland, from the Earliest Period to the Present Day* (Baltimore, 1879), 1:45; Codignola, *The Coldest Harbour*, 96. For more on the little ice age, see Hubert H. Lamb, "Climatic Variation and Changes in the Wind and Ocean Circulation: The Little Ice Age in the Northeast Atlantic," *Quarternary Research* 11 (1979): 1–20.
24. John M. Lenhart, "An Important Chapter in American Church History (1625–1650)," *Catholic Historical Review* 8 (1929): 504–505.
25. "Examination of Erasmus Stourton, Late Preacher to the Colony of Ferryland in Newfoundland, October 9th, 1628," in *Calendar of State Papers, Colonial Series, 1574–1660*, ed.

W. Noel Sainsbury et al. (London, 1860), 1:94; Baltimore to Charles I, August 19, 1629, in Scharf, *History of Maryland*, 1:45.
26. Lenhart, "An Important Chapter in American Church History," 504–505.
27. Baltimore to an unnamed friend, probably Francis Cottington, August 18, 1629, in Lawrence Counselman Wroth, "Tobacco or Codfish: Lord Baltimore Makes his Choice," *Bulletin of the New York Public Library* 58 (1954): 527; Baltimore to Charles I, August 19, 1629, and Baltimore to the Duke of Buckingham, August 25, 1628, in Scharf, *History of Maryland*, 1:45, 42; Krugler, *English and Catholic*, 95–101.
28. Ibid., 105; "Governor Pott and Others to the Council," in *Archives of Maryland*, ed. William Hand Brown et al. (Baltimore, 1883–present), 3:16.
29. Baltimore to Charles I, August 19, 1629, in Scharf, *History of Maryland*, 1:45; Baltimore to Francis Cottington, August 18, 1629, in Wroth, "Tobacco or Codfish," 527. Avalon remained in the Calvert family's possession, and several dozen colonists continued to live there with Cecilius Calvert as their very uninvolved proprietor until 1637, when King Charles I rescinded the charter his father had given to Lord Baltimore and gave the territory to David Kirke. Kirke later insisted that "the air of Newfoundland agrees perfectly well with all God's creatures except Jesuits and schismatics." See "Preface," *Calendar of State Papers, Colonial Series, America and West Indies, 1661–1668*, ed. W. Noel Sainsbury (London, 1880), 5:xxxvii.
30. Krugler, *English and Catholic*, 107, 103; Wroth, "Tobacco or Codfish," n. 5, 530.
31. Virginia's original charter ran from "four and thirty and one and forty Degrees of the said Latitude." See "The First Charter of Virginia, 1606," in *The Federal and State Constitutions, Colonial Charters, and Other Organic Laws of the States, Territories, and Colonies, Now and Heretofore Forming the United States of America*, ed. Francis Newton Thorpe (Washington, DC, 1909), 7:3784, *The Avalon Project, Yale Law School*, April 12, 2009, http://avalon.law.yale.edu/17th_century/va01.asp; "Satellite View and Map of the United States," *One World, Nations Online*, April 12, 2009, http://www.nationsonline.org/oneworld/map/google_map_usa.htm; Krugler, *English and Catholic*, 107.
32. Ibid., 117; Dermot B. Fenlon, "Wentworth and the Parliament of 1634," *Journal of the Royal Society of Antiquaries of Ireland* 94 (1964): 159–175.
33. Fr. Simon Stock approached the Propaganda on Calvert's behalf. For a translation of his correspondence with the office, see Codignola, *The Coldest Harbour*, 69–140.
34. "Father Andrew White to Lord Baltimore, February 20th, 1638," in *The Calvert Papers*, ed. John Wesley Murray Lee (Baltimore, 1889), 1:205. Shortly before Calvert left Newfoundland to travel to Virginia, two Jesuits, Alexander Baker and Lawrence Rigby, arrived in Avalon, having been sent there by Andrew White. See Simon Stock to the Propaganda Fide, July 2, 1629, in Codignola, *The Coldest Harbour*, 114.
35. "Cecilius, Lord Baltimore, Declaration to the Lords," n.d., in *Calvert Papers*, 1:222–225. The boundaries of Maryland were modified one other time, in June 1632, in response to Virginia Governor Plott's assertion that the southernmost tip of the Chesapeake's eastern shore had already been surveyed and settled by Virginians. Hence, what is known as the "Delmarva Peninsula" today includes the Virginia counties of Accomack and Northampton. See Lois Green Carr and Edward C. Papenfuse, "The Charter of Maryland," *Archives of Maryland*, 550:19.
36. "Will of Sir George Calvert Lord Baltimore," *Calvert Papers*, 1:48–50.
37. "Lord Baltimore's Instructions to Colonists," November 13, 1633, in *Calvert Papers*, 1:134, 136–137; Robert Wintour, *A Short Treatise Sett Downe in a Letter Written by R.W. to His Worthy Friend C.J.R. concerning the New Plantation Now Erecting under the Right Ho[nora]ble the Lord Baltemore in Maryland*, reproduced in facsimile from the original document in the Hugh Hampton Young Collection of the Enoch Pratt Free Library, ed. John D. Krugler (Baltimore, 1976), 38.
38. *Modus Vivendi hominum Societatis*, 1616, rpt. in *Records of the English Province of the Society of Jesus*, ed. Henry Foley (London, 1875), 2:5.
39. When Samuel Johnson challenged the sincerity of the colonists' reaction to the Quebec Act in 1774, he noted that Maryland, under the Catholic Lords Baltimore, had been "distinguished

with Immunities superior to all other Colonies," and that the "whole executive power of the State was centered in... the popish proprietor." See Samuel Johnson, *Hypocrisy Unmasked; or, a Shorty Inquiry into the Religious Complaints of our American Colonies* (1774), 6–7.

40. "Charter of Maryland," *Archives of Maryland*, 657:64–65; W. S. Holdsworth, *A History of English Law* (London, 1903), 1:50; Gaillard Thomas Lapsley, *The County Palatine of Durham: A Study in Constitutional History* (London, 1900). Durham was not considered to be a separate kingdom. It was, rather, a kingdom within a kingdom. Henry VIII actually reduced some of the autonomy that the bishops of Durham had been given by William Rufus, but the leaders of the palatinate still had far more power than any of the local leaders in counties that were closer to London.

41. For more on the similarities between Durham and Maryland, see Tim Thornton, "The Palatinate of Durham and the Maryland Charter," *American Journal of Legal History* 45 (2001): 235–255.

42. John Tracy Ellis, *American Catholicism* (Chicago, 1969), 25; Mark A. Noll, *A History of Christianity in the United States and Canada* (Grand Rapids, MI, 1992), 35. Edward Fox describes Charles as a "Catholic monarch" in an article about the Royal Stuart Society, which has been publically marking the anniversary of Charles's execution every year since 1926. See Edward Fox, "Tales of the City: Head of a Divine Cult; Followers Keep Faith with Spirit of Charles I," *The Independent (London)*, February 1, 1995, 22. See also Arnold Oskar Meyer's old, but surprisingly modern and viable article, "Charles I and Rome," *American Historical Review* 19 (1913): 13–26.

43. "Baltimore's Four Points. Submitted to the English Provincial, and to be issued in the name of the latter," 1641, in Thomas Hughes, *History of the Society of Jesus in North America, Colonial and Federal, Documents* (New York, 1907), 1:167.

44. Carr and Papenfuse, "Charter of Maryland," *Archives of Maryland*, 657:75, 550:13.

45. Jerome Hawley and John Lewger, *A Relation of Maryland; together with a Map of the Countrey, the Conditions of Plantation, with his Majesties Charter to the Lord Baltemore, translated into England* (1635), in *Archives of Maryland*, 657:42–44. Initially, Baltimore offered 2,000 acres for every five men an individual transported to the colony, but that offer was halved shortly after the first crop of settlers arrived in Maryland. See Carr and Papenfuse, "Charter of Maryland," *Archives of Maryland*, 550:13.

46. John D. Krugler, "Captain Robert Wintour and the Maryland Design, 1633–1638," in *To Live Like Princes*, ed. John D. Krugler (Baltimore, 1976), 8; Robert Wintour, *A Short Treatise Sett Downe in a Letter Written by R.W. to His Worthy Freind C.J.R. concerning the New Plantation Now Erecting under the Right Ho[nora]ble the Lord Baltemore in Maryland*, reproduced in facsimile from the original document in the Hugh Hampton Young Collection of the Enoch Pratt Free Library, ed. John D. Krugler (Baltimore, 1976), 31.

47. According to William Peasley, the first treasurer of Maryland and Lord Baltimore's brother-in-law, *A Relation of Maryland* was "written and conceived by Mr. Jerome Haulie and Mr. John Lewgar." See L. Leon Bernard, "Some New Light on the Early Years of the Baltimore Plantation," *Maryland Historical Magazine* 44 (1947): 100. For more on Lewger, see Arthur Pierce Middleton and Henry M. Miller, "'Mr. Secretary': John Lewgar, St. John's Freehold, and Early Maryland," *Maryland Historical Magazine* 103 (2008): 132–136. For more on Hawley, see Edward D. Neill, *The Founders of Maryland, as Portrayed in Manuscripts, Provincial Records, and Early Documents* (Albany, NY, 1876), 83–86; James Walter Thomas, *Chronicles of Colonial Maryland* (Cumberland, MD, 1913), 70; and Ernest M. Wiltshire, "Descendants of James Hawley," genealogical notes provided to the author.

48. Jerome Hawley and John Lewger, "A Relation of the Lord Baltemore's Plantation in Maryland," *Archives of Maryland*, 657:25, 22, 18, 25. For more on the various techniques used by the authors of colonial promotional literature in the seventeenth century, see Howard Mumford Jones, "The Colonial Impulse: An Analysis of 'Promotional' Literature of Colonization," *Proceedings of the American Philosophical Society* 90 (1946): 131–161.

49. Edward Duffield Neill, *Virginia Carolorum: The Colony under the Rule of Charles I and Second* (Albany, 1886), 200–201.
50. Andrew White, S.J., *A Relation of the Success-full beginnings of the Lord Baltemore's Plantation in Mary-land* (1634), 3, 8.
51. Russell R. Menard, "Immigrants and their Increase: The Process of Population Growth in Early Colonial Maryland," in *Law, Society and Politics in Early Maryland*, ed. Aubrey C. Land, Lois G. Carr, and Edward C. Papenfuse (Baltimore, 1977), 93; Wesley Frank Craven, *The Colonies in Transition, 1660–1713* (New York, 1968), 15–16.
52. Maris A. Vinovskis, "Mortality Rates and Trends in Massachusetts before 1860," *Journal of Economic History* 32 (1972): 195, 201; Russell R. Menard, *Economy and Society in Early Colonial Maryland* (New York, 1985), 143; Russell R. Menard, "Immigration to the Chesapeake Colonies in the Seventeenth Century: A Review Essay," *Maryland Historical Magazine* 68 (1973): 323–329.
53. Vicenzo Gussoni, Venetian Ambassador in England, to the Doge and Senate, October 28, 1633, in *Calendar of State Papers and Manuscripts Relating to English Affairs, Existing in the Archives and Collections of Venice, and in Other Libraries of Northern Italy*, ed. Allen B. Hinds (London, 1921), 23:158; Cecilius Calvert to Thomas Wentworth, January 10, 1634, in *The Earl of Strafforde's Letters and Dispatches, With an Essay Towards His Life, by Sir George Radcliffe, From the Originals in the Possession of His Great Grandson, The Right Honourable Thomas Earl of Malton*, ed. William Knowler (London, 1739), 1:178–179; Krugler, *English and Catholic*, 145, 121.
54. "Lord Baltimore's Instructions to Colonists," November 13, 1633, *Calvert Papers*, 1:134, 136–137; Wintour, "A Short Treatise," 38.
55. Cecilius Calvert to Thomas Wentworth, January 10, 1634, in *The Earl of Stafforde's Letters and Dispatches*, 1:178; Robert Brenner, *Merchants and Revolution: Commercial Change, Political Conflict, and London's Overseas Traders* (London, 2003), 121.
56. "Lord Baltimore's Instructions to Colonists," *Calvert Papers*, 1:132. The mandate that Baltimore gave his brother was, of course, not what Monsignor John Fox had in mind 270 years later, when he warned his parishioners about the dangers of "Americanism." Nevertheless, Fox's warning does seem ironic, when juxtaposed with the letter and spirit of Baltimore's warning from 1633. Fox's homily is discussed in the Introduction to this book.
57. Ibid.
58. Andrew White to Cecilius Calvert, December 12, 1638, *Calvert Papers*, 1:201; Henry Foley, *Records of the English Province of the Society of Jesus* (London, 1882), 3:338; Robert Emmett Curran, ed., *American Jesuit Spirituality: The Maryland Tradition, 1634–1900* (New York, 1988), 10, 13; Earl Arnett, Robert J. Brugger, and Edward C. Papenfuse, *Maryland: A New Guide to the Old Line State* (Baltimore, 1999), 16; Christopher Haigh, "From Monopoly to Minority: Catholicism in Early Modern England," *Transactions of the Royal Historical Society* 31 (1981): 139–141. See also chapter 1.
59. James Axtell, *The Invasion Within: The Contest of Cultures in Colonial North America* (New York, 1985), 49–90; *The European and the Indian: Essays in the Ethnohistory of Colonial America* (New York, 1982), 39–86.
60. Christopher Morris to Edward Knott, July 27, 1640, in Curran, *American Jesuit Spirituality*, 57. The Society's Constitutions clearly defined an evangelical mission for the Jesuits. "Our vocation," Ignatius wrote, "is to travel through the world and to live in any part of it whatsoever where there is hope of greater service to God and of help of souls." See George E. Ganns, trans., *The Constitutions of the Society of Jesus* (St. Louis, MO, 1970), 170, 172.
61. John J. Gerard, *Stonyhurst College: Its Life beyond the Seas, 1592–1794, and on English Soil, 1794–1894* (Belfast, 1894), 3.
62. Russell R. Menard and Lois G. Carr, "The Lords Baltimore and the Colonization of Maryland," in *Early Maryland in a Wider World*, ed. David B. Quinn (Detroit, 1982), 180; Michael A. Smolek, *Archeological Investigations at Fort Point, St. Inigoes, Maryland* (St. Mary's City, MD, 1983), 7.
63. *Archives of Maryland*, 1:2.
64. Thomas Copley to Lord Baltimore, April 3, 1638, *Calvert Papers*, 1:163.

65. *Archives of Maryland*, 1:16–17. The clerical situation was far worse for the Church of England in seventeenth-century Maryland than it was for the Catholic Church. By 1696, there were just four more Anglican clergy in Maryland than there were Catholic priests, even though Quakers and Catholics combined made up just 10 to 15 percent of the white population at the time. Anglicanism did not have an inherently evangelical impulse, so the opportunity to convert the Indians held no particular attraction for ministers of the Church of England, many of whom had wives and children who would have had to make the journey to Maryland with them. For more on the number of Anglican clergy in seventeenth-century Maryland, see Carol Lee van Voorst, "The Anglican Clergy in Maryland, 1696–1776" (Ph.D. dissertation, Princeton University, 1978), 110.
66. Ganns, *The Constitutions of the Society of Jesus*, 170–172; Thomas O'Brien Hanley, *Their Rights and Liberties: The Beginnings of Religious Toleration and Political Freedom in Maryland* (Westminster, MD 1959), 85–86.
67. Alfred Pearce Dennis, "Lord Baltimore's Struggle with the Jesuits, 1634–1649," *Annual Report of the American Historical Association* (1899), 113; Dennis Pogue and Karlene B. Leeper, *Archeological Investigations at the "Old Chapel Field," St. Inigoes, Maryland* (St. Mary's City, MD, 1984), 7; Edwin Warfield Beitzell, *The Jesuit Missionaries of St. Mary's County, Maryland* (Abell, MD, 1976), 20.
68. *Archives of Maryland*, 4:35–36.
69. Ibid., 36.
70. Thomas Cornwallis to Lord Baltimore, April 16, 1638, in *Calvert Papers*, 1:172.
71. See Henry Smith, "The Church of Rome is Not the True Church of God," *God's Arrow Against Atheists*, in *The Sermons of Mr. Henry Smith, Sometime Minister of St. Clement Danes, London*, ed. Thomas Fuller (London, 1866), 2:381–414.
72. *Archives of Maryland*, 4:36.
73. Ibid., 38–39.
74. John Cooper to Edward Knott, July 17, 1640, in Hughes, *History of the Society of Jesus, Text*, 1:473; Lawrence Worsley to Edward Knott, in William P. Treacy, *Old Catholic Maryland and its Early Jesuit Missionaries* (Swedesboro, NJ, 1889), vi–vii; Christopher Morris to Edward Knott, July 27, 1640, in Curran, *American Jesuit Spirituality*, 57.
75. "Annual Letter of the English Province of the Society of Jesus," 1639, in *Original Narratives of Early American History: Narratives of Early Maryland, 1634–1684*, ed. Clayton Colman Hall (New York, 1910), 124; Andrew White to Lord Baltimore, February 20, 1638, *Calvert Papers*, 1:202. White's manuscript in Piscataway is one of the treasures occasionally on display in the Special Collections library at Georgetown University. A photostat of the manuscript can be found at the Maryland State Archives (MSA), S455-222. For more on the importance this rare, surviving example of the Piscataway language, see Lisa Mackie's Master's thesis, "Fragments of Piscataway: A Preliminary Description" (Oxford University, 2006).
76. *Archives of Maryland*, 3:162 and 4:264.
77. "An Act for the Authority of Justices of the Peace," in ibid., 1:53. Fr. John Brooke would later downplay the Jesuits' disagreement with Calvert, insisting that the governor feared for the safety of the Jesuits, and that this was the reason he did not want White living among the Indians. See "Annual Letter of the English Province of the Society of Jesus," 1639, in *Narratives of Early Maryland, 1633–1684*, ed. Clayton Colman Hall (New York, 1946), 125.
78. The list of delegates in the 1638 Assembly can be found in Edward Papenfuse's *A Biographical Dictionary of the Maryland Legislature, 1635–1789* (Baltimore, 1979), 1:15. The biographical information about the sixty-one men and one woman (Margaret Brandt) who served in that assembly is available alphabetically in Papenfuse's volumes. Almost 20 percent of the Catholic estates valued in the latter half of the seventeenth century in St. Mary's County were worth more than £500. That compares with just slightly more than 5 percent of the estates in St. Mary's County as a whole. Fifty-nine percent of the Catholics in St. Mary's had estates worth less than £100, as compared to 74 percent of the population overall. Thus, it would seem that Catholics in seventeenth-century Maryland were not

only wealthier than their Protestant neighbors, they were also less poor. See Michael Graham, "Meetinghouse and Chapel: Religion and Community in Seventeenth-Century Maryland," in *Colonial Chesapeake Society*, ed. Lois Green Car, Philip D. Morgan, and Jean B. Russo (Chapel Hill, NC, 1988), 268–269.
79. Edward F. Terrar, "Social, Economic, and Religious Beliefs among Maryland Catholic Laboring People during the Period of the English Civil War" (Ph.D. dissertation, University of California at Los Angeles, 1991), 412; Thomas Copley to Cecilius Calvert, April 3, 1638, *Calvert Papers*, 1:162–165. It should be noted that English Catholics, whether they were in England or Maryland, were not the only Catholics in the seventeenth century who felt entitled to criticize their priests. As R. Po-Chia Hsia has shown, Catholics in Continental Europe criticized their priests, too, accusing them of hypocrisy and immorality whenever they engaged in the surprisingly common practice of "clerical concubinage." No matter how vocal the laity in Continental Europe were, however, they never assumed it was their right or responsibility to instruct their clergy or to discipline them. See R. Po-Chia Hsia, *The World of Catholic Renewal, 1540–1770* (New York, 1998), 106–121.
80. *Archives of Maryland*, 3:100.
81. Hall, *Narratives of Early Maryland*, 124.
82. Thomas Copley to Lord Baltimore, April 3, 1638, *Calvert Papers*, 1:162.
83. Ibid., 167.
84. Ibid., 166. The papal bull, *In Coenae Domini*, was a list of seven censures originally issued in 1323. The list was added to over the years, and by 1627, the number had risen to twenty. See John Prior, "In Coenae Domini," *The Original Catholic Encyclopedia* (New York, 1907–1912), 7:717–718.
85. Thomas Cornwaleys to Lord Baltimore, April 16, 1638, in *Calvert Papers*, 1:171–172.
86. Copley to Lord Baltimore, April 3, 1638, in *Calvert Papers*, 1:168, 159.
87. Krugler, *English and Catholic*, 145–146.
88. Lord Baltimore to Edward Knott, 1641, in Hughes, *History of the Society of Jesus, Documents*, 1:166–167.
89. Knott's letter to Rosetti, November 17, 1641, in Hughes, *History of the Society of Jesus, Text*, 1:505.
90. Lord Baltimore to Leonard Calvert, November 23, 1642, in *Calvert Papers*, 1:217–218; William Peasely to Fr. Gervits, S.J., September 30, 1642, and Ann Calvert Peasley to Fr. Gervits, S.J., October 5, 1642, in "Applications for the Maryland Mission—1640," *Woodstock Letters* (Woodstock, MD, 1872–1969), 9:91–93.
91. For more on the trial and execution of Charles I, see Geoffrey Robertson's *The Tyrannicide Brief: The Story of the Man Who Sent Charles I to the Scaffold* (New York, 2005), 151–176.
92. Carr and Papenfuse, "The Charter of Maryland," *Archives of Maryland*, 550:19.
93. Timothy B. Riordan, *The Plundering Time: Maryland and the English Civil War, 1645–1646* (Baltimore, 2004), 11, 29, 131–139, 172, 184, 206–211; *Archives of Maryland*, 4:435–436; Graham, "Meetinghouse and Chapel," 268–269.
94. Riordan, *Plundering Time*, 263–267, 296–298.
95. Hughes, History of the Society of Jesus, Text, 2:13; Documents, 1:191–196.

Chapter 3

1. James I, *The Trew Law of Free Monarchies* (1598), in *The Political Worlds of James I*, ed. Charles H. McIlwain (Cambridge, MA, 1918), 69; John Milton, *The Tenure of Kings and Magistrates*, ed. William Talbot Allison (New York, 1911), 15, 40, 11.
2. John Locke, *The Second Treatise of Government* (1690), rpt., ed. Joseph Carrig (New York, 2004), 57. For more on the rise of contractarianism in seventeenth-century English political thought, see Michael Zuckert's *Natural Rights and the New Republicanism* (Princeton, NJ, 1994), 49–118.
3. *Archives of Maryland*, ed. William Hand Brown et al. (Baltimore, 1883–present), 4:527; Percy G. Skirven, "Seven Pioneers of the Colonial Eastern Shore," *Maryland Historical Magazine* 15 (1920): 230–232; Henry C. Peden, *Colonial Maryland Soldiers and Sailors*,

1634–1734 (Westminster, MD, 2008), 283; Edward Papenfuse, *A Biographical Dictionary of the Maryland Legislature, 1635–1789* (Baltimore, 1979), 2:660–661.
4. Charles Haywood Stone, *The Stones of Surry* (Charlotte, NC, 1955), 22.
5. Timothy B. Riordan, *The Plundering Time: Maryland and the English Civil War, 1645–1646* (Baltimore, 2004), 320–323.
6. Lois Green Carr, "Sources of Political Stability and Upheaval in Seventeenth-Century Maryland," *Maryland Historical Magazine* 79 (1984): 55.
7. Chris Beneke has observed that the introduction of civility to the discourse on religion in early America played an instrumental role in the creation of religious pluralism. At the turn of the nineteenth century, "the standards of public expression changed," such that it became fashionable for educated Americans to extend a "presumption of equal worth" to people whose religious beliefs were different from theirs. Beneke notes, however, that the "routine denigration of Catholics" was "one of the more glaring exceptions" to the development he charts. It is noteworthy, therefore, that the first formal, if failed effort to achieve the civility that Beneke describes was launched by a Catholic 150 years before the turn of the nineteenth century. See *Beyond Toleration: The Religious Origins of American Pluralism* (New York, 2006), 9–10.
8. "An Act Concerning Religion," April 21, 1649, *Archives of Maryland*, 1:244–247.
9. Ibid., 246.
10. *Archives of Maryland*, 1:318–319.
11. Ibid., 10:354–355; "Luke Gardiner," Saint Mary's City Men's Career Files, Maryland State Archives (MSA), SC5094.
12. "Thomas Brook," Saint Mary's City Career Files, MSA, SC5094; "Will of Thomas Brooke," *Maryland Calendar of Wills*, ed. Jane Baldwin (Westminster, MD, 2007, rpt.), 1:181.
13. John Langford, *A Just and Cleere Refutation of a False and Scandalous Pamphlet Entitled Babylons Fall in Maryland* (1655), rpt. in Clayton Colman Hall, *Narratives of Early Maryland, 1633–1684* (New York, 1910), 255; "An Act Concerning Religion," *Archives of Maryland*, 1:245.
14. Edward Lloyd et al., *Virginia and Maryland, or The Lord Baltamore's printed CASE, uncased and answered. Shewing, the illegality of his Patent, and Usurpation of Royal Jurisdiction and Dominion there* (1655), rpt. in Hall, *Narratives*, 203; *Archives of Maryland*, 1:304; John D. Krugler, *English and Catholic: The Lords Baltimore and the Seventeenth Century* (Baltimore, 2004), 193.
15. John Hammond, *Leah and Rachel, or, Two Fruitfull Sisters Virginia and Maryland; Their Present Condition, Impartially states and Related* (London, 1656), rpt. in Hall, *Narratives*, 303; *Archives of Maryland*, 3: 311.
16. *Archives of Maryland*, 3:312–313.
17. Ibid., 1:341.
18. Lloyd, *Virginia and Maryland*, 203–204; Hammond, *Leah and Rachel*, 304–306.
19. "Oliver Cromwell's Speech to Parliament, September 12th, 1654," in *The Letters and Speeches of Oliver Cromwell*, ed. S. C. Lomas (New York, 1904), 2:382; "Oliver Cromwell to the Governor of Ross, October 19th, 1649," in *Oliver Cromwell's Letters and Speeches*, ed. Thomas Carlyle (New York, 1846), 132; Samuel Rawson Gardiner, *Oliver Cromwell* (London, 1899), 117; and James D. Tracy, *Europe's Reformations, 1450–1650: Doctrine, Politics, and Community* (Lanham, MD, 2005).
20. Wallace Notestein and Helen Frances Relf, eds., *Commons Debates, 1621* (New Haven, CT, 1935), 1:318–319. Also, see chapter 2 of this book.
21. Lloyd, *Virginia and Maryland*, 206, 220, 219, 190–191.
22. It was still a little early in the 1650s for philosophers to be talking about a "right" to property as something government was obliged to protect, but in outlining what he called "the History of Tyrannicide," Milton wrote of how the sixth-century Greek poet, Theognis of Megara, "was deprived of his property by a tyrant and forced into exile." Milton also called Charles I "a true tyrant, who holds our life and property in his power." See, *The Tenure of Kings and Magistrates* (1650), and *A Defence of the People of England* (1651), in *Milton: Political Writings*, ed. Martin Dzelzainis (New York, 1991), 127.

23. Cecilius Calvert, *The Lord Baltemore's Case, Concerning the Province of Maryland, adjoining to Virginia in America, With full and clear Answers to all material Objections, touching his Rights, Jurisdiction, and Proceedings there, And Certaine Reasons of State, why the Parliament should not impeach the same* (1653), in Hall, *Narratives*, 167, 169, 175; Edward C. Papenfuse et al., "Cecilius Calvert," in *A Biographical Dictionary of the Maryland Legislature, 1635–1789* (Baltimore, 1979), 1:186.
24. Oliver P. to Richard Bennett, Esq., Governor of Virginia, January 22, 1655, rpt. in John Hammond, *Hammond vs. Heamans; or, An Answer to an Audacious Pamphlet, published by a ridiculous and impudent fellow, named Roger Heamans* (1655).
25. For more on the convoluted negotiations that led to the restoration of Baltimore's control, see Krugler, *English and Catholic*, 204–207.
26. For more on Jewish "converts" to Christianity in early modern Portugal, see Antonio Jose Saraiva, *The Marrano Factory: The Portuguese Inquisition and its New Christians, 1536–1765*, trans. H. P. Salomon and I. S. D. Sassoon (Boston, 2001), 1–42; and David L. Graizbord, *Souls in Dispute: Converso Identities in Iberia and the Jewish Diaspora, 1580–1700* (Philadelphia, 2003), 19–142.
27. *Archives of Maryland*, 1:341, 244.
28. Ibid., 41:203, 258–259, 591, and 3:488; J. H. Hollander, "Some Unpublished Material Relating to Dr. Jacob Lumbrozo," *Publications of the American Jewish Historical Society* 1 (1893): 25–40.
29. David W. Jordan, "Josias Fendall," *American National Biography Online*, July 28, 2009, %3ca href=http://www.anb.org.resources.library.brandeis.edu/articles/01/01-00281.html?a=1&g=m&n=Fendall%2C%20Josias&ia=-at&ib=-bib&d=10&ss=0&;q=1(subscription only); Krugler, *English and Catholic*, 215.
30. *Discipline of the Society of Friends, Indiana Yearly Meeting* (Cincinnati, 1835), 50; "The Sermon on the Mount," Matthew, 5:34–37.
31. *Archives of Maryland*, 3:352–355; 362.
32. Krugler, *English and Catholic*, 185–186; Robert Wintour, in *To Live Like Princes*, ed. John D. Krugler (Baltimore, 1976), 38.
33. *An Homily Against Disobedience and Willful Rebellion* (London, 1837), 5.
34. John Milton, *A Defence of the People of England* (1651), in *The Prose Works of John Milton*, ed. James Augustus St. John and Charles Richard Sumner (London, 1881), 1:108.
35. Krugler, *English and Catholic*, 185–186, 201, 210–211.
36. *Archives of Maryland*, 1:36, 94–95, 107; Edward F. Terrar, *Social, Economic, and Religious Beliefs among Maryland Catholic Laboring People during the Period of the English Civil War* (Bethesda, MD, 1997), 145, 153.
37. David W. Jordan, *Foundations of Representative Government in Maryland, 1632–1715* (New York, 2002), 53.
38. David S. Lovejoy, *The Glorious Revolution in America* (New York, 1972), 78.
39. Edward C. Papenfuse, *A Biographical Dictionary of the Maryland Legislature, 1635–1789* (Baltimore, 1979), 1:25; *Archives of Maryland*, 2:168–169, 137, 142.
40. *Archives of Maryland*, 2:174–175.
41. At least seventeen of the twenty-seven men who served in the Upper House between 1666 and 1669 were Catholic. Not all of these Catholics were wealthy; William Evans, who served in the Upper House from 1664 to 1668, owned just two hundred acres at the time of his election to the Lower House in 1658. In general, however, the Catholic members of the Upper House came from the more prosperous families in Maryland. Of the other ten men who served in the Upper House, only eight can be identified as having been Protestant. Of those eight, three—Benjamin Rozer, William Digges, and William Burgess—were related in some way to the Calvert family. Additionally, Henry Coursy was a close friend of Philip Calvert, Lord Baltimore's nephew. See Papenfuse, *Biographical Dictionary*, 1:23, 25.
42. Lord Culpeper to the Lords of Trade and Plantations, December 12, 1681, in *Calendar of State Papers, Colonial Series, America and West Indies, 1681–1685*, ed. J. W. Fortescue (London, 1898), 11:156.

43. *Archives of Maryland*, 7:118; Michael Kammen, "The Causes of the Maryland Revolution in 1689," *Maryland Historical Magazine* 55 (1960): 298; Lois Green Carr and David William Jordan, *Maryland's Revolution of Government, 1689–1698* (Ithaca, NY, 1974), 33.
44. Maria A. Day, "Charles Calvert, Third Lord Baltimore, 1637–1714/15," *Biographical Series*, Maryland State Archives (MSA), SC 3520-193; John H. B. Latrobe, "The History of Mason and Dixon's Line," *Annual Address before the Historical Society of Pennsylvania* (Philadelphia, 1854), 5–9.
45. Fourteen of the twenty-one men Charles Calvert appointed had either been raised as Catholics, or else had converted to Catholicism. See Carr and Jordan, *Maryland's Revolution*, 50; Papenfuse, *Biographical Dictionary*, 1:27, 29, 30.
46. Francis Edgar Sparks, *Causes of the Maryland Revolution of 1689* (Baltimore, 1896), 50; Graham, "Meetinghouse and Chapel, 268–269.
47. For a contemporary analysis of the causes and consequences of Bacon's Rebellion, see John Berry, Francis Moryson, and Herbert Jefferys, *A True Narrative of the Rise, Progress and Cessation of the Late Rebellion in Virginia, Most Humbly and Impartially Recorded by His Majesties Commissioners, Appointed to inquire into the Affairs of the Said Colony* (1677), in *Narratives of the Insurrections, 1675 to 1690*, ed. Charles Andrews (New York, 1915), 99–142.
48. *Archives of Maryland*, 5:134, 137–139.
49. Ibid., 5:300–301.
50. *Archives of Maryland*, 5:353–355; Francis Edgar Sparks, *Causes of the Maryland Revolution of 1689* (Baltimore, 1896), 40, 70.
51. The Dominion of New England, which encompassed all of present-day New York, New Jersey, and New England, was James II's effort to implement a more centralized and controlled method of colonial governance, along the lines of what France had with Quebec. See John Miller, *James II* (New Haven, CT, 2000), 146–147; Joseph A. Conforti, *Imagining New England: Exploration of Regional Identity from the Pilgrims to the Mid-Twentieth Century* (Chapel Hill, NC, 2001), 51–59.
52. John Childs, *The Army, James II, and the Glorious Revolution* (Manchester, UK, 1980), 1–3; Tim Harris, *Revolution: The Great Crisis of the British Monarchy, 1685–1720* (New York, 2008), 95–100; "English Bill of Rights, 1689," *The Avalon Project: Documents in Law, History and Diplomacy*, Lillian Goldman Law Library, Yale University, August 31, 2009, http://avalon.law.yale.edu/17th_century/england.asp.
53. Ibid., Thomas Babington Macaulay, *The History of England from the Ascension of James II* (London, 1889), 1:242.
54. Quoted in and from Lois G. Schwoerer, "Propaganda in the Revolution of 1688–89," *American Historical Review* 82 (1977): 843, 848–850.
55. Ibid., 851; Maurice Ashley, *The Glorious Revolution of 1688* (New York, 1867), 255. As it turns out, Thomas Ken, John Lake, William Sancroft, Francis Turner, and Thomas White were among nine Anglican bishops who refused to recognize William as the head of the Church, launching the Nonjuring Schism in the Church of England, which lasted until 1788, when James II's grandson, Charles Edward Stuart, died in exile, and his brother formally recognized the legitimacy of the Hanoverian succession.
56. The real title of Foxe's book is *Actes and Monuments of these Latter and Perillous Days, Touching Matters of the Church*. William Haller, *The Elect Nation: The Meaning and Relevance of Foxes' Book of Martyrs* (New York, 1963), especially 224–250. Catholicism's "otherness" in Stuart England is also discussed in Caroline M. Hibbard's "Early Stuart Catholicism," *Journal of Modern History* 52 (1980): 1–34. According to the *Oxford English Dictionary*, Robert Copland did use the word "popery" as early as 1536, in his *Hye way to Spytell Hous*. The next known use of the word does not occur, then, until 1551, when Thomas Cranmer uses it in his *Answer to S. Gardiner*. After Foxe's use of the word in 1563, the next known reference is in 1593, when Richard Hooker insists that "the name of Popery is more odious than very Paganism amongst . . . the more simple sort."
57. Schwoerer, "Propaganda," 856–857; Lawrence Stone, "Literacy and Education in England, 1640–1900," *Past and Present* 42 (1969): 109, 112. More than 2,000 political and

ecclesiastical tracts and pamphlets were published in England in 1689. William also managed to gain editorial control of at least eight newspapers in England, all of which reported news of his invasion favorably. See Jonathan Israel, "General Introduction," in *The Anglo-Dutch Moment: Essays on the Glorious Revolution and its World Impact*, ed. Jonathan Israel (New York, 1991), 6–7.
58. Frederic George Stephens, ed., *Catalogues of Prints and Drawings in the British Museum, Division 1: Political and Satirical* (London, 1870), 1:726, n. 1186; M. Dorothy George, *English Political Caricature to 1792: A Study of Propaganda and Opinion* (New York, 1959), 63.
59. Stephens, *Catalogues*, 1:719, n. 1174; Schwoerer, "Propaganda," 861.
60. *Archives of Maryland*, 8:102. For more on the dearth of Anglican leadership in seventeenth-century Maryland, see Carol Lee van Voorst, "The Anglican Clergy in Maryland, 1692–1776" (Ph.D. dissertation, Princeton University, 1978).
61. *Archives of Maryland*, 17:142, 239.
62. For more on how incredibly labor-intensive tobacco farming was, see T. H. Breen's *Tobacco Culture: The Mentality of the Great Tidewater Planters on the Eve of Revolution* (Princeton, NJ, 1985), 46–58. For more on indentured servitude in the Chesapeake Bay region, see Kenneth Morgan's *Slavery and Servitude in Colonial North America* (New York, 2001), 8–25.
63. Papenfuse, *Biographical Dictionary*, 1:234, 138.
64. Beatriz Bentacourt Hardy, "Papists in a Protestant Age" (Ph.D. dissertation, University of Maryland, 1993), 35; Carr and Jordan, *Maryland's Revolution*, 49.
65. Ibid., 49; Lovejoy, *The Glorious Revolution*, 94–95; *Archives of Maryland*, 8:41–43.
66. Ibid., 13:150–153.
67. Ibid., 8:55–56.
68. Ibid., 56, 77–78; 13:65.
69. Fortescue, *Calendar of State Papers*, 13:137, 143.
70. *Archives of Maryland*, 8:101–107.
71. Ibid., 107, 122, 125, 212, 188; *Records of the American Catholic Historical Society of Philadelphia* (Philadelphia, 1906), 210.
72. *Archives of Maryland*, 8:371–374, 503; 13:342; "The Morgan Family," *Maryland Historical Magazine* 2 (1907): 373.
73. Annie Leakin Siossat, "Lionel Copley, First Royal Governor of Maryland," *Maryland Historical Magazine* 17 (1922): 163–177.
74. Carr and Jordan, *Maryland's Revolution*, 161; *Archives of Maryland*, 20:3.
75. Ibid., 8:276–277; Nelson Rightmyer, "The Anglican Church in Maryland: Factors Contributory to the American Revolution," *Church History* 19 (1950): 190.
76. David William Jordan, "The Royal Period of Colonial Maryland, 1689–1715" (Ph.D. dissertation, Princeton University, 1966), 172–173.
77. Ibid., 276, 279–280.

Chapter 4

1. Sydney E. Ahlstrom, *A Religious History of the American People* (New Haven, CT, 1972), 339.
2. Jon Butler, *Awash in a Sea of Faith: Christianizing the American People* (Cambridge, MA, 1990), 31; Olwen Hufton, "The French Church," in *Church and Society in Catholic Europe in the Eighteenth Century*, ed. William J. Callahan and David Higgs (Cambridge, 1979), 13–33. According to Butler, the late seventeenth and early eighteenth centuries were a time when a "persistent, even deepening, lay indifference to institutional Christianity" characterized the European population.
3. *Account of the Condition of the Catholic Religion in the English Colonies of America* (1763), rpt. *Catholic Historical Review* 6 (1920–21), 517–524; Curran, *American Jesuit Spirituality*, 10, 13.

4. *The Great Law, or the Body of Laws of the Province of Pennsilvania and Territories there unto belonging* (1682), in *Charter to William Penn and Laws of the Province of Pennsylvania*, ed. George Staughton, Benjamin N. Nead, and Thomas McCamant (Harrisburg, PA, 1879), 107; "A List of the Number of Papist inhabiting in the Several Countys of this Province," in *Archives of Maryland*, ed. William Hand Brown et al. (Baltimore, 1883–present), 25:258; *Account of the Condition of the Catholic Religion*, 521–522. New York had approximately 1,500 Catholics—what the report called "a Catholic here and there." There were no priests serving the Catholic community in that colony, however. In 1740, John Ury was accused by officials in New York of "being a Roman Catholic priest, exercising his religion, and seducing the people." Ury denied the charge, however, and in his private journal, he specifically denied the legitimacy of the Catholic Sacrament of Penance, insisting that it was "the prerogative only of the Great God" to forgive sins. Ury was probably an Anglican who simply failed to recognize the legitimacy of the Hanoverian Succession. See Jason K. Duncan, *Citizens or Papists? The Politics of Anti-Catholicism in New York, 1685–1821* (New York, 2005), 22–23.
5. In 1773, when the Society of Jesus was suspended by Pope Clement XIV, there were twenty-one priests serving in Maryland—the largest number the colony ever saw. See "Regulations for the Maryland Mission, 1759, by Father Corbie, English Provincial," Maryland Province Archives (MPA), Special Collections, Georgetown University, Box 2, Folder 9; Box 18, Folder 6. Of course, the priest-to-layperson ratio in 1763 looks pretty good when compared to the ratios today. In 2009, there were 749 priests serving the 1.8 million Catholics in the Archdiocese of Boston. That is a ratio of 1:2,403. Unlike the Maryland Mission, however, the Archdiocese of Boston has 310 primary and secondary schools, six colleges, forty Councils of the Knights of Columbus, three newspapers, and a public access television station to sustain the Catholic community in Massachusetts. See Robert O'Grady, ed., *The Boston Catholic Directory, 2009* (Braintree, MA, 2009), 235.
6. The entire population of Maryland in 1708, white and black, was 33,833. *Archives of Maryland*, 25:258; Lois Green Carr and David William Jordan, *Maryland's Revolution of Government, 1689–92* (Ithaca, NY, 1974), 33.
7. *Archives of Maryland*, 9:315; Ronald Hoffman, *Princes of Ireland, Planters of Maryland: A Carroll Saga, 1500–1782* (Chapel Hill, NC, 2000), 267; "Will of Garrett van Sweringen, St. Mary's County, proved October 25, 1698," Maryland State Archives (MSA), S538–11; "Gerard Slye, Jr.," Men's Career Files, MSA SC 5094; James Everett Schwartz and Lorna Belle Schwartz, "Roman Catholic Diocese of Owensboro, Family Histories," in *The Roman Catholic Diocese of Owensboro, Kentucky*, ed. Sister Joseph Angela Boone (Nashville, TN, 1994), 204; "Mary Gardiner Slye," Women's Career Files, MSA, SC 4040. Although there is some disagreement among historians about the point at which an individual achieved "planter" status in the colonial Chesapeake, most scholars feel that by the mid-eighteenth century, an individual was considered to be a prominent and influential member of his society if he owned at least 500 acres and twenty slaves. See Edward J. Perkins, *The Economy of Colonial America* (New York, 1988), 81.
8. *Archives of Maryland*, 8:159; 2:90.
9. Beatriz Bentancourt Hardy, "A Papist in a Protestant Age: The Case of Richard Bennett, 1667–1749," *Journal of Southern History* 60 (1994): 204; Oswald Tilghman, *History of Talbot County, Maryland, 1661–1861* (Baltimore, 1915), 2; Christopher Johnston, "Lloyd Family," *Maryland Historical Magazine* 7 (1912): 424; Thomas J. Peterman, "Catholics on the Eastern Shore of Maryland," *Catholic Historical Review* 89 (2003): x; John Bozeman Kerr, *Genealogical Notes of the Chamberlaine Family of Maryland* (Baltimore, 1880), 26.
10. Ibid., 26–28; George A. Hanson, *Old Kent: The Eastern Shore of Maryland* (Baltimore, 1876), 29; Henry C. Peden, Jr., *Revolutionary Patriots of Anne Arundel County* (Westminster, MD, 2006), 33. It is not completely clear that Margaretta Freeman and her daughter, Henrietta Maria Lloyd, were Protestants. Henrietta Maria did marry a Protestant, however, and her son, Samuel Chew, must have been Protestant, since he was a Justice of the Peace in Anne Arundel County from 1757 to 1776.

11. Fr. George Hunter arranged passage for at least thirty-one young women from Maryland who joined convents in France in the mid-eighteenth century. See Fr. George Hunter to John Tichbourne, no date (but some time between 1747 and 1756), "Hunter Letterbook," MPA, Box 2, Folder 10. Margaret Lloyd is the only one of Philemon and Henrietta Maria's children for whom the nineteenth-century genealogist, John Bozeman Kerr, was not able to find a burial plot; see Kerr, *Genealogical Notes*, 26–28. For more on the gender imbalance in the colonial Chesapeake, see Lois Green Carr and Lorena S. Walsh, "The Planter's Wife: The Experiences of White Women in Seventeenth-Century Maryland," *William and Mary Quarterly* 34 (1977): 542–571, and Russell R. Menard, "Immigrants and their Increase," in *Law, Society, and Politics in Early Maryland*, ed. Aubrey C. Land, Edward C. Papenfuse, and Lois Green Carr (Baltimore, 1977), 88–110.
12. Thomas J. Peterman, "Catholics on the Eastern Shore of Maryland, up to 1868," Robert O. McMain Annual Lecture of the Catholic Historical Society, October 27, 2002, Washington, DC, text available online at *St. Dennis Church, Galena, MD*, October 6, 2009, http://www.stdennischurch.org/COLONIALDELMARVA.htm; Kerr, *Genealogical Notes*, 26; Beatriz Bentacourt Hardy, "Papists in a Protestant Age" (Ph.D. dissertation, University of Maryland, 1993), 567.
13. Steve Gilland, *Early Families of Frederick County, Maryland and Adams County, Pennsylvania* (Westminster, MD, 1997), 4; Elise Greenup Jourdan, *Early Families of Southern Maryland* (Westminster, MD, 2007), 2:129–130; William W. Warner, *At Peace with All their Neighbors: Catholics and Catholicism in the National Capital, 1787–1860* (Washington, DC, 1994), 41–42.
14. Marriage register for St. Joseph's Parish, Cordova, Talbot Co., and St. Francis Xavier, Bohemia, Cecil County, MSA SC4649.
15. William Hunter, "Whether Disparity of Cult is a Diriment Impediment to Matrimony in Maryland," rpt. in Gerald P. Fogarty, "Slaves, Quakers, and Catholic Marriage in Colonial Maryland," *The Jurist* 35 (1975): 149, 153–154; 156–157; John Carroll to Charles Plowden, February 12, 1803, in *The John Carroll Papers*, ed. Thomas O'Brien Hanley (Notre Dame, IN, 1976), 2:408; Hardy, "Papists in a Protestant Age," 606.
16. "Thomas Brooke," Men's Career Files, MSA SC 5094; Warner, *At Peace with All their Neighbors*, 43.
17. Scharf, *History of Maryland*, 1:215; Dr. Charles Carroll to Charles Carroll, July 21, 1739, Letterbook, 1731–1748, Maryland Historical Society (MHS), MS 208.1.
18. Scharf, *History of Maryland*, 1:215.
19. *Archives of Maryland*, 50:51–54.
20. Theodore Bland, ed., *Report of Cases Decided in the High Court of Chancery of Maryland* (Baltimore, 1840), 2:566–569; Marylynn Salmon, *Women and the Law of Property in Early America* (Chapel Hill, NC, 1986), 62–63; Hoffman, *Princes of Ireland*, 92–93.
21. Ibid., xxiv. Digges's letter to the proprietor is undated and unsigned. At one point, however, it mentions that it has been "sixty years since the law was enacted for fixing the succession to the crown of the realm in the House of Hanover," indicating that the letter was written around 1774. The letter is among Clement Hill's papers at the Maryland Historical Society, and the handwriting is strikingly similar to that of Hill's nephew, Charles Digges, who was related to Hill's wife, Mary Digges. MHS MS446, Box 5, Folder 158, Item 25.
22. "List of Converts, St. Joseph's, Cordova, Talbot County," MPA, Box 31, Folder 4; "Proclamation of Francis Nicholson," in *Historical Collections Relating to the American Colonial Church*, ed. William Stevens Perry (Hartford, CT, 1871), 4:24–25; N.N., *An Epistle of a Catholicke young gentleman, (being for his religion imprisoned.) To his Father a Protestant.* (London, 1623), 12–13.
23. Maryland colonial records are filled with countless recitations of this oath. One such recitation can be found in the vestry minutes from Queen Anne's Parish in Prince George's County, 1705–1717, MSA M687: "I do from my heart abhor, detest, & abjure as Impious & Heretical, that Damnable Doctrine by the Pope, or any authority of the See of Rome." According to the "Act for the Better Security of the Peace and Safety of

his Lordship's Government, and the Protestant Interest within This Province," the governor did have the power to ask officeholders to swear the Oaths of Allegiance and Abjuration again. Such reaffirmations were not mandated, however, and so long as the governor had no reason to be suspicious, there was no reason to ask an officeholder to retake the oaths. See *Archives of Maryland*, 30:617.

24. Ibid., 662:144–146; 31:14; September 8, 1770, MPA, Box 1, Folder 8.
25. Edward C. Papenfuse lists Benjamin Young as one of two sons born to Anne Rozer and Benjamin Young, Sr. The *Archives of Maryland* clearly state that the "Benjamin Young, Jr." who served as the clerk of St. Mary's County from 1755 to 1770 had a Catholic mother—and a father, of course, who was named Benjamin Young. In spite of his name, Benjamin must have been the younger of the two sons, because Notley inherited their father's estate. He shared this inheritance, Cerne Abbey Manor, with his half-brother from his mother's first marriage, Daniel Carroll of Duddington. The two Catholic brothers eventually sold the estate to the federal government, and the Capitol building sits on that property today. See Edward C. Papenfuse, *A Biographical Dictionary of the Maryland Legislature, 1689–1785* (Baltimore, 1989), 2:929. *Archives of Maryland*, 662:84, 63, 146; 663:75; Robert Emmet Curran, *The Bicentennial History of Georgetown University: From Academy to University* (Washington, DC, 1993), 1:37; Margaret Brent Downing, "The American Capitoline Hill and its Early Catholic Proprietors," *Catholic Historical Review* 2 (1916): 270; "List of Converts," MPA, Box 31, Folder 4.
26. *Archives of Maryland*, 662:176; Edwin F. Beitzell, *The Jesuit Missions of St. Mary's County, Maryland* (Abell, MD, 1976), 246; Geoffrey Holt, *The English Jesuits: 1650–1825, A Biographical Dictionary* (Norfolk, UK, 1975), 264; "Notley Rozer, 1727" Probate Records, 1634–1777, Inventories, Prince George's County, MSA, Box 7, Folder 23; American Catholic Sermon Collection (ACSC), Special Collections, Georgetown University, Le-5.
27. Beitzell, *Jesuit Missions*, 246, 316; Papenfuse, *Biographical Dictionary*, 1:271–272; George Henning, "The Mansion and Family of Notley Young," *Records of the Columbia Historical Society, Washington* 16 (1912): 4; Hardy, "Papists in a Protestant Age," 595.
28. Joseph Mosley to Mrs. Dunn, July 5, 1773; September 8, 1758; and October 14, 1766, MPA, Box 1, Folders 7 and 11. Carroll is quoted in Curran, *American Jesuit Spirituality*, 100.
29. Papenfuse, *Biographical Dictionary*, 2:929. The entry for Benjamin Young, Sr. contains many biographical details about Anne Rozer and the couple's children—including Benjamin Young, Jr. The younger Young's various governmental positions are all discussed, as is the embezzlement scandal he was a part of in 1761. There is no mention of his conversion to Catholicism, however.
30. Mosley converted twenty-eight slaves and one free black between 1766 and 1786. Yet, baptismal records indicate that he baptized ninety-five free or enslaved black people, nearly all of them adults, between December 1766 and December 1770. Mosley probably did not consider all of these ninety-five people to be converts, since many of them would have held prior religious beliefs that the priest did not recognize as "religious." The fact that he called twenty-nine of the people "converts" suggests that some of the blacks he baptized may have been baptized by Protestant ministers beforehand. See "List of Converts," MPA, Box 31, Folder 4; "Baptisms for St. Joseph's Parish, Talbot Co., includes present-day Queen Anne's, Dorchester, Caroline, and Kent (MD and DE) Counties; aka 'Tuckaho' and 'Wye,'" MSA M11706.
31. T. Vaughan, *Roots of American Racism: Essays on the Colonial Experience* (New York, 1995), 141; Alan Taylor, *American Colonies: The Settling of North America* (New York, 2002), 336.
32. Charles Colcock Jones, *The Religious Instruction of the Negroes in the United States* (Savannah, GA, 1842), 197; Charles F. Irons, *The Origins of Proslavery Christianity* (Chapel Hill, NC, 2008), 23–30; Albert J. Raboteau, *Slave Religion: The "Invisible Institution" in the Antebellum South* (New York, 1978), 99–107, 126–127, 132.
33. Thomas Murphy, *Jesuit Slaveholding in Maryland, 1717–1838* (New York, 2001), 131, 147–149; Stephen F. Brett, *Slavery and the Catholic Tradition: Rights in the Balance* (New York, 1994), 192.

34. "Baptisms for St. Joseph's Parish," MSA M11706.
35. Hoffman, *Princes of Ireland*, 240, 250, 253; Hardy, "Papists in a Protestant Age," 583, 593; Charles Carroll of Annapolis (CCA) to Charles Carroll of Carrollton (CCC), April 16, 1759, and November 12, 1773; CCC to CCA, October 30, 1769, in Ronald Hoffman, Sally D. Mason, and Eleanor S. Darcy, eds., *Dear Papa, Dear Charley: The Peregrinations of a Revolutionary Aristocrat* (Chapel Hill, NC, 2001), 1:98, 2:700, 480.
36. Address of George Hunter, Jesuit retreat, December 20, 1749, MPA, Box 57, Folder 1, Number 202A7; Hoffman et al., *Dear Papa, Dear Charley*, 2:707, n 5.
37. "List of Lands Held by Papists for the Year 1758, Dorchester County Rent Rolls," rpt., *Maryland Historical Magazine* 5 (1910): 202; "Baptisms for St. Joseph's Parish," MSA M11706; "Baptisms, St. Francis Xavier and St. Inigoes Congregations," rpt. in *Catholic Families of Southern Maryland*, ed. Timothy J. O'Rourke (Baltimore, 2001), 25.
38. Hanson, *Old Kent*, 39.
39. The few exceptions to this rule almost always grew up in Maryland after religious liberty had been restored to Catholics by the state's constitution in 1776. Ignatius Dairs, for instance, wrote to his "respected friends" in 1798 to explain why he had chosen to marry a woman who was not a Methodist. "I have no wish to leave the Methodist society," he assured his friends. He simply was not able to find a Methodist woman who pleased him. MSA S1005-15926, 1/5/8/75.
40. Gaius Marcus Brumbaugh, ed., *Maryland Records: Colonial, Revolutionary, County and Church, from Original Sources* (Baltimore, 1975), 1:300, 306; "George Hunter's Census of the Catholics in St. Mary's County, 1765–1797," rpt. in Beitzell, *Jesuit Missions*, 102–107; "Baptismal and Marriage Records, St. Inigoes, 1767–69," MPA, Box 15, Folder 10, "Sodality of the Perpetual Adoration of the Bd. Sacrament," MPA, Box 57, Folder 2, No. 202A14.
41. "List of the Congregation at St. Inigo, 1768," MPA, Box 15, Folder 10; O'Rourke, *Catholic Families of Southern Maryland*, 35.
42. Chancery Papers, June 13th, 1795, MSA 512-4-3907, Accession No. 17898-3785; O'Rourke, *Catholic Families*, 35.
43. Ibid.; "Will of Monica Ford," November 26, 1751, Prerogative Court Wills, MSA S538-40; Linda Reno, "A Journey Through Time," *County Times*, June 4, 2009, 23; "Will of Ignatius Combs," September 16, 1790, St. Mary's County Wills, MSA Liber JJ 1, p. 520; "Sodality of the Perpetual Adoration of the Bd. Sacrament," MPA, Box 57, Folder 2, No. 202A14; "Diary of Brother Joseph Mobberly," Brother Joseph P. Mobberly, SJ Papers (Mobberly Papers), Special Collections, Georgetown University, 5:72.
44. Henry C. Peden, *Revolutionary Patriots of Calvert and St. Mary's Counties* (Westminster, MD, 1996), 91, 288.
45. When defined simply as the ability to read and write one's name, literacy rates were around 60 percent throughout the colonial period—a little higher in New England; a little lower in the South. David Henkin points out that "literacy is a tricky concept," though, and that "one can learn to write one's name without being able to comprehend a newspaper." In order to comprehend some of the complex texts that colonial America's Catholics were either purchasing or borrowing from the Jesuits, the ability to read and comprehend a simple newspaper would have been essential. This might suggest that only educated—that is, upper class—Catholics were actually reading these religious books. Tamara Plakins Thornton has argued, however, that reading and writing were two very different skill sets, and while the latter was deemed necessary only for the sake of public commerce, the former was often taught within the family specifically as a way of facilitating religious study. The ability to sign one's name, in other words, came after one learned how to read, and writing was a skill that was less widespread. See David M. Henkin, *City Reading: Written Words and Public Spaces in Antebellum New York* (New York, 1998), 20; Tamara Plakin Thornton, *Handwriting in America: A Cultural History* (New Haven, CT, 1996), 5; Barbara E. Lacey, *From Sacred to Secular: Visual Images in Early American Publications* (Newark, DE, 2007), 21.
46. Ferdinand Farmer, "Letter to his Brother," 1755, MPA, Box 25, Folder 5; Hardy, "Papists in a Protestant Age," 596.

47. Memorandum from Peter Atwood, August 1716, MPA, Box 57, Folder 1, No. 203A4. The quote comes from the subtitle of Kellison's book, which was first published in 1687.
48. John LaFarge, "The Survival of the Catholic Faith in Southern Maryland," *Catholic Historical Review* 21 (1932): 14; Robert Manning, *The Shortest Way to End Disputes about Religion* (1716), rpt. (Boston, 1855), 259; Edwin Burton, "Richard Challoner, Bishop of Debra, Vicar Apostolic of the London District, Author of Spiritual and Controversial Works (1691–1781)," *Original Catholic Encyclopedia* (New York, 1907–1912), 3:564–565.
49. "Preface," Richard Challoner, *The Garden of the Soul: A Manual of Spiritual Exercises and Instructions for Christians* (London, 1856), iii.
50. Mary Heimann, *Catholic Devotion in Victorian England* (New York, 1995), 1, 3, 79–80; Bill McSweeney, *Roman Catholicism: The Search for Relevance* (New York, 1980), 38; Derek Holmes, *The Triumph of the Holy See: A Short History of the Papacy in the Nineteenth Century* (Shepherdstown, WV, 1978), 135.
51. John T. McGreevy, *Catholicism and American Freedom* (New York, 2003), 27–29; Ann Taves, "Context and Meaning: Roman Catholic Devotion to the Blessed Sacrament in Mid-Nineteenth-Century America," *Church History* 54 (1985): 482–495. Taves mistakenly states that devotions to the Blessed Sacrament "were introduced into the United States during the nineteenth century." While it is true that Rome became interested in introducing American Catholics to this devotion in the nineteenth century, the Jesuit order had been promoting it as early as the mid-eighteenth century.
52. Lance Gabriel Lazar, *Working in the Vineyard of the Lord: Jesuit Confraternities in Early Modern Italy* (Buffalo, NY, 2005); Mieko Nishida, "From Ethnicity to Race and Gender: Transformations of Black Lay Sodalities in Salvador, Brazil," *Journal of Social History* 32 (1998): 329–349; Mark Thiel, "Catholic Sodalities among the Sioux, 1882–1910," *U.S. Catholic Historian* 16 (1998): 56–77. For more on the mystical and individualistic orientation of Ignatius's *Spiritual Exercises*, see Michael J. Buckley, "Ecclesiastical Mysticism in the *Spiritual Exercises* of Ignatius," *Theological Studies* 56 (1995): 441–463.
53. Lazar, *Working in the Vineyard of the Lord*, 4–5.
54. For more on the role that keeping kosher plays in defining and maintaining Jewish identity in religiously pluralist societies, see Eton Diamond, *And I Will Dwell in their Midst: Orthodox Jews in Suburbia* (Chapel Hill, NC, 2000), 118–125; Andrew Buckser, "Keeping Kosher: Eating and Social Identity among the Jews of Denmark," *Ethnology* 38 (1999): 191–209; and A. D. Smith, "Chosen Peoples: Why Ethnic Groups Survive," *Ethnic and Racial Studies* 15 (1992): 436–456.
55. Ari L. Goldman, *Being Jewish: The Spiritual and Cultural Practice of Judaism Today* (New York, 2000), 224–229; Sue Fishkoff, "Women Kosher Supervisors on the Rise, Earning Respect," *Baltimore Jewish Times*, June 30, 2009, 3.
56. "Sodality of the Sacred Heart of Jesus at St. Aloysius," MPA, Box 57, Folder 2; Fr. J. Walton's Diary, MPA, Box 4, Folder 1; "A List of the Congregation at St. Inigoes, 1768," and "Names of the Congregation at St. Inigoes, 1769," MPA, Box 15, Folder 10.
57. "Sodality of the Perpetual Adoration of the Bd. Sacrament," MPA, Box 57, Folder 2; Harry Wright Newman, *The Maryland Semmes and Kindred Families* (Westminster, MD, 2007), 242–243, 45; Elise Greenup Jourdon, *Early Families of Southern Maryland* (Westminster, MD, 2005), 1:163–164. For more on the decision to allow women to join sodalities, see Joseph Hilgers, "Sodality," *Original Catholic Encyclopedia*, 14:128–129.
58. Fr. Joseph Mosley to Mrs. Dunn, September 8, 1758, and September 1, 1759, MPA, Box 1, Folders 3, 4; Hugh Neill to Dr. Bearcroft, September 1, 1751, in *Records of the Society for the Propagation of the Gospel in Foreign Parts, Series B*, ed. Walter Pinchinton (Yorkshire, England, 1965), 19:121; Robin Briggs, *Communities of Belief: Cultural and Social Tension in Early Modern France* (New York, 1995), 285–286.
59. *History of the Society of Jesus in North America, Colonial and Federal, from the First Colonization till 1645, Documents*, ed. Thomas Hughes (New York, 1907), 1:207–208; Thomas J. Peterman, *Bohemia, 1704–2004: A History of St. Francis Xavier Catholic Shrine in Cecil County, Maryland* (Devon, PA, 2004), 16–19.

60. E. I. Devitt, "Bohemia: Mission of St. Francis Xavier, Cecil County, Maryland," *Records of the American Catholic Historical Society of Philadelphia* 24 (1913): 112; Hardy, "Papists in a Protestant Age," 584. Fr. John Lewis wrote a poem in 1730, in which he described the itinerate life of a Catholic priest in Maryland: "In this soft season, were the dawn of day / I mount my Horse, and lonely take my way / From woody hills that shade Patapsko's head / (In whose deep vales he makes his stony bed / From when he rushes with resistless force / Tho' huge rough Rocks retard his rapid course,) / Down to Annapolis, on that smooth stream / Which took from fair Anne Arundel her name." See MPA, Box 2, Folder 9, No. 2T3.
61. ACSC, Be-4, Be-9, Se-9, Ne-3.
62. Perry Miller, *The New England Mind: From Colony to Province* (Cambridge, MA, 1939); and *Errand into the Wilderness* (Cambridge, MA, 1956); Edmund Morgan, "New England Puritanism: Another Approach," *William and Mary Quarterly* 23 (1966): 236–242; Robert G. Pope, "New England Versus the New England Mind: The Myth of Declension," *Journal of Social History* 36 (1969): 95–108; Increase Mather, *The Day of Trouble is Near* (1674), 6.
63. Sacvan Bercovitch, *The American Jeremiad* (Madison, WI, 1978), xi, 18.
64. Ibid.; ACSC, Nea-4, Li-3. Throughout the colonial period, settlers from Virginia to New England consumed more than 15 gallons of hard cider per capita annually. See W. J. Rorabaugh, *The Alcoholic Republic: An American Tradition* (New York, 1979), 9–10, 95, 99.
65. "Five regulations about the observance of Holydays by Catholics in Maryland," 1722, MPA, Box 2, Folder, 9, No. 2T10; "Regulations concerning the observance of Holydays in Maryland," in "The Old Records," MPA, Box 2, Folders 4–6. Priests could only grant dispensations on an individual basis. Large-scale dispensations, such as the one that they wanted to give to all Catholic farmers, required the approval of the Vicar Apostolic. The Church's designation of Holy Days of Obligation has consistently confused the laity throughout the centuries, because up until the seventeenth century, each bishop had the right to add his own feast days to the calendar that his diocese followed. Even today, Canon Law allows the bishops of every country to meet as a group to determine which of the ten feast days, as designated by the 1917 Code of Canon Law, will be celebrated in their country. Since 1992, Catholics in the United States have been obliged to observe just six of the ten Holy Days of Obligation. Throughout the seventeenth and most of the eighteenth centuries, Catholics in British North America observed the thirty-six feasts celebrated by Catholics in England. In 1777, Pope Pius VI reduced the Holy Days of Obligation for England and its colonies to just eleven, and in 1789, Bishop John Carroll of Baltimore, the only Catholic bishop in the United States at the time, removed the Feast of St. George from the list of days that American Catholics were expected to observe. He probably did this because St. George was the Patron Saint of England. See Richard Challoner, *The Catholic Christian Instructed* (1737), 199–209; and "Our Observance of Holy Days is Still Evolving," *St. Anthony Messenger Magazine* (April 1997): 14.
66. See William Cronon, *Changes in the Land: Indians, Colonists, and the Ecology of New England* (New York, 1983).
67. MPA, Box 2, Folder 9, No. 2T10.
68. Hoffman, *Princes of Ireland*, 109–100. Ten years or so after the founding of the Baltimore Company, Ralph Faulkner, a Protestant, and Edward Neale, a Catholic, also partnered up to open an ironworks. That company failed after several years, however. See Dr. Charles Carroll to Edward Neale, October 20, 1750, Letterbook, 1716–1769, MHS, MS 208; Maryland *Gazette*, May 1, 1751.
69. John Bossy, *The English Catholic Community, 1570–1850* (New York, 1976), 112–115. When the wife was the Catholic partner in the marriage, the English clergy tended to be more lenient.
70. John Carroll to Charles Plowden, September 26, 1783, and J.C. to an unidentified priest, August 18, 1785, in *The John Carroll Papers*, ed. Thomas O'Brien Hanley (Notre Dame, IN, 1976), 1:77, 195.
71. *Archives of Maryland*, 4:35–36.

72. Charles County Court Record, MSA, Liber A, No. 2, 136–137; Christopher Johnston, "Neale Family of Charles County," *Maryland Historical Magazine* 7 (1912): 207.
73. Hunter, "Disparity of Cult," 153; Bossy, *English Catholic Community*, 113.
74. *Archives of Maryland*, 26:46, 340; Hardy, "Papists in a Protestant Age," 91, 556.
75. Ibid., 583–584; 593, 595, 601–602, 628; William P. Treacy, *Old Catholic Maryland and its Early Jesuit Missionaries* (Swedesboro, NJ, n.d.), 177; Will of Richard Marsham, April 14, 1713, in Baldwin, *Maryland Calendar of Wills*, 3:240.
76. Narrative of Alexander Stuart and Letter of Donal MacPherson to his Father, in "Two Jacobite Convicts," *Maryland Historical Magazine* 1 (1906): 349–352 and 346–348; MPA SCGU, Box 26, Folder 8. Stuart was originally purchased by a Catholic second cousin of Lord Baltimore, but Edward Digges purchased Stuart's contract from Benedict Calvert, and then released Stuart two months later. For more Jacobites who were purchased by Catholics in Maryland, see David Dobson's *Directory of Scots Banished to American Plantations, 1650–1775* (Baltimore, 1983).
77. Vaughan, *Roots of American Racism*, 141.
78. John Mack Faragher, *A Great and Noble Scheme: The Tragic Story of the Expulsion of the French Acadians from their American Homeland* (New York, 2005); Henry Wadsworth Longfellow, "Evangeline," in *Evangeline and Other Poems*, ed. Thomas Crofts (Mineola, NY, 1995), 33.
79. CCA to CCC, July 26, 1756, in Hoffman et al., *Dear Papa, Dear Charley*, 1:30; Bohemia Day Book, 1735–1761, MPA, Box 3, Folder 10.
80. Elisabeth Louise Roark, *Artists of Colonial America* (Westport, CT, 2003), 73–74; 79–80.
81. Although the Immaculate Conception of Mary was not defined as dogma by the Catholic Church until 1854, the concept had a strong following in the Church in the eighteenth century, and the Feast of the Immaculate Conception had been a Universal feast since 1476. In contrast, the Anglican Church considered December 8th to be a Lesser feast that honored "The Conception of the Blessed Virgin Mary," implying that that conception did not avoid the reality of Original Sin. The doctrine of the Perpetual Virginity of Mary is defined as a *de fide* doctrine in Catholicism—that is, one that is essential to the faith. Martin Luther continued to believe that Mary never had relations with her husband, but John Calvin rejected that notion on the basis of scriptural references to Jesus' "brothers and sisters." See Ludwig Ott, *The Fundamentals of Catholic Dogma* (Charlotte, NC, 1974), 199–203; W. J. Sparrow Simpson, *The Minor Festivals of the Anglican Calendar* (London, 1901), 451–458; Martin Luther in Jaroslav Pelikan, ed., *Luther's Works* (Philadelphia, 1955), 22:23; 214–215; John Calvin, *Calvin's Bible Commentaries: Matthew, Mark, and Luke, Part 1* (Charleston, SC, 2007), 54–59.
82. Ibid., 84; G. Richard Dimler, "Short Title Listing of Jesuit Emblem Books," *Emblematica: An Interdisciplinary Journal of Emblem Studies* 2 (1987): 139–187; David S. Russell, "Emblem," *Encyclopedia of the Renaissance* (New York, 1999), 2:65–67; Wolfgang Lottes, "Henry Hawkins and *Partheneia Sacra*," *Review of English Studies* (1975): 144–153; Karl Joseph Höltgen, "Henry Hawkins: A Jesuit Writer and Emblematist in Stuart England," in *The Jesuits: Culture, Sciences, and the Arts, 1540–1773*, ed. John W. O'Malley (Toronto, 1999), 1:600–626; Beverly Seaton, *The Language of Flowers: A History* (Charlottesville, NC, 1995), 45–46.
83. Henry Hawkins, "The Plat-Forme of the Garden," in *Partheneia Sacra, or The Mysterious and Delicious Garden of the Sacred Parthenes* (1633), 9, 22.
84. Hardy, "Papists in a Protestant Age," 456–457; Richard Trappes-Lomax, ed., "Records of the English Canonesses of the Holy Sepulcher at Liege, Now at New Hall, Essex, 1652–1793," in *Miscellanea Records of the Catholic Record Society* (London, 1915), 17:208–209.
85. Peterman, *Bohemia*, 16–19; Newtown Memoranda, 1740–1745, MPA, Box 3, Folder 15.
86. Hardy, "Papists in a Protestant Age," 190; Elizabeth Carroll to CCC, September 30, 1754, and September 8, 1756, in Hoffman et al., *Dear Papa, Dear Charley*, 1:24, 37; Colin Haydon, *Anti-Catholicism in Eighteenth-Century England, c. 1714–80* (Manchester, UK, 1993), 204.
87. *Archives of Maryland*, 46:549–550, 52:358; Hardy, "Papists in a Protestant Age," 315.

88. Robert Bireley, *The Refashioning of Catholicism, 1450–1700: A Reassessment of the Counter Reformation* (Washington, DC, 1999), 121–146; CCC to CCA, October 22, 1761, December 19, 1761, and March 22, 1750, in Hoffman et al., *Dear Papa, Dear Charley*, 1:231, 240, 6. To be fair, many educational historians do consider the Jesuits' *Ratio* to be a precursor to our modern-day liberal arts education, in that it emphasized Renaissance Humanism. Most scholars agree, however, that the *Ratio* also discouraged innovative thinking. See John W. O'Malley, "Introduction." *Ratio Studiorum: Jesuit Education, 1548–1773.* 1999. Boston College. July 29, 2011, http://www.bc.edu/sites/libraries/ratio/ratiointro.html.
89. CCC to CCA, March 22, 1750, in Hoffman, *op. cit.*, 1:6.
90. James Lawson to Hugh Matthews, May 16, 1779, "Papers of Hugh Matthews, 1770–1791," MSA, M-1340. Lawson settled in Port Tobacco upon his return to Maryland and became a merchant who did extensive business with the Jesuits. Matthews may have been the grandson of Hugh Matthews, a prominent planter in Cecil County in the 1730s. In 1801, the Jesuits at Bohemia hired a Hugh Matthews to do some surveying for them. See MPA, Box 1, Folder 67 and Box 30, Folder 4; June D. Brown, ed., *Abstracts of Cecil County Maryland Land Records, 1673–1751* (Westminster, MD 1998), 205.
91. Quoted in John Algeo, ed., *The Cambridge History of the English Language: English in North America* (New York, 2001), 6:168. Although the dialectical differences that separated the colonists from the British were not nearly as great in the mid-eighteenth century as they would be fifty or sixty years later, historian David Hackett Fischer asserts that the mid-Atlantic region, more so than New England, had developed a distinctive way of speaking by the mid-eighteenth century, thanks, in part, to the wide immigration from non-English-speaking countries and from various parts of England and Ireland that the region experienced. See his *Albion's Seed: Four British Folkways in America* (New York, 1989), 470–475. For more on the differences between American and British English that were apparent in the eighteenth century, see Seth Lerer, *Inventing English: A Portable History of the Language* (New York, 2007), 181–192.
92. CCC to CCA, March 23, 1764, and June 10, 1761, in Hoffman et al., *Dear Papa, Dear Charley*, 1:356, 213.
93. CCA to CCC, October 9, 1752, in ibid., 19–20.
94. Hardy, "Papists in a Protestant Age," 615–617; Leonard Neale to Ann Neale, February 15, 1770, MPA Box 57, Folder 2.
95. CCC to CCA, December 26, 1759, in Hoffman et al., *Dear Papa, Dear Charley*, 142, 212; Fr. George Hunter to John Tichbourne, no date (but some time between 1747 and 1756), "Hunter Letterbook," MPA, Box 2, Folder 10; Peter Guilday, *The English Catholic Refugees on the Continent, 1558–1795* (New York, 1914), 372; "Notes and Comments," *Catholic Historical Review* (Washington, DC, 1917), 2:238–239. The Ursuline Nuns built a convent in New Orleans in 1727, but in 1790, New Orleans was not yet a part of the United States.
96. Roger Finke and Rodney Stark, *The Churching of America, 1776–2005: Winners and Losers in Our Religious Economy* (New Brunswick, NJ, 2006), 1–155.

Chapter 5

1. Victor Tanner and Ashraf al-Khalidi, "Sectarian Violence: Radical Groups Drive Internal Displacement in Iraq," *Brookings Institute Papers*, July 29, 2011, http://www.internaldissplacement.org/8025708F004CE90B/(httpDocuments)/32A4EE04F73CD176C125720B004F151A/$file/10112006_Tanner_Iraq_FINAL.pdf; "World Economic Outlook Database: Iraq," *International Monetary Fund*, July 29, 2011, http://www.imf.org/external/pubs/ft/weo/2009/01/weodata/weorept.aspx?sy=2006&ey=2009&scsm=1&ssd=1&sort=country&ds=.&br=1&c=433&s=NGDPD%2CNGDPDPC%2CPPPGDP%2CPPPPC%2C; Lois Green Carr, "Sources of Political Stability and Upheaval in Seventeenth-Century Maryland," *Maryland Historical Magazine* 79 (1984): 55; Russell R. Menard, P. M. G. Harris, and Lois Green Carr, "Opportunity and Inequality: The Distribution of Wealth in the Lower Western Shore of Maryland, 1638–1705," *Maryland Historical Review* 82 (1974): 172.

2. Babak Dehghanpisheh, Rod Nordland, and Michael Hastings, "Love in a Time of Madness," *Newsweek*, March 13, 2006, 32. Out of 6 million marriages in Iraq, an estimated 2.5 million involve Sunni and Shia partners.
3. A great deal has been written about the connection between anti-Catholicism and British identity. See, for example, Owen Stanwood, "The Protestant Moment: Antipopery, the Revolution if 1688–89, and the Making of an Anglo-American Empire," *Journal of British Studies* 46 (2007): 481–508; Colin Haydon, "'I love my King and my Country, but a Roman catholic I hate': Anti-Catholicism, Xenophobia, and National Identity in Eighteenth-Century England," in *Protestantism and National Identity: Britain and Ireland, c. 1650–c.1850*, ed. Tony Claydon and Ian McBride (New York, 1998), 33–52; Jeremy Black, "Confessional State or Elect Nation? Religion and Identity in Eighteenth-Century England," ibid., 53–74; Linda Colley, "Britishness and Otherness, an Argument," *Journal of British Studies* 31 (1992): 309–329; and J. C. D. Clark, *The Language of Liberty: Political Discourse and Social Dynamics in the Anglo-American World* (New York, 1994), especially 237–257.
4. William Blackstone, "Of the Rights of Persons" and "On Private Wrongs," *Commentaries on the Laws of England, in Four Volumes* (Oxford, 1765–1769), rpt. (New York, 1853), 1:89, 140; 2:337.
5. Griffith Williams, *The Triumph of the Israelites Over the Moabites, or Protestants Over Papists* (1763), 5.
6. John D. Krugler, *English and Catholic: The Lords Baltimore in the Seventeenth Century* (Baltimore, 2004), 117; Dermot B. Fenlon, "Wentworth and the Parliament of 1634," *Journal of the Royal Society of Antiquaries of Ireland* 94 (1964): 159–175; John Evelyn, *Memoirs of John Evelyn, Comprising his Diary from 1641 to 1705–06* (London, 1827), 3:208, 127.
7. John Adams, "A Dissertation on Canon and Feudal Law," in *The Works of John Adams, Second President of the United States*, ed. Charles Francis Adams (New York, 2008, rpt.), 3:456; Francis D. Cogliano, "Exposing the Idolatry of the Romish Church: Anti-popery and Colonial New England," in *Critical Issues in American Religious History: A Reader*, ed. Robert R. Mathisen (Waco, TX, 2006), 63; Pauline Maier, "The Pope at Harvard: The Dudleian Lectures, Anti-Catholicism, and the Politics of Protestantism," *Proceedings of the Massachusetts Historical Society* 97 (1985): 18.
8. In a report he sent to London in 1678, New York's governor Edmund Andros noted that there were Jews in the colony, along with a host of Protestant denominations, but he did not mention any Catholics. In 1687, Thomas Dongan, an Irish Catholic whom James II appointed as governor in 1682, reported that New York had "some Jews," but "few Roman Catholics." See Michael Kammen, *Colonial New York: A History* (New York, 1975), 85–87, 118–119. For more on Leisler's Rebellion and the role of anti-Catholicism, see Randall Balmer, *A Perfect Babel of Confusion: Dutch Religion and English Culture in the Middle Colonies* (New York, 1992), 28–50.
9. *Archives of Maryland*, ed. William Hand Brown et al. (Baltimore, 1883–present), 8:107, 448; 20:144; 22:487; 26: 289, 349; 27:371; 33:109.
10. Ibid., 26:46, 340.
11. Ibid., 25:582. Nicholson's proclamation is printed in *Historical Collections Relating to the American Colonial Church*, ed. William Stevens Perry (New York, 1969), 4:24–25.
12. *Archives of Maryland*, 19:36–37, 389–390.
13. Ibid., 27:146.
14. Margaret Sankey, *Jacobite Prisoners of the 1715 Rebellion: Preventing and Punishing Insurrection in Hanoverian England* (Burlington, VT, 2005), 67–69.
15. Ronald Hoffman, *Princes of Ireland, Planters of Maryland: A Carroll Saga, 1500–1782* (Chapel Hill, NC, 2000) 82–90; *Archives of Maryland*, 30: 373–376, 612–617.
16. Ibid., 30:334; Sankey, *Jacobite Prisoners*, 69.
17. John Krugler, Gerald Fogarty, and Tricia Pyne have all written about the claim that Maryland's Catholics made to the rights of Englishmen. Their work, while extremely important, fails to explore the extent to which Catholics staked their claim to English rights not as Englishmen, but as "Marylandians." See Krugler, *English and Catholic*; Gerald Fogarty,

"Property and Religious Liberty in Colonial Maryland Catholic Thought," *Catholic Historical Review* 72 (1986), 573–600; Tricia Pyne, "The Politics of Identity in Eighteenth-Century British America: Catholic Perceptions of their Role in British Society," *U.S. Catholic Historian* 15 (1997): 1–14.

18. *Archives of Maryland*, 33:288–289; "William III, 1998–99: An Act for the Further Preventing the Growth of Popery" (11 and 12 William III, c. 4), in *Statutes of the Realm, 1695–1701*, ed. John Raithby (London, 1820), 7:586–587.
19. Peter Atwood, "Liberty and Property, or the Beauty of Maryland Displayed," rpt., *United States Catholic Historical Magazine* 3 (1889–90): 248, 249, 252, 242.
20. "Letter from the Spanish Ambassador, 1718," Maryland Province Archives (MPA), Special Collections, Georgetown University, Box 3, Folder 10.
21. *Archives of Maryland*, 27:243. Part of the reason the Lower House wanted to establish a precedent for applying England's penal laws to Maryland was that the application of parliamentary law to the colony would have challenged proprietary prerogative. The Lower House, more so than the Upper House, was at odds with the proprietor throughout most of the eighteenth century.
22. *History of the Society of Jesus in North America, Colonial and Federal, from the First Colonization till 1645, Documents*, ed. Thomas Hughes (New York, 1907), 1:225.
23. Dr. Charles Carroll to James Carroll, March 12, 1750, in "Letterbook and Business Account," 2:301, Maryland Historical Society (MHS), MS208; Charles Carroll of Annapolis (CCA) to Clement Hill, n.d., MPA, Box 3, Folder 10.
24. CCA to Charles Carroll of Carrollton (CCC), July 26, 1756, in Ronald Hoffman, Sally D. Mason, and Eleanor S. Darcy, eds., *Dear Papa, Dear Charley: The Peregrinations of a Revolutionary Aristocrat* (Chapel Hill, NC, 2001), 1:28; *Archives of Maryland*, 9:316; "The Governor's Council of Maryland Orders the Magistrates to Inquire into the Conduct of the Negros and Catholics," rpt. in *The American Catholic Historical Records*, ed. Martin I. J. Griffin (Philadelphia, 1908), 264–265.
25. Basil Sollers, "The Acadians (French Neutrals) Transported to Maryland," *Maryland Historical Magazine* 3 (1908): 7; Maryland *Gazette*, September 4, 11, and 25, 1755.
26. "Replies of the Magistrates that They Can Find No Cause of Complaint," rpt. in Griffin, *Historical Records*, 266–273; *Archives of Maryland*, 9:317–319.
27. This renewed effort to apply England's recusancy laws to Maryland, had it passed, would not have resulted in the deportation of Catholics to England because the new proposal gave Maryland's governor and the colony's court system the authority to determine violations of English law. See Beatriz Bentacourt Hardy, "Papists in a Protestant Age" (Ph.D. dissertation, University of Maryland, 1993), 265; *Maryland Gazette*, November 13, 1755; Thomas Hughes, *History of the Society of Jesus in North America, Colonial and Federal, from the First Colonization till 1645, Text* (New York, 1908), 2:533.
28. "Petition of Roman Catholics of Maryland Against a Bill Depriving Them of all Civil and Religious Rights," rpt. in Griffin, *Historical Records*, 264; "An Act to oblige papists to register their names and real estates" (1 George I, stat. 2, c. 55) and "An Act for granting an Aid to his Majesty by laying a tax upon Papists" (9 George I, stat. 1, c. 18) in *The Statutes at Large, from Magna Carta to the thirtieth year of King George the Second*, ed. John Cay (London, 1758), 4:130, 445.
29. "Petition of the Roman Catholics," 261–264; George Hunter, "A Short Account of the proceedings of the Maryland Assembly in regard to Roman Catholicks settled there," n.d., but sometime in 1750s, MPA, Box 3, Folder 10.
30. "Charles Carroll Protests Against the Assembly's Act," rpt. in Griffin, *Historical Records*, 261–264.
31. "English Bill of Rights, 1689," *The Avalon Project: Documents in Law, History and Diplomacy*, Lillian Goldman Law Library, Yale University, March 30, 2010, http://avalon.law.yale.edu/17th_century/england.asp; Atwood, "Liberty and Property," 248.
32. *Archives of Maryland*, 9:316.
33. Ann Arundel County Court (Judgment Record), 03/1746–03/1748, Liber IB6, Folders 138–143, Maryland State Archives (MSA) C91-19; *Archives of Maryland*, 28:355–357;

Maryland *Gazette*, July 22, 1746; Hardy, "Papists in a Protestant Age," 173–174, 246; Grace L. Tracey and John P. Dern, *Pioneers of Old Monocacy: The Early Settlement of Frederick County, Maryland, 1721–1743* (Baltimore, 1987), 251–252; "Address of the Roman Catholics to the Governor Against the £40,000 Act as Double Taxing Them, with Copies of Former Addresses to His Majesty and the Proprietor," rpt. in *United States Catholic Historical Magazine* 3 (1890): 3:214.

34. Hester Dorsey Richardson, *Side-lights on Maryland History* (Charlottesville, VA, 1913), 17–18. Samuel Ogle was the fourth man to serve as governor during this period. The rector of St. Omer's College reported that Charles Calvert, the third Lord Baltimore, tried to keep his grandsons enrolled in the school after his son, Benedict Leonard, "turned Protestant." Benedict Leonard, however, was good friends with Robert Harley, the Lord of the Treasury, who threatened to have every Jesuit in England expelled if the boys were not returned to their father. Officials at St. Omer's insisted that Benedict Leonard's oldest son, Charles, had told them he would "rather loose his estate than his Religion." This was not a choice the Calvert boys were allowed to make, however. See "The Letter Book of Lewis Sabran, S.J. (Rector of St. Omers College, October 1713 to October 1715," *Publications of the Catholic Record Society*, ed. Geoffrey Hold (Hertford, England, 1971), 62:34, 54.
35. "Address of the Roman Catholics of Maryland to Charles, Lord Baltimore,1727," MPA, Box 3, Folder 11; "The Humble Address of the Roman Catholic Inhabitants of the Province of Maryland," rpt., *United States Catholic Historical Magazine* 3 (1890): 213.
36. Hardy, "Papists in a Protestant Age," 221–227; *Archives of Maryland*, 46:75–77; 50:52, 54.
37. Joy Gary, "Patrick Creagh of Annapolis," *Maryland Historical Magazine* 48 (1953): 310–326; St. Paul's Parish Collection, "Vestry Minutes," 1733, MSA, M255; King George's Parish Vestrymen to Bishop Gibson, July 6, 1731, and Giles Rainsford to Bishop Gibson, July 22, 1725, in *The Fulham Papers in the Lambeth Palace Library, American Colonial Section, Calendar and Indexes*, ed. William Wilson Manross (Oxford, UK, 1965), 3:150, 76–77; Arthur Holt to Samuel Smith, May 21, 1734, in ibid. I found no actual evidence that Catholics attended Anglican services in the 1730s and 1740s, but they definitely attended in the 1770s, when a Catholic heard the Anglican minister Jonathan Boucher preach and turned Boucher, who was a Loyalist, in to the Annapolis Committee of Safety. If Catholics attended Anglican services in the 1770s, it is not unreasonable to assume that they attended in the 1730s and 1740s. See Jonathan Boucher, *A View of the Causes and Consequences of the American Revolution* (New York, 1967; orig., 1797), 243.
38. *Archives of Maryland*, 42:13, 16–17, 19.
39. Ibid., 50:51–54; *Maryland Gazette*, March 25, 1746, and March 18, 1746.
40. Ibid., July 31, 1755.
41. Memorial to the Earl of Halifax, 1751, MPA, Box 3, Folder 13; *Archives of Maryland*, 50:54, 177–178; 198–205; 249–250; *Maryland Gazette*, July 31 and November 6, 1755.
42. Ibid., October 17, 1754; *Archives of Maryland*, 50:513–519.
43. Edward Papenfuse, *A Biographical Dictionary of the Maryland Legislature, 1635–1789* (Baltimore, 1979), 1:55; Hardy, "Papists in a Protestant Age," 279.
44. Frederick Calvert's secretary, Cecilius Calvert, told Maryland's governor, Horatio Sharpe, of the pressure Thomas Robinson was placing on the proprietor. See Cecilius Calvert to Horatio Sharpe, September 9, 1755, in Sharpe Papers (1754–1769), MHS, MS 1414.
45. *Archives of Maryland*, 52:325, 508–510; Timothy Bosworth, "Anti-Catholicism as a Political Tool in Mid-Eighteenth-Century Maryland," *Catholic Historical Review* 61 (1975): 558–559.
46. Benedict Calvert to CCA, May 11, 1756, and "Petition of the Roman Catholics," (1756), MPA, Box 3, Folder 12; CCC to CCA, February 13, 1761, in Hoffman et al., *Dear Papa, Dear Charley*, 1:195.
47. *Archives of Maryland*, 52:358–360, 6:419. After signing the bill, Governor Sharpe wrote to Lord Baltimore to explain that if he had not signed it, he would have been accused of favoring popery.
48. The annual salary that CCA paid to Fr. John Ashton was £33, 6s, 8d, and because his estates were spread out along the western shore, it was not usual for Carroll to have more

than one priest on the payroll. By the mid-1760s, Carroll's net worth was around £90,000. See Hoffman et al., *Dear Papa, Dear Charley,* 707, n. 5; Hoffman, *Princes of Ireland,* 240, 100–101, 176.
49. It is not clear what happened with the bill that the Upper House proposed, but it did not pass. See *Archives of Maryland,* 52:376, 441–449.
50. Ibid., 6:539–540; 9:117; 11 and 12 William III, c. 4, in Raithby, *Statutes of the Realm,* 7:586–587; Fogarty, "Property and Religious Liberty," 595; Hardy, "Papists in a Protestant Age," 291–292.
51. MPA, Box 3, Folders 10 and 11.
52. American Catholic Sermon Collection (ACSC), Special Collections, Georgetown University, Mos-1, Be-10, Ca-3.
53. George Hunter, "A Short Account of the state and condition of the Roman Catholics in the Province of Maryland, collected from authentic copies of the provincial records and other undoubted Testimonies," n.d., rpt., *Woodstock Letters* (1881), 10–11; 15–16.
54. Frederick Calvert to Horatio Sharpe, April 7, 1757, in *Archives of Maryland,* 6:539–540.
55. MPA, Box 3, Folder 10; Maryland *Gazette,* May 27, 1756; Hoffman, *Princes of Ireland,* 263. CCA estimated his loans to be in excess of £24,000 in 1760, four years after he placed the ad.
56. Ibid., 275–276, n. 19.
57. CCC to CCA, February 30 [sic], 1760, and December 10, 1759, in Hoffman et al., *Dear Papa, Dear Charley,* 1:150, 140.
58. CCC to CCA, January 1, 1761, in ibid., 192–193.

Chapter 6

1. John Adams to Thomas McKean, August 31, 1813, in *The Works of John Adams, Second President of the United States: With a Life of the Author, Notes and Illustrations,* ed. Charles Francis Adams (Boston, 1865), 10:62.
2. Adams's problem with histories like Warren's was that they failed to show any "instances of the friendship of Great Britain toward this country from 1600 to 1813." Histories that emphasized England's friendship with the colonies did exist; alas, they were all written by Loyalists who tended to be less-than-complimentary toward John Adams. Peter Oliver, for instance, blamed the war on a small gang of men from Massachusetts who "understood human Nature, in low life, so well" that they could "turn the minds of the great Vulgar" to "seditious Associations." See Peter Oliver, *Origin and Progress of the American Rebellion,* ed. Douglass Adair and John A. Schutz (1781, rpt. Stanford, CA, 1961), 39, 44–45.
3. Jonathan Boucher, *A View to the Causes and Consequences of the American Revolution, in Thirteen Discourses* (London, 1797), xxxi; Jonathan Boucher to John James, December 9, 1765, and March 9, 1767, in the Jonathan Boucher Papers (JBP), Special Collections, College of William and Mary, Box 1, Folder 3. For more on the Proclamation Line, see Colin G. Calloway, *The Scratch of a Pen: 1763 and the Transformation of North America* (New York, 2006), 47–65.
4. Boucher, *Causes and Consequences,* 241–242; vii.
5. Ibid., xxv; "Junius," Maryland *Journal,* May 3, 1775.
6. Boucher, *Causes and Consequences,* 242, 255, 241.
7. Ibid., 243.
8. Samuel Johnson, *Hypocrisy Unmasked; or, a Short Inquiry into the Religious Complaints of our American Colonies* (1774), 9.
9. Charles Albro Barker, *The Background of the Revolution in Maryland* (New Haven, CT, 1940), 291–293, 315–316; Ronald Hoffman, *A Spirit of Dissension: Economics, Politics, and the Revolution in Maryland* (Baltimore, 1973), 37–43; 60–88.
10. Robert Middlekauff, *The Glorious Cause: The American Revolution, 1763–1789* (New York, 1982), 58–62.
11. Hoffman, *Dissension,* 36, 80, 90.
12. Daniel Dulany, *Considerations on the Propriety of Imposing Taxes in the British Colonies, for the Purpose of raising Revenue, by an Act of Parliament* (Annapolis, 1765), 6–11, 34, 31, 5. Dulany's

pamphlet was written in response to Thomas Whatley's *The Regulations Lately Made concerning the Colonies and the Taxes Imposed Upon Them, Considered* (1765). Whatley was Secretary to the Treasury, and his argument that the colonists were "virtually represented" in the same way that the inhabitants of Leeds, Halifax, Manchester, and Birmingham were virtually represented was quickly taken up by Prime Minister George Grenville.

13. John Joachim Zubly, *An Humble Inquiry into the Nature of the Dependency of the American Colonies* (1769), quoted in Bernard Bailyn, *The Ideological Origins of the American Revolution* (Cambridge, 1967), 169; John Dickinson, "Letter IV: Letters from a Farmer," in *The Political Writings of John Dickinson, Esquire* (Wilmington, DE, 1801), 1:174; Hoffman, *Dissension*, 80–82, 98–100.

14. David Curtis Skaggs, "Maryland's Impulse toward Social Revolution, 1750–1776," *Journal of American History* 54 (1968): 771–786. See also Skaggs's *Roots of Maryland Democracy, 1753–1776* (Westport, CT, 1973); Hoffman, *Dissension*; Barker, *Background*; and Aubrey C. Land, *Colonial Maryland: A History* (Millwood, NY, 1981).

15. For more on proprietary politics and the coming of the Revolution in Pennsylvania, see Carl and Jessica Briedenbaugh's dated, but still useful *Rebels and Gentlemen: Philadelphia in the Age of Franklin* (New York, 1942); Stephen Brobeck, "Revolutionary Change in Colonial Philadelphia: The Brief Life of the Proprietary Gentry," *William and Mary Quarterly* 33 (1976): 410–434; and Lorett Treese, *The Storm Gathering: The Penn Family and the American Revolution* (State College, PA, 1992). On the coming of the Revolution in Virginia, see Rhys Isaac, *Landon Carter's Uneasy Kingdom: Revolution and Rebellion on a Virginia Plantation* (New York, 2004); Jack P. Greene, "Society, Ideology, and Politics: An Analysis of the Political Culture of Mid-Eighteenth-Century Virginia," in *Society, Freedom and Conscience: The American Revolution in Virginia, Massachusetts, and New York*, ed. Richard M. Jellison (New York, 1976), 14–76; and Jack P. Greene, "'Virtus et Libertas': Political Culture, Social Change, and the Origins of the American Revolution in Virginia, 1763-1766," in *The Southern Experience in the American Revolution*, ed. Jeffrey J. Crow and Larry E. Tise (Chapel Hill, NC, 1978), 55–108.

16. "A Church of England Man," *New York Journal*, November 19, 1774.

17. Jack P. Greene, *Peripheries and Center: Constitutional Development in the Extended Polities of the British Empire and the United States, 1607–1788* (Athens, GA, 1986), 12, 95–97, 103–104; 110–124. The Franklin quote is on p. 12.

18. When they insisted that Parliament had authority in Maryland, lawmakers in the Lower House also challenged Lord Baltimore's authority in the colony. The historians mentioned in n. 14 have all written about this aspect of the Lower House's deference to Parliament, but they have missed that the lawmakers' deference was also an attempt to preserve Maryland's English identity by keeping Catholic influence in the colony in check. Additionally, scholars have missed that the tactic of deferring to Parliament, whether it was to cement Maryland's English identity or to challenge the proprietor, rendered Maryland's lawmakers incapable or responding positively, at first, to the anti-parliamentary rhetoric coming out of other colonies.

19. Dulany, *Considerations*, 28, 30, 21, 4–6.

20. Beginning in the 1740s and 1750s, assemblymen in Massachusetts and New York began to articulate a constitutional understanding of their legislative prerogatives, arguing—as "Zacharias Plaintruth" did in 1752—that it would be "slavish" to insist that "we have no Constitution in the Colonies but what the King is pleased to give us." Legal historians have debated whether the colonists were actually on solid ground when they made this argument—with many experts insisting they were not. See "Zacharias Plaintruth," *New-York Gazette*, January 27, 1752; Greene, *Peripheries and Center*, 28–42; *Negotiated Authorities: Essays in Colonial Political and Constitutional History* (Charlottesville, 1994), 25–42; and "From the Perspective of Law: Context and Legitimacy in the Origins of the American Revolution. A Review Essay," *South Atlantic Quarterly* 51 (1986): 56–77.

21. A more detailed description of the circumstances leading up to Governor Eden's fee proclamation is available in Hoffman, *Dissension*, 92–103, and Peter S. Onuf, *Maryland and Empire, 1773: The Antilon-First Citizen Letters* (Baltimore, 1974), 13–16.

22. *Maryland Gazette*, January 7, 1773, rpt. in Onuf, *Maryland and Empire*, 45, 47, 48, 51.
23. Hoffman, *Dissension*, 94.
24. *Maryland Gazette*, June 14, 1773; Lloyd Dulany to Charles Carroll of Carrollton (CCC), September 29, 1769, Charles Carroll Papers, 1731–1833, Maryland Historical Society (MHS), MS 206 (microfilm MS 81); Ronald Hoffman, *Princes of Ireland, Planters of Maryland: A Carroll Saga, 1500–1782* (Chapel Hill, NC, 2000), 202–206, 288–290.
25. Antilon's *Third Letter*, April 8, 1773, and *Fourth Letter*, June 3, 1773; First Citizen's *Third Letter*, May 6, 1773, in Onuf, *Maryland and Empire*, 122, 186, 188, 125.
26. Antilon's *Fourth Letter*, ibid., 157.
27. Antilon's *Second Letter*, February 18, 1773, and *Third Letter*, in ibid., 71, 101; Nicholas B. Wainwright, "Tale of a Runaway Cape: The Penn–Baltimore Agreement of 1732," *Pennsylvania Magazine of History and Biography* 87 (1963): 251–293.
28. First Citizen's *Second Letter*, March 11, 1773, in Onuf, *Maryland and Empire*, 87.
29. First Citizen's *Third Letter*, in ibid., 134–135, 78.
30. First Citizen's *First Letter*, February 4, 1773, in ibid., 57. "The King can do no wrong" is a fundamental maxim in Blackstone's *Commentaries on the Laws of England*, rpt. (London, 1821), 1:246.
31. First Citizen's *First Letter*, in Onuf, *Maryland and Empire*, 57.
32. Antilon's *Second Letter*, in ibid., 66–67; consult Onuf's introduction, 17, 26–27.
33. First Citizen's *Fourth Letter*, July 1, 1773, in ibid., 206–207.
34. Bernard Bailyn, *The Origins of American Politics* (New York, 1967), 11. See also Pauline Maier, *From Resistance to Revolution: Colonial Radicals and the Development of American Opposition to Britain, 1765–1776* (New York, 1972); and Edward Countryman, *The American Revolution* (New York, 1985).
35. Antilon's *Second Letter*; First Citizen's *Second Letter*, in Onuf, *Maryland and Empire*, 73–75, 78–79. John Dickinson actually refused to sign the Declaration of Independence, because in July 1776, he still believed that the king, unlike his ministers, was not corrupt. When George III authorized the British navy's occupation of New York City in the fall of 1776, however, Dickinson finally embraced independence. See Joseph C. Morton, *Shapers of the Great Debate at the Constitutional Convention of 1787* (Westport, CT, 2006), 74–75.
36. Pauline Maier has noticed that the editors of a number of colonial newspapers were articulating anti-monarchical sentiments as early as 1771 and 1772. She believes these sentiments were a reaction to George III's unwillingness to respond to a series of petitions that the colonists had sent to the king in the wake of the Boston Massacre. Maier calls these early criticisms of the king "proto-revolutionary," and she notes that although they were expressed in newspapers as far south as South Carolina, it was really only in Massachusetts that they manifested themselves in local acts of defiance against the king—at least prior to 1774. See *From Resistance to Revolution*, 198–227, especially 211 and 218.
37. The decision to extend toleration to the Catholics in Canada may have been as much a matter of pragmatism, as it was an assertion of George III's authority. In August 1770, Governor Guy Carleton wrote to George III and warned the king that Catholics were likely to outnumber Protestants in Canada for many years to come. Echoing George and Cecilius Calvert's experiences with colonization, Carleton told the king that Quebec desperately needed people, regardless of their religious affiliation, and he worried that if George III did not give Catholics an incentive to stay, Quebec would soon experience massive depopulation. See Karen Arnita Stanbridge, "British Catholic Policy in Eighteenth-Century Ireland and Quebec" (Ph.D. dissertation, University of Western Ontario, 1998), 178.
38. In 1784, there were approximately 132,000 people of European descent living in Quebec. In 1763, the year the territory became an English colony, there were 70,000 French Catholics in Quebec. See Massimo Levi-Bacci, *A Concise History of World Population* (Malden, MA, 1992), 49; and A. Fournet, "Canada," *The Catholic Encyclopedia*, ed. George Herberman (New York, 1908), 3:234.
39. Bailyn, *Ideological Origins*, 19. For a more honest appraisal of the colonial reaction to the Quebec Act, see Brendan McConville, *The King's Three Faces: The Rise and Fall of Royal America, 1688–1776* (Chapel Hill, NC, 2006), 282, 288–290.

40. Samuel Adams, *Writings of Samuel Adams, 1773–1777*, ed. Harry Alanzo Cushing (New York, 1907), 3:213; John Adams, *Works*, 2:252; Ezra Stiles, *The Literary Diary of Ezra Stiles*, ed. Franklin Bowditch Dexter (New York, 1901), 1:455.
41. Alexander Hamilton, *A Full Vindication of Matters of Congress from Calumnies of their Enemies* (1774), rpt. in *The American Catholic Historical Researches* 6 (1889): 160; William Henry Drayton, "Charge of William Henry Drayton," in *American Archives, Fourth Series*, ed. Peter Force (Washington, DC, 1837), 6:959; C. H. Van Tyne, "The Influence of the Clergy, and of Religious and Sectarian Forces on the American Revolution," *American Historical Review* 19 (1914): 59–62.
42. *Maryland Gazette*, October 13, 1774; December 22, 1774; November 10, 1774; *Maryland Journal*, September 7, 1774. Mary Katherine Goddard was the first printer to publish copies of the Declaration of Independence that included the signers' names. See Ward L. Miner, "Mary Katherine Goddard," in *Notable American Women, 1607–1950*, ed. Edward T. James (Cambridge, 1971), 2:55–56.
43. *Journal*, May 3, 1775; *An Englishman's Answer to the Address from the Delegates to the People of Great Britain* (Rivington, NY, 1775), 21–22.
44. *New England Chronicle*, May 18, 1775; *New York Gazette*, March 2, 1775; David A. Copeland, *Debating Issues in Colonial Newspapers* (Westport, CT, 2000), vi–xvi.
45. *Proceedings of the Conventions of the Province of Maryland Held at Annapolis, 1774, 1775, 1776* (Baltimore, 1836), 210–215. In July 1776, when the convention was convened yet again, the Quebec Act was listed as a grievance, but the focus of the complaint was the extension of Canada's boundaries. Delightful though this fact is to Neo-Whig historians, Maryland's convention was quite unusual in its failure to mention the religious implications of the Quebec Act.
46. *Archives of Maryland*, ed. William Hand Brown et al. (Baltimore, 1883–present), 78:209, 168, 10; Thomas O'Brien Hanley, *Revolutionary Statesman: Charles Carroll and the War* (Baltimore, 1983), 42. Maryland's representatives to the First Continental Congress were Thomas Johnson, William Paca, Samuel Chase, Matthew Tilghman, and Robert Goldsborough.
47. *Archives of Maryland*, 28:363.
48. The religious identities of most of the "Patriots" from Maryland are unknown. However, Henry Peden has identified 2,035 men from St. Mary's County who aided the independence movement, and I have determined that at least 51 percent of them were probably Catholic. Some of them were married, baptized, or buried in the Church, left money or property to the Church, or had their children baptized in the Church. Others are not listed in the surviving Church records, but they were probably the fathers, sons, or brothers of known Catholics, as evidenced not just by their names but also by their residence in the same hundreds and their involvement in the probate records of known Catholics (sometimes as witnesses or executors, and other times as heirs). We do not know what percentage of the St. Mary's County population, overall, was Catholic in the 1770s. Governor Horatio Sharpe estimated that around 7 percent of Maryland's entire population was Catholic in 1758, but the only surviving county-by-county census of the Catholic population prior to the Revolution was done in 1708. At that time, 32 percent of the households in St. Mary's County were Catholic, and around 9 percent of the colony's entire white population was Catholic. The overall Catholic population in 1758, therefore, was 23 percent smaller than it had been fifty years earlier, when Catholic households made up 32 percent of the population in St. Mary's County. If we reduce the Catholic population of St. Mary's County by 23 percent, then, we arrive at an estimate that puts the Catholic population at 25 percent. See "Maryland Catholic Subscribers to Boston Relief," "Baptisms, Marriages, St. Francis Xavier and St. Inigoes Churches," "Census, St. Inigoes, St. Mary's County, 1768, 1769," and "Presumed Catholic Births Recorded at St. Andrew's Episcopal Church," rpt. in Timothy J. O'Rourke, *Catholic Families of Southern Maryland* (Baltimore, 2001, 1–40, 52–70; "Non-Jesuit Wills, 1694–1840," MPA, Box 25, Folder 8; Henry C. Peden, *Revolutionary Patriots of Calvert and St. Mary's Counties, Maryland, 1775–1784* (Westminster, MD, 2006); Gaius M. Brumbaugh, *Maryland Records: Colonial, Revolutionary, County and*

Church from Original Sources (Baltimore, 1885), 2:63–78; Lois Green Carr and David William Jordan, *Maryland's Revolution of Government, 1689–92* (Ithaca, NY, 1974), 33n.
49. Robert M. Calhoon, "Loyalism and Neutrality," in Jack P. Greene and J. R. Pole, *A Companion to the American Revolution* (Malden, MA, 2000), 235; *Archives of Maryland*, 9:315, 25:258–259; M. Christopher Newton, *Maryland Loyalists in the American Revolution* (Centreville, MD, 1996); Hoffman, *Dissension*, 80–82, 98–100; Skaggs, "Maryland's Impulse toward Social Revolution," 771–786.
50. "Muster Rolls and Other Records of Service of Maryland Troops in the American Revolution, 1775–1783," *Archives of Maryland*, 18:25, 384, 410, 30–32; S. Eugene Clements and F. Edward Wright, *The Maryland Militia in the Revolutionary War* (Silver Spring, MD, 1987), 210, 213, 158, 160; Henry C. Peden, Jr., *Marylanders to Kentucky, 1775–1825* (Westminster, MD, 1991), 96; Ben J. Webb, *The Century of Catholicity in Kentucky* (Louisville, KY, 1884), 67–87. The Diocese of Bardstown was formed in 1808, the same year the Dioceses of New York and Boston were formed.
51. *Woodstock Letters* (Woodstock, MD, 1913), 42:146–147; John Thomas Scharf, *History of Maryland from the Earliest Period to the Present Day* (Hatboro, PA, 1967), 2:442.
52. Joseph Willcox, "John Willcox of Pennsylvania and North Carolina," *American Catholic Historical Researches* 19 (1902): 17–18; Walter George Smith, "Pennsylvania," *Catholic Encyclopedia*, 11:644. There were twenty-two Irish and fifteen Germans in the original congregation at St. Joseph's, but Germans dominated the Catholic population in Pennsylvania overall. A census from 1757 counted 949 German Catholics and 416 English or Irish Catholics in Pennsylvania. See John Tracey Ellis, *Catholics in Colonial America* (Baltimore, 1965), 376.
53. "Governor's Council Proceedings, July 25th, 1734," rpt. in *American Catholic Historical Researches* 15 (1895): 181–182; Earl Arnett, Robert J. Brugger, Edward C. Papenfuse, *Maryland: A New Guide to the Old Line State* (Baltimore, 1999), 21.
54. Ragnhild Marie Hatton, *George I: Elector and King* (London, 1978), 131–136; Jeremy Black, "George II and all that Stuff: On the Value of the Neglected," *Albion* 4 (2004): 588–589.
55. Captain Robert MacKenzie to Lt.-Col. Alfred Clifton, October 7 and 14, 1777, rpt. in Martin I. J. Griffin, "The Roman Catholic Regiment in the Service of Great Britain," *American Catholic Historical Researches, New Series*, 3 (1907): 327. There is other evidence that some Catholics in Philadelphia had loyalist tendencies, even if they were not among the 180 or so men who enlisted in the Roman Catholic Volunteers. After the war was over, Isaac Atwood, a comb-maker in the city, testified that "Isaac Lort, late become Roman Catholic, told me that the Roman Catholics were generally against the American Cause." Lort, himself, does not seem to have been against the American Cause, however. He swore his allegiance to the state of Pennsylvania on July 12, 1777, and in April of that year, he provided the state's navy with supplies. See John B. Linn and William H. Egle, eds., *Pennsylvania Archives, Second Series* (Harrisburg, 1876), 1:614; "Catholic Loyalists of the Revolution," *American Catholic Historical Researches, New Series*, 4 (1908): 298.
56. Arthur O'Leary, *Address to the Common People of the Roman Catholic Religion* (1777), rpt. in *The Life and Writings of Rev. Arthur O'Leary*, ed. Michael Bernard Buckley (Dublin, 1868), 105; Vincent Morley, *Irish Opinion and the American Revolution, 1760–1783* (New York, 2002), 97–169.
57. We can probably conclude that Leary's loyalist convictions were not very strong, since he was still living in Philadelphia in 1795, when he became John and Thomas Donnelly's godfather in a double baptism that Leonard Neale performed at St. Joseph's Church. Many of the staunchest Loyalists from Philadelphia found that their lives became insufferable after British troops left the city in June 1778; it is unlikely, therefore, that anyone who was fiercely loyal to the king would have still been living in the city in the 1790s. Additionally, the Roman Catholic Volunteers were never very effective. The unit was disbanded after a year, and at least two captains, John McKinnon and Martin McAvoy, were court-martialed for "plundering in the Jerseys, taking horse and cow and behaving indecently." See "Sacramental Registers at St. Joseph's Church, Philadelphia, Pennsylvania, from January to

December 1795," *Records of the American Catholic Historical Association of Philadelphia* 16 (Philadelphia, 1905), 211; Wilbur H. Siebert, *The Loyalists of Pennsylvania* (Columbus, OH, 1905), 68–70; and Griffin, "The Roman Catholic Regiment in the Service of Great Britain," 335–336.

58. Michael Burleigh, *Earthly Powers: The Clash of Religion and Politics in Europe, from the French Revolution to the Great War* (New York, 2005), 23–66.

59. Alan Virta, *Prince George's County: A Pictorial History* (Norfolk, VA, 1991), 68.

60. "Peter Muhlenberg, a Soldier of the Revolutionary War," *Concordia Historical Institute Quarterly* (1968): 94; Abraham Keteltas, *God Arising and Pleading His People's Cause* (Newburyport, MA, 1777), 29. For more on the involvement of Protestant ministers in the war effort, see Mark Noll, *Christians in the American Revolution* (Washington, DC, 1977), 163–175.

61. In a letter that he wrote to his sister in April 1776, Joseph Mosley told her that he did not know if he should stay in Maryland or return to England to avoid the impending violence. "I am truly between Hawk and Buzzard," he wrote "and no [sic.] not which step best to take." Ultimately, Mosley stayed in Maryland and swore his allegiance to the state in 1779. In February 1782, John Bolton wrote to Elizabeth and Mary Hagan, two sisters from Maryland who were safely ensconced in a convent in France, and told them that the war as "unfortunate" and "painful." See Maryland Province Archives (MPA), Special Collections, Georgetown University, Box 1, Folder 14; Box 57, Folder 11; Curran, *American Jesuit Spirituality*, 100.

62. Joseph Mosley to his sister, October 3, 1774, MPA, Box 1, Folder 13; John Carroll to Daniel Carroll, September 11, 1773, in Peter Guilday, *The Life and Times of John Carroll* (New York, 1922), 44. For more on the suppression of the Society of Jesus, see Bertrand N. Roehner, "Jesuits and the State: A Comparative Study of their Expulsions, 1590–1990," *Religion* 2 (1997): 165–181.

63. Thomas O'Brien Hanley, *The John Carroll Papers* (Notre Dame, IN, 1976), 1:171–172, 176–177, 2:614; Ronald A. Binzley, "Ganganelli's Disaffected Children: The Ex-Jesuits and the Shaping of Early American Catholicism, 1773–1790," *U.S. Catholic Historian* 26 (2008): 60.

64. *John Carroll Papers*, 1:64, 142, n. 21; Binzley, "Ganganelli's Disaffected Children," 71.

65. Brantz Mayer, "Introductory Memoir upon the Expedition to Canada," in Charles Carroll, *Journal of Charles Carroll of Carrollton during his Visit to Canada in 1776*, ed. Brantz Mayer (Baltimore, 1876), 30; "Commission of Dr. Franklin, Samuel Chase, and Charles Carroll, as Commissioners to Canada," March 20, 1776, in *American Archives, Fourth Series*, 5:411; Bernard U. Campbell, "Life and Times of Archbishop Carroll," *U.S. Catholic Magazine* 3 (1844): 244.

66. Hoffman, *Princes of Ireland*, 304–305.

67. Carroll, *Journal*, 93.

68. "To the Inhabitants of the Province of Quebec," October 26, 1774, in *Journals of the Continental Congress, 1774–1789*, ed. Worthington Chauncey Ford et al. (Washington, DC, 1904), 1:105–113; Claude Galarneu, "Fleury Mesplet," *Dictionary of Canadian Biography Online*, University of Toronto, accessed June 6, 2010, http://www.biographi.ca;. Fleury Mesplet was Catholic, but he was not deferential. In the late 1780s, a bilingual newspaper that he printed and edited in Montreal, the *Gazette*, called Quebec's Bishop Jean-Francois Hubert a "Christian despot" and criticized Hubert's opposition to a mixed, Catholic-Protestant college in Montreal.

69. "To the People of Great Britain" and "To the Inhabitants of the Colonies," October 21, 1774, in Ford, *Journals of the Continental Congress*, 88, 99–101.

70. "Extract of a Letter from Canada, dated Montreal, March 24th, 1775," *American Archives, Fourth Series*, 2:229.

71. Massachusettensis (Daniel Leonard), "To The Inhabitants of Massachusetts Bay," *Boston Gazette*, March 27, 1775, rpt. in John Adams and Jonathan Sewall, *Novanglus and Massachusettensis: Political Essays Published in the Years 1774 and 1775* (Boston, 1819), 221; *An Englishman's Answer*, 24; Johnson, *Hypocrisy Unmasked*, 17. Adams mistakenly thought

that Massachusettensis was Jonathan Sewall, the colony's attorney general, and so when he published the exchange of letters in 1819, he put Sewall's name on the collection. See Lorenzo Sabine, *Biographical Sketches of Loyalists of the American Revolution* (Boston, 1864), 11.

72. Steven Waldman, *Founding Faith: Providence, Politics, and the Birth of Religion Freedom in America* (New York, 2008), 50; John Lathrop, *A Discourse preached, December 15th, 1774: being the day recommended by the Provincial Congress to be observed in thanksgiving to God* (Boston, 1774), 31.

73. Clements and Wright, *The Maryland Militia*, 211; Edwin W. Beitzell, *Calendar of Events in St. Mary's County in the American Revolution* (Leonardstown, MD, 1975), 149; "Register of Baptisms and Marriages, Congregations of St. Francis Xavier and St. Inigoes," rpt. in O'Rourke, *Catholic Families*, 36; Beatriz Bentancourt Hardy, "Papists in a Protestant Age" (Ph.D. dissertation, University of Maryland, 1993), 587; Henry C. Peden, *Revolutionary Patriots of Charles County, Maryland* (Westminster, MD, 1997), 33; Daniel Barber, *The History of My Own Times* (Washington, DC, 1827), 17.

74. Thomas Sim Lee to Ignatius Digges, July 9, 1771, and n.d., 1771; Philip Thomas Lee to Thomas Sim Lee, December 30, 1771, Maryland State Archives (MSA), SC 773. The exact date of Lee's conversion is unknown, and earlier biographers mistakenly put it as late as 1800. Most scholars nowadays, however, believe that Lee's conversion happened shortly after he was married in October 1771. See Edward C. Papenfuse et al., *Biographical Dictionary of the Maryland Legislature, 1635–1789* (Baltimore, 1979), 2:529–530; and Arnet et al., *Guide to the Old Line State*, 570–571. Lee was related to Catholics on his mother's side; his great-grandfather was Thomas Brooke, whose parents, Elinor Hatton and Thomas Brooke, converted to Catholicism after they were married in 1658. Lee took his own conversion to Catholicism quite seriously. In his will, he left $1,000 to "build a Roman Catholic church in the vicinity of my farm Needwood"; that church, St. Mary's, Petersville, is still operational today. Thomas Sim Lee and Mary Digges Lee are buried in a common grave in Mt. Carmel Roman Catholic Cemetery in Prince George's County.

75. "Junius," *Maryland Journal, and the Baltimore Daily Advertiser*, May 3, 1775; *Maryland Gazette*, September 8, 1774, and April 21, 1781. Interestingly, the *Maryland Journal* was one of only two American newspapers that did not celebrate the Catholic Church's misfortunes during the French Revolution. The *Journal* offered no commentary in favor of the Church's treatment, and on November 17, 1789, it mistakenly reported that the Bishop of Rodez was so in favor of republican reform that he actually called for the abolition of the clerical tithe. The other newspaper that refused to celebrate the demise of popery in France was the *Massachusetts Centinel*. See Beatrice F. Hyslop, "The American Press and the French Revolution of 1789," *Proceedings of the American Philosophical Society* 104 (1960), 76–77.

INDEX

Absolutism, 11, 95–96, 112–114, 119–121, 250
Acadians, 177–178, 193, 203
Act Concerning Religion (original), 104, 109
    selective enforcement of, 108–112
    tests of, 99–102, 108–112
Act Concerning Religion (Puritans'), 104, 109
Act for the Better Discovering and Suppressing of Popish Recusants, 42
Act for the Further Preventing the Growth of Popery (England), 194, 198, 201–202
Act to Prevent the Growth of Popery in this Province, 194–195, 198, 201–202, 226–227
Acts of Uniformity and Supremacy, 1559, 13, 21
Adams, Abigail, 219
    John, 6, 15, 182, 191, 219, 238, 249, 252
    Nabby, 219
Adams, Sam 6, 17, 220, 238
Afghanistan, 188
Albemarle Sound, 61
Algonquian language, 83 (*see also* Piscataway Indians)
Allen, William, 29–30
Altham, John, 74, 76–78
Anabaptists, 99, 105
Andrew's Air Force Base
Anglicanism, 15, 51, 65, 145, 147, 157, 202, 209–210 (*see also* Church of England)
    establishment in Maryland, 133–134, 174
    disestablishment in Maryland, 12, 255
Anne, Queen of England, 130, 134, 195–196
Anne, wife of James I, 55
Anne Arundel County, 102, 110–111,114, 116, 130, 146, 154, 182, 207–209
Annapolism 102, 145, 195, 221–222, 224, 239–240, 255
Anti-Catholicism (*see also* Popery and Pope's Day)
    as different from a fear of Catholics 18, 190–192, 253–255

legislation in England, 42–43, 198, 205
legislation in Maryland, 134, 136, 193–201, 204–207, 211–215
in New England, 191, 254
in state constitutions, 253–254
apostasy (*see* Conversion)
Aquinas, Thomas, 506, 153
Ark, 13, 70–72, 76, 141
Arnold, Benedict, 249
Artwork, 178–181
Arundel, Anne, 62, 80, 102
    Thomas (Baron Arundel of Wardour), 32, 62, 191
Ashton, John, 153–154, 172
Atwood, Peter, 159, 198–201, 203, 233
authority
    Catholic challenges to, 9–15, 41, 46
Axtell, James, 75
Avalon, 55, 61, 64, 66, 75–76

Badin, Stephen, 10
Bacon, Francis, 36–37
Bacon, Nathaniel, 118
Bacon's Rebellion, 118
Bailyn, Bernard, 235
Baltimore, Lord (*see* Calvert)
Baltimore Company, 171, 230
Baltimore *Sun*, 4
Baptism, 23, 84, 136, 144, 155, 175
    (*see also* Sacraments)
Barbados, 161
Barlow, William Rudesind, 43
Barton, Thomas, 175
Battle of Brooklyn, 241, 243, 247
Battle of the Severn, 102, 104–105
Beadnall, James, 167–169, 214–215
    arrest of, 214–215
Bedford, Dukes of, 24–25
Bellarmine, Cardinal Robert, 43, 144

295

Benedictines, 25, 34, 43, 45, 68
Bennett, Richard, 104–106, 108, 140
    Richard, Jr., 140–141
    Richard III, 141, 208, 210
Beothuk Indians, 56 (*see also*
        Native American Indians)
Bercovitch, Sacvan, 168–169
Berkeley, William, 118, 120
Berkshire, Earl of (*see* Howard, Charles)
Birchmore, Ann (*see* Wheeler, Ann Birchmore)
Bishop of Chalcedon (*see* Smith, Richard)
Bishop of London (*see* Challoner, Richard)
Blakiston, Nathaniel, 192
Blakiston, Nehemiah, 128–129, 131, 192–193
        (*see* also Protestant Associators)
Blackwell, Archpriest George, 43–44
Blackstone, William, 189–190, 215, 234
Bladen, Thomas, 207
Blake, Charles Henry, 141
    Dorothy (*see* Carroll, Dorothy Blake)
    Henrietta Maria Lloyd, 141, 153
    Henrietta Maria, 141
    John 141, 153
    Philemon, 141, 153
    Philemon Lloyd, 141
Blake, George Leddle, 153
"Blue Nuns" (*see* Order of the Immaculate
        Conception of our Lady)
Boarman, Mary Matthews, 142
    Sarah (*see* Matthews, Sarah Boarman)
    Sarah Linle, 142
    William, 139, 142
Bohemia Manor, 167, 178, 243, 254
Bolton, John, 142
Book of Common Prayer, 23, 133
Book of Martyrs (*see* Foxe, John)
Brandt, Randolph, 132
Boston, 11–12, 202, 222, 237, 240, 252, 254
        (*see* also Massachusetts)
Boston Port Act, 237 (*see* also Intolerable Acts)
Boston Tea Party, 202, 236
Boucher, Jonathan, 219–221, 247
Braddock, Edward, 203, 210
Brent, Giles, 83, 92
Brent, Margaret, 92
British Military Intelligence, 37
Brook, Baker, 254–255
    Ignatius, 254–255
Brooke, Elinor Hatton, 101–102
    Robert, 201–202
    Thomas, 102
    Thomas, Jr., 145, 147, 157, 201–202
        lawsuit against brother's heirs, 201–202
Brooke, Elizabeth (*see* Carroll, Elizabeth
        Brooke)
Brooke, John, 86
Brooke, Henry, 205

Brown, Ann Mattingly, 254
    Basil, 254–255
Browne, Anthony, 32
    Magdelen, 31
Brownson, Orestes, 7
Buckingham, First Duke of (*see* Villiers, George)
Bulla Coenae, 87, 89
Burgess, Susannah, 117
    William, 117, 120

Calvert, Cecilius (second Lord Baltimore), 22,
        27, 38, 46–51, 54, 62–63, 65–74,
        76–117, 120, 128–129, 134–135, 138,
        140, 206, 233
    and the Act Concerning Religion, 63, 94,
        98–100, 108–110
    conversion to Catholicism, 66
    dealings with Jesuits, 78, 82–91
    dealings with Oliver Cromwell, 105–108
    desire to live in Maryland, 63, 71
    inconsistency of, 95–96
    instructions to his brother, 71–74, 81
    political ecumenism of, 96–98, 102–103, 114
Calvert, Benedict Leonard (Governor), 207, 213
Calvert, Charles (third Lord Baltimore), 15, 16,
        116–120, 128, 135, 145
    poor diplomatic skills, 116, 120
Calvert, Charles (fifth Lord Baltimore), 134,
        145, 196–197, 207–208
    visit to Maryland, 208
Calvert, Charles (Governor), 207
Calvert, Frederick (sixth Lord Baltimore), 134,
        204, 212, 215, 225
Calvert, Christopher, 28, 64
Calvert, George (first Lord Baltimore), 28, 38,
        48–66, 75–76, 106, 191
    conversion to Catholicism, 51–52, 55
    debate over motives for Maryland, 49–51
    ecumenism, 56–57
    elevation to peerage, 55
    experiences in Canada, 56–60
    family, 54, 56, 59
    interest in New World colonization, 53, 55, 58
    service to James I, 52–55
    and the Spanish Match, 52–54
Calvert, George (Cecilius's brother), 107
Calvert, Leonard (Governor), 51, 61–62,
        66–67, 89, 92, 113
Calvert, Leonard (George's father), 28
Calvert County, 114
Calvin, John, 40
Calvinism, 24
Calvinists, 25, 48, 59, 61, 72, 75, 79, 81, 91, 94,
        97–99, 102–106, 109, 111, 116,
        120–121, 123, 140–142, 144, 168–169,
        188, 192, 195
Cambridge University, 35–39

Index

Campion, John, 39
Canada, 10, 48, 55–60, 63, 177, 220, 237–240, 249, 253 (*see also* Avalon, Montreal, Quebec, Renews)
    diplomatic mission to, 10, 248–250
    reaction to address from Continental Congress, 250–252
    weather in, 55–58
capital punishment, 78
Caplin Bay, 53
Carroll, Charles (the Settler), 132, 147, 196–197, 200
    Daniel, 171, 205
Carroll, Charles of Annapolis, 34, 153, 159, 171, 175, 178, 183, 185, 196, 205, 208, 210, 212–213, 215
    and the Acadians, 178
    and the double-tax, 213–213, 215
    keeping of priests, 153–154, 175
    intention to move to Louisiana, 215–216
    lawsuit against Dr. Charles Carroll, 202–230
    slaves, 154
    understanding of Maryland's history, 203, 205–206, 214
    Elizabeth Brooke, 181–182
Carroll, Charles of Carrollton, 18, 34, 147, 154, 178, 181, 183, 186, 216–218, 227–228, 230–236, 240–241, 246, 248–250, 253, 256
    Antilon-First Citizen letters, 227–228, 230–236
    Continental Congress, 240, 253
    diplomatic mission to Canada, 248–250
    homesickness, 181, 184–185
    opinion of Catholic government, 216–217
    opinion of Jesuit education, 34, 183
    personal animosity for Daniel Dulany, Jr., 230
Carroll, Charles Dr., 141, 145–147, 171, 202–203, 209–210, 214
    anti-Catholic rhetoric and tactics, 203
    conversion, 145–146
    lawsuit against Charles and James Carroll, 202–203
    Charles, the Barrister, 145–146
    Dorothy Blake, 141, 145
    John Henry, 145
    Mary Clare, 145
Carroll, James, 202
Carroll, James Fr., 159, 202, 209, 214
    lawsuit against Dr. Charles Carroll, 202–203
    reaction to double tax, 214–215
Carroll, John, 9–11, 143, 151, 172–174, 181, 183, 185, 243, 248–250
    diplomatic mission to Canada, 10, 248–250
    First Amendment, 10
    suppression of the Society of Jesus, 248
    theological leniency of, 143, 172–174

Carroll, Margaret (*see* Macnamara, Margaret Carroll)
Cartwright's Creek (*see* Kentucky)
Cary, Elizabeth Tanfield, 39–40
    Henry, 39–40
The Case Stated (*see* Leslie, Charles)
Catherine of Aragon, 23
The Catholic Christian Instructed (*see* Challoner, Richard)
Cecil County, 132, 142–143, 150, 167, 181, 183, 243
Cecil, Anastasia (*see* Wheatley, Anastasia Cecil)
Cecil, William, 54
Challoner, Richard, 14, 138–139, 160
Champney, Anthony, 33
Character (*see* William of Orange)
Charles I of England, 38–40, 46, 52, 54, 57–59, 62, 64–65, 67, 72, 88, 90–92, 95–98, 103, 105, 113, 121, 155, 206
    crypto-Catholicism of, 65, 91
    execution of, 91, 96, 103, 105, 113, 121
Charles II of England, 116, 118
Charles V of the Holy Roman Empire, 23
Charles County, 116, 132, 139–140, 143, 165–166, 174, 243, 254–256
Chase, Thomas, 249
    Samuel, 248–249
Chesapeake, 11, 13, 27, 40, 46, 48, 50, 57, 59, 61–63, 66, 70, 72, 76, 95, 97, 106, 131, 139, 141, 149–152, 192, 220, 225, 240
Chew, Henrietta Maria Lloyd, 155
    Henrietta Maria, 155
    Samuel, 156
        Henrietta Maria, 156
Chowan River, 61
Christ's College, 35
Church of England, 25–26, 28, 38, 42, 55, 65, 78, 112, 117, 122, 127, 133–134, 141, 145–147, 155, 196, 207, 213, 221 (*see also* Anglicanism)
Church Papist, 26, 42, 46, 65 (*see also* Schismatic)
Church-State separation, 5, 7, 22, 44, 48, 90, 95
Churchill, Arabella, 34
Cisalpine Club, 12–13
Civil War (English), 90–91, 94, 124
Civility, 93, 95, 98–100
Claiborne, William, 59, 61, 67, 69, 72, 91–94, 96–99, 103–106, 108, 113–114, 116, 128, 140, 188
Clifton, Alfred, 244 (*see also* Loyalists, Catholic)
Cole, Elizabeth, 244
Cole, Josias, 109, 111
Combs, Mary Manning, 157
    Ignatius, 157
    Mary Fenwick, 157
Committee of Ten, 105, 108

Commonwealth, The, 103, 107–108
(*see also* Cromwell, Oliver)
Communion (*see also* Eucharist, Sacraments)
Communist Party (*see* Marxism)
Conditions of Plantation, 76–77, 85, 88, 105, 110, 128–129
Confraternities (*see* sodalities)
Connell, John, 245 (*see also* Loyalists, Catholic)
Considerations on the Propriety of Imposing Taxes in the British Colonies, 229
(see also Dulany, Daniel Jr.)
Constitution
  England, 191, 198, 206, 213–214, 217, 224, 227, 230, 232–235
  Maryland, 12, 134–135, 158, 189, 198–199, 201, 204, 206, 208, 213–214, 217, 226–227, 230–236, 238, 240–241, 255
  other colonies/states, 201, 226, 235, 253–254, 256
  U.S., 187
Continental Army, 155, 242–243, 247, 249, 254–255
Continental Congress, 238, 241, 247, 249–253
  addresses to
    the king, 250
    the inhabitants of the colonies, 250–252
    the inhabitants of Great Britain, 250–252
    the inhabitants of Quebec, 250–252
contractarianism, 96, 106–107, 115–116, 121, 135
conversion
  Catholic to Protestant, 57, 80, 101–102, 137, 141–142, 144–148, 194, 196, 201–202, 207, 209–210, 213
  Protestant to Catholic, 38–40, 51–52, 54–55, 66, 69, 116, 149–152, 189, 210, 213, 255
  Native American, 22, 75, 82–86
Coode, John, 128–129, 131–132
  (*see also* Protestant Associators)
Cooper, John, 82
Copernicus, Nicolaus, 35–37
Copley, Thomas, 76–79, 81–82, 84, 86–89, 92–93, 138
Copley, Lionel, 133, 145, 192
Cornwallis, Thomas, 72, 79–80, 87
Cotton, John, 97
  William, 97
  Verlinda, 97
Country Party, 225
Countryman, Edward, 235
Coursey, Henry, 120
Craycroft, Susannah
  (*see* Matthews, Susannah Craycroft)
Croft, Herbert, 39
Cromwell, Oliver, 103, 105–108, 122
Crosby, John, 214
Culpeper, Thomas, 116
cultural relativism, 75

Darnall, Henry II, 181
  Henry III, 146–147, 181, 205, 208–210, 213
    conversion of, 146–147
  Eleanor, 179–181
  John, 146–147, 181, 201–202, 209–210
    conversion of, 146–147
    defense of Robert Brooke's heirs, 201–202
Darnall, Philip, 205
Davis, Peter, 175
Declaration of Independence, 18, 49, 141, 145, 147, 186, 221, 230, 243, 255
Declaration of Right, 121, 206
"Defender of the Faith" (*see* Henry VIII)
Delaware, 167
Denmark (*see* Anne, wife of James I)
Dent, John, 255
devotions, 24, 34, 160–167, 180
Dickenson, John, 224, 250
Diderich, Bernard, 153–154
Digby, Kenelm, 39
Digges, Edward, 176
Digges, William, 117, 120, 129, 175
  Charles, 148
  Jane (*see* Rozer, Jane Digges)
  William, Jr., 151
    Ignatius, 175, 205, 213, 255 Mary
    (*see* Lee, Mary Digges)
  Thomas, 139, 151–152, 175
Digges, Jane (*see* Young, Jane Digges)
Dignitatis Humanae, 90
Discalced Carmelites, 185
dispensations, 136, 169–170, 172–174
Dixon, Jeremiah, 117
Dolan, Jay, 6, 8–9
Dominicans, 75
Dorchester County, 150–151, 154
Douai, College at, 29, 33–34
double-tax, 212–215
Dove, 13, 70–72, 141
Doyne, Mary, 165
Doyne, Jane, 165
  Mary Ann, 165
  Sarah, 165
Drayton, William Henry, 239
Duggins, Eleanor, 164–165
Duke of York (*see* James I)
Dulany, Daniel Sr., 171–172
  Daniel Jr., 223–236
    Antilon-First Citizen letters, 227, 229–236
    Stamp Act, 224–226
  Lloyd, 230
  Walter, 228
Durham, 64–65
Durham Clause, 64–65, 67, 93–94, 98, 104, 134, 244

eastern shore, 97, 143–151, 167, 203, 248
Ecclesiastical Appeals Act, 23
Eden, Robert, 228–229, 231–235
education, Catholic in Europe, 34–35, 76, 181–185
   Catholic in Maryland, 126, 181
   Protestant in Europe, 35–38
Elizabeth I of England, 25, 29, 43, 55, 81, 112, 190
emblem books, 180–181
Enlightenment Catholicism, 9, 12
Establishment Clause, 10
Eton College, 146
Eucharist, 14, 23, 26–28, 42, 137, 139, 159, 166–167, 169, 241 (*see also* Sacraments)
Evelyn, John, 191
   Mary, 191

Falkland, Viscountess (*see* Cary, Elizabeth Tanfield)
Farmer, Ferdinand, 158–159, 164, 244
Farnaby, Thomas, 39
fee proclamation controversy (*see* Eden, Robert)
Fendall, Josias, 110–111
Fielding, Margaret, 39
Fenwick, James, 157
   Catherine, 157
   Athanasius, 157
Fenwick, John, 157
   Monica Ford, 157
      Mary (*see* Combs, Mary Fenwick)
   Mary Thomson, 157
Fenwick, Ignatius, 157–158, 240–241, 255–256
First Amendment, 10, 248
FitzJames, Henrietta, 34
FitzRedmond, William, 196
Ford, Athanasius, 157
   Monica (*see* Fenwick, Monica Ford)
Fox, John, Monsignor, 3–4
Foxe, John, 123–124
Framback, James, 151
France, 6, 9, 11–13, 16, 19–20, 34, 38, 40, 54, 73, 76, 95, 124, 126, 130–131, 137, 144, 157, 161, 177, 182, 186, 190, 193–194, 203–204, 210–214, 216–217, 223, 237–239, 242, 245–247, 250, 256
Franciscans, 75, 175
Franklin, Benjamin, 226, 248–250
Frederick County, 146, 154, 240
Freeman, Margaretta (*see* Lloyd, Philemon, Jr.)
Freeman, William, 28
French and Indian War, 16, 203–204, 211, 213, 217, 237, 256

Garden of the Soul (*see* Challoner, Richard)
Gardiner, Elizabeth, 101
   Luke, 101–102

Garnet, Henry, 26, 42
General Assembly (Maryland), 14, 38, 49, 66–67, 77–78, 83–86, 93–94, 96, 98–100, 102–106, 108, 110, 113–118, 120, 130, 132, 134–136, 140, 145–146, 175, 182, 192–199, 201, 204–212, 215, 222, 225–226, 228–229, 232–233, 235, 241, 244, 255
Gentry, 13, 21–22, 29, 31–33, 35, 38, 172, 174–175, 178, 181–183, 186
George I of England, 205, 244
George II of England, 207–208, 212–213, 244
George III of England, 11, 220, 224, 234, 236, 238–240, 244, 251
Georgetown College, 141
Gerard, John, 26, 28, 30–32
German Catholics, 20, 151, 243–245 (*see also* Loyalists, Catholic)
Gervase, Thomas, 74, 76
Gleason, Philip, 5
Glorious Revolution, 13–14, 16–17, 23, 42, 94, 96, 120–127, 135, 177, 189, 193, 196, 204, 208, 234, 236
   propaganda literature for, 122–127
Goddard, Mary Katherine (*see* Maryland *Journal*)
   William (*see* Maryland *Journal*)
Gordon, James, 33
Gray, Francis, 81–82
Greaton, Joseph, 243–244
Green, Ann (*see* Maryland *Gazette*)
   Frederick (*see* Maryland *Gazette*)
Greene, Thomas, 96
Greenwell, Bennett, 157
   George, 157
   Ignatius, 157
   Joseph, 157
      Elizabeth Newton, 157
   Justinian, 157
   Nicholas, 157
Grenville, George, 224
Gunpowder Plot, 42, 60
Guy Fawkes Day (*see* also Pope's Day, Gunpowder Plot)

Haddock, James, 175
Hall, Francis, 205
Hamilton, Alexander, 239
Hamilton, Dutchess of (*see* Fielding, Margaret)
Hancock, John, 220
Hanly, Mathias, 245
   (*see also* Loyalists, Catholic)
Hanoverian Succession, 13, 244
Harding, Robert, 175
Hardwicke, Philip Lord, 231–234
Hart, John, 196–197, 207
Harvard College, 182, 191–192

Hatton, Elinor (*see* Brooke, Elinor)
　Elizabeth (*see* Gardiner, Elizabeth)
　Margaret, 101–102
　Thomas, 97–98, 101–102, 105
Hawkins, Henry, 180
Hawley, Jerome, 69, 72, 79
headright system, 68, 128
Hearn, Daniel, 207
Hearst, William Randolph, 4
Heath, James, 132, 167
Hecker, Isaac, 7
Henricopolis, 53
Henrietta Maria (wife of Charles I), 38–40, 54, 155
Henry VIII of England, 21–25, 40
Henry, Patrick, 17–18
Hill, Christopher, 37
Hill, Clement, 175, 203, 205, 213
Historie of the World (*see* Raleigh, Walter)
History of the Rise, Progress, and Termination of the American Revolution (*see* Warren, Mercy Otis)
Hobbes, Thomas, 37–38
Hoffman, Ronald, 148
Holmes, Richard, 176
Holt, Arthur, 209
Holy Days, 170–172
Holy Roman Empire, 23
House of Burgesses, 17, 118
House of Commons (*see* Parliament)
Houston Baptists, 6
Howard, Charles, 39
　Robert, 39
Howard, Francis, 130
Howe, William, 244
Hunter, George, 215, 243
Hunter, William, 143–144, 174

identity
　American, 4, 6, 8, 12, 236
　Catholic, 5, 7, 10–16, 20–21, 40, 44–45, 63, 74, 138, 142, 149, 155, 163–164, 171, 174, 177–178, 183, 186–187, 195, 197, 206, 208–209, 257
　English, 14, 16–17, 42, 126, 131, 134, 192–193, 197, 200, 209, 211, 213, 217, 226–228, 241, 256
　Protestant, 121, 123, 148
Impartial Administration of Justice Act, 237 (*see also* Intolerable Acts)
indentured servants, 66, 76, 79, 82, 88, 91, 115, 118, 128, 147, 176–177, 193, 196
individualism, 4, 7, 187
Infanta, 52, 54
Independent Maryland Company, 242
Ingle, Robert, 67, 91–94, 96–99, 103–104, 113–114, 116, 128, 188

Ingle-Claiborne Rebellion, 67, 69, 93–94, 96–99, 103, 113–114, 128, 188
internal taxation, 223–224
Interregnum, 115 (*see also* Commonwealth, The)
Intolerable Acts, 236, 240
Iraq, 188
Ireland, 7–8, 11, 20, 40, 55, 60, 68, 71, 95, 103, 105, 122, 124, 129, 131, 145, 147–148, 153, 176, 191, 196, 203, 211, 245–246
Ireland, John, 7

Jacobites, 176–178, 193, 196–197, 207
James I of England, 21, 25, 32–33, 41, 46–45, 52–56, 60, 74, 95, 103–107, 149
James II of England, 12–13, 16, 96, 116, 120–124, 126, 129–130, 176, 192, 194, 196, 234
　arrest of Anglican bishops, 123
　conversion to Catholicism, 116
　relations with Parliament and the Army, 121
James VI of Scotland (*see* James I of England)
James River, 58–59, 61, 72
Jamestown, 53, 61
Jarboe, Robert, 155
Jefferson, Thomas, 9, 36, 182, 220
Jesuits, 14, 21–22, 25, 27–32, 34, 43, 45–46, 60–61, 74–79, 81–90, 92–93, 126, 131, 141–146, 151–152, 154, 156–157, 159, 162, 164, 167–173, 175–176, 180–181, 183–185, 207–208, 211, 213, 217, 242–243, 247–248 (*see also* Society of Jesus)
John V of Portugal, 190
Johnson, Samuel, 184, 222, 252–253
Joseph, William, 129–131
Judaism, 163 (*see also* Lumbrozo, Jacob)
justification by faith, 23

Kellison, Mathew, 159
Kennesaw, Georgia, 59
Kent County, 114,116, 130
Kent Island, 72, 91, 97, 104
Kentucky, 8, 10, 12, 173–174, 243
Keteltas, Abraham, 247
King George's War, 210
Kitamaquund, Mary, 83 (*see also* Piscataway Indians)
Knott, Edward, 82, 88
Kühn, Justus Engelhardt, 178–179

laity (Catholic), 8–10, 12–15, 20, 22, 25–31, 44, 46, 77–79, 93–94, 154–158, 160–182, 187
　clashes with clergy, 10, 21–22, 30–31, 77–79, 82–90, 167
　cooperation with clergy, 90–91, 93–94, 143–144, 161–171

disproportionate wealth of, 20, 33–33, 40, 42, 50, 66, 84, 118
expectations of clergy in Maryland, 83–85
geographic distribution in England, 21–28
geographic distribution in Maryland, 139–140
maintenance of Catholic identity, 154–158, 164–166, 174–182
"popular" Catholicism, 23–24
Lancaster, John, 176
  Joseph, 176
Last Rites, 78 (*see also* Sacraments)
Lawson, James, 183–184
Le Mirroir du Monde (*see* Ortelius, Abraham)
Leary, Cornelius, 245–246
  (*see also* Loyalists, Catholic)
Lee, Richard Henry, 15, 250–251, 253
Lee, Mary Digges, 175, 255
  Thomas Sim, 255–256
    conversion, 255
    election as governor, 256
Leisler, Jacob, 192–193
Leonard, Daniel, 252
Leopold I of Austria, 190
Leslie, Charles, 160
Lewger, John, 38, 69, 77, 80, 113
Lewis, John, 139, 150–152, 178
Lewis, William, 79–82, 87, 93, 173
liberalism, 5–6, 9–12, 36–38, 42, 46–49, 134–135
liberty, 3, 5–7, 12, 14, 16–18, 37, 50, 100–102, 104–105, 107, 109–110, 138, 143, 157, 190, 199, 210, 217, 224, 227, 229–230, 241, 250–253, 256
Liege, College at, 83–181, 185
Linle, Sarah (see Boarman, Sarah Linle)
Lisbon, College at, 33, 146
Lister, Thomas, 43
Livers, Arnold, 169
Lloyd, Anna Maria, 141
  Edward, 141
  Henrietta Maria Neale Bennett, 140–141, 155, 173
  Henrietta Maria (*see* Blake, Henrietta Maria Lloyd)
  James, 141
  Margaret, 141
  Philemon, 140
  Philemon, Jr., 141, 155
    Henrietta Maria (*see* Chew, Henrietta Maria Lloyd)
    Margaretta Freeman, 141
Locke, John, 38, 42, 46, 48, 90, 96
London, 13, 14, 24, 27, 41, 52–54, 58, 61, 64, 90, 94, 104, 108, 119, 122, 135, 146, 160, 170, 181, 184, 195, 199, 216, 252
Long Parliament, 90

Longford, County (*see* Ireland)
Lord Protector (*see* Cromwell, Oliver)
Lords of Trade, 119–120, 128, 133, 138, 195
Louis XIII of France, 54
Louis XIV of France, 126, 190
Louis XV of France, 210
Louvain, Jesuit University in, 183
Lord Deputy of Ireland (*see* Cary, Henry and Wentworth, Thomas)
Loyalists, 21, 221, 240, 242
  Catholic, 243–246
Loyola, St. Ignatius of, 31, 78, 84, 157
Luckett, Henry, 243
  Ignatius, 243
Lumbrozo, Jacob, 109–110
Luther, Martin, 36, 41
Lutheranism, 23, 55, 99
Lynch, John, 245 (*see also* Loyalists, Catholic)

Macnamara, Margaret Carroll, 1470148
  Thomas, 147–148
MacPherson, Donal, 176
Macquacomen (*see* Patuxent Indians)
Maier, Pauline, 235
Manning, Mary (*see* Combs, Mary Manning)
Manning, Robert, 159–160
Mansell, Thomas, 167
Maria Anna of Spain (*see* Infanta)
marriage
  inter-faith, 140–144, 171, 174, 188–189
  Jesuit attitudes toward, 143–144
  of Charles I, 52–54
Marxism, 37
Mary II of England, 121–123, 131, 134, 145, 182, 192
Mary of Modena, 130
Maryland Designe, 112–113, 115 (*see also* Conditions of Plantation)
Maryland
  charter, 46, 59–68, 77, 191, 96, 98, 103–105, 115, 120, 133, 135–136, 145, 191, 196, 206, 215, 227, 253
  suspension of, 120, 133–134
  depopulation of, 98, 188
  motivations for founding, 14, 22, 49–51, 73
  population of, 70–71
Maryland *Journal*, 239–241
Maryland *Gazette*, 18, 203, 207–208, 210–211, 215, 227, 229–230, 239–241
Marylandian, 17, 148, 183, 199–200, 205–206, 229–230, 233, 240, 248, 256
Martineau, Harriet, 9
Marvell, Andrew, 39
Mason, Charles, 117
Massachusetts, 168, 179
Massachusetts Government Act, 237
  (*see also* Intolerable Acts)

material culture, 158–161, 164
Mattapany, 86
Mather, Increase, 168
Matthews, Hugh, 183
Matthews, Joseph, 185
   Ann Teresa, 185–186
   Susannah Craycroft, 185
Matthews, Mary (*see* Boarman, Mary Matthews)
   Sarah Boarman, 142
   Thomas, 142
Matthews, Martha Doyne, 165
   Jane, 165
   Jesse, 165
Matthews, William, 165
Mattingly, Ignatius, 243
   Luke, 243
   William, 243
Mattingly, Anne (*see* Brown, Anne Mattingly)
Maury, James, 220
McCullock, Kenneth, 245 (*see also* Loyalists, Catholic)
McEvoy, Martin, 245 (*see also* Loyalists, Catholic)
McGreevy, John, 6, 8
McKean, Thomas, 219
Mead, Joseph, 35
Meekins, Abraham, 154
   Henry, 153
   Matthew, 154
Melhorn, Frances, 164–165
memory, 15–16
Mencken, Henry Louis, 4
Mesplet, Fleury, 250
Micmac Indians, 56 (*see also* Native American Indians)
Middleton, Nicholas, 34–35
Milton, Christopher, 39
   John, 39, 95–96, 106–107, 113, 115
miscegenation, 71
Mobberly, Joseph, 157
Molasses Act, 223–224
Molyneaux, Richard, 207
Monacacy Valley, 46, 207
Montague, Viscounte of (*see* Browne, Anthony)
   Viscountess of (*see* Browne, Magdalen)
Montgomery, Richard, 249
Montreal, 248–250, 252
Morely, Walter, 86
Morris, Christopher, 75
Mosley, Joseph, 142, 148–154, 167, 248
Mother Bernardina Teresa Xavier of St. Joseph (*see* Matthews, Ann Teresa)
Muhlenberg, Peter, 247–248
Mumford, Joseph, 159
Murray, John Courtney, 5–6, 8–9, 11–12, 18–19
Mynne, Anne, 54

naming, 137, 156–158
National Assembly, 246
Native American Indians, 75, 162
Neale, Anthony, 173–174
   Bennett, 139, 168
   Charles, 186
   Edward, 282
   Henry, 242, 246
Neale, James, 140
   Henrietta Maria (*see* Lloyd, Henrietta Maria Neale Bennett)
Neale, Leonard, 140, 169, 185–186
Neale, Raphael, 157
Neill, Hugh, 167
Neo-Whig School, 238
New Atlantis (*see* Bacon, Francis)
New Cabriol, 53
New England, 70, 103, 168–169, 191, 194, 200, 219–220, 239
New-Yeares Gift for English Catholikes (*see* Preston, Thomas)
New Ross (*see* Taaffe, Lucas)
New York, 7, 12, 59, 192–194, 207, 222, 226–227, 239–240, 252
New York *Journal*, 226
New York *Times*, 3–4
Newark, NJ, 3, 49
Newfoundland, 53, 55–56, 58, 60, 106 (*see also* Renews, Avalon)
Newton, Elizabeth (*see* Greenwell, Elizabeth Newton)
Newtown, 156, 159, 167, 181, 185
Nichols, Thomas, 176
Nicholson, Francis, 148, 192, 194–195, 207
   sullied reputation of, 194–195
nonimportation agreements, 202, 222, 240, 242
North Carolina, 61
Norton, John, 168

Oad, Ann, 164–165
Oath of Abjuration, 149–150, 197, 211
Oath of Supremacy and Allegiance (to James I), 21, 42–45, 71, 74, 149
Oath of Allegiance (to Lord Baltimore), 103, 110–112, 119
Ochs, Adolph, 3
O'Connell, Daniel, 8
O'Daniel, Mary Ann, 167
O'Leary, Arthur, 245–246
Order of the Immaculate Conception of Our Lady, 34
Ortelius, Abraham, 40
Otis, James, 17, 223
Outer Banks, 61
Oxford University, 35–39, 54, 191
Oxfordshire, 28

Paine, Tom, 16
Pakes, Walter, 100
papal authority, 13, 21, 23, 44–45
Parliament
  jurisdiction in the colonies, 53, 105–108, 202, 224–226
Parsons, Robert, 43, 153
Passamagnus River (*see* Chowan River)
Partheneia Sacra (*see* Hawkins, Henry)
Patuxent Indians, 83, 85–86 (*see also* Native American Indians)
Pecci, Vincenzo (see Pope Leo XIII)
Penance, 23, 65, 167 (*see also* Sacraments)
Penn, Thomas, 244
Penn, William, 50, 117, 129, 226
Pennsylvania, 14, 16, 49–50, 117, 121, 132, 138, 159, 201, 215, 219, 224, 226, 231, 237, 243–246, 250
Peter I of Russia, 190
Philadelphia, 7, 49, 158, 175, 222–223, 241, 244, 249–250 (*see also* Pennsylvania)
Philip III of Spain, 52
Pile, John, 96
Piscataway Indians, 83, 85 (*see also* Native American Indians)
The Plea of the Roman Catholics (*see* Mumford, Joseph)
Plains of Abraham, 37, 249
pluralism, 5, 9, 48, 56–57, 93–94, 98–99
Plowden, Charles, 143, 172
Plunkett, Francis, 182
Plymouth, 53, 70, 131 (*see also* Massachusetts)
Pope Clement XIV, 247
Pope Innocent XI, 191
Pope Leo XIII, 4–5, 7–8, 10
Pope Paul V, 21, 44–45
Pope Urban VIII, 74, 87
Popery, 11, 18, 104, 123, 189, 191, 194–195, 198, 201–203, 207, 210, 213, 217, 221, 226–227, 238–243, 247, 253–256 (*see also* anti Catholicism and Pope's Day)
population, Catholic
  in British North America, 138
  in England, 27
  in Maryland, 138
Porter, Olivia, 38
Posey, Elizabeth, 156
  Francis, 156
  Rhody, 156
  Thomas, 156
Potts, John, 58–59
Presbyterians, 4, 98, 103, 105, 224 (*see also* Calvinism)
Preston, Thomas, 44–45
Pretender, The (*see* Stuart, James Edward Francis)

Price, John, 97
Primogeniture, 68
Prince George's County, 151, 154, 175, 179, 208, 220–221, 255
Privy Council, 39–40, 57, 61
Propaganda Fide, 60
Protestant Associators, 131–133, 192–193, 195–196
Providence (*see* Annapolis)
Pulitzer, Joseph, 4
Puritans, 70, 81, 90–92, 97–99, 102–105, 109–111, 113–114, 122, 140, 168–169, 191, 219 (*see also* Calvinism)
Puritan Uprising, 103–108, 113–114, 140

Quakers, 48, 109, 11–112, 127, 138, 142, 144, 201, 244 (*see also* Society of Friends)
  imprisonment in Maryland, 111–112
Quartering Act, 237 (*see also* Intolerable Acts)
Quebec, 11, 18, 75, 194, 237–238, 242, 248–253 (*see also* Montreal)
Quebec Act, 220–221, 237–240, 251–254 (*see also* Intolerable Acts)
Queen Anne's County, 142–143, 145, 150, 153
quit-rents, 68, 84, 88

Raleigh, Walter, 36
Ratio Studiorum (*see* education, Catholic in Europe)
Reade, Captain John, 68, 112
Recollects, 75
recusancy, 25–26, 31–32, 40, 42, 108, 198, 201, 204, 206
Relatio Itineris in Marylandiam (*see* White, Andrew)
Relation of the Lord Baltemore's Plantation in Maryland (*see* Hawley, Jerome and Lewger, John)
republicanism, 5, 7–10, 17, 103, 187, 219, 221–222, 254, 259
religiosity
  decline in Europe, 137
  among lay Catholics in Maryland, 15, 136–138
Reformation, 21, 23–24, 29, 46, 65, 180
Renews, 53
Revenue Act of 1767, 222
Rhemish Testament, 159
rights of Englishmen, 17–18, 189–190, 197–199, 233 (*see also* Constitution, England)
Robinson, Lawrence, 207
Robinson, Thomas, 212
Rome, College at, 33
Roman Catholic Relief Act, 1791, 13
Roman Catholic Volunteers, 244–245 (*see also* Loyalists, Catholic)
Roos, William, 39
Rousby, Christopher, 129

Royal Proclamation of 1763, 220
Rozer, Ann (*see* Young, Ann Rozer)
Rozer, Benjamin, 117, 120
Rozer, Henry, 205
Rozer, Jane Digges, 150–151
Rozer, Notley, 175
Russell, John (*see* Bedford, Dukes of)

Sacraments, 23, 65, 78, 133, 137, 143, 160, 162, 164–169, 171
Sayer, Peter, 132–133, 175
Scantling, Cornelius, 207
Schismatic, 26, 46, 98 (*see also* Church Papist)
Scientific Method, 36
Scientific Revolution, 36
Scrope, Emmanuel, 32
Sears, William, 154
seasoning, 98, 107
secular clergy, 21–22, 25–29, 43–44, 56, 60, 75, 89
   clashes with Jesuits, 21–22, 25, 28–29, 43
Sedgwicks of Massachusetts, 178–179
seigneurial Catholicism, 21, 29, 31, 46, 56, 63, 88, 138, 175
Semmes, Joseph, 185
Semmes, Marmaduke, 176
   Violetta, 165
Semmes, Thomas, 240–241, 246, 255–256
Sepulchrine nuns, 181
Sermon on the Mount, 111
Seven Years War (*see* French and Indian War)
Severn River (*see* Battle of the Severn)
Sewall, Ann, 117
   Elizabeth, 117
   Nicholas, 117
Sewall, Charles, 168
Seymour, John, 145, 156, 194, 207
Sharpe, Horatio, 139, 203–204, 213, 215
Shea, John Gilmary, 49, 59
Shirley, James, 39
The Shortest Way to End Disputes About Religion (*see* Manning, Robert)
Slavery
   and Catholic conversion, 152–155
   and Christianity, 152
Sleakam, George, 153
Slye, George, 139
Smith, Henry, 81
Smith, Nicholas, 43
Smith, Richard, 31, 33
Smith, Samuel, 209
Smith, Thomas, 78
Society of Friends, 109–11 (*see also* Quakers)
Society of Jesus
   clashes with Lord Baltimore's government, 89–90
   clashes with Protestants, 28–29, 42, 60

   commitment to mission work, 60, 75, 82–83
   cooperation with laity, 90–91, 93–94, 143–144, 161–174
   desires for martyrdom, 75, 82–83
   differences between Maryland and England, 143–144, 172–173
   relations with Native American Indians, 83–86
   residence in laypeople's homes, 29–30, 56, 153–154, 175–176
   suppression, 182, 247–248
   tendency to focus on gentry, 21–22, 29, 31
   sodalities, 162–166, 174
Sola Scriptura, 41, 186
South America, 162, 209
Spain, 12–13, 16, 20, 52, 54, 57, 69, 72, 140, 144, 150, 186, 200, 223, 242, 247–248
Spanish Match, 52–54
St. Alban's School, 39
St. Catherine's College, 39
St. George's, 53
St. Inigoes, 77, 79–82, 85–86, 92–93, 156, 159, 164, 173, 242
St. John's, 53
St. Mary's City, 70, 76–77, 83, 91–92, 102–104, 130, 132, 176, 194, 244
St. Mary's County, 91–92, 97–98, 100, 116–117, 130, 139–140, 143, 150–151, 156–158, 164, 167, 181, 185, 188, 194–195, 240, 242–243, 255
St. Mary's County militia, 155, 242–243, 254
St. Omer's College, 34, 143, 144, 146, 175, 181–186
Stamp Act, 53, 201–202, 206, 217, 220, 222–226, 231, 239, 242
Stevens, William, 120
Stiles, Ezra, 238, 247
Stone, William, 97–98, 100–102, 104–105, 110
Stourton, Erasmus, 57
Strafford, Earl of (*see* Wentworth, Thomas)
Stuart, Alexander, 176
Stuart, Charles, 176
Stuart, James Edward Francis, 12–13, 196
Summa theologica, 6
Sunderland, Earl of (*see* Scrope, Emmanuel)
Susquehannock Indians, 113
   (*see also* Native American Indians)

Taaffe, Lucas, 105
Talbot County, 132, 150, 175, 214
Talbot, George, 129
Tasker, Benjamin Sr., 171–172
Taylor, Thomas, 120
Terra Mariae, 61
Testem Benevolentiae Notrae, 4
Thirty-Nine Articles of Religion, 23
Thomson, Agnes, 153

Thomson, Mary (*see* Fenwick, Mary Thomson)
Three Conversions of England (*see* Parsons, Robert)
Time Magazine, 8
tobacco, 12, 58, 77, 82, 84, 92, 110, 128, 133, 176, 200, 208, 210, 220, 223, 225, 228, 231
   inspection and prices in Maryland, 223, 225, 228, 231
   stinting bill, 208, 210
Tocqueville, Alexis de, 19
toleration, 15–17, 46, 48–51, 63, 67, 94–95, 100, 196, 199, 206, 221, 233, 246
Townshend Duties (see Revenue Act of 1767)
The Touchstone of the Reformed Gospel (*see* Kellison, Matthew)
tract literature, 32–33, 44, 69–70, 122
transubstantiation, 149, 159, 197, 211
Treaty of Utrecht, 177
The Triumph of the Israelites over the Moabites (*see* Williams, Griffith)

Ultramontanism, 7–8, 160–161
Uriah Forrest's Flying Camp, 243
Ursulines, 75
U.S. Naval Academy, 105

Valladolid, College at, 33
Van Sweringen, Garrett, 139, 207
   Anne, 207
Vann, Bennett, 156
Vatican, 9, 60, 75, 162, 248
Vatican I, 160
Vatican II, 7, 90
Vaughan, Robert, 96
Vaughan, William, 53, 106
Venner, Robert, 39
A View to the Causes and Consequences of the American Revolution (*see* Boucher, Jonathan)
Villiers, George, 38–39
Villiers, John, 39
Virginia, 9, 17–18, 50, 58–59, 61, 63, 65, 67, 70, 72–73, 78–81, 92, 97, 102–104, 107, 116, 118–120, 128, 130–131, 140, 152, 173, 179, 200–201, 211, 217, 223, 226, 247, 250, 255
Virginia Company of London, 53, 58–59
virtual representation, 224

Waldegrave, Henry, 34
Waldman, Steven, 254
Wales, 27
Walton, James, 164
Wappeler, William, 185
Waring, Basil, 205, 213
Waring, Marsham, 175
Warren, Mercy Otis, 219
Washington, George, 237
Wathen, Francis, 243
   Ignatius, 243
   John Baptist, 243
Wentworth, Thomas, 59–60, 191
Wexford, County (*see* Taaffe, Lucas)
Wharton, Justinian, 176
Wheatley, Francis Xavier, 156–157
   Anastasia Cecil, 157
Wheeler, Francis Xavier, 156–158
   Ann Birchmore, 157
Whetenhall, Henry, 150, 175
   John, 175
White, Andrew, 60–61, 69–70, 74, 76–78, 83–85
White Marsh, 159
Wieregan, Nicols, 245 (*see also* Loyalists, Catholic)
Willcox, Thomas, 244
William of Orange, 121–126, 130–134, 145, 192, 194, 198
Williams, Griffith, 190
Williams, Roger, 50, 97
Wills, Garry, 7
Wilson, James, 49
Wimsatt, Janice, 164–165
Woburn Abbey, 24
Wintour, Robert, 68, 112
Woodyard, 179
Wooster, David, 250
Worsley, Lawrence, 83
Wye River, 151

Young, Ann Rozer, 150–151
   Benjamin, 150–152
   Jane Digges, 150–151
   Notley, 150–151
Yonkers, NY, 59
Yorkshire, 20, 24, 27–28, 31, 51, 64, 137

Zubly, John Joachim, 224

main ✓

SEP 18 2012

PORTLAND PUBLIC LIBRARY SYSTEM
5 MONUMENT SQUARE
PORTLAND, ME 04101

09/03/2012 $35.0

WITHDRAWN